ELLIPSIS:

DUAL VISION

Photographs by Stephen Posen

with texts by ALEXANDRA POSEN,
COLIN CHENEY, SCOTT INDRISEK,
and ZAC POSEN

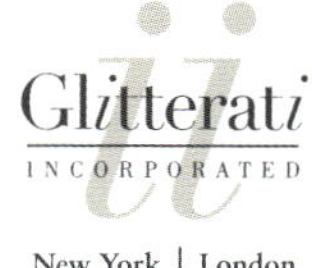

New York | London

First published in 2015 by

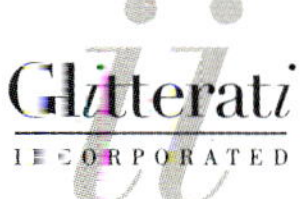

New York Office:
630 Ninth Ave, Ste 603
New York, NY 10036
Telephone: 212 362 9119

London Office:
1 Rona Road
London NW3 2HY
Tel/Fax +44 (0) 207 267 9739

www.GlitteratiIncorporated.com | media@GlitteratiIncorporated.com for inquiries

First edition, 2015

Library of Congress Cataloging-in-Publication data is available from the publisher.

Hardcover edition ISBN 13: 978-0-9903808-4-9
Design: Sarah Morgan Karp | smk-design.com
Printed and bound in China by C P Printing, Limited

10 9 8 7 6 5 4 3 2 1

CONTENTS

PREFACE:

METAPHORA

A deep look into the path that my father's work has taken reveals a fascinating lifelong conversation between the flat plane of a canvas, the painterly illusion of sculptural space, and the paradoxical power of drawing to sew these two realities together as one.

Throughout his career, the camera and photograph have been steadfast companions on his artistic quest. His early work in hard-focus realism painting drew on photographic representations of shallow sculptural spaces. In addition to the meticulous and sensuous modeling of the painted plane, Posen added quixotic dimension by entwining draped lines to the vertical landscapes. These cloth lines were also translated into photorealistic paint; however, their voice signified the artist's drawn line amidst the objectivity of the surface. These marks both reinforced the illusionistic space and simultaneously proposed a wily rebuttal to it.

The masterful playfulness of this dialogue describes my father's quintessential essence. While he has defined himself as a painter for most of his career, in recent years the camera has become an enthusiastic accomplice to his paintbrush.

The camera permits my father to share the passionate act of observation and habitual visual analysis that defines his being in the world. Ironically, it is perhaps his work in photography that has allowed my father to most fluidly elucidate his profound love of drawing, and his dependence on its magic as a central metaphor for life itself. Just as the poet relishes the fruit of the word, and juices every drop of potentiality through measured usage, so does my father approach the photographic image. He lovingly toys with the substance of each captured picture—its perceptual bones, contextual flesh and the mystery it exhales.

Within the series *Ellipsis: Dual Visions,* he constructs poetic phrases by pairing images—each image receiving its full weight and identity face-to-face with its chosen twin. In his book, *The Poetics of Space,* French philosopher Gaston Bachelard quotes Rilke: "These trees are magnificent, but even more magnificent is the sublime and moving space between them, as though with their growth it too increased."

With visual avarice and wit, my father's camera grabs at the incessant aesthetic happenings of everyday. The act of seeing becomes a giddy festivity of abundance. In a more contemplative space, my father redoubles his work of perception and pairs photo to photo, finding unexpected parallels and echoes amongst his visions.

There is much at play in these pairs and, on principle my father makes no effort to restrain the creative and intellectual gymnastics that characterize the complexity of his work in painting, drawing and photography. He mischievously leaps from the sublime to the mundane, from the absurd to the philosophic and from riddle to rhyme.

Within *Ellipsis: Dual Visions*, there are pairs that function like enchanted mirrors—the pleasure of two perceptual experiences see themselves in each other's distinctive beauty, and yet are hardly recognizable even to themselves. These lyrical works communicate the sheer joy of the experience of sight that fills my father's heart.

Some pairs conduct a more haunting conversation: one image stares back at the other, subverting its content into a rude revelation. In these interesting cases, the photographic diptych sets up an irreverent collision, where the distillation of formal information and its harmony or repetition causes a brutally loaded obliteration of meaning and context. In the strongest examples, my father's work can make death look like life at first glance. In other more gentle and humorous clashes, the revered marble sculpture is visually equalized with the plastic dregs from a flea market.

The works can also seek completion in each other: the images are fractions of life and inseparable halves of a dimensional whole. The two photographs rope together literal and figurative spaces, pushing and pulling on each other to conjure the illusion of volume and completion. In these examples, I am most reminded of his early paintings—the truth of the images both underscored and belied by drawing.

For all of the myriad logics of pairing, the works in *Ellipsis: Dual Visions* share the fact that they are reflexive metaphors: there is no subject, no object, no words. Instead, the images find poetic revelation in each other's sameness, difference and wholeness.

"Then the sea and heaven rolled as one and from the two came fresh transfigurings of freshest blue."

—Wallace Stevens

Ellipsis: Dual Visions brings the gift of intelligent vision and delivers a perceptual feast made with love. I am grateful to my father for this lasting and generous meal.

—Alexandra O. Posen
New York City

FOREWORD:

THE TENOR AND THE VEHICLE

I have a memory of my father holding his light meter above a prickly pear blossoming in the parking lot of a Motel 6—or maybe it was Econo Lodge—on the outskirts of Capitol Reef, Utah. I'd grown accustomed to this gesture. Invariably it meant delayed departure, my mother's tolerance drifting toward impatience, children antsy in the backseat. But it's a peculiar memory to hold onto. Here was no grand event, no incident. I know now that the act of taking his old analog light meter out of his rawhide camera case signaled that something beckoned to be captured. Something called to be translated from a glimpse into an image: a matrix of negative spaces between the jumbled stems, crosshatch of needles against green, matte skin. The fleshy flower, like a heart born in violent beauty outside an infant's body, opening toward my father's eye, his seeing.

I know now that the gesture signaled how the cacti had already been at work on him, on his imagination—even if all I could see was an overgrown parking island. He wouldn't always take such lengths, of course, to make certain that the particular quantum of the world he'd aimed his camera toward was translated on his slide or print film exactly as desired, as he'd seen. He would drive through hours of landscape—badlands, switchbacks down a mountainside in the Rockies—with one of his cameras perched on the steering wheel, or holding the lens out the window in an attempt to capture some fleeting vista while keeping the truck on the road.

Before digital photography, before he could know whether he'd gotten the shot (whether chanced upon, or the product of careful calculation of film speed, aperture and exposure, lens, angle), I know he must have carried around the echoes, the fleeting possibilities of those encounters. Until the film could be developed, until he knew what was there, on that negative, he carried around the memory of what he'd seen, of that iota of reality he'd tried to harness as image. Wondering: what have I gleaned? Did I capture some part of what existed between my seeing and what I saw?

Stephen Posen's vibrant and beguiling collection of photographs, *Ellipsis: Dual Vision,* leaves me charged with wondering and possibility. With resonant distances and uncommon intimacies. Traversing these eighty-six images—each composed of a pair of photographs—I was reminded of Mark Doty's comment about the later still lifes of the Dutch Masters. The significance of the objects found in each of the paintings—the translucency of a lemon, light of white damask—lies in "a poetry of relation." Here, too, in Posen's book, we feel the resonance, the thrum, the yearning that opens up between the two photographs comprising each of

his images. We feel it even when the subjects of a pair—a flag in a golf green, a model having her make-up done (#62); a rotting fruit beset by bumblebees, a Members Only jacket on the hood of a car (#43)—so often have little to recommend one to the other.

But such is the nature of metaphors—and I came to understand at least part of the relationship between Posen's photographs as that of the two parts of a metaphor, the tenor and the vehicle. "I say moon is horses in the tempered dark," writes the poet Jack Gilbert in his poem "Finding Something," "because horse is the closest I can get to it." As in Gilbert's poem, viewers of Posen's photographs are left to decipher precisely how a child's hand grasping a brilliantly pink, sunlit toy relates to a swan—by what energy "moon" (the tenor) is bound to "horses in the tempered dark" (the vehicle). The answer is, of course, at least partially because Posen has placed them together for us to behold. But, as with a metaphor, the viewer is left to close the connection.

I've been trying to reckon the mechanics of this yearning I feel between the photographs. Posen told me that he's "interested in the space between the images," and while spending time with his collection I was reminded of something I'd once read about the peculiarity of the relationship between the former ninth planet, Pluto, and its moon, Charon. Most planets in the solar system are so massive that their moons are held in orbit around them. But Pluto and Charon are more equally matched in size and mass: they exert a more equal measure of gravity on the other. As a result, the two icy rocks orbit a point of gravity—a barycenter, it's called—that they create together in the space between them. They are a spinning system of twin worlds that at once influence and are influenced by each other's mass.

So, too, are Posen's photographs locked into a synchronous orbit with each other. In #15, a glass case of unsettling plastic fingers displaying false nails—floral punctuation, starbursts—tugs at the accompanying photograph's fossilized ammonites' spiral shells; in each other's echoes I hear an anxiety of impermanence. This seabed record of ancient dead lends the mall counter stilllife a melancholy urgency. Caught in the space between the quiet fossils and the vapid terror of the human beauty industry I hear the poet Rilke, in the presence of his headless statue of Apollo, imploring "you must change your life." The force the photographs have on each other—and the contemplation they force us into—makes it nearly impossible to decouple them from each other. Separated, they would ache for each other, for the image—the spinning, tidal system—they are together. For the metaphor they become.

I've returned frequently to the second image in the book, uncertain not about what I see in each photograph (though in other instances that's the case), but about the gravity that sets them spinning about that point between them. One photograph gives a homeless man huddled on an MTA subway car bench; the other offers some garish pinwheels, the door of a van or truck in the background. Little or nothing of the photographs' subjects initially calls out toward each other. But, after a moment, certain formal echoes begin to emerge. The curves of the

window frame reach toward the vehicle's wheel well. The sickle of red, white, and blue vanes between the two concentric windmills draw the eye toward a crescent between the sweatshirt and the hefty bag wherein the man's face can be glimpsed. Plucked out of the current of our daily lives—commutes, suburban yards—each image threatens a kind of banal transience. The eye might move from each photograph's quotidian subject swiftly were it not for these rhymes: curves, negative space, transecting lines.

And these rhymes beckon me into contemplation. A sense of impossibility wells up when I register the cowled man's white cane as that of a blind person. How does a blind man endure, homeless, a New York City winter? Or, sighted, did this man—enveloped in the mass of his possessions, seeking sleep or privacy—take up this symbol of blindness to serve some other, private purpose? At once terribly dull in their plastic, rural patriotism and mundane psychedelic flora, the pinwheels are alive in the force of their color against the washed-out metal. I am caught between the two photographs, held in an unease bound up in ideas of home, gestures toward tentative solace and vibrant light, if not joy. And it is form that makes this happen.

But how did these photographs come together? In spite of myself, I can't help but wonder which photograph Posen took first, or how a formal element—the hunter orange of a backyard mosquito tent; the same color, faded, glimpsed inside a tent pitched on a dune (#20)—became an open nerve, almost painfully alive with potential. A holstered handgun resting on a gray plastic bag; a newly chainsawn tree stump rising from a field of tar (#42): did Posen carry the memory of one of these photographs around in his head, charged with an openness, a desire? In his essay, "Souls on Ice," Mark Doty writes, "our metaphors go on ahead of us, they know before we do." I can imagine the shape of that handgun, that shade of blaze orange "knowing" before Posen does—a memory stirring him towards the discovery of the other, tuning his seeing toward a photograph not yet taken. But I can also as easily imagine that the realization of connection occurs only later, when he shuffles through the photographs amassed on the computer, spread across his desk in New York.

The answer doesn't matter to me, not really. Because I have been left to play in the music of each duet, to thrum to the resonances awakened between the two photographs. However the individual photographs were initially taken, however they were brought into concert, their work together is vibrant and immediate. Not a single pairing is obvious. No single photograph is in thrall to the other—each exerts a force on the other that simultaneously clarifies and complicates my reading of them. While there is a metaphorical relationship between them, it is a reciprocal one: each is both tenor and vehicle to the other. Indeed, the images exist in a kind of parataxis, if I can borrow that term from grammar: Posen has placed the photographs side by side without any explicit guidance to how they relate to one another. We must hunt, or perhaps simply be open to the surprise of what formal and tonal details allow us to "grok" their relationship. A system

of wires and suspended lamps in a high-vaulted room—a church? museum?—develops an uncanny intimacy with the inner space of a hot air balloon's ropes and metal skeleton (#6). Each photograph emphasizes the logarithmic dynamics of a nautilus shell that can now be seen in the other. The curve of a gold-tasseled curtain echoes a winter branch tangled with a spider's gossamer: the formal echo is clear, yet so subtle that my eye lingers in the hope of glimpsing something more elusive that holds the two photographs together (#4). Of seeing into the mechanics of the poetry at work here.

But my uncertainty about this poetry of relation is, I think, essential to Posen's work in his book. Consider how the viewer looks down into the two worlds given in #16—the alligator enclosure and the efficiency bathroom—and immediately experiences the formal echoes across the photographs: rectilinear space, kindred colors, the tapered head of the gator and the squat-toilet drain. The first might have been taken out on Tonlé Sap Lake in Cambodia, one stop on a package tour that allows the visitor to gawk at the reptiles in their underwater cages and witness the Vietnamese refugees in their floating village of political limbo. The bathroom's ugliness is somehow honest and brutally vibrant, but I doubt myself as soon as my mind reaches for a narrative or thematic link between the two (water and effluent? enclosure?). I like feeling an ache between the two photographs without feeling compelled to riddle out a particular story. I like that to try to consider the photographs independent of each other would do some violence to what they have become together, the image they combine to create.

As the reader falls deeper into the book, some of Posen's preoccupations come into focus. He is drawn, I think, to the perfect strangeness of our species' impulse to create images: plastic fir boughs decking the front of a farm truck; a growling wolf on a polyester blanket (#37); the distorted musculature of a child's action figures; the plastic solemnity of a Virgin Mary clock (#45); an Assyrian frieze depicting a roaring lion; a Kiss impersonator in full regalia, tongue lolling (#52). Some of these pairings help us read the way we gather our symbols, our objects together in deliberate, if questionable aesthetic statements; others reveal the way our view, indeed, our experience of the world is cluttered and mediated by the productions and reproductions we surround ourselves with. The first image in the book—tchotchke ceramic statuary and dancers in shimmery taffeta—calls attention to our everyday enactments of (culturally specific) ideas of beauty, how different societies tune our sensibilities. Without a sense of either praise or condemnation, Posen remains fascinated by the resonant patterns these pairings awaken formally and thematically. He invites the viewer in, to participate—comfortably or otherwise—in the play between the images.

I'm intrigued how some of the pairings leave me disturbed, enlivened by a violence that somehow isn't quite there. In #9, glass bulbs and needles mar a landscape of scarred, rose-mottled skin—a practice of Chinese medicine known as "cupping." Then: a ghostly, blurred shape intimates a hanged man—no, that's not it, more the hooded prisoner on a stool at Abu Ghraib—before I realize it's simply an unopened lawn umbrella with a Lichtenberg figure of a

winter deciduous tree radiating behind it. It's wonderful, and disorienting, what happens here without anything—without any literal brutality—happening between the images.

However, in a later pairing, #50, the violence is palpable and explicit, unsettling in a quite different way. By thrusting the window of stacked skulls into this nearly absurd, cruel contrast with the vending machine of gumballs, Posen is able to make what's become a banal—and thus easy, too easy to turn away from—photographic remnant of the Khmer Rouge atrocity disturbingly fresh again. The gumballs burgeon in size, their supermarket foyer made strange as it is forced to accept the echo of those skulls, the innocent Cambodian dead. The eye sockets, nasal cavities, the gaping wound of a bullet: they all pick up the slapdash rainbow patterns—diamonds, ammonia clouds of Saturn—emblazoned on the balls. Only in this juxtaposition do questions come that might not otherwise, so familiar are we with this species of atrocity image: how do you even begin accounting for such loss? Do these skulls belong here, behind glass, on display, offered up? Shouldn't they be in the ground, in a grave? But if they were, would I be asked—forced—to carry this image away with me?

I realize that the images that keep pulling me back are those that make me joyfully uneasy. They provoke laughter and discomfort, tentative understanding and lingering mystery. In #56, the rhyme between the nature morte of a slaughtered goat, arranged on blood-soaked cardboard, and the photograph that might be entitled "Still Life with Jabba the Hut and Winter Gourds" makes the butchery somehow playful, the (found? staged?) scene of unusual harvest inexplicably unsettling. The veins and cells of overexposed cabbage leaves re-jig how I see the patchwork of fields, snows, and roads framed by a jet-engine at 30,000 feet (#5). And my favorite duet—tadpoles caught in green, stagnant water on a bleached tarpaulin; a somehow planetary glimpse of, maybe, a koi fish—I still resist even describing for fear that doing so, taking the nearly abstract image and drawing it into figurative reality, will make something vanish for me. As though locating the barycenter between Pluto and Charon would somehow send those worlds spinning away from each other, or crashing together in cataclysm. I don't want to know too much for fear that my wonder will pale; I want to remain with the chimera born of these two images' (almost) ineffable intimacy.

In his book, *Still Life with Oysters and Lemon*, Mark Doty explores the elusive force that this one small still life by Jan Davidsz de Heem has somehow had on him. He writes, "I have been pulled into the orbit of a painting, have allowed myself to be pulled into its sphere by casual attraction deepening to something more compelling. I have felt the energy and life of the painting's will; I have been held there, instructed." One result of this attraction, this instruction, is that once he's left the painting's vivid world of resonant, minute detail, once he's left the museum, the rest of Doty's world, the city itself, is enlivened. The painting has re-tuned his seeing: "the air of the Upper East Side full of rising plumes of smoke from furnaces and steaming laundries, exhaust from the tailpipes of idling taxis, flapping

banners, gangs of pigeons." For a spell, Doty is able to see and feel the overwhelming stimulus of the city as though it were a still life.

After spending another afternoon looking at Stephen Posen's photographs in the cafe of a design center sequestered on the sixth floor of one of Bangkok's many malls, I make my way out into the city. Normally I struggle to block out the persistent and pernicious advertisements the storefronts pummel me with, must brace myself for their visual klaxon as I run the gauntlet of brands. But today, Posen's photographs have tuned my mind's eye, my anxiety. In his book, *The Necessary Angel: Essays on Reality and the Imagination*, poet Wallace Stevens writes that "Reality is a cliché from which we escape by metaphor." Today, I think, Posen's images, their resonant patterns and particular gravities, provide me with the metaphors to escape the disorienting tumult of manipulated desires and plundered signs I encounter in the mall. Posen gives me: a cataract of green felt emptying into a billiard pocket; ripples radiating about a swan's neck, diving for food (#85). And here I find: the cascading blue fabric of a Gucci coat, spangled with stars; a two-story living wall of ferns, orchids, and unopened peace lilies. "Sometimes," Doty writes in 'Souls on Ice,' "it seems to me as if metaphor were the advance guard of the mind; something in us reaches out, into the landscape in front of us, looking for the right vessel, the right vehicle, for whatever will serve." The eighty-six pairings of *Ellipsis: Dual Visions* have charged me with seeing, with yearning, with an openness that allows me to reach out into the world in front of me in all its forms, uglinesses, aching, and psalms. And when I walk out into the hothouse air of Thailand's rainy season I feel nothing but rhymes and echoes: bottles of strawberry Fanta left for the spirits; duck-heads grilling under a billowing, greasy fan. The torn blue shirt of the construction workers walking home; the patchwork tarpaulins—cobalt, zaffre, Tiffany blue, azure—shrouding the abandoned building at the top of our street.

I know that if I held my iPhone up to what I see there I might hold, for a moment, what I have seen. But that it couldn't hold, not really, the gravity of attention and attraction Posen's images have awakened me to. Images themselves don't ever really contain what we want them to—not really. That's what I admire so much about this collection of photographs. Posen provokes us to inhabit not just the photographs, but the quick, uncertain poetry of their relation: The spirit of attraction between them, an attraction that is only made palpable through the viewer's presence. It's the spirit, I imagine, my father carried between the moment he glimpsed something and when he took out his light meter and flipped it open. Between when he took the photograph and when it was developed—the wondering, the longing between his seeing and what he'd seen. Between what our minds reach for, and what we grasp. If only for a moment.

—Colin Cheney
Bangkok, Thailand

INTRODUCTION:

STRANDED MEANINGS

Painting has been at the throat of photography since the latter's inception, and at best they now exist in a state of conflicted truce. Stephen Posen has spent the past four decades working between the two mediums—painting from photographs, painting on photographs, and, more recently, letting the photographs stand on their own, unadorned with any mark-making. In the '70s, he was making oil-and-acrylic paintings like *Cooper Square:* a black-and-white photorealistic background (of an industrial, decaying interior), over which float colorful, dimensional bulges of fabric. (It was prescient for its pre-PhotoShop age—by now our eye is better trained for layered juxtapositions of images that shouldn't really make sense together.) Confronted by those canvases, the viewer struggles to parse two distinct sets of visual information that don't quite align.

After these "Fabric on Photo" paintings, Posen eventually began using actual photographs in his practice—compositions that he'd taken himself, often searching for an image, like the nave of a church, that had a central blankness that he would then augment with oil paint sticks. The layering aspect is similar to the earlier paintings, with the artist's marks mirroring certain shapes or general movements already present in the underlying photograph. It's not hard to see how Posen made the leap from these painted-on photos (made mostly between 2006 and 2012) and the photographic pairings that he began creating in 2009, which are collected here in this volume.

All of these works upend certain expectations the human eye has, and ask the viewer to linger, to parse, to translate or compute. Posen's paintings and painted photographs combined two distinct sets of visual information, but layered one atop the other, in a single image; the works in Ellipsis: Dual Visions separate the related-but-distinct images, placing them into couplings in parallel conversation with each other. An ellipsis, in grammatical terms, is a way of removing a piece of text that is extraneous, that is not necessary to comprehend the meaning of the two remaining parts of a sentence, stranded on either side of those three eliding dots. In the case of Posen's photographs, the ellipsis is instead the integral sinew between each

image in the pair: Meaning effaced, obscured, or withheld just out of reach. It's the missing piece, the relational key; it's up to you.

And so there is a rhythm to this book, and to this series, which asks the viewer to simultaneously analyze two distinct pictures—considering them as a pair, equally weighted, rather than a visual story or as an A to B transition. As a result, experiencing this work can be jarring; one's eye *wants* to read from left to right, building a narrative or a progression that simply isn't there (the child's hand on a pool toy does not move with any chronological logic toward the swan and its bright orange beak). The work is associative, but the nature and tenor of those associations varies, from the straightforward to the oblique, the formal to the poetic. There may not be a narrative flow from one image to the next, or within the series—nothing happens, nothing changes—but there is a distinctive thematic and tonal flow, an expertly contoured series of movements, styles, image-rhymes and registers.

It's in making those associations that Posen cements the artistry of this series; the role of editing and organization replaces that of physical mark-making on the surface of the photograph. He is both executor of these images and self-curator, culling a personal archive to uncover unexpected linkages. With few exceptions, the individual photos are incorporated into these pairings as they were taken, without additional cropping. The moment in which Posen takes each shot is of course important, but the moment in which he realizes the *connection* between two of those photographs—taken, in some cases, months or even years apart—is perhaps more important. Cartier-Bresson's oft-repeated idea of the "decisive moment" is relocated: From the snapping of the shutter to the instant at the editing table when two images collide and, in tandem, begin speaking a new language.

If the associations binding these image pairs together were all of the same stripe, viewing "*double* decisive moments" would degrade to the level of a game: Look, find the connection, move on. It's the richness and variety of the image parallels that is rewarding, and that binds these eighty-seven pairs into a single body of work, with contours, peaks and valleys, musical flights, trills, the connections occasionally echoing within the larger series, shouting back to a geometry or color or subtle pun established earlier.

In some cases this involves drawing a conceptual line between the organic and the manmade, or challenging the viewer to make the distinction between the two: A stuffed bear before a wall mural of a seagull on the left; an actual seagull on the right, perched by the rearview mirror of the artist's car in Ireland. Elsewhere it's more oblique, a sense of movement, slippery alignments—as in the pairing of a golf hole, its flagpole casting a stark line of shadow, with a shot of a fashion model in the midst of having her make-up applied. A taxonomy of *Ellipsis: Dual Visions* would have to categorize all the ways in which Posen's images settle next to each other, from gallows humor jokes (a children's gumball machine sidled up with stacks of human skulls in a window), to dense screens of conflicting information overload

towels featuring wrestlers and Winnie the Pooh at a flea market next to an anatomical diagram of the human septum) and perverse similarities (an open-mouthed lion on an Istanbul museum wall with a long-tongued Gene Simmons impersonator in Las Vegas). In a few rare cases things get exceedingly *meta*, as in one instance where we see, on the right of the double pages, a photograph of one of Posen's previous painted-on photographs. Some of the more astounding pairs hit multiple registers simultaneously. One of my favorites combines a close-up of acupuncture's "cupping" practice (in which the skin is drawn up into a plastic or glass bulb, forming a sort of inadvertent ripple) with an out-of-focus photo of a folded patio umbrella, the blurriness giving it the appearance of a statuesque monument in some anonymous public square.

I like that Posen has taken a good number of these shots while touring flea markets in Pennsylvania. As someone who grew up in New Jersey I'm comfortable within that vernacular, the hodgepodge of the yard sale, that unexpected mix of beauty and ugliness, unintentional irony, kitsch and cast-offs. He assumes the role of image-hunter, stalking the moments (or plastic figurines, or China-produced bath towels with wolf faces) that might otherwise go neglected. Other photographs were taken in the countryside near New York City, or on the Manhattan streets of SoHo, where the artist has long lived. Many additional images in the series were taken on travels around the world, which lends a certain diaristic edge, a personal record.

But by taking these images and recombining them, the artist elevates them to a universal level; they're not about Stephen Posen, where he's been or what he's seen, but they instead address a shared desire to tease connections, to make sense out of the visual glut that is the modern world. As such, *Ellipsis: Dual Visions* is an exercise in delight and recognition. Distinct photographs are made into strange bedfellows, and that's the joy: Finding connections where many see only a random chaos of image.

—Scott Indrisek

ESSAY:

AN ABSTRACTING LENS

I feel as if I was raised to view the world through an abstracting lens. I learned to see what was materially present but also what was possibly an interpretation, a blurring, a questioning, and a new vision. Everything was context, relationships, formal understanding, and frequently through seeing life in its many uncanny variations, I learned to perceive the world. This was something that we learned to do automatically, like a game, shifting from one way of seeing to another, ecstatic that we could move weights in the visual field at will. This was a gift from my father, who has been a painter his whole life. His more recent work in photography takes that lens and applies it in fascinating ways to this world.

I grew up in a Soho loft with African fertility sculptures set against giant Italian wooden winepress screws. The negative space between mirrors became a positive extension of the loft's cast-iron columns, not in a didactic way, but as a visual proposal for any who might care to look. Office chairs stripped of their upholstery would reveal fine bones with elegant lines and be juxtaposed to others with their original upholstery—fat in their ordinariness. A series of floor lamps with inflating mushroom-shaped tops were an inspired acquisition. My father placed them to form a triangle that would be completed by another architectural element in the room. He would (and still does) bring objects into the loft and then, through some magical alchemy that only he can conceive, transform them by placing them in juxtaposition to one another. Or he will take a vintage industrial object and repurpose it for modern use. His rather vast collection of pre-industrial wooden tools and objects at his eighteenth-century farmhouse in Bucks County, Pennsylvania reflects his passion for the "hand," or tools that are extensions of the hand, and a deep respect for the inventors and creators of these very imaginative, somewhat primitive, objects that were created to serve a specific need. All of these objects—from the most primitive to those of cutting-edge design—are treated with equal respect.

Life's journey began early in my father's travels across Turkey and the Mideast as a young Fulbright Scholar out of Yale. I see the influence of his upbringing in St. Louis, Missouri to his years painting in Florence, studying Giotto and Piero, an Abstract Expressionist painter walking a half block to visit the Medici Tombs on a break from his studio. The rawness of his first loft on Avenue B on New York's Lower East Side in the late 60s contrasted with my comfort in the family home and studio in Soho where he was an original urban homesteader. From his trompe l'oeil paintings of boxes under cloth in the 1970s or his paintings of the 90s utilizing cartoon imagery like George Herriman's cartoon character, Krazy Kat, my father has consistently looked hard—with both humor and pathos—at the contrasts in his surroundings. So, his work in

Ellipsis: Dual Visions bridges the line between the abstract and figurative. My father's "paired" photographs contain juxtapositions that allow and encourage the kind of mixed metaphors in which he has always delighted.

Take for example the pairing of photographs of the road and the pool-cleaning jet. What has a horizon, what are the barriers? Are the lines an illusion? The pairing blurs the edge between what defines a photo or a painting. It distills to emotional association and reaction.

Small details are positioned against large-scale exploration of color, form and perspective, for example the submerged crocodile that looks dangerous and iconic as it emerges from a murky green pool in Cambodia to the bathroom stall found on a train in the middle of China. It's not only a relation of form, texture and shape of the scales of the croc to the linoleum-tiled floor: There is a forced perspective and underlying fear of the dangerous pre-historic animal in the depths and the ominous urinal hole.

Or in the first photograph in *Ellipsis: Dual Visions,* the porcelain dancing ladies whose movements are still and abstract but completely in scale with the human proportions of the photograph with which this image is paired. The relationship of the pristine porcelain beside the plastic organza sparkles of dancing princesses in a Beijing opera is the result of his brilliant selection process and his amazing through-the-lens editing (he doesn't crop). This and other pairings provide a delightful play on which of the two images is more present: the close-up figurine or the stage-lit dancers from afar.

Or look at the neon-pink inflated plastic object positioned next to the beautiful swan, which offers a humorous regard for contour. The child's hand reaching out to the pool toy creates an interesting perspective on negative shape. The swan breaking through its pristine ivory body is the same alarming color. It's both abrupt and gentle, fragile yet ferocious.

There is something very freeing, visceral and uniting about the work my father has created here. It is a new proposition in the use of photographic information. Side-by-side, image-by-image, he challenges the viewer to take the leap of imagination and fill the "information gap," to bridge what our objects and places can mean when two images become one metaphor. The photographic pairing of the gumballs and skulls: Is it a commentary about the disposable nature of our lives? Is it about the empty skulls that blend together like a stamp motif with slight surface and color subtleties that are similar yet essentially different from the balls being dispensed from a gumball machine?

These are some of the questions raised as you travel through the pairs of photographs in *Ellipsis: Dual Visions,* a powerful and expressive collection in an age when not just images are disposable, but from these photographs it is clear that much of the physical content of life is as well. *Ellipsis: Dual Visions* shares my father's idiosyncratic, yet universal, vision and encourages the viewer to make his or her own connections.

—Zac Posen
New York City

"In the final analysis, a drawing simply is no longer a drawing, no matter how self-sufficient its execution may be. It is a symbol, and the more profoundly the imaginary lines of projection meet higher dimensions, the better."

—Paul Klee

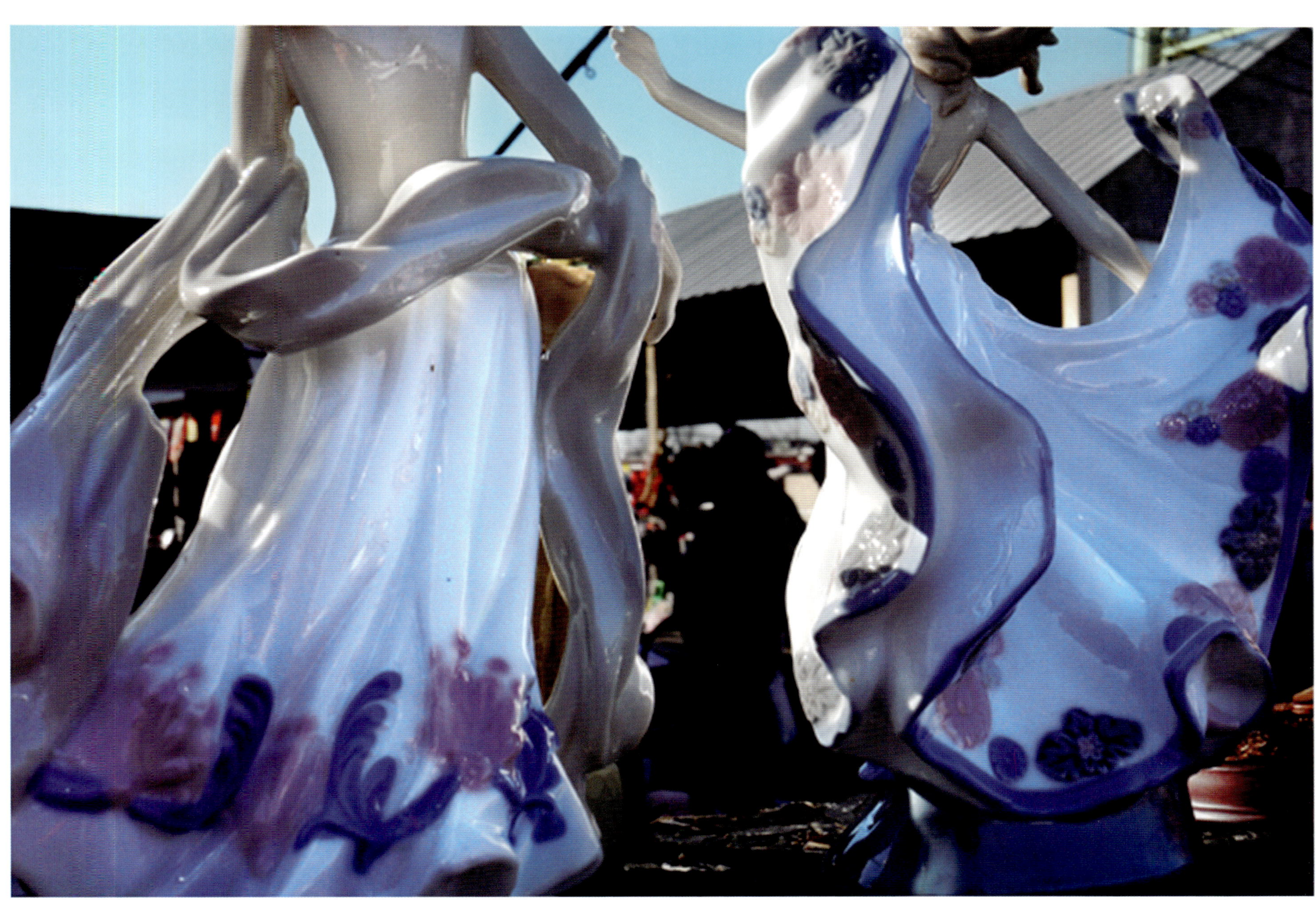

2C

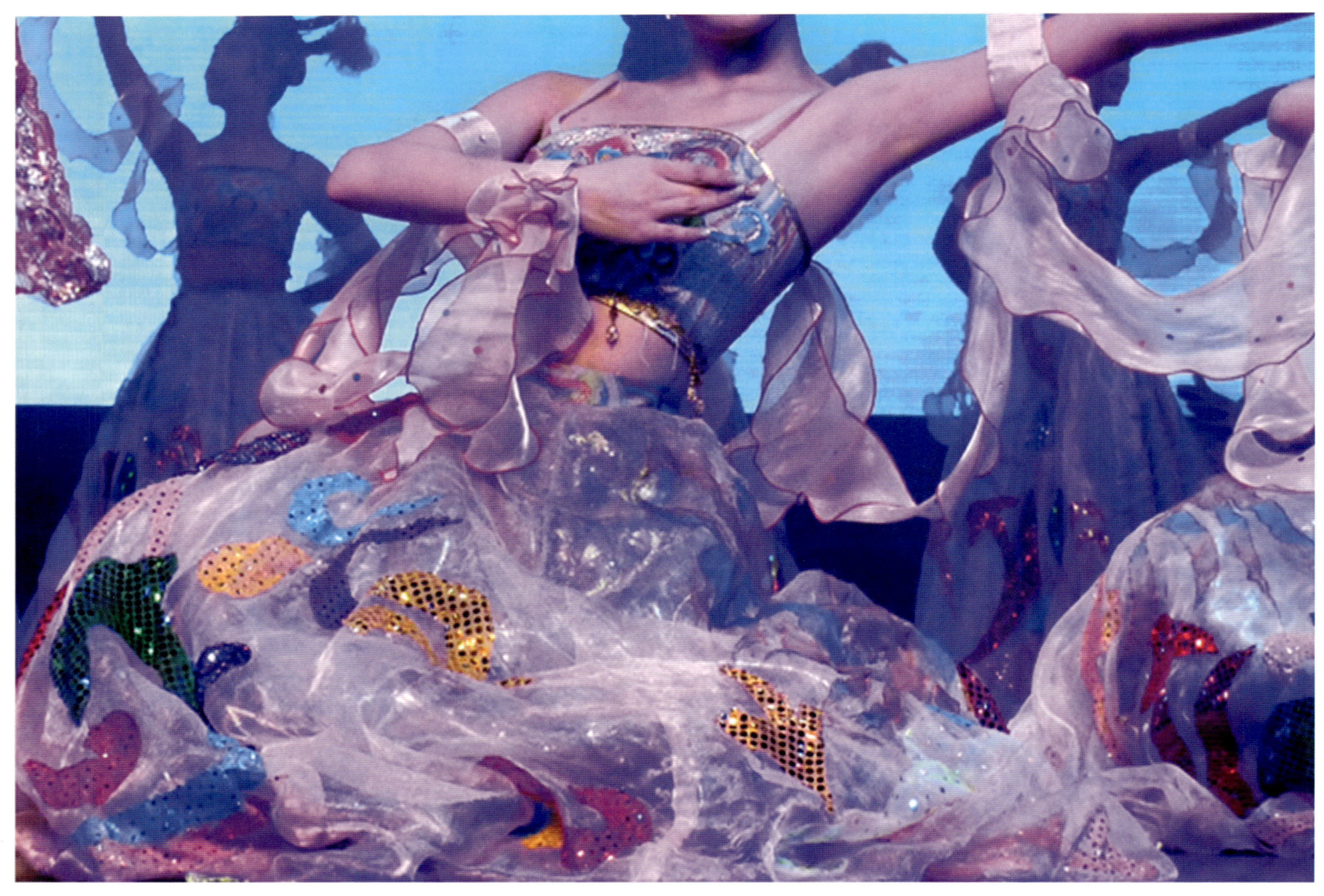

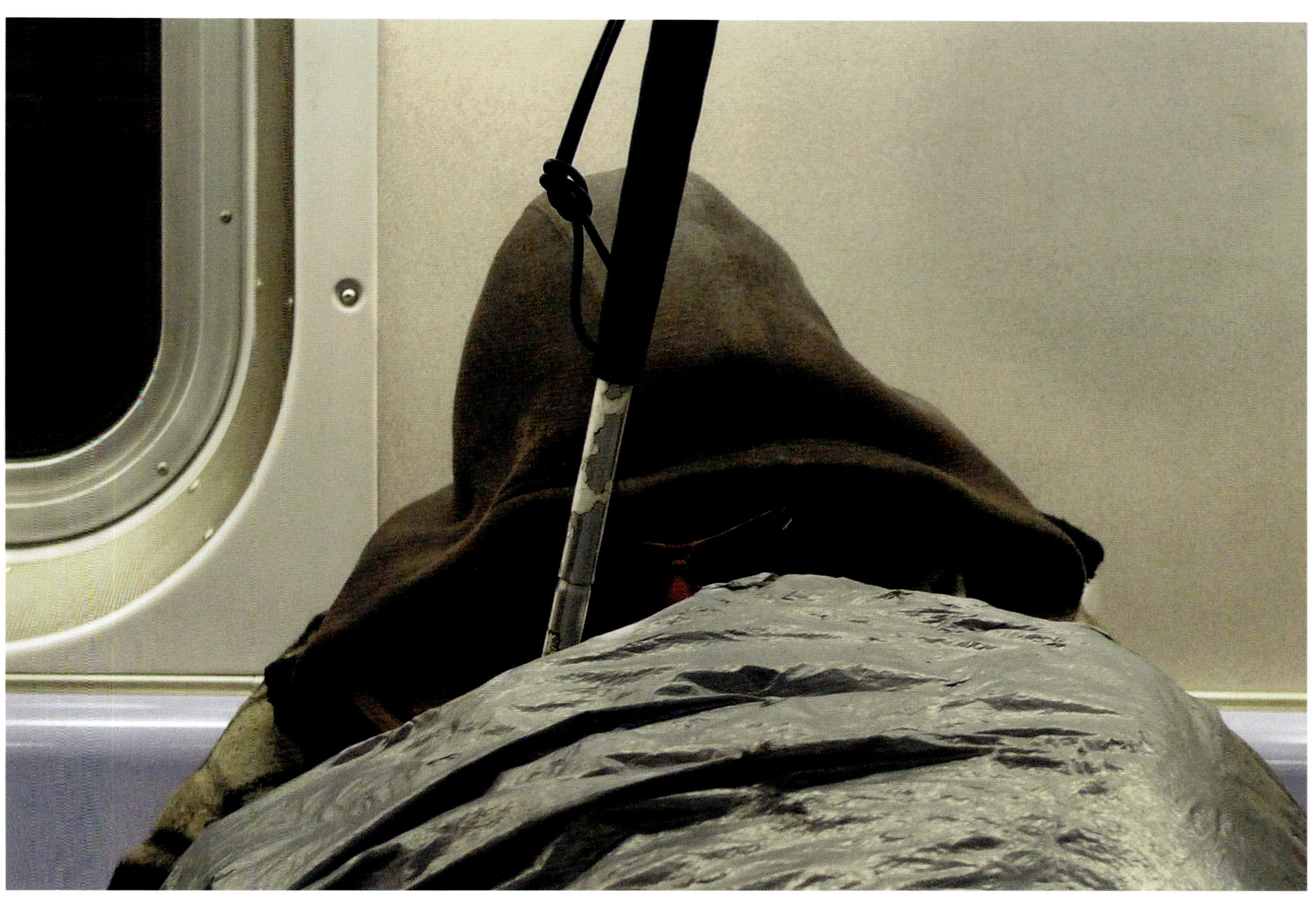

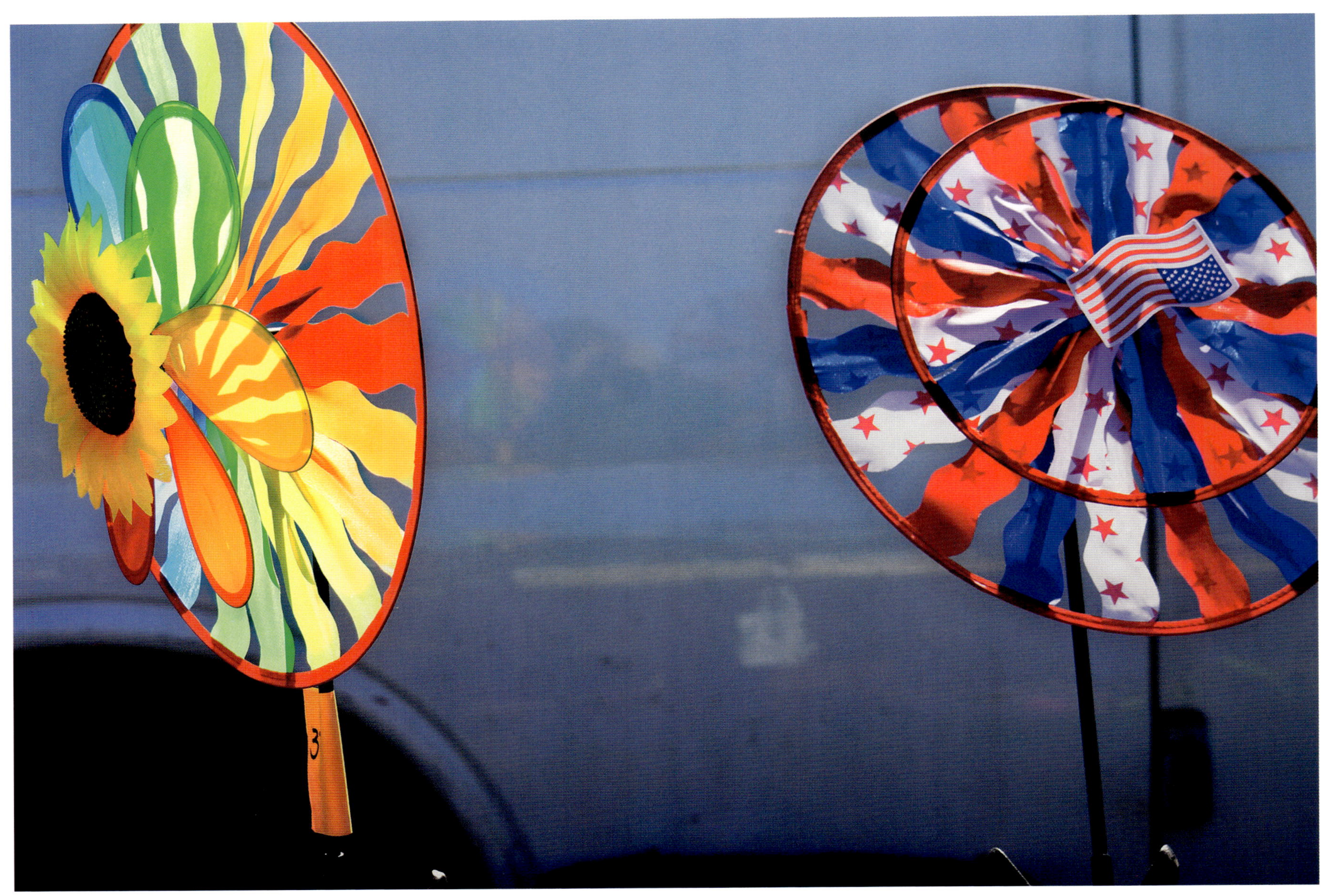

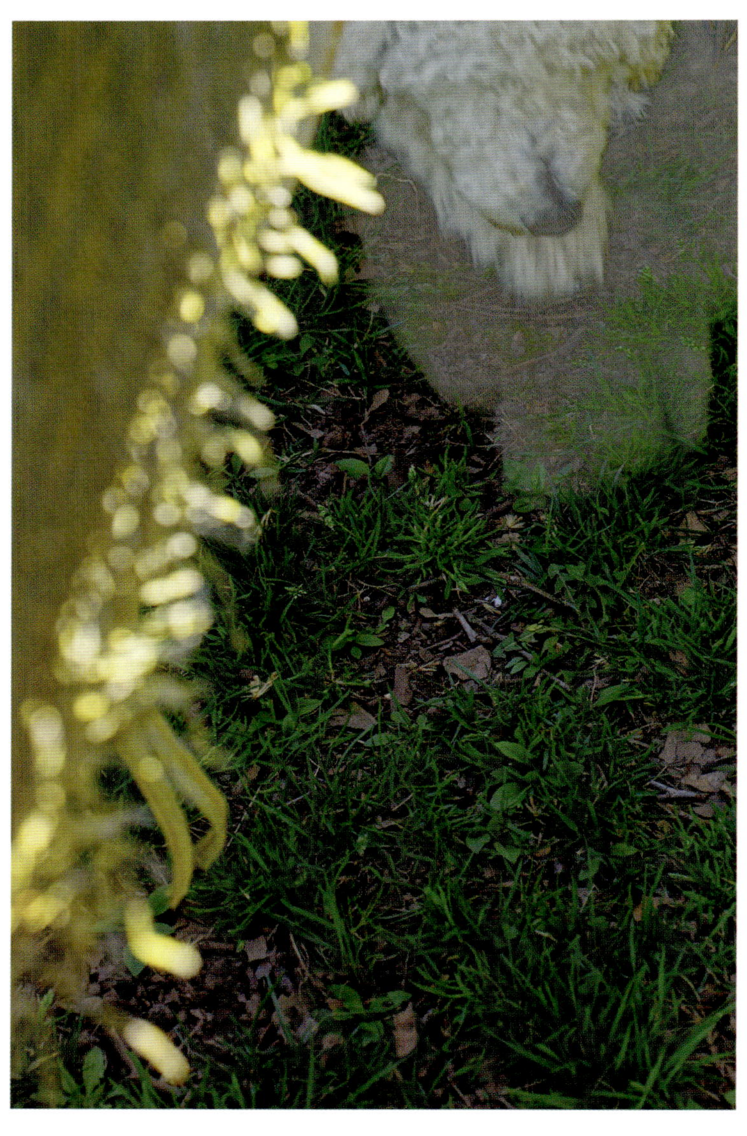

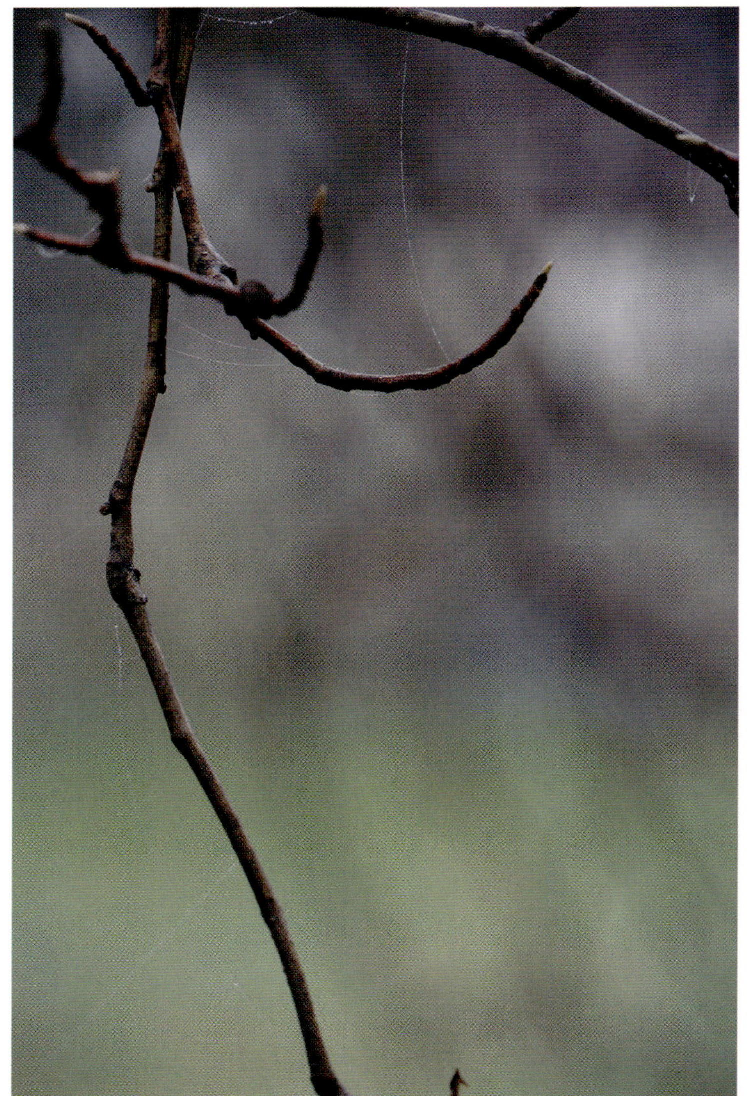

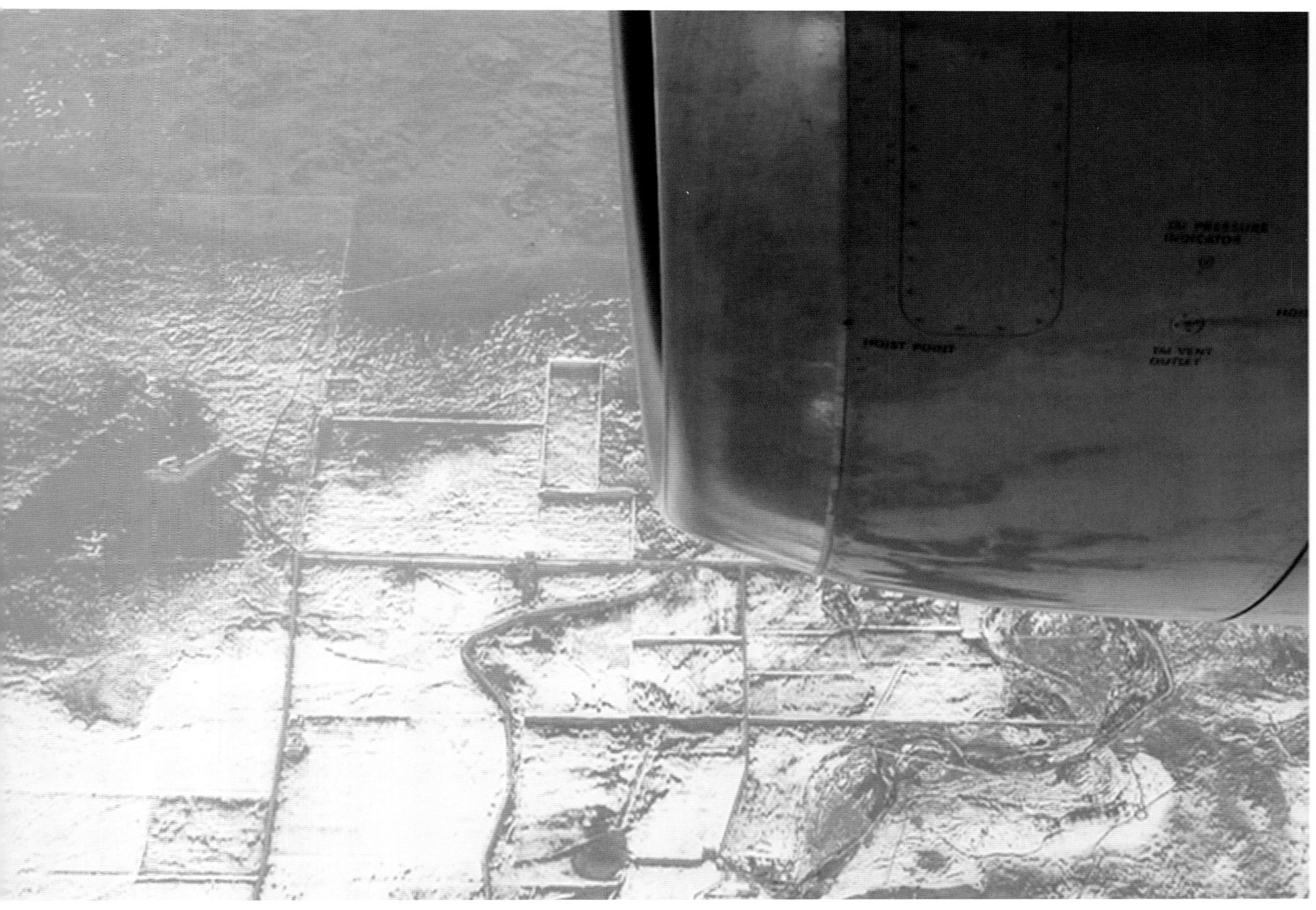
PRESSURE
INDICATOR
HOIST POINT
TM VENT
OUTLET

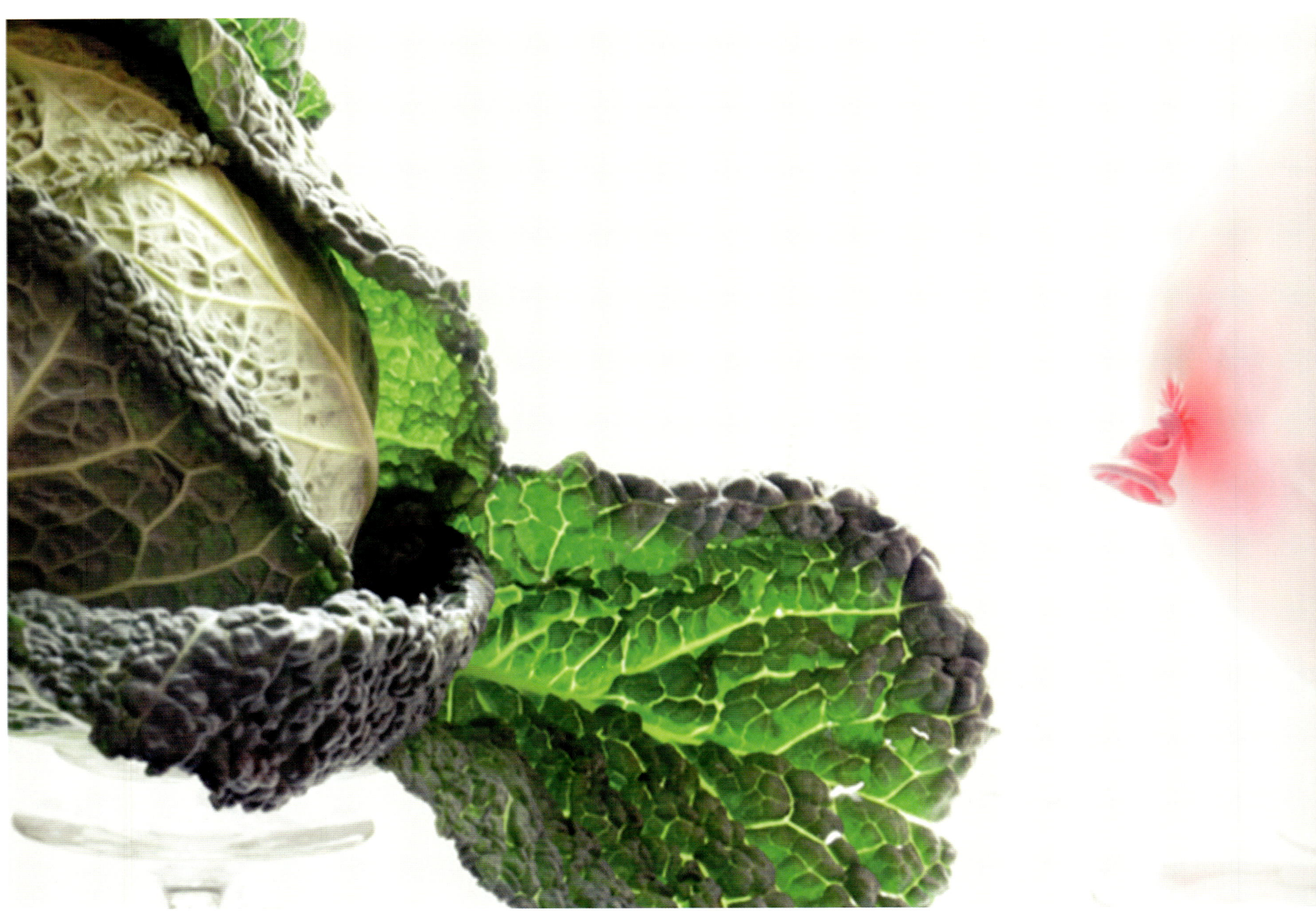

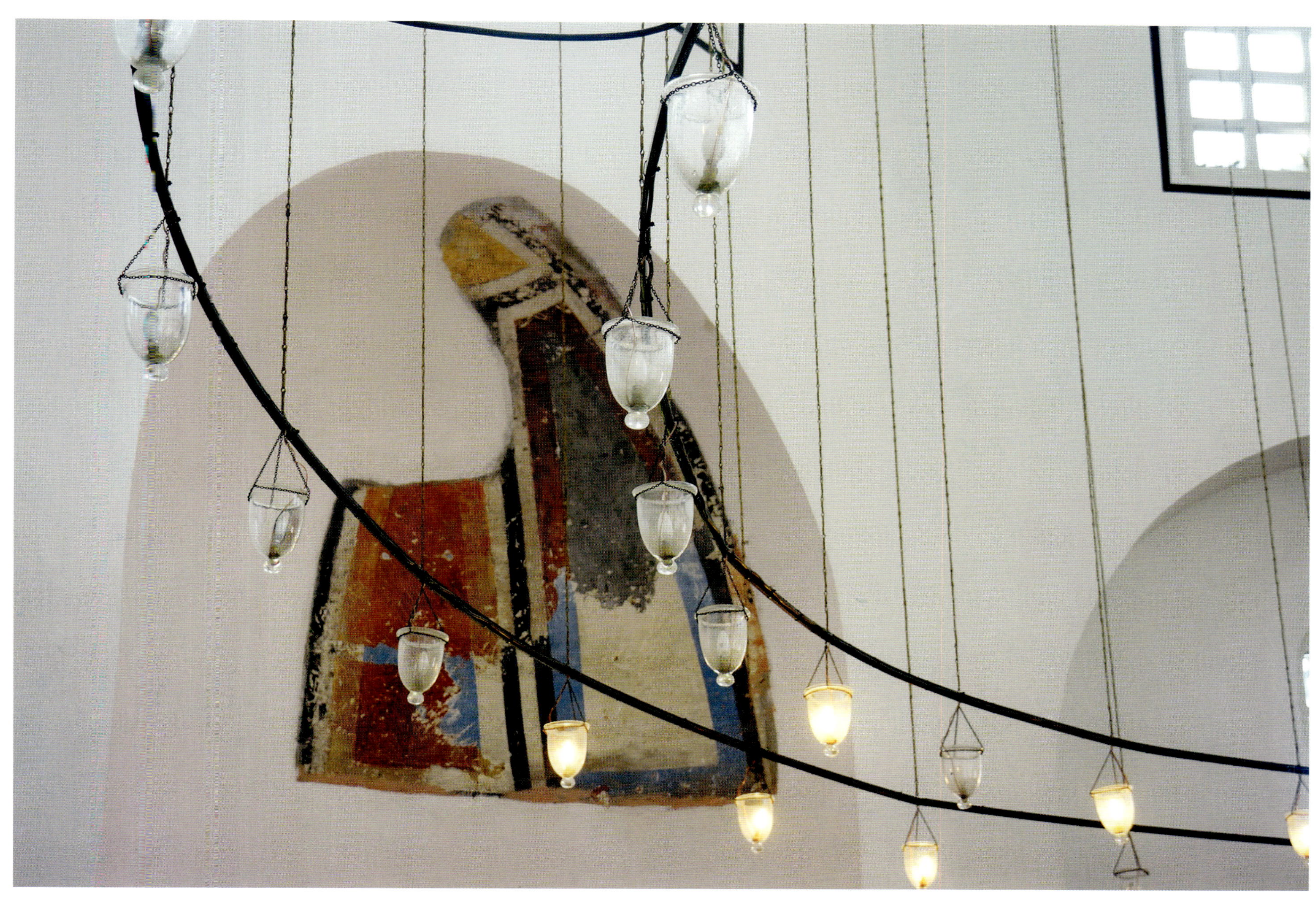

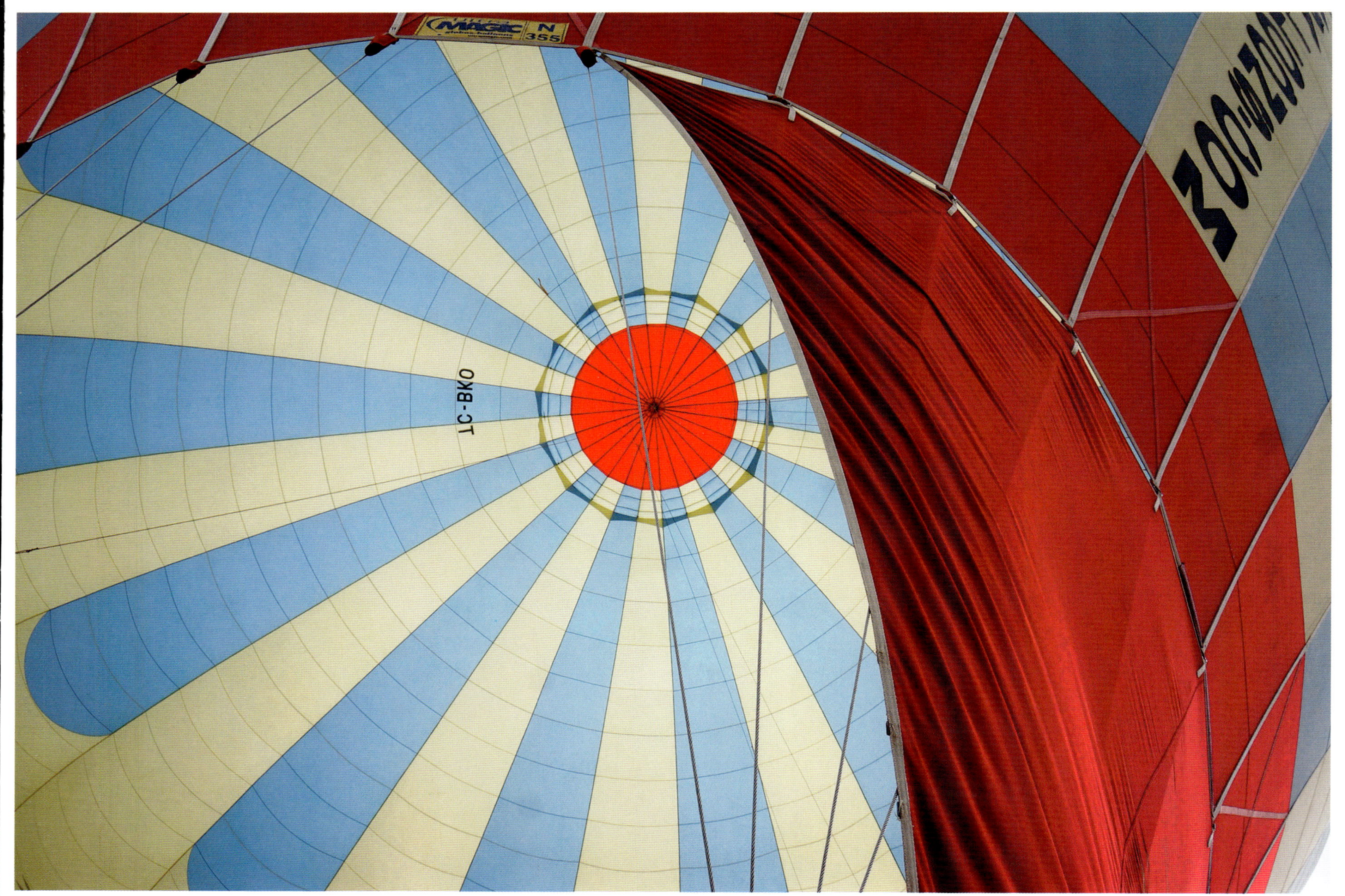
MAGIC
N
355

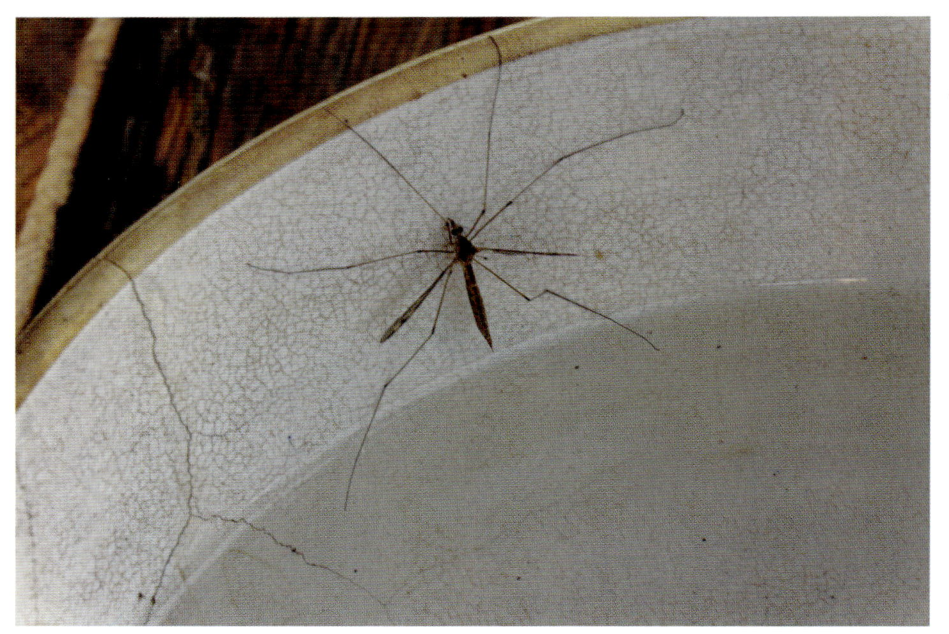

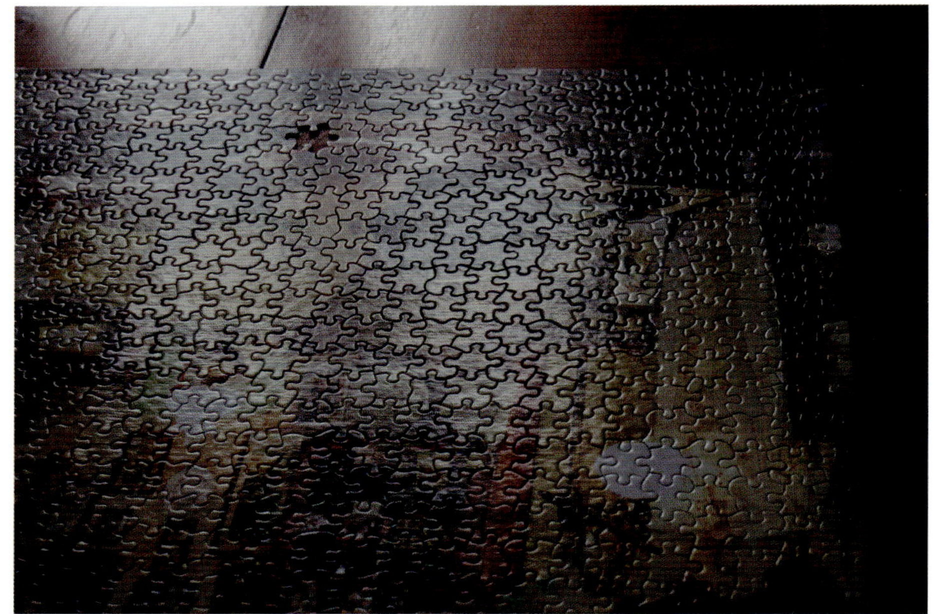

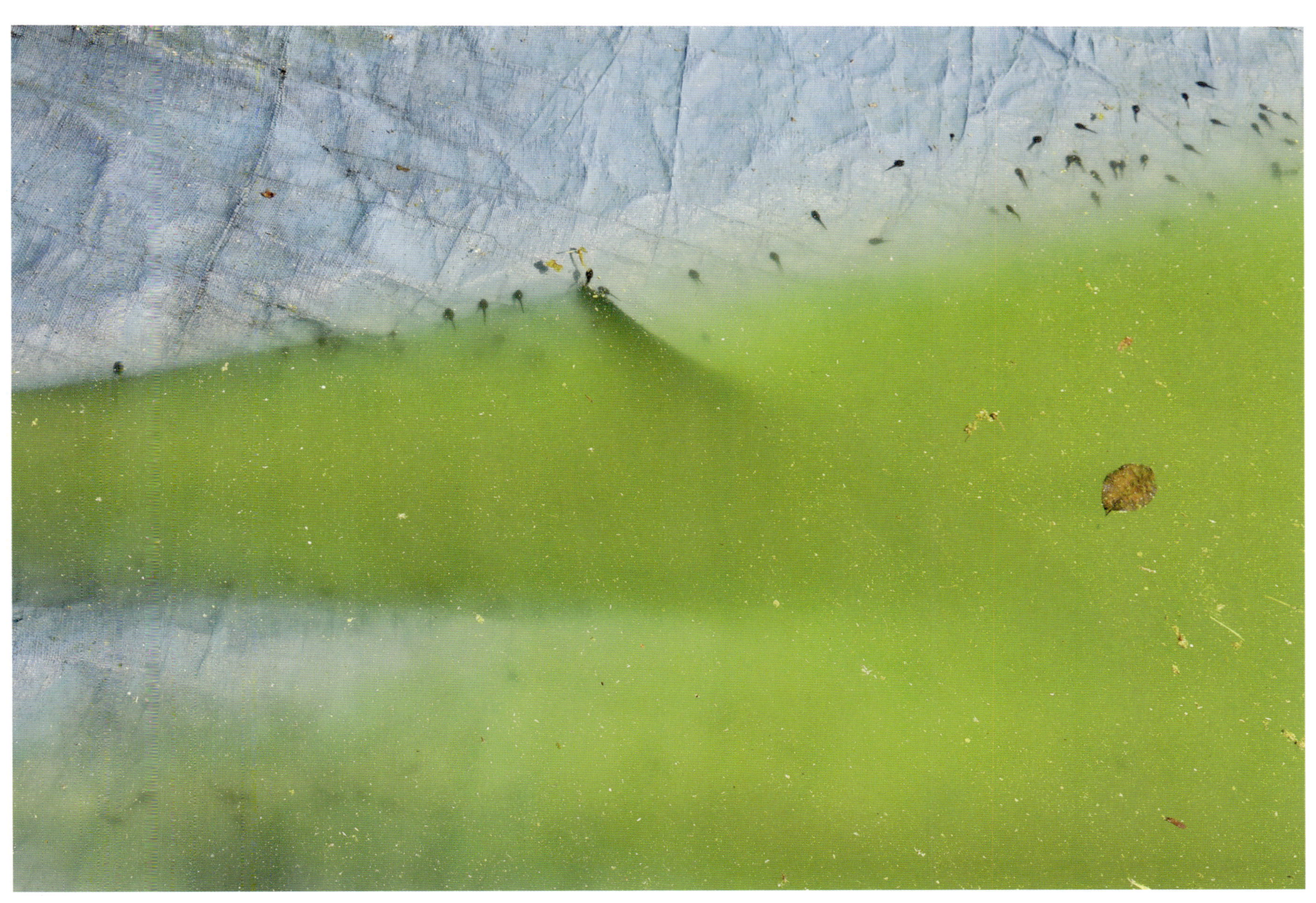

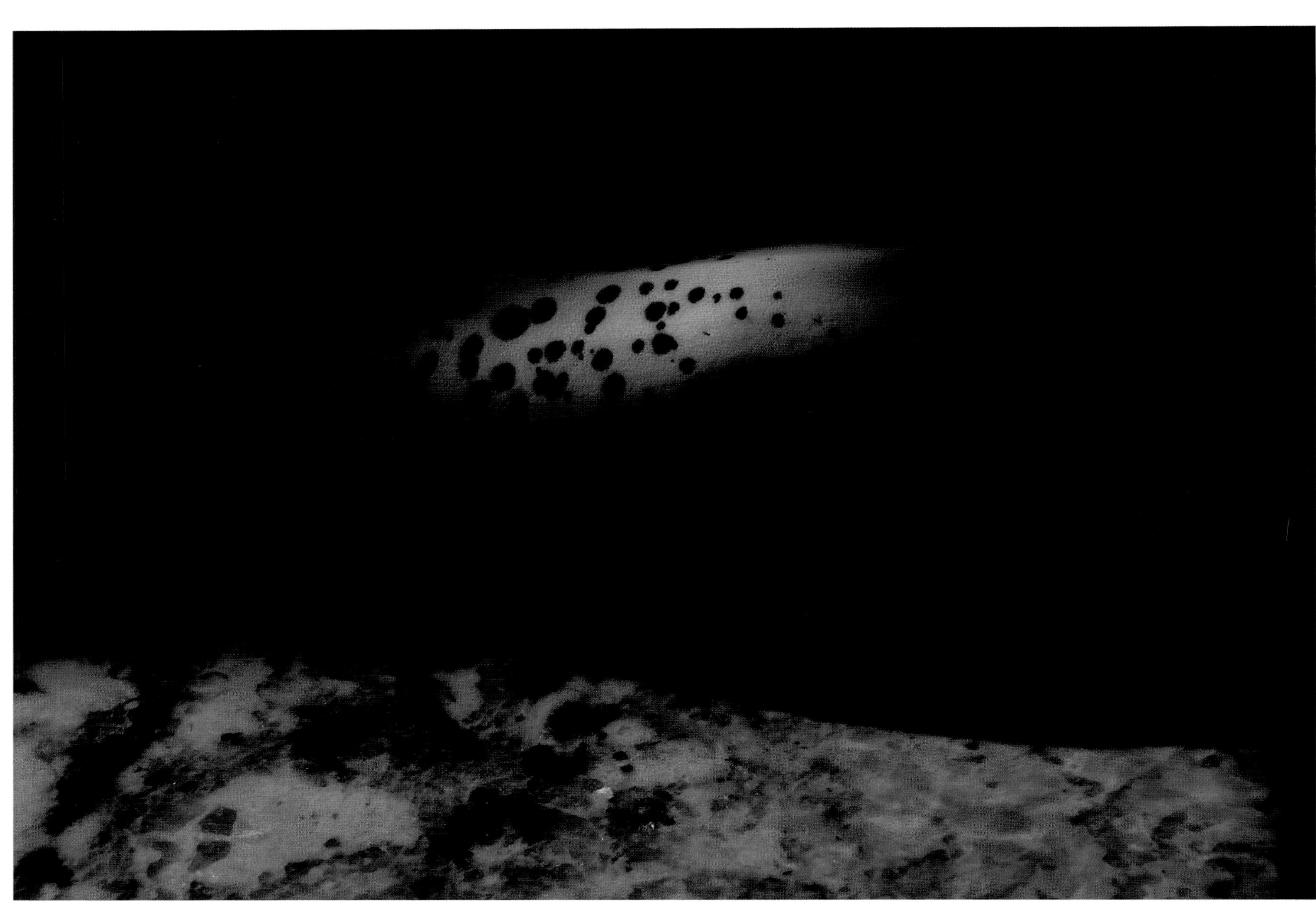

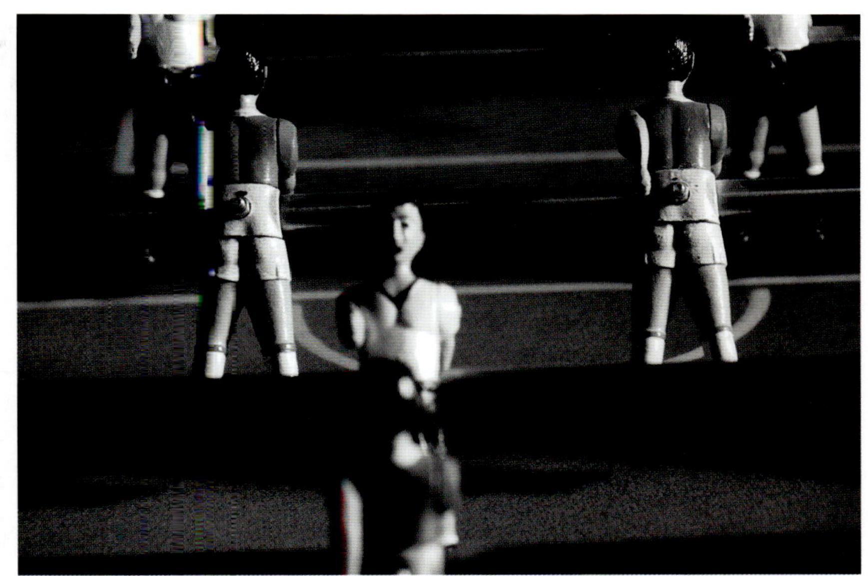

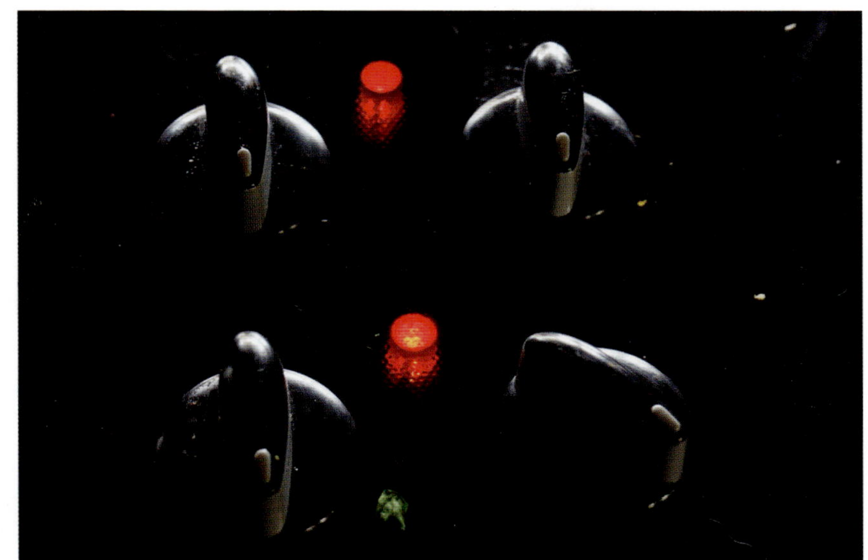

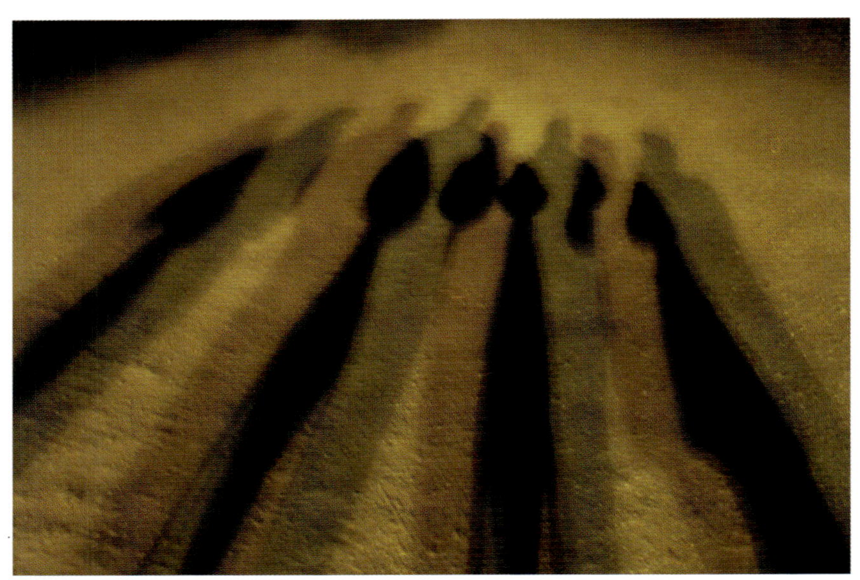

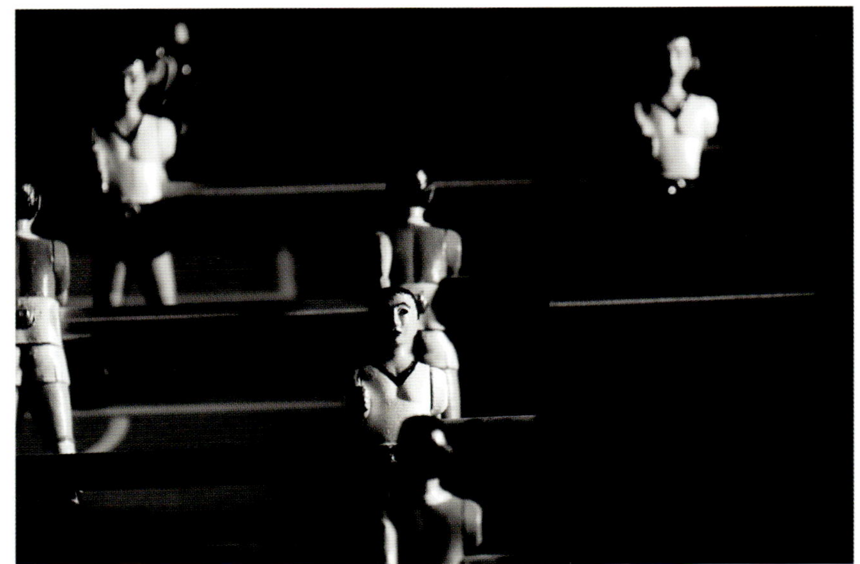

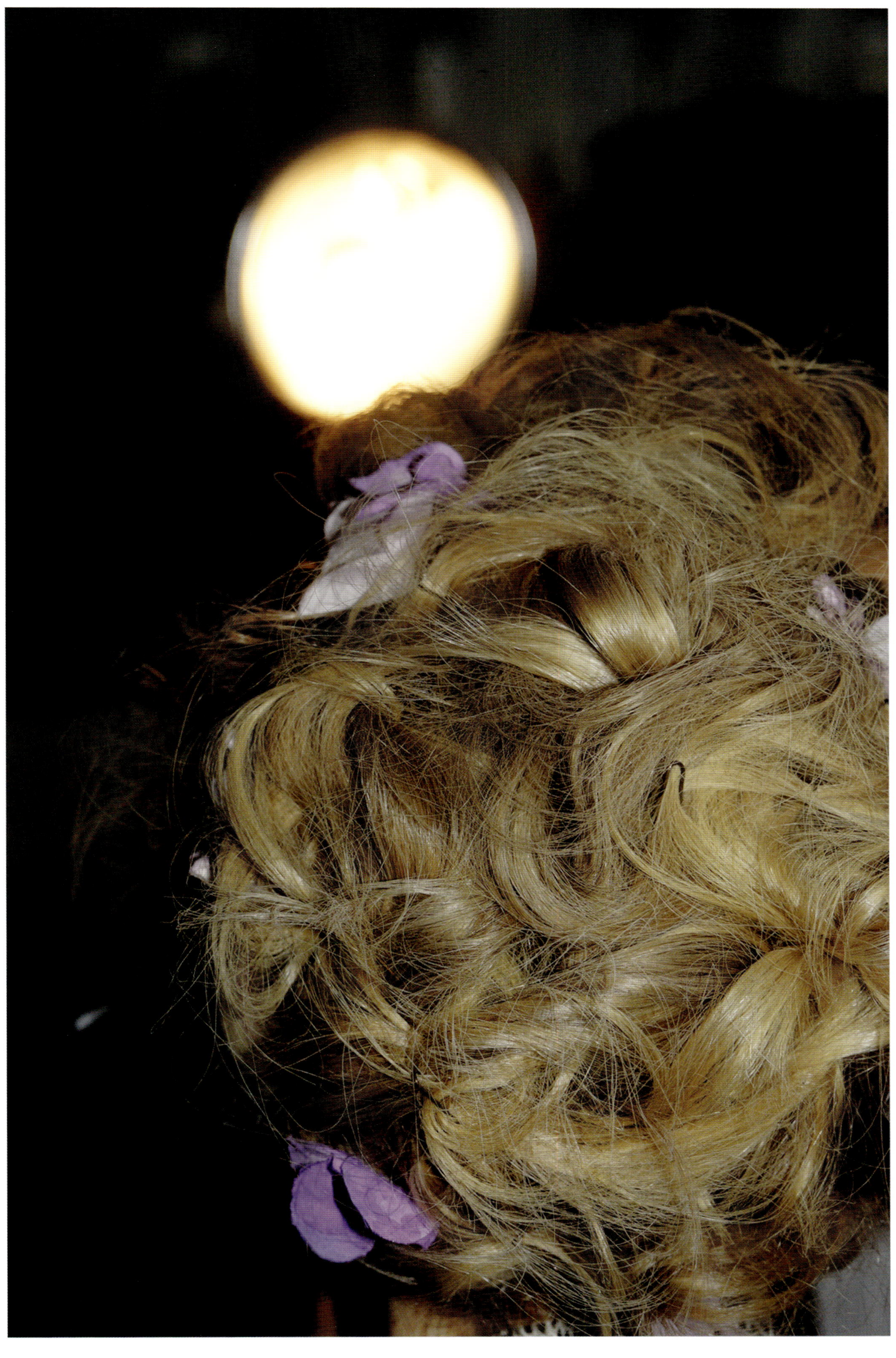

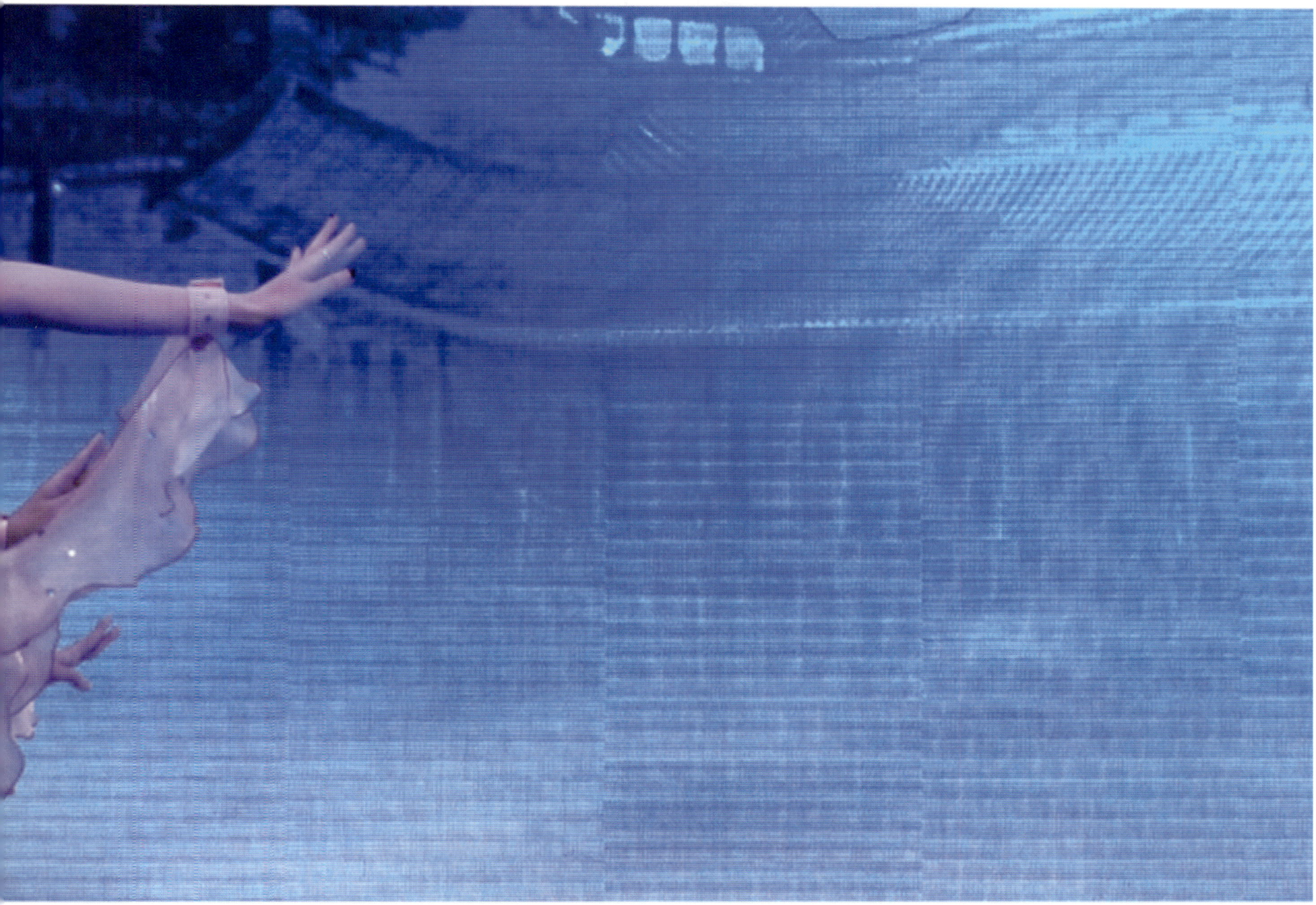

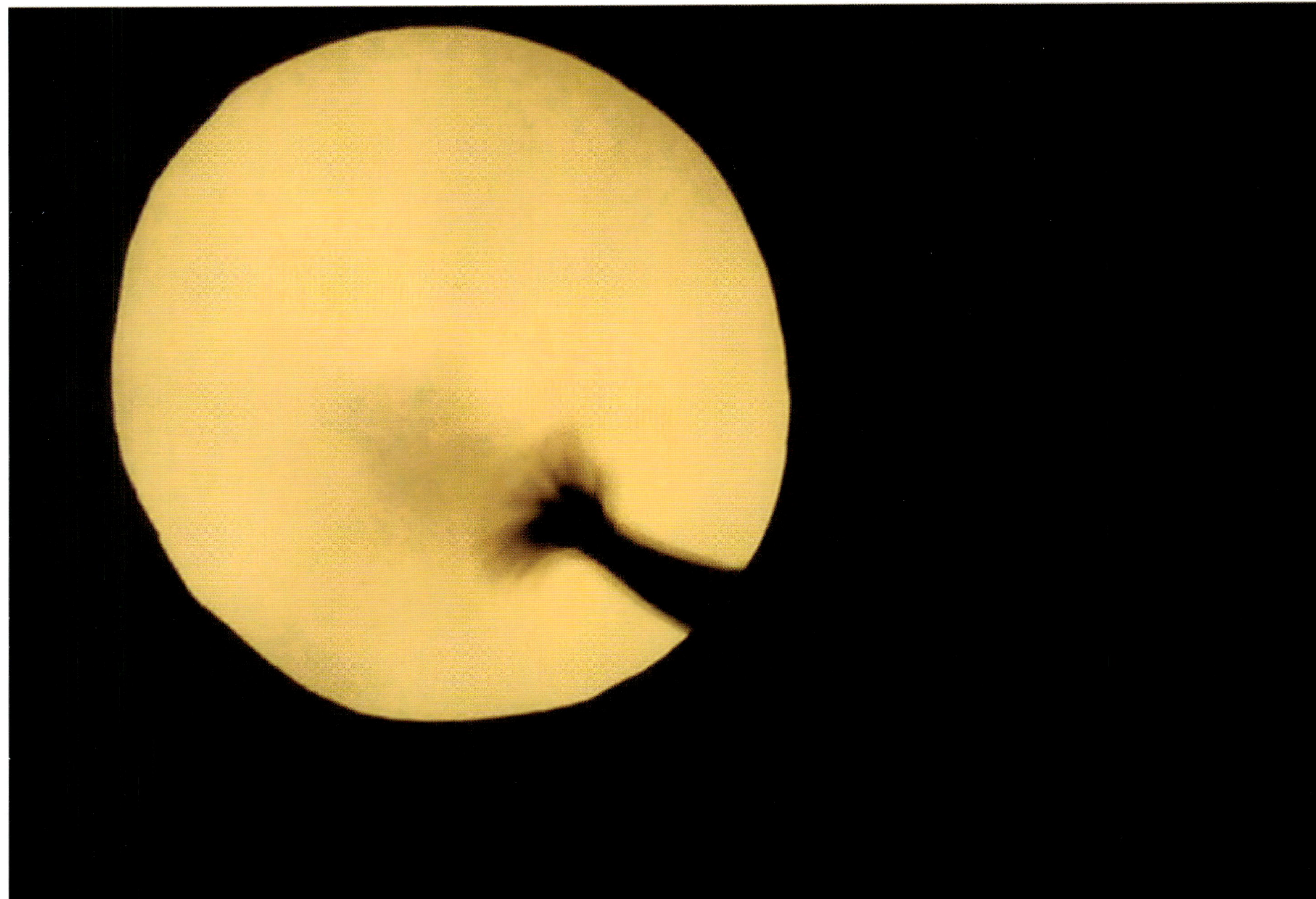

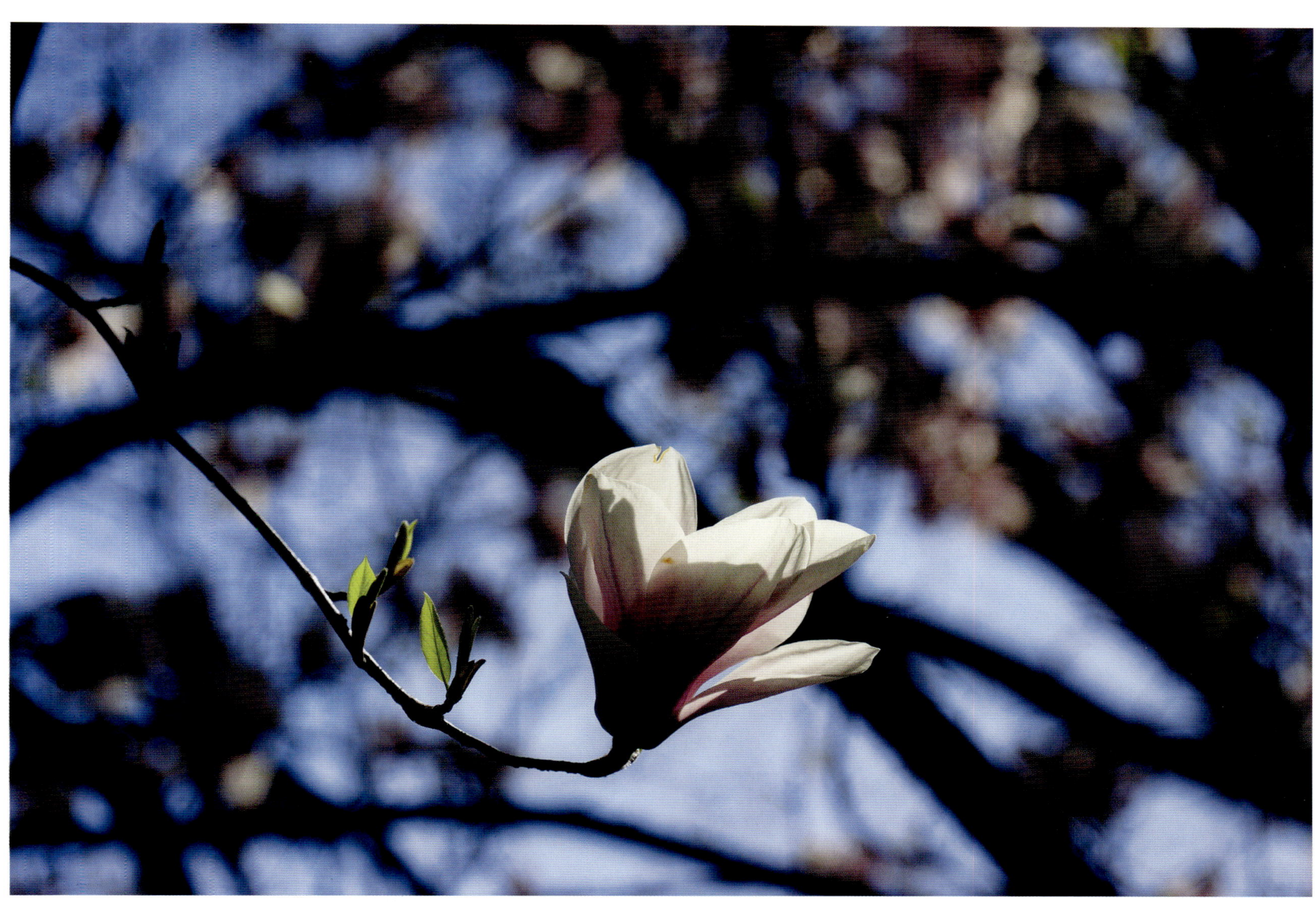

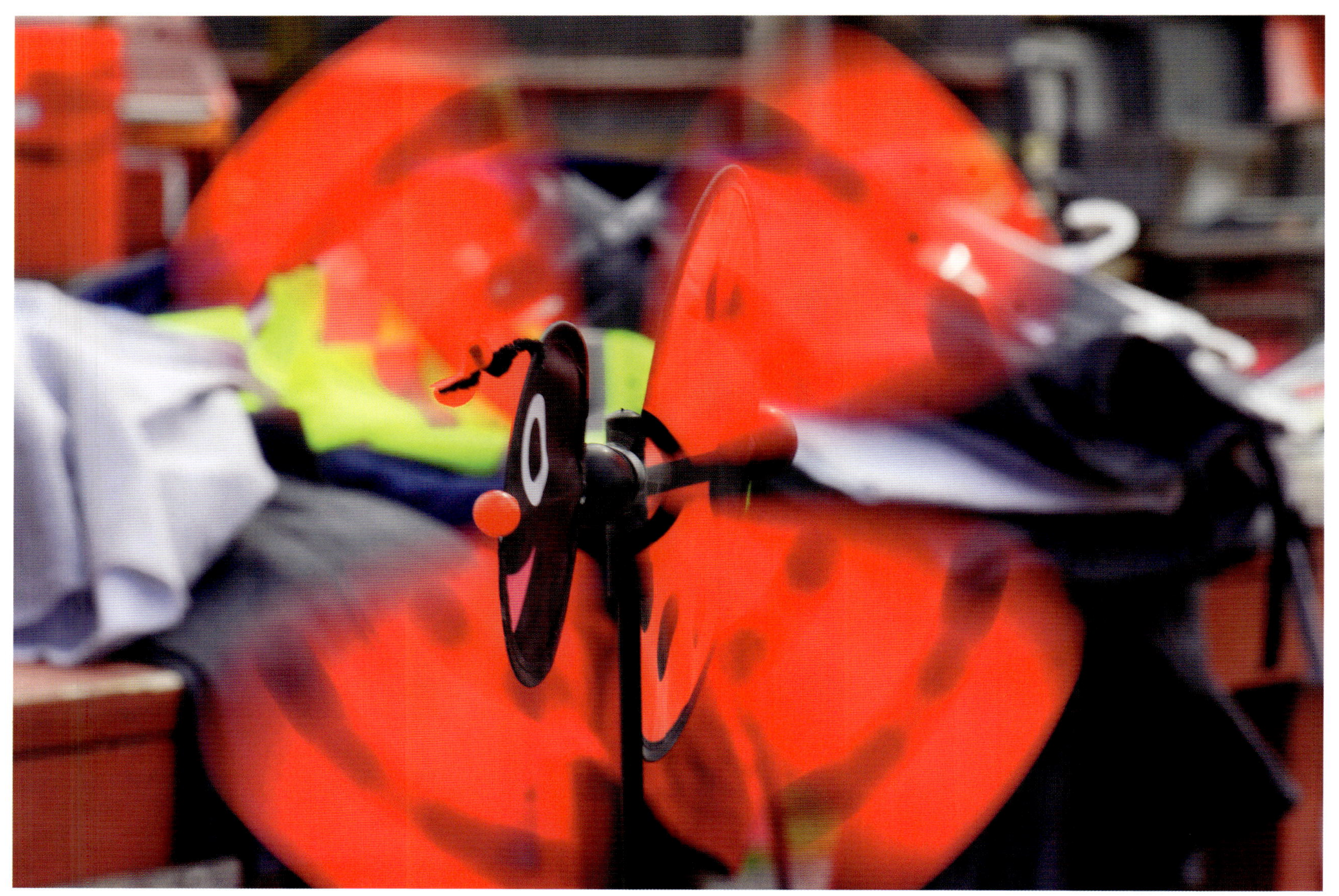

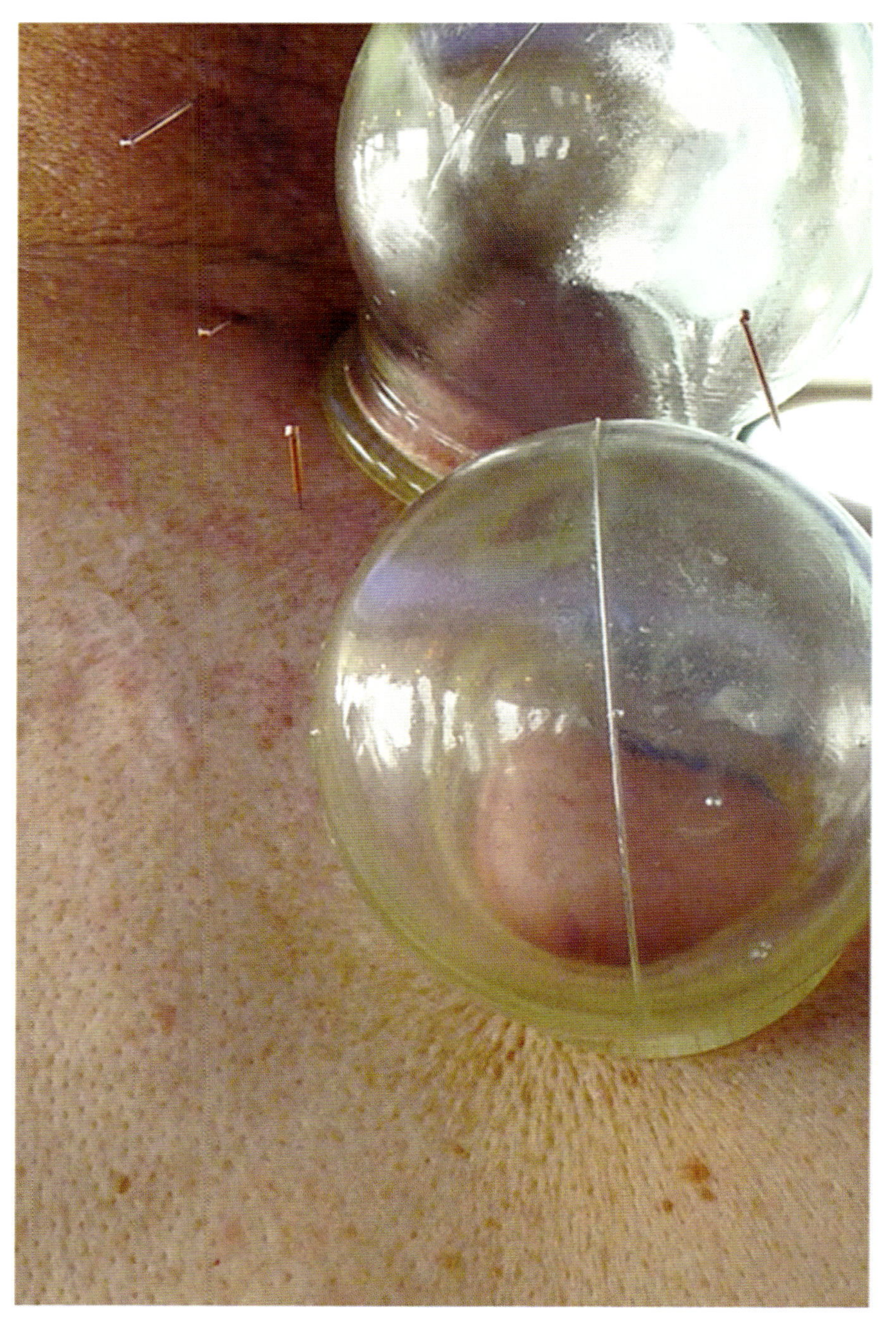

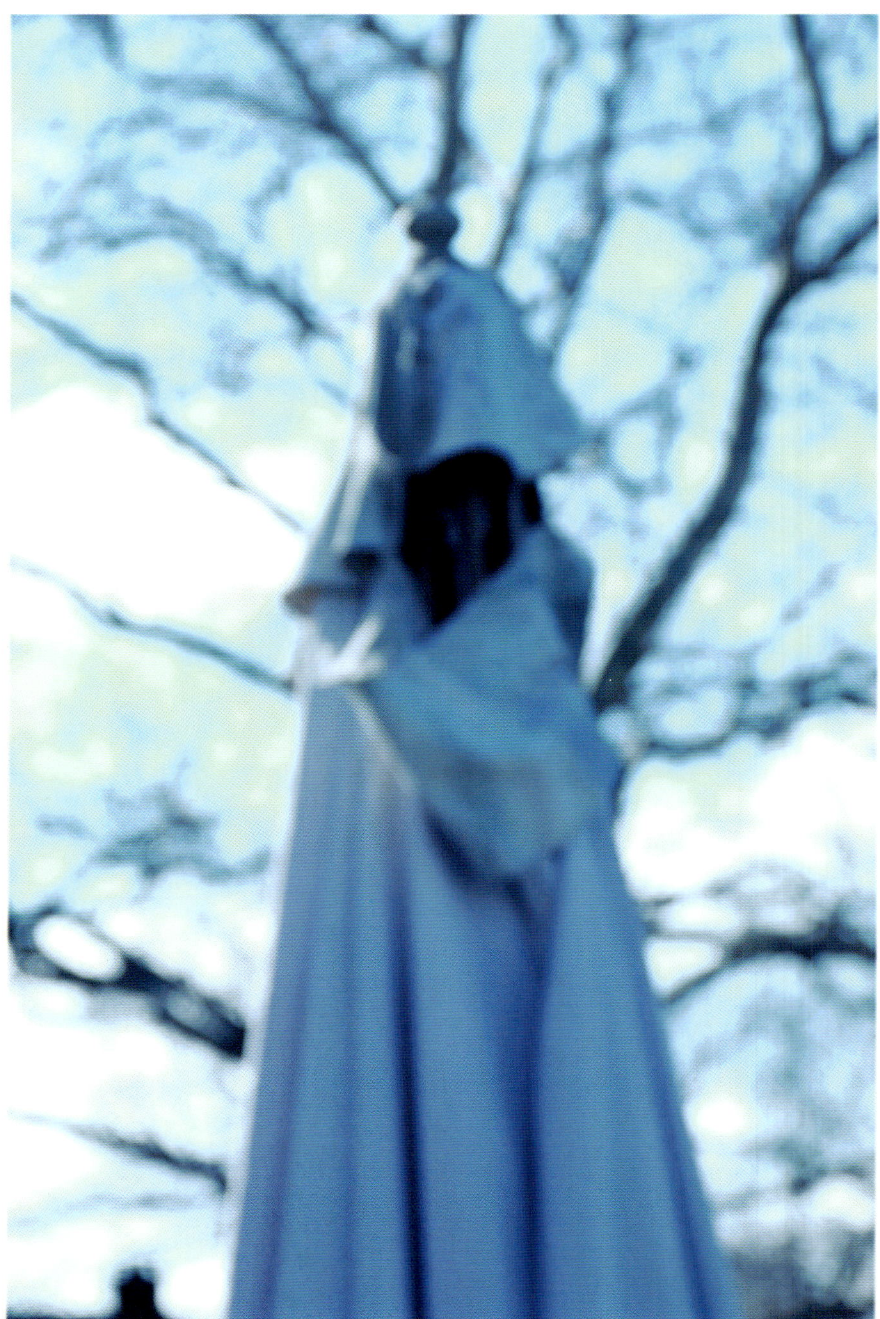

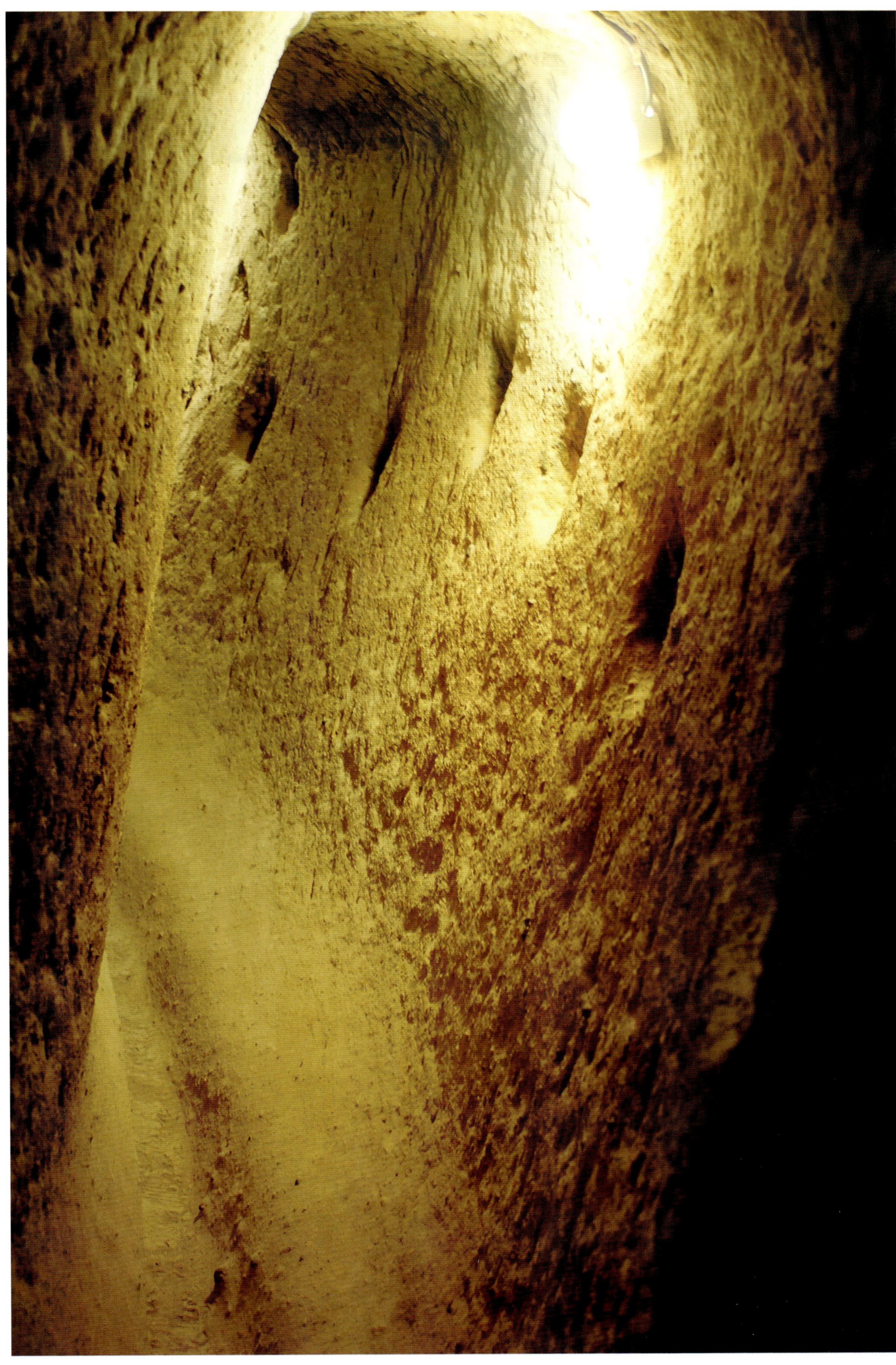

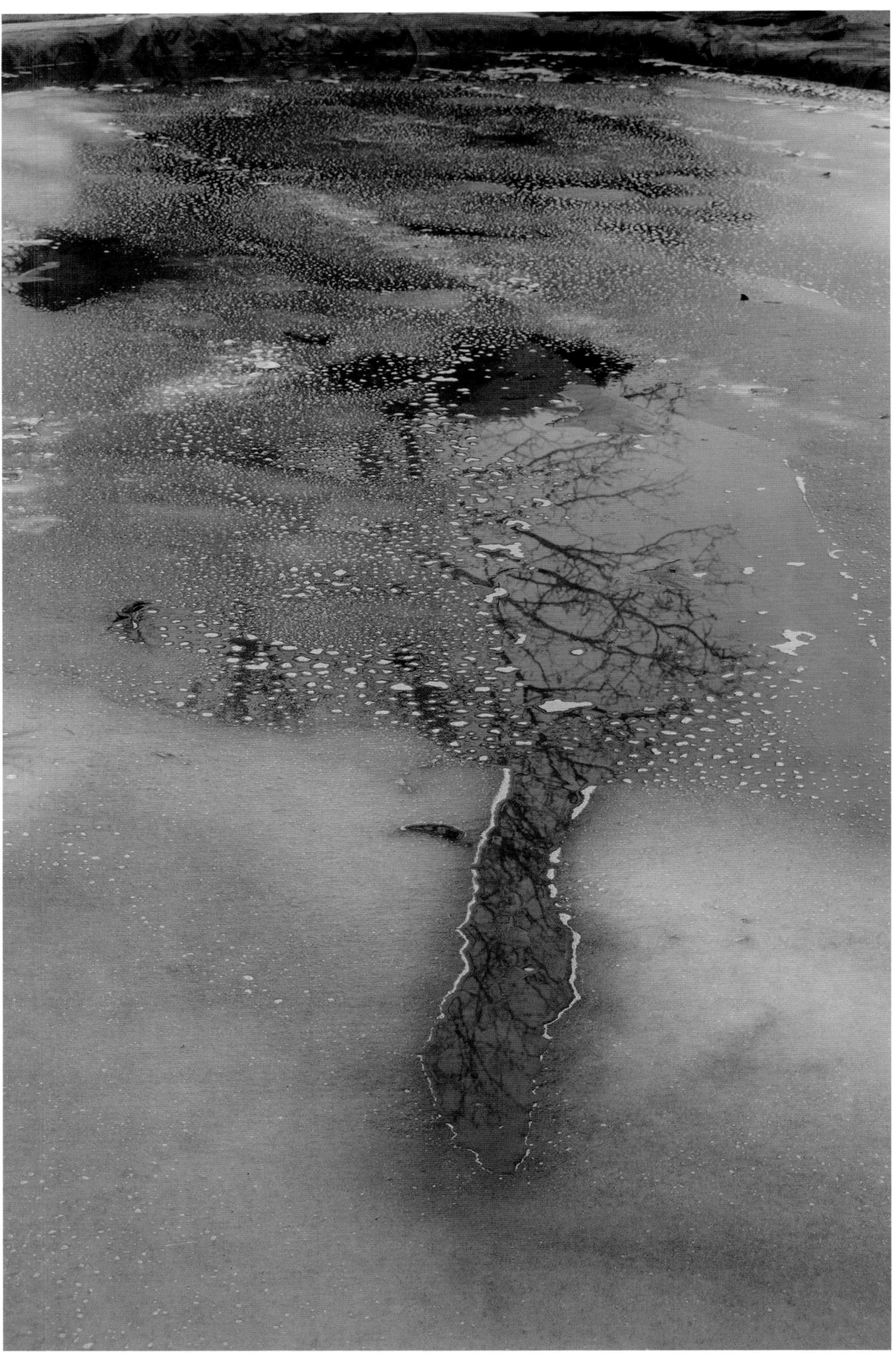

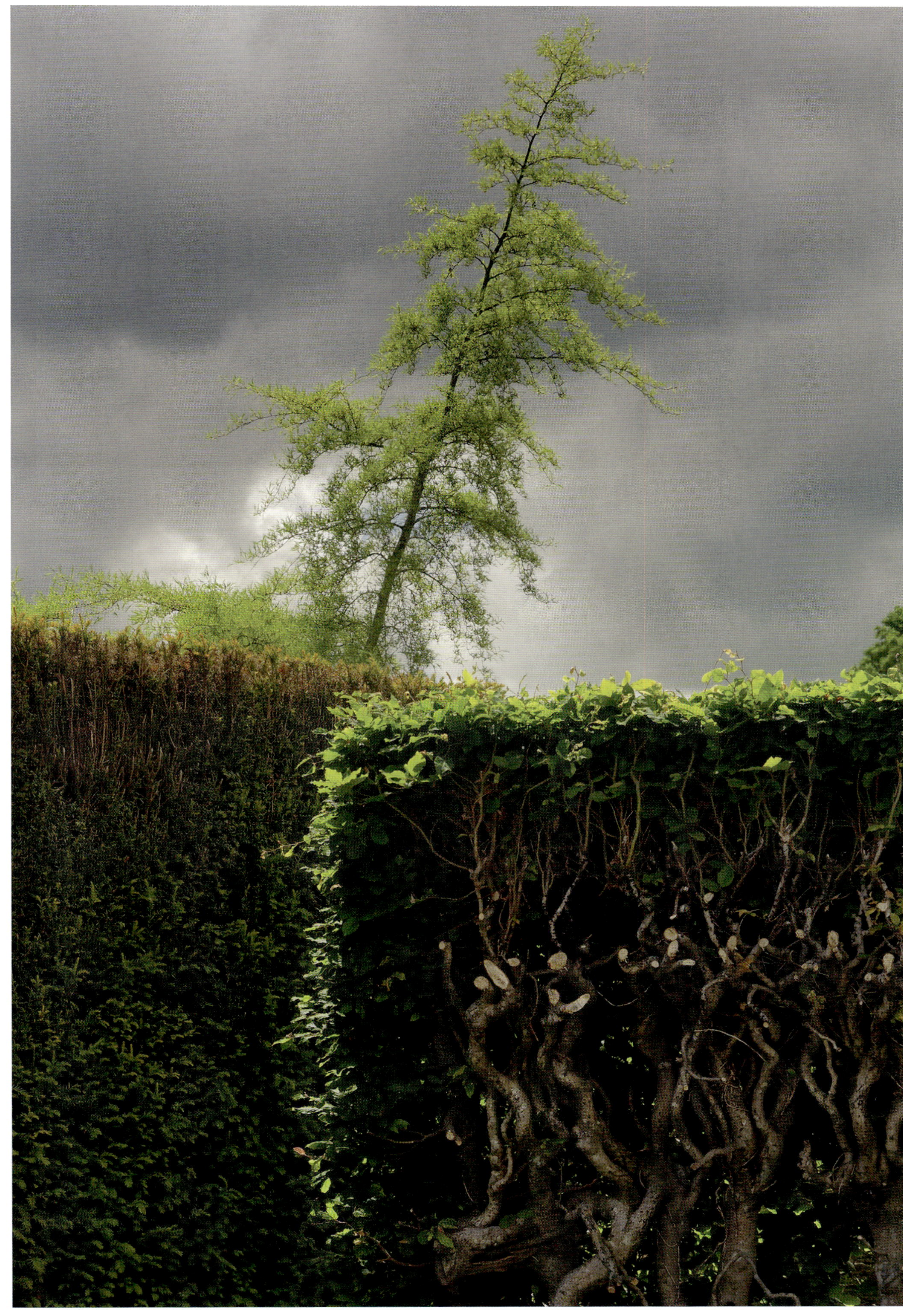

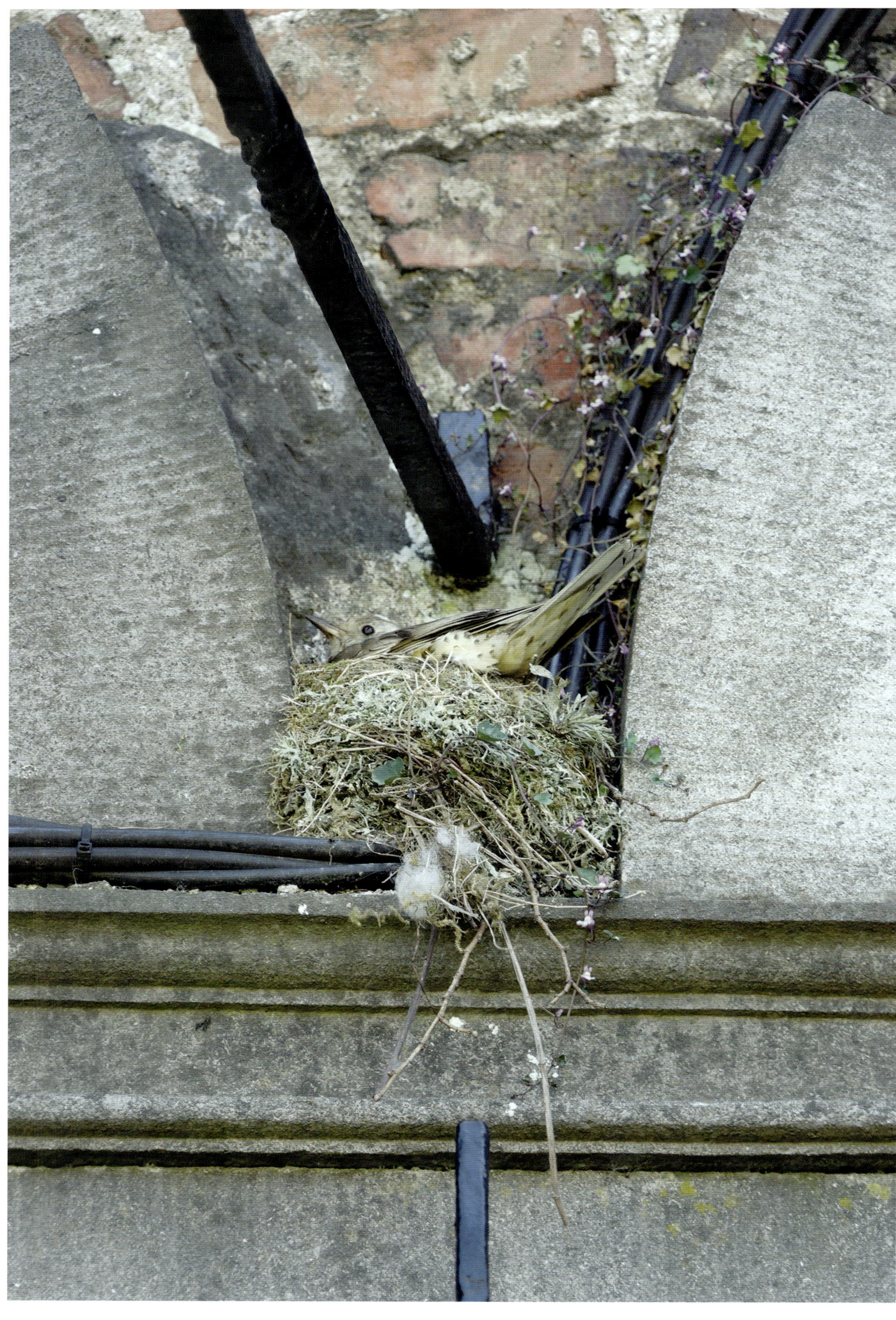

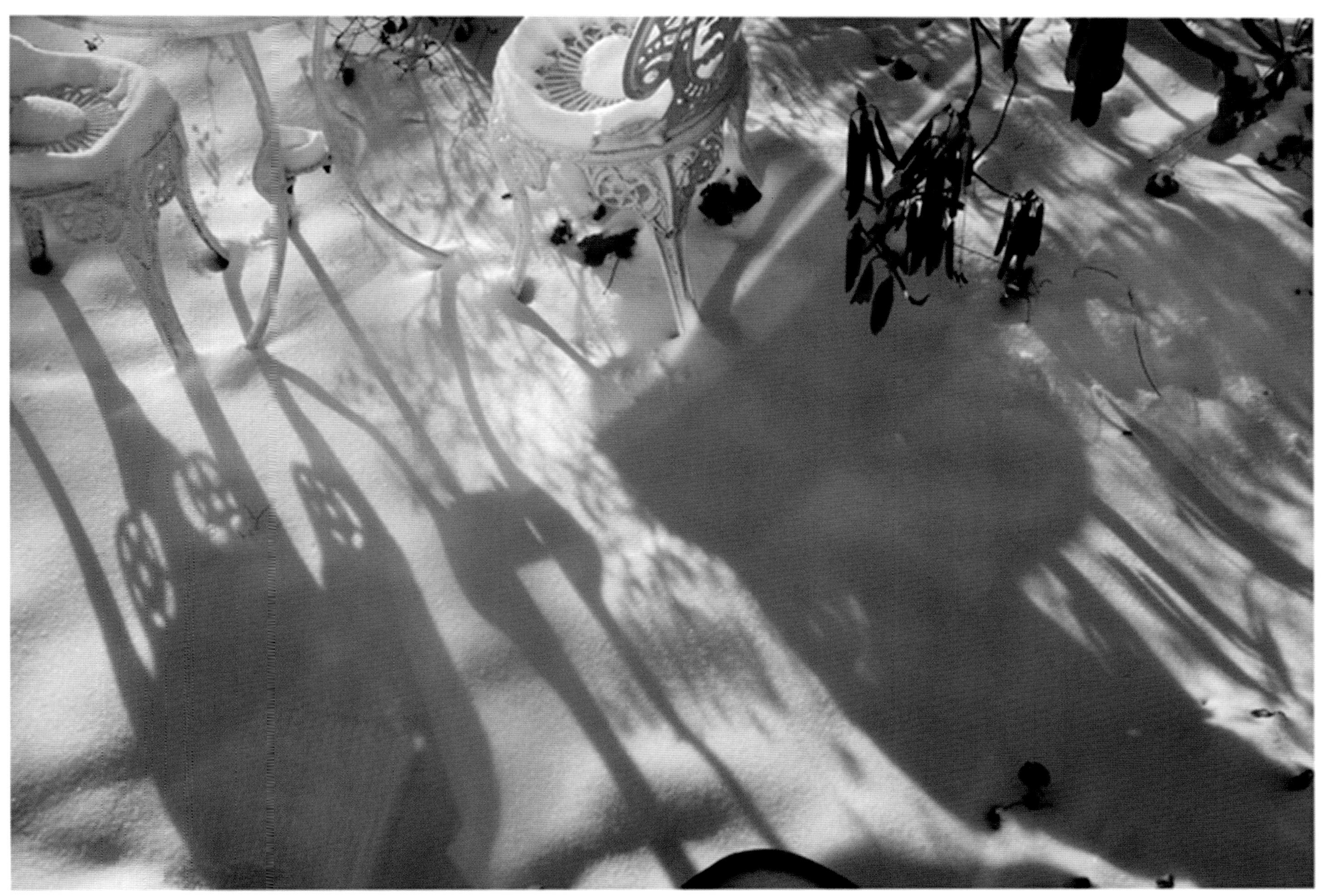

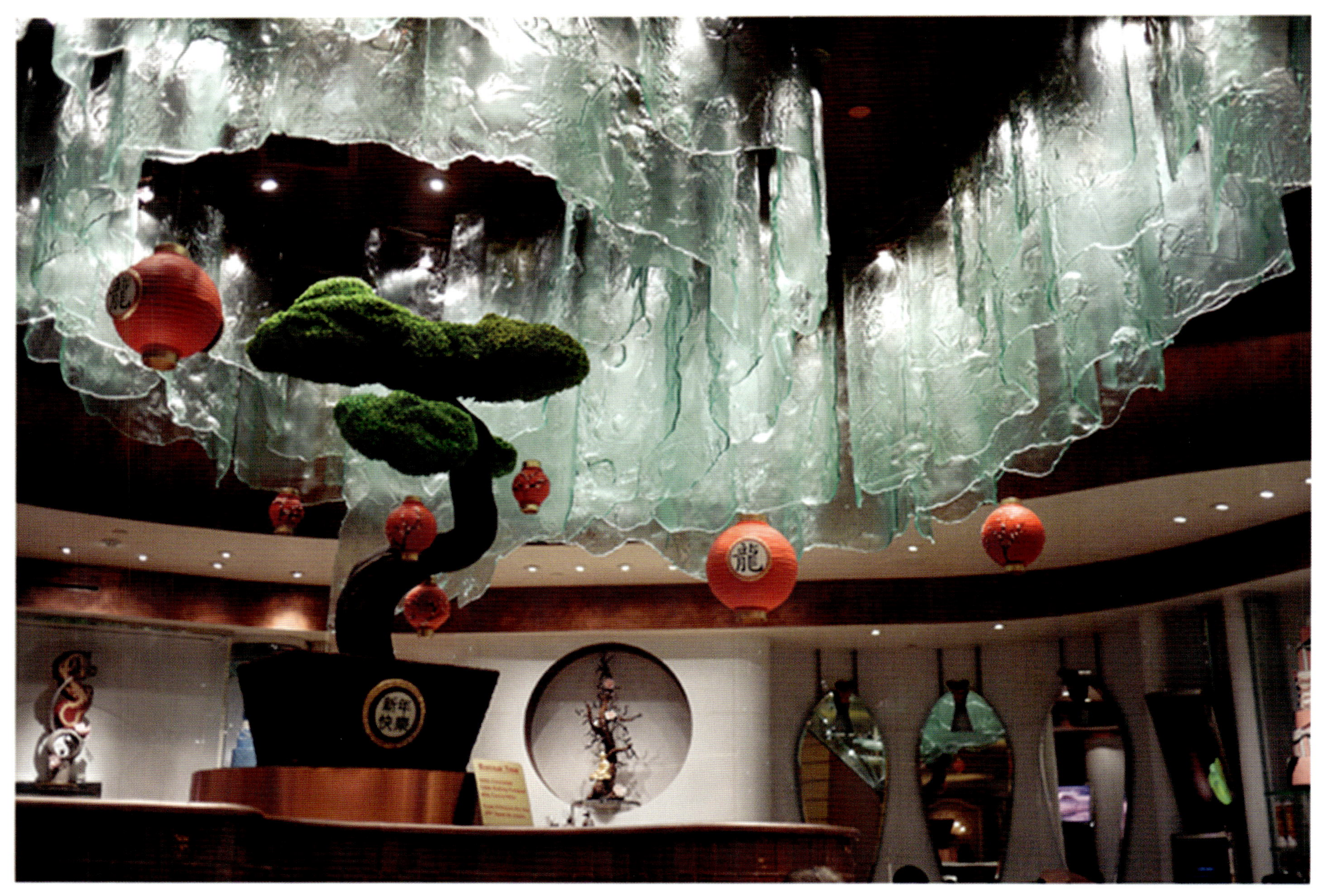
龍
龍

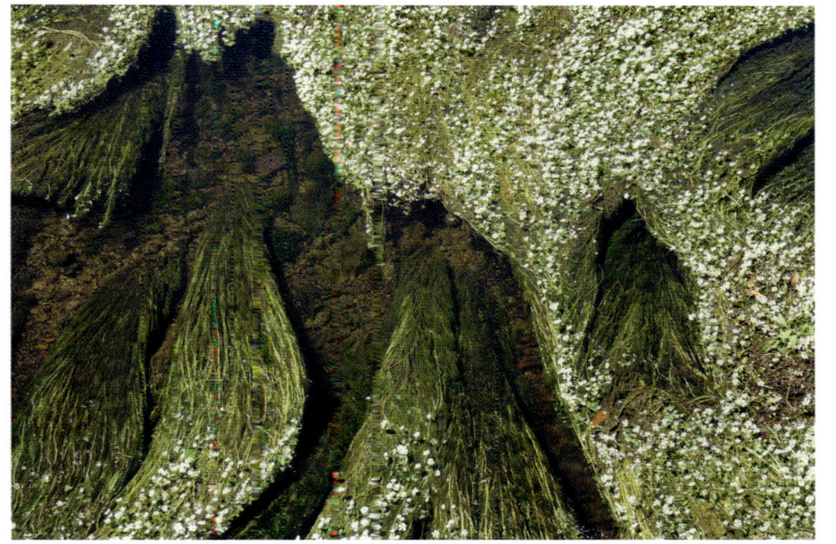

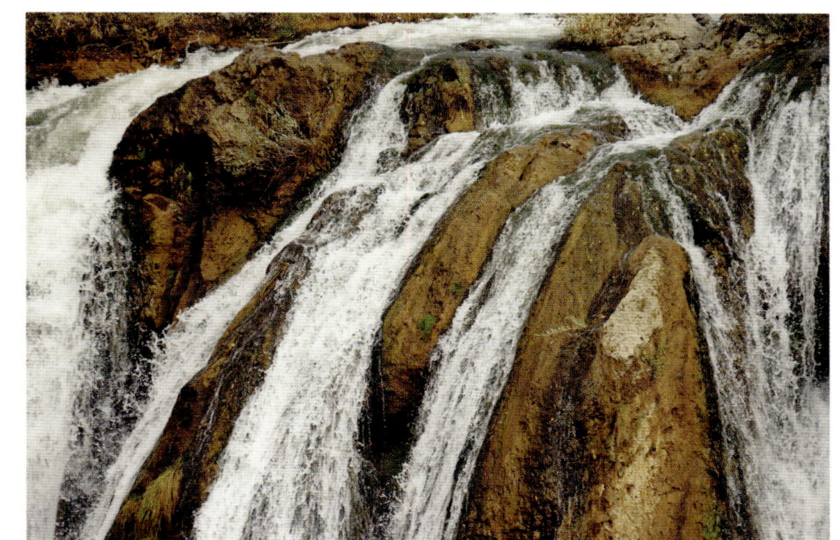

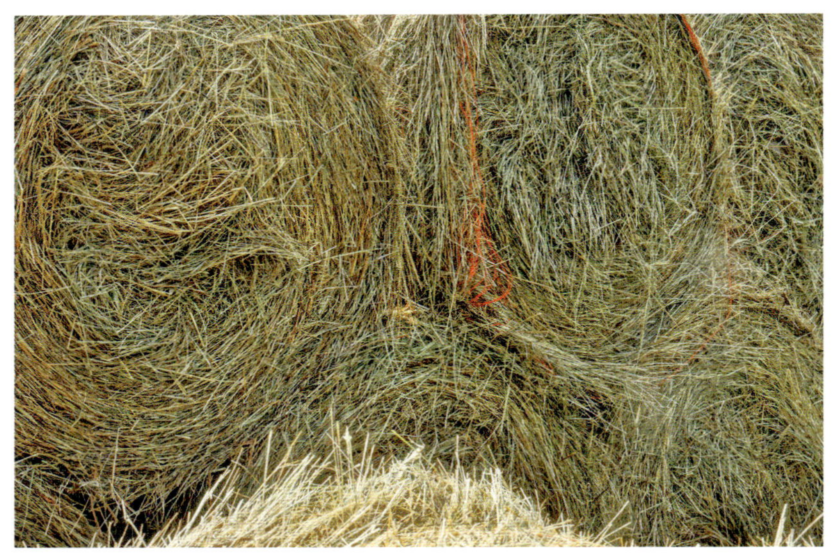

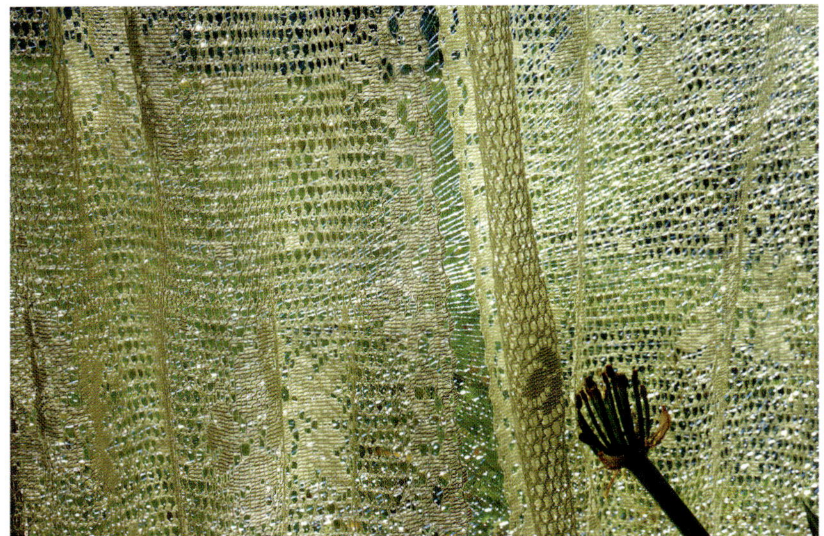

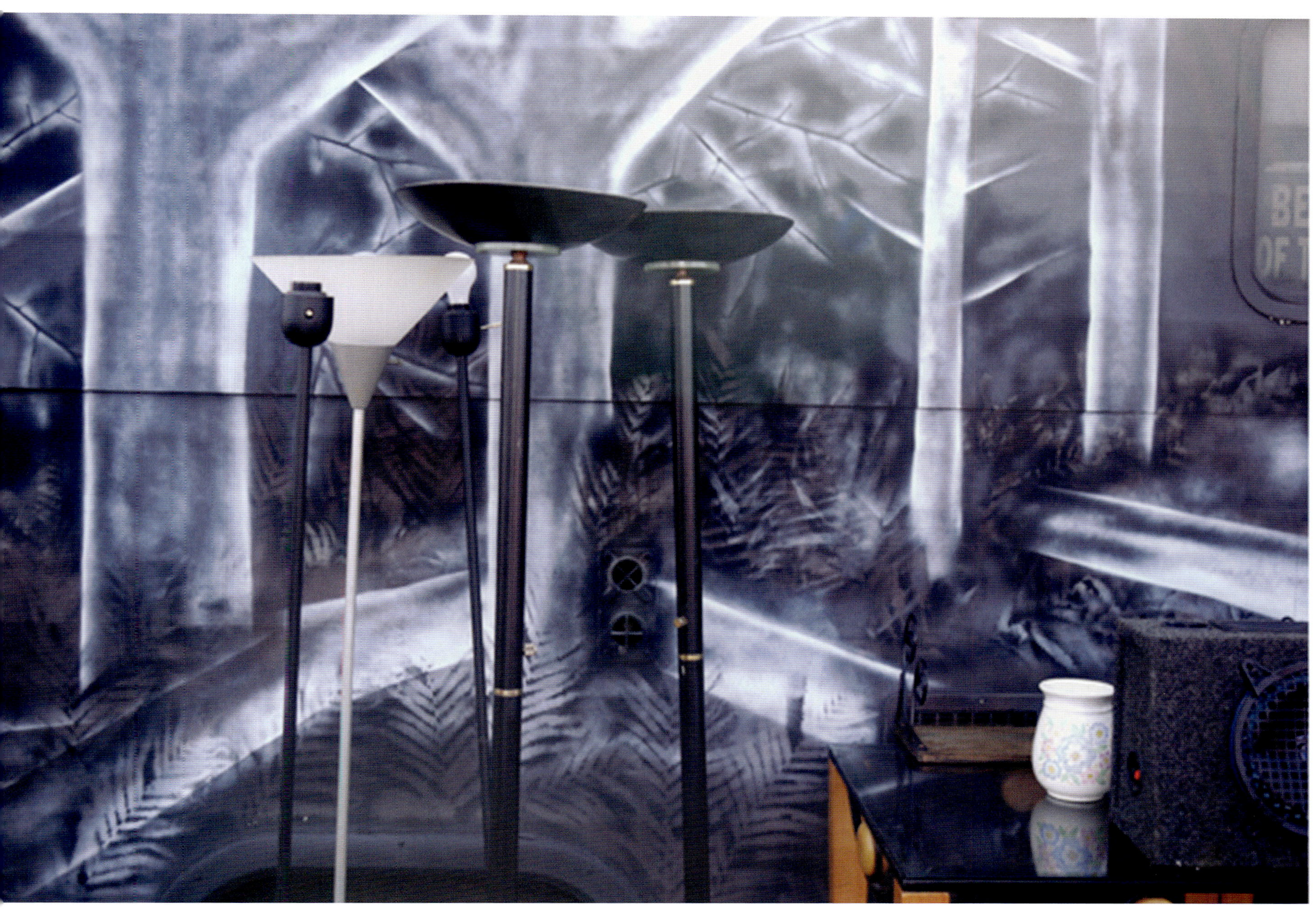

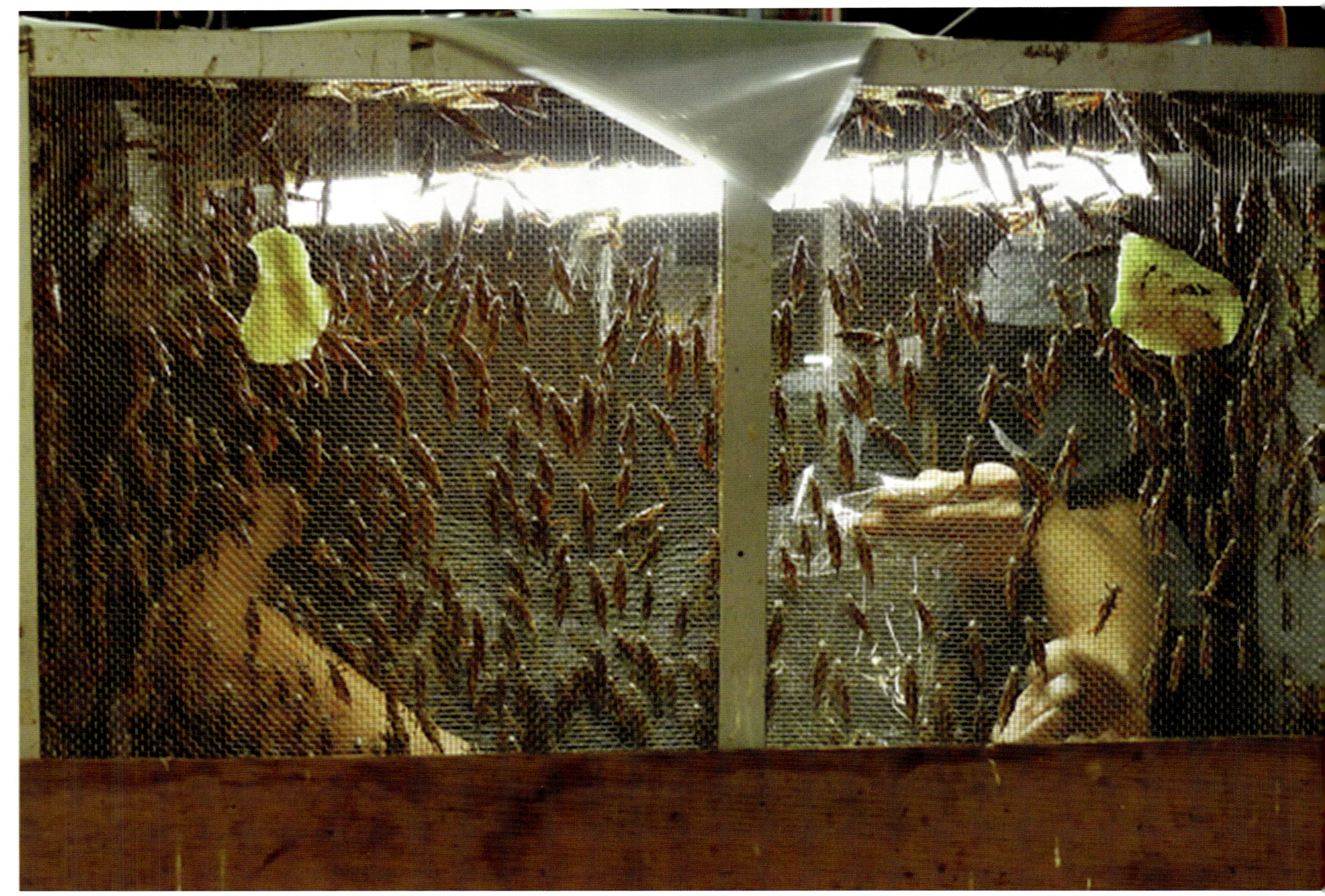

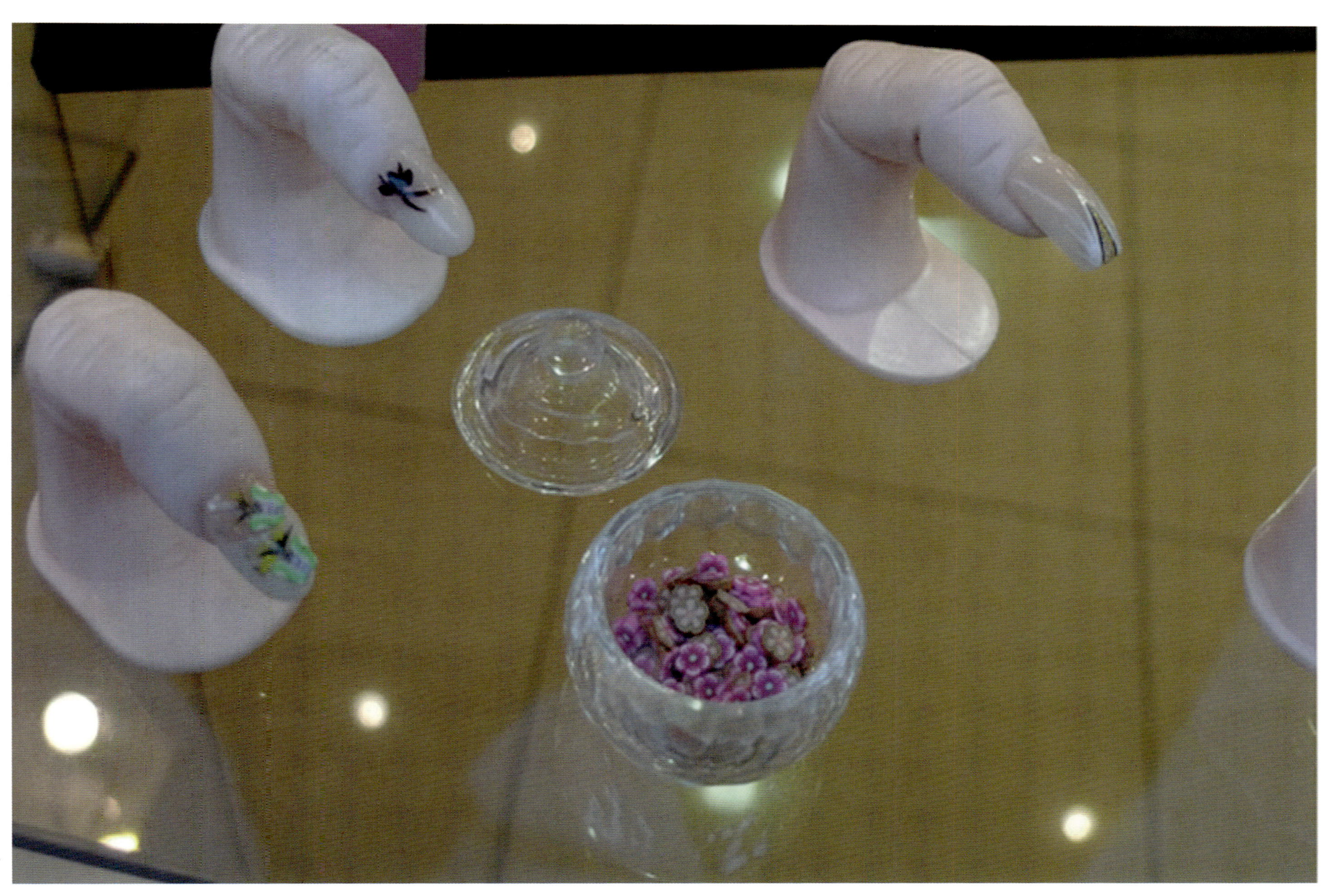

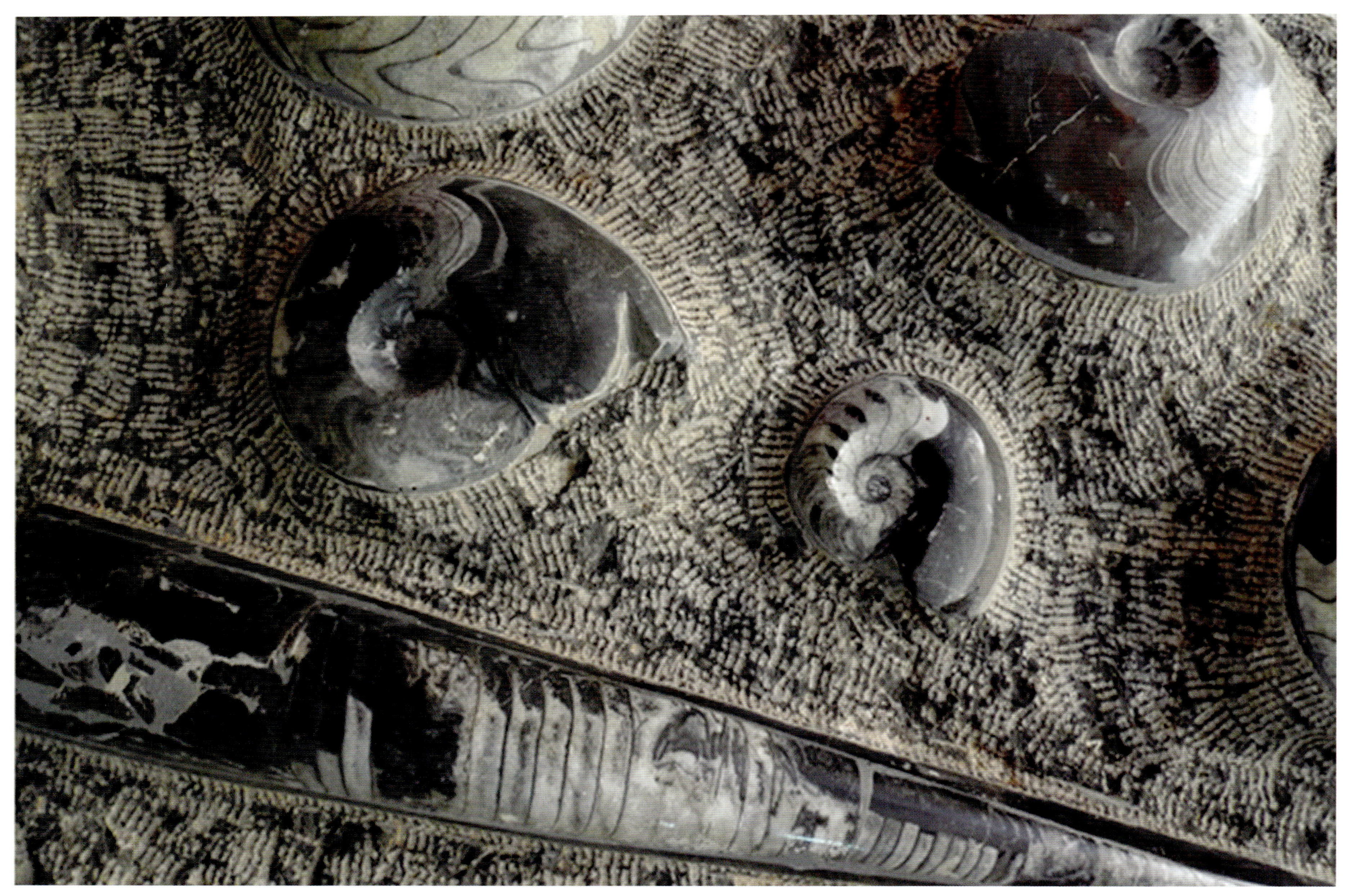

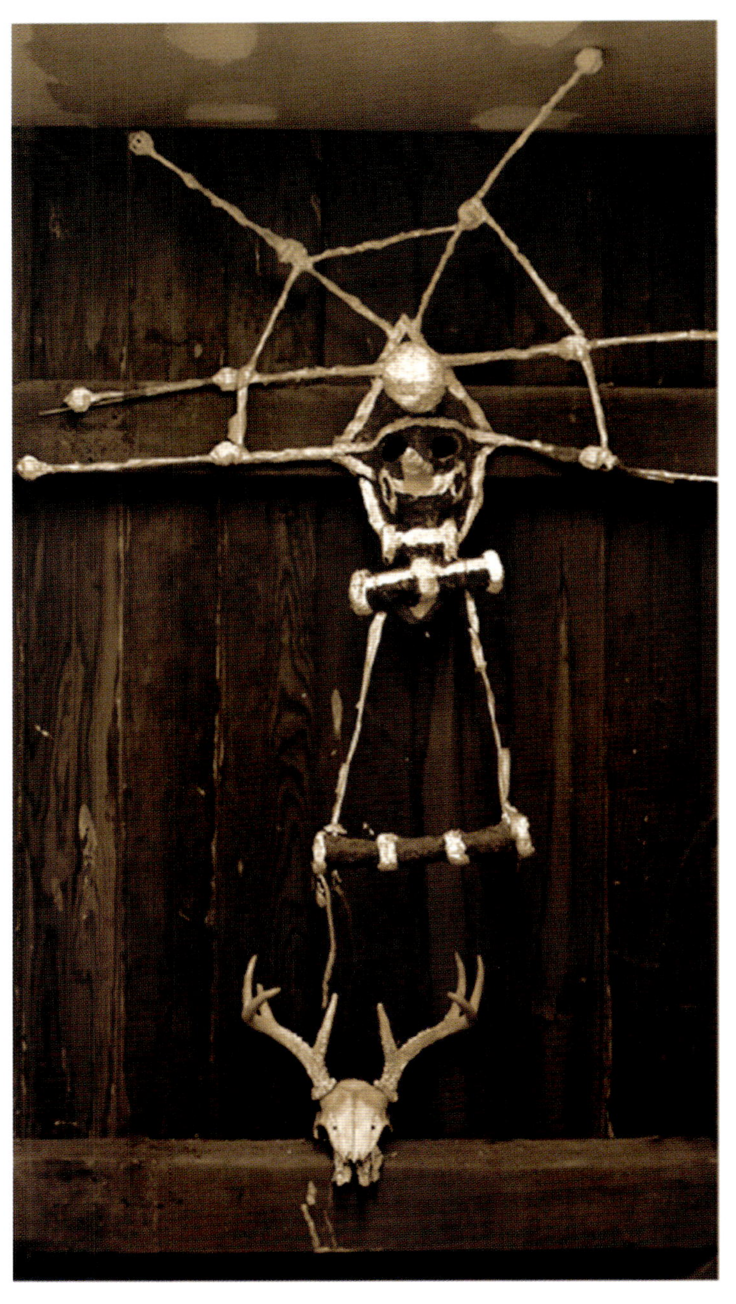

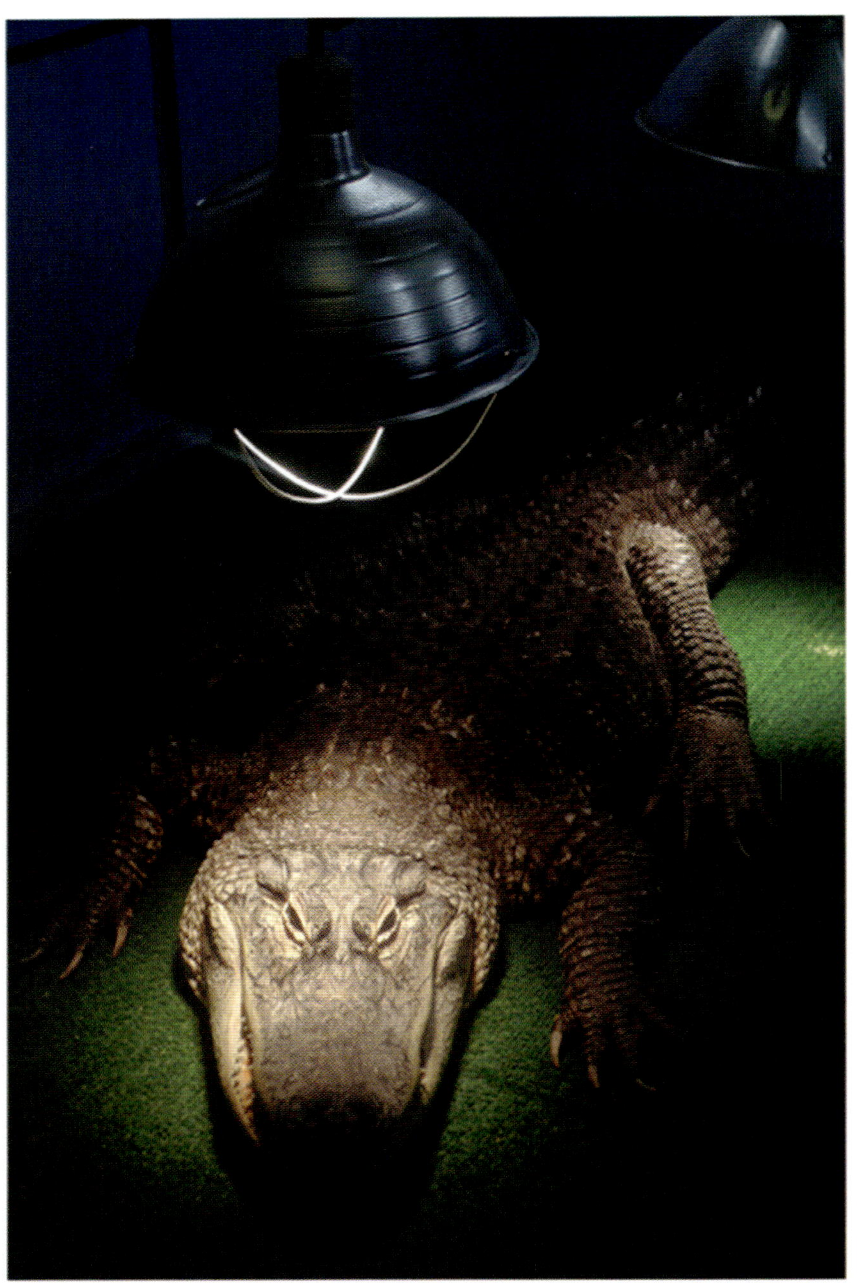

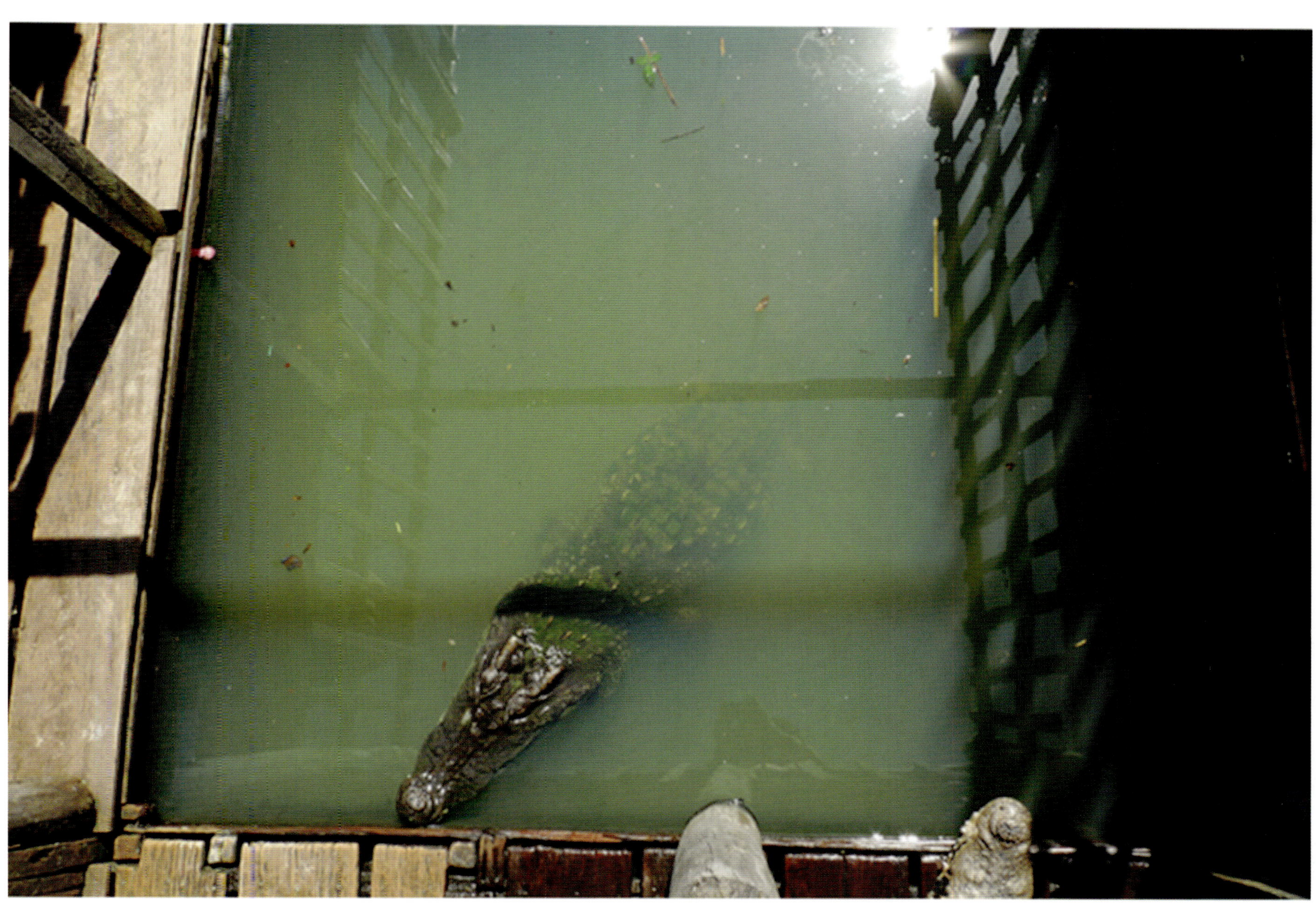

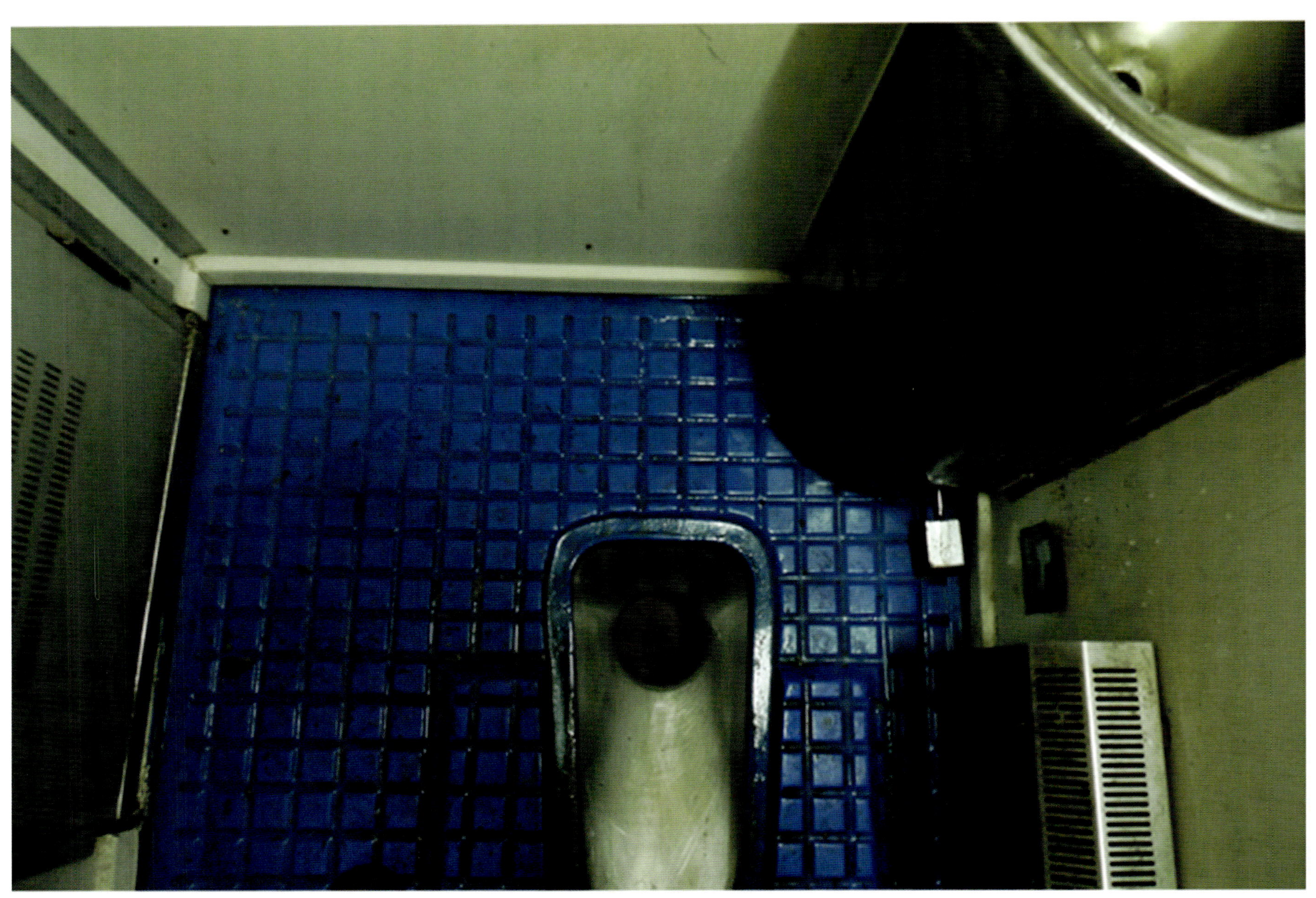

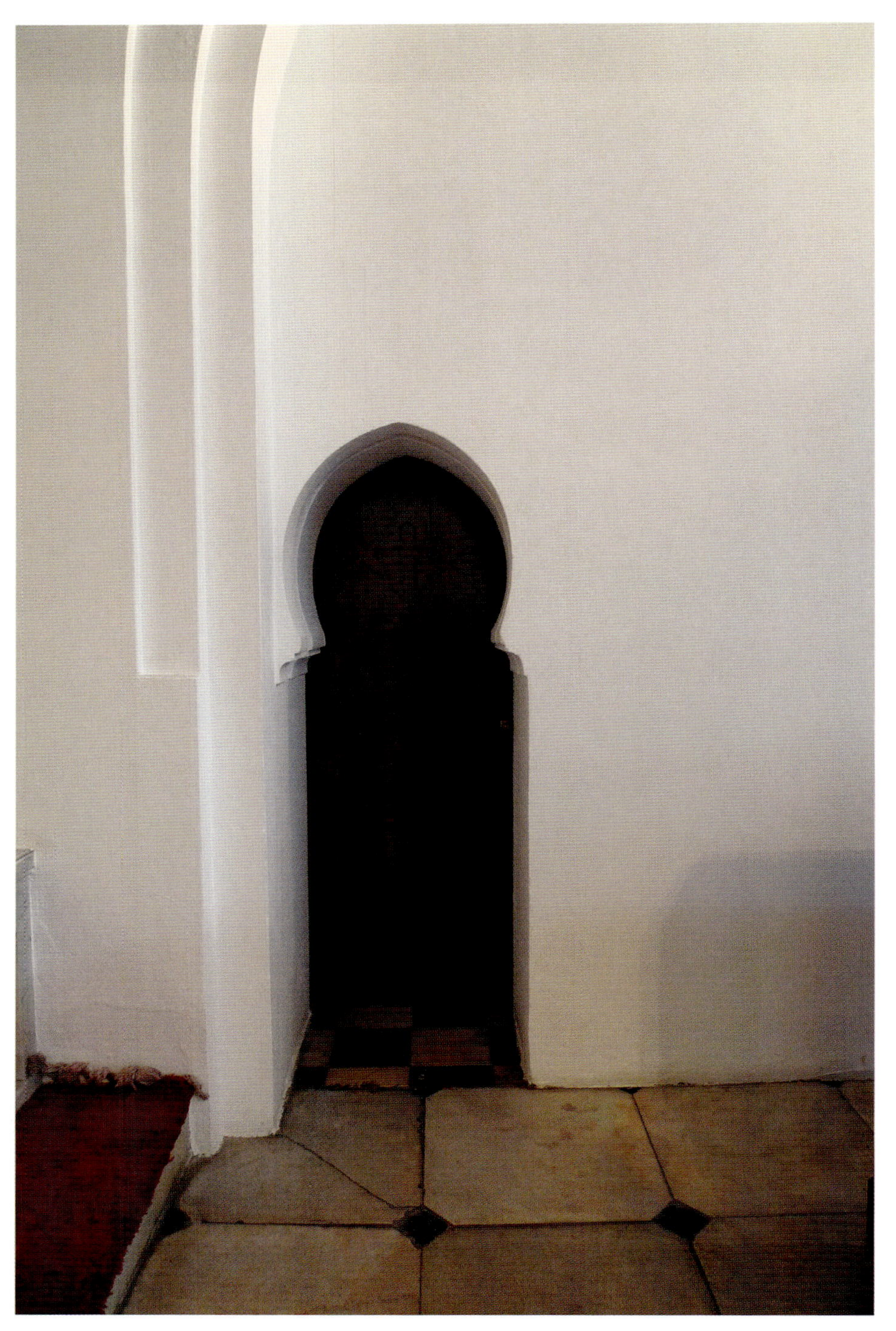

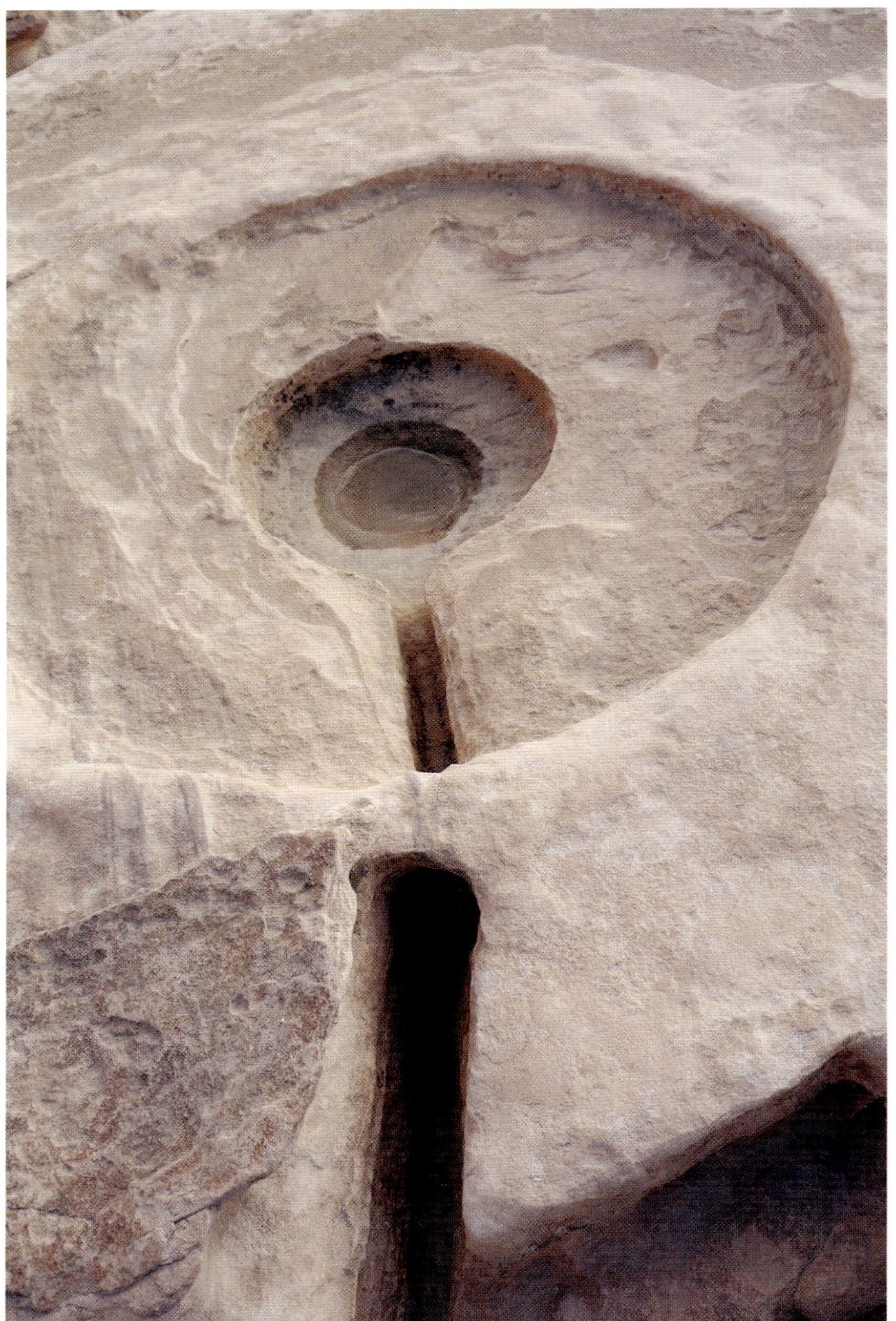

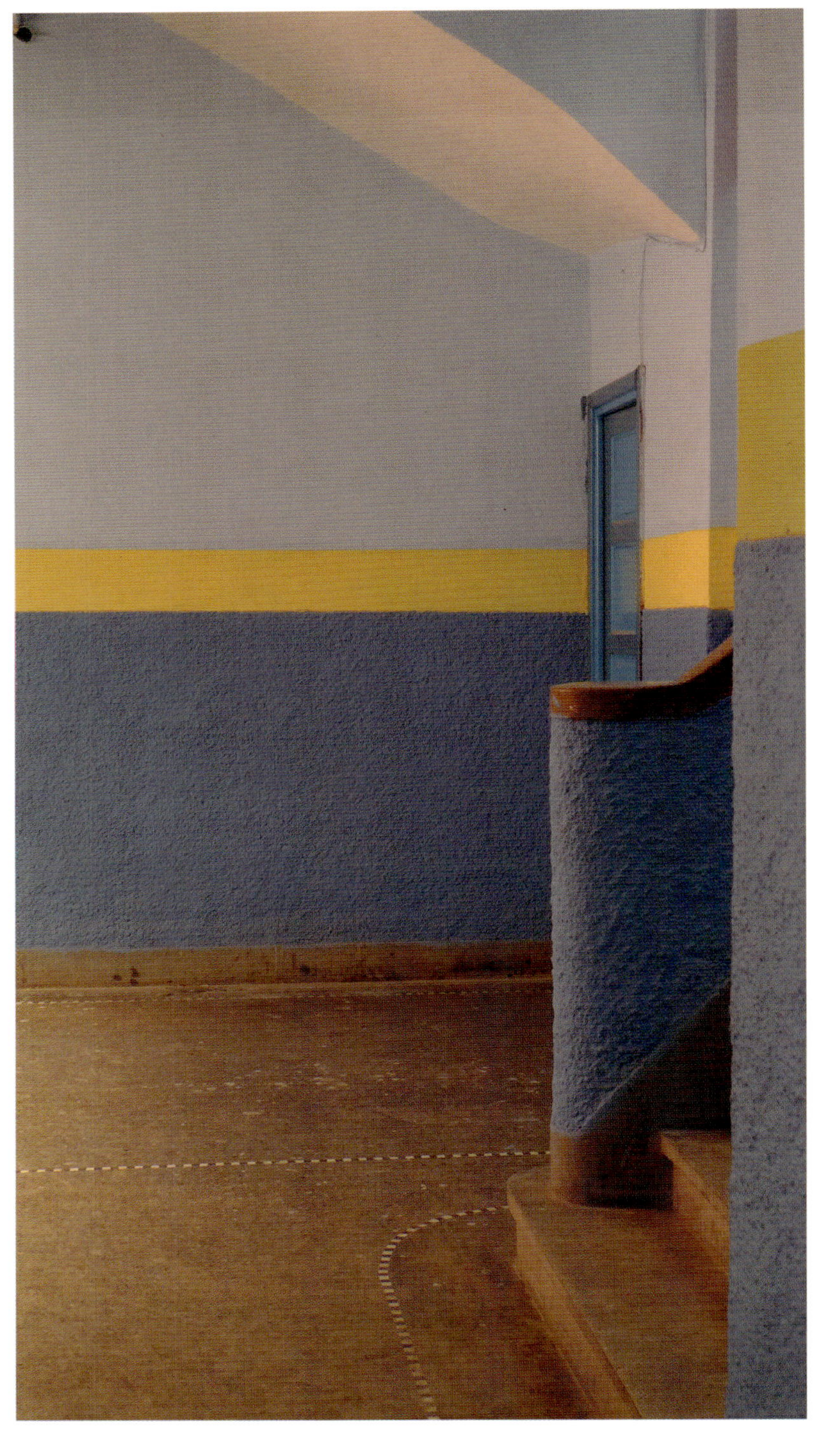

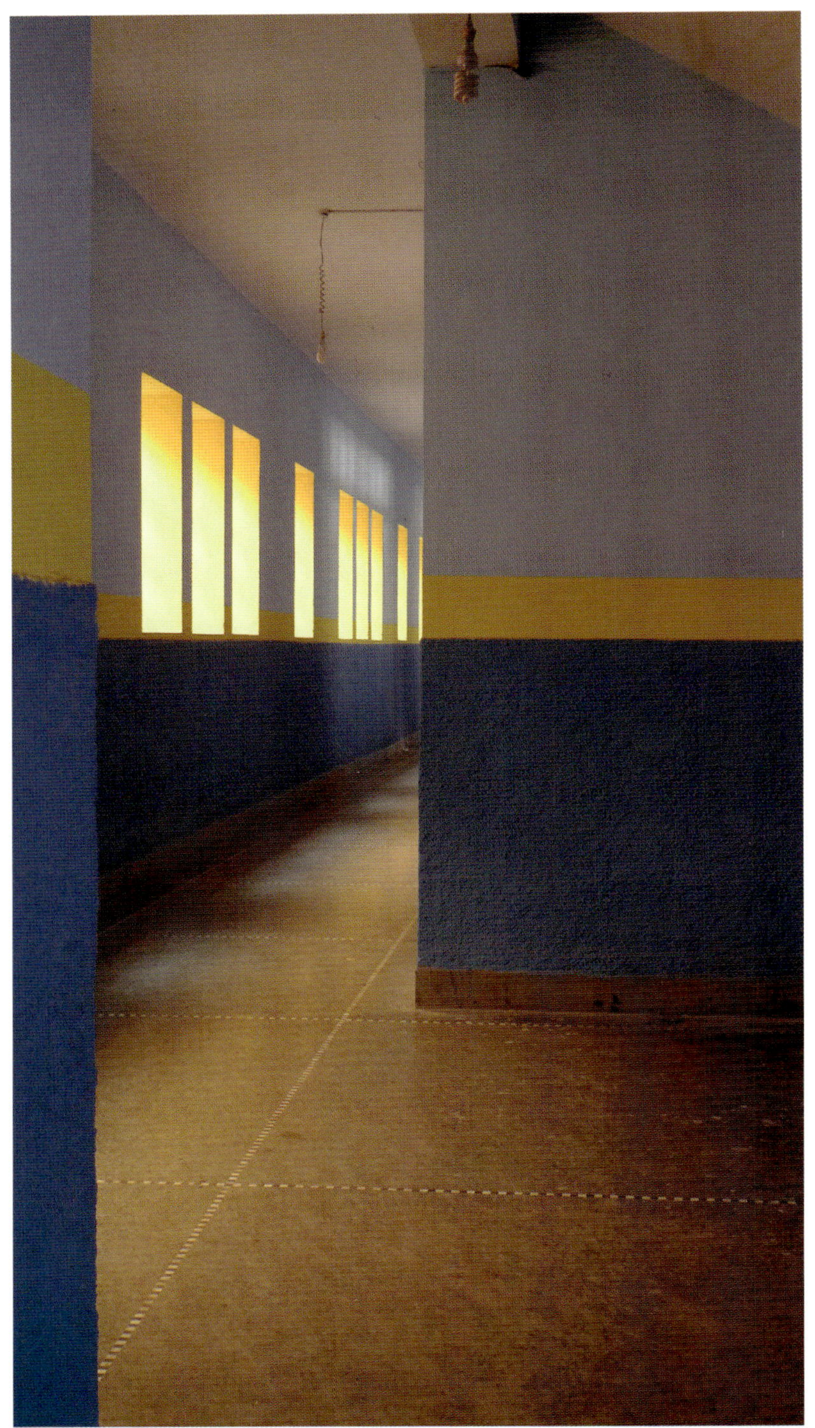

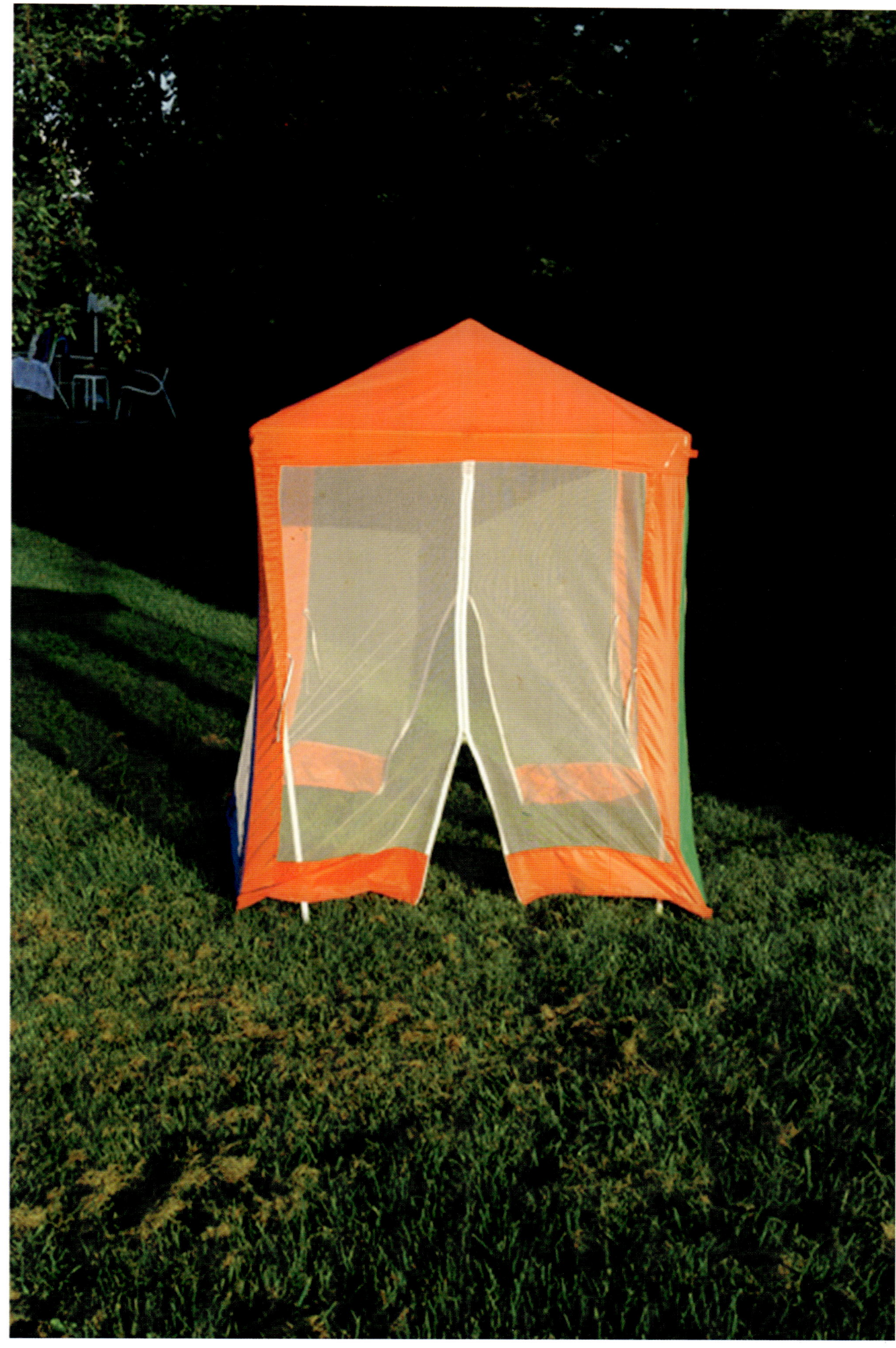

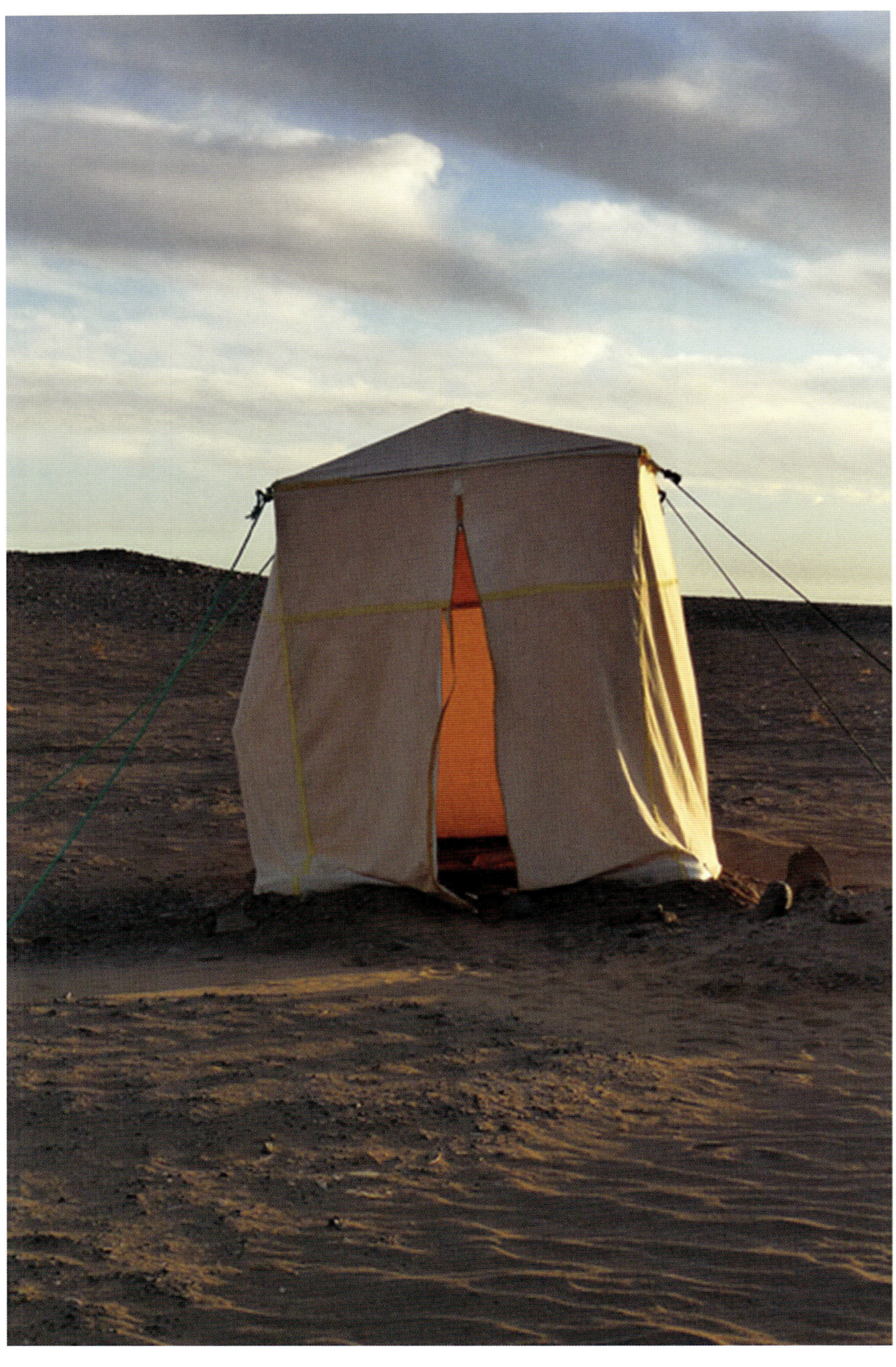

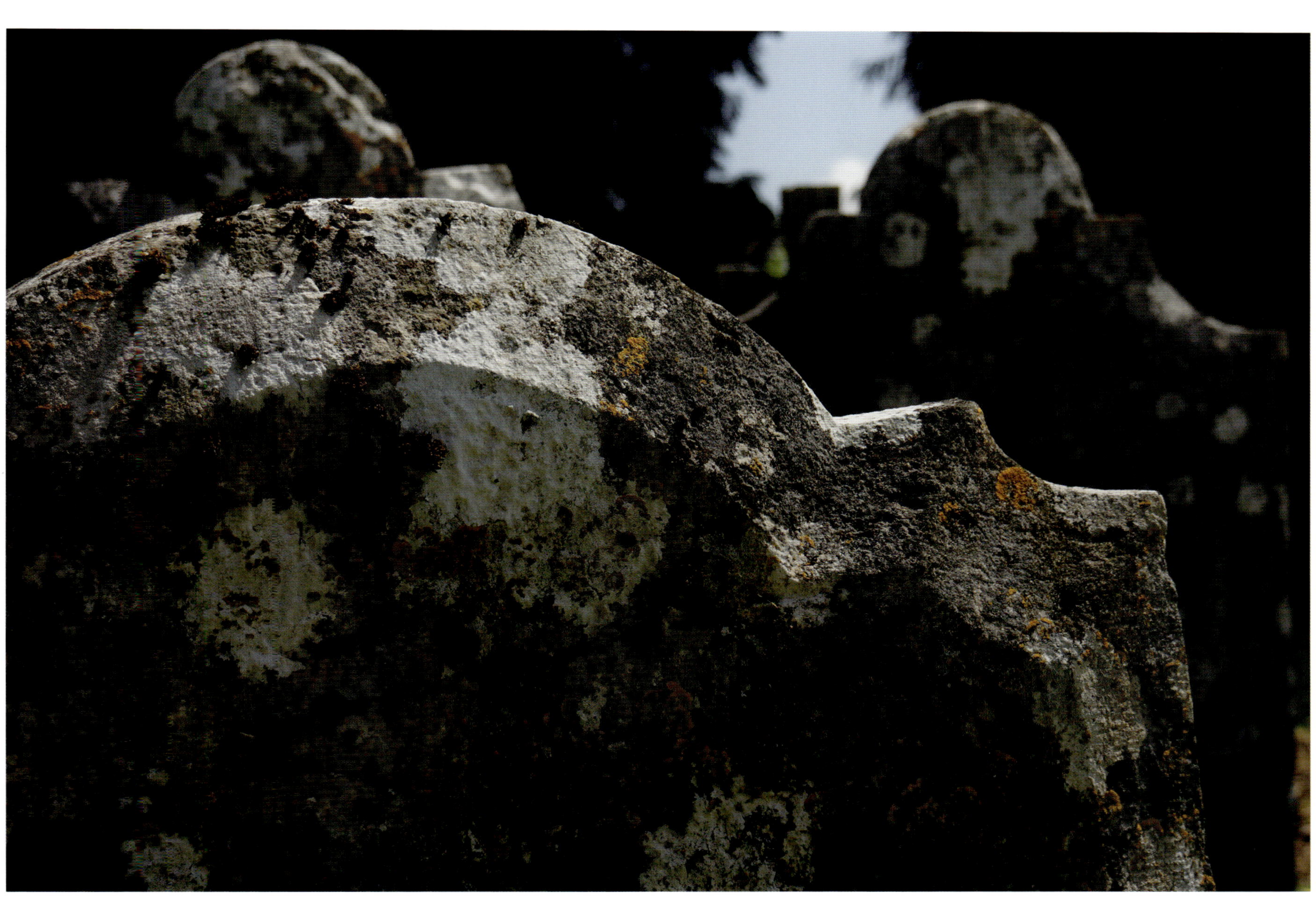

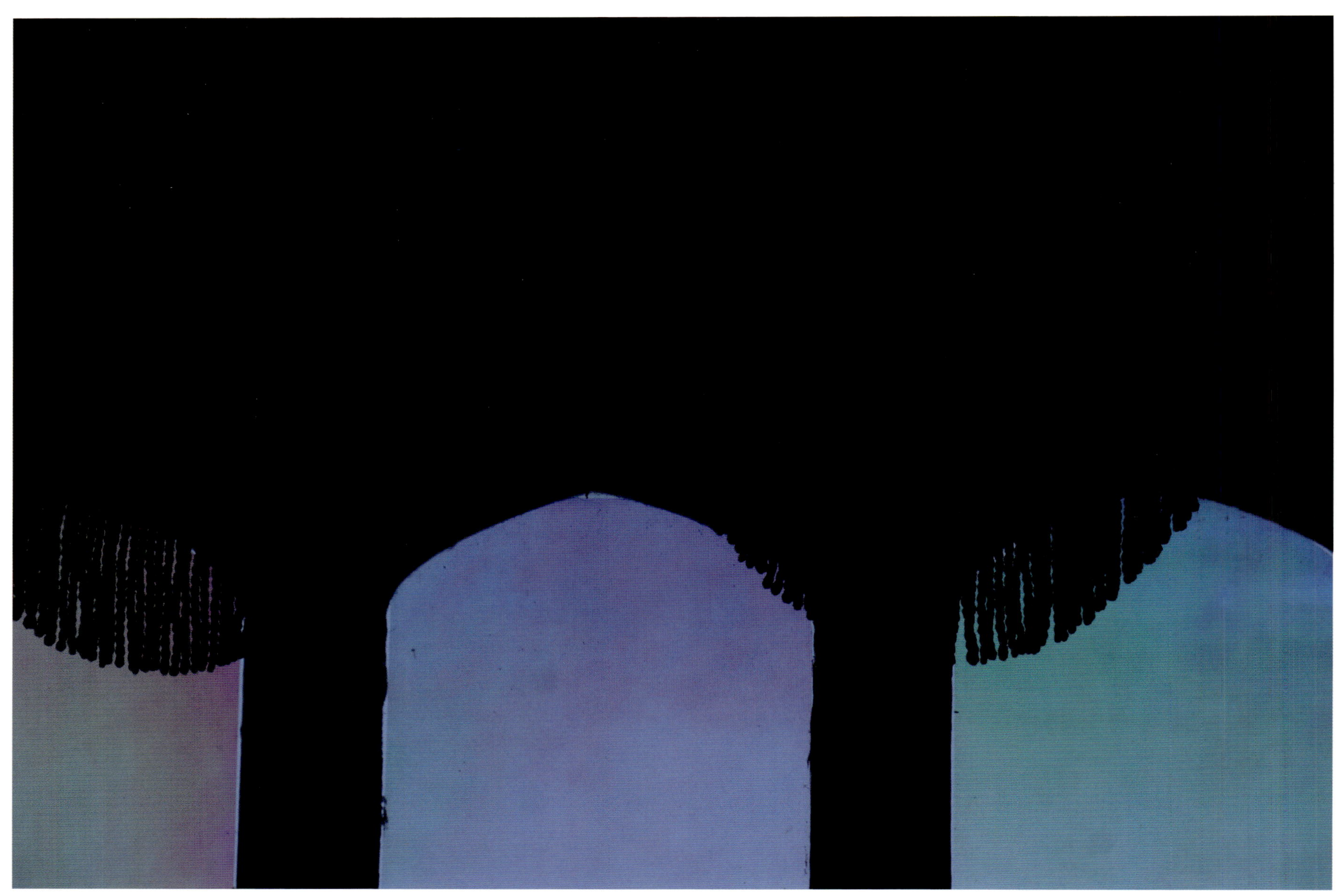

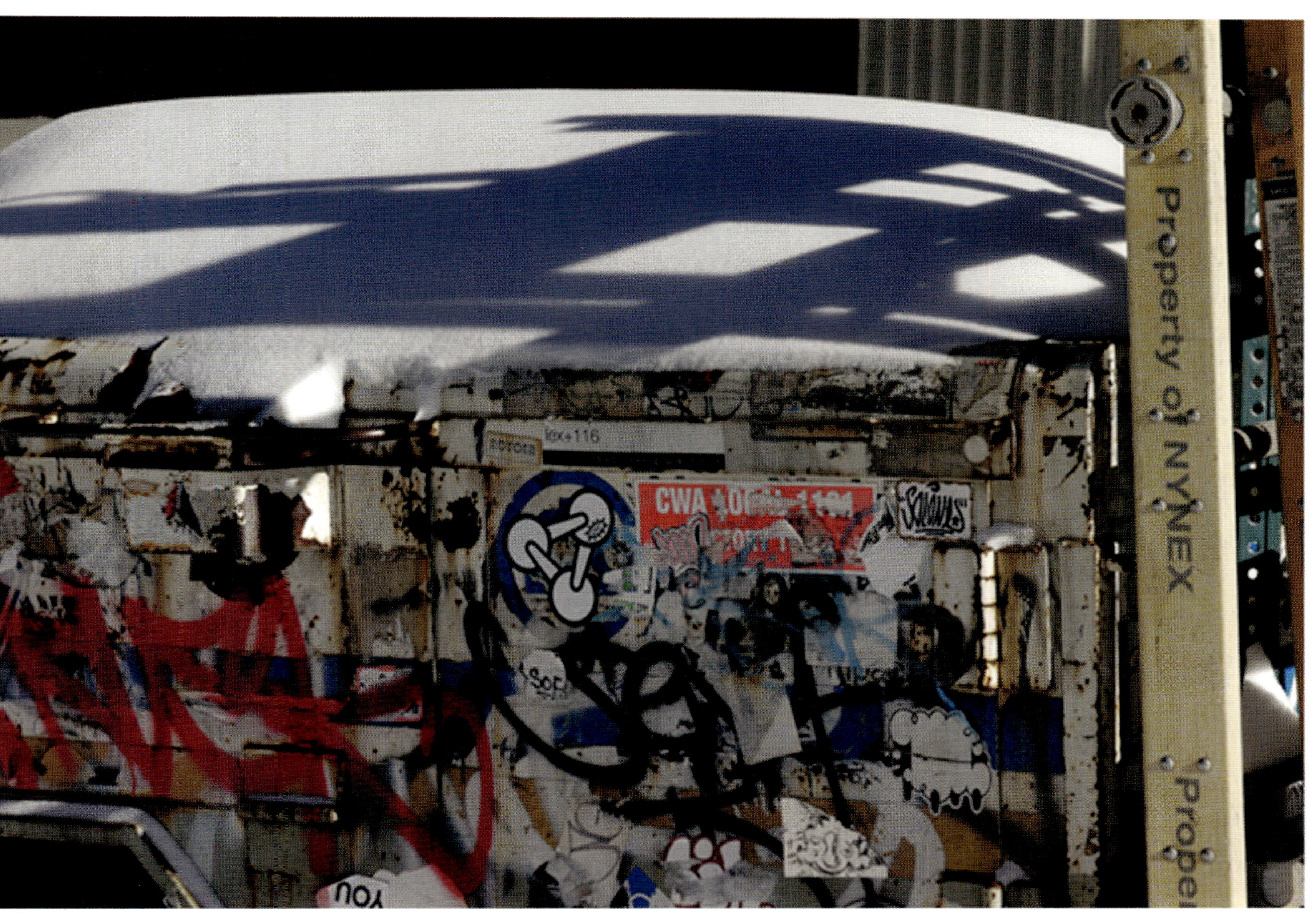
lex+116
CWA
Property of NYNEX

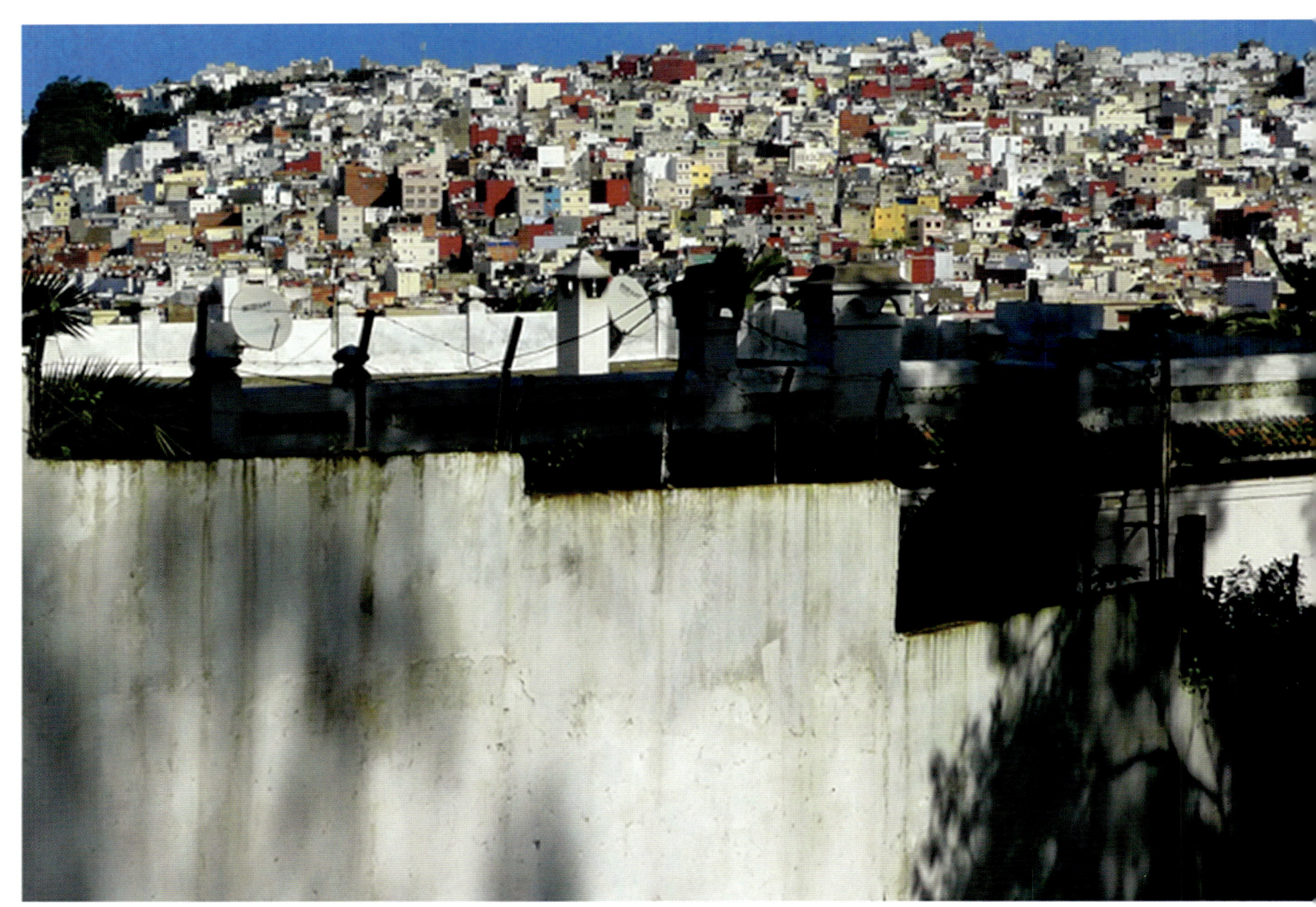

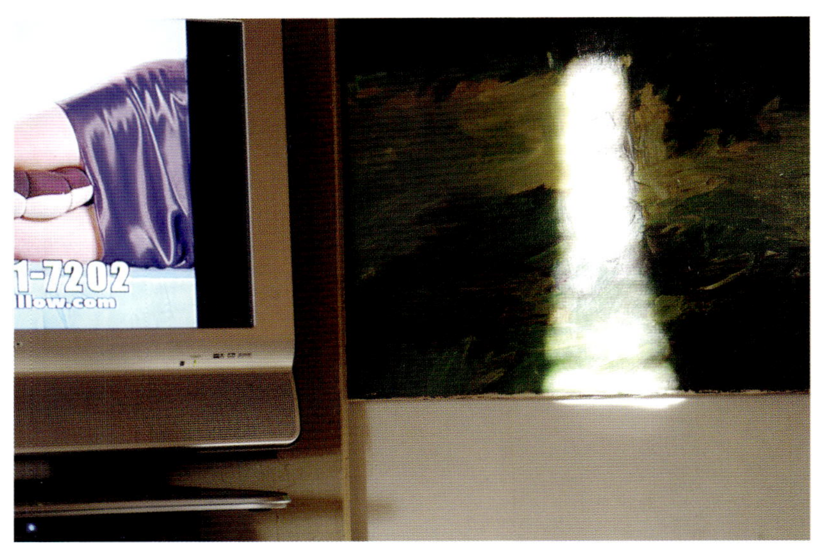
1-7202
llow.com

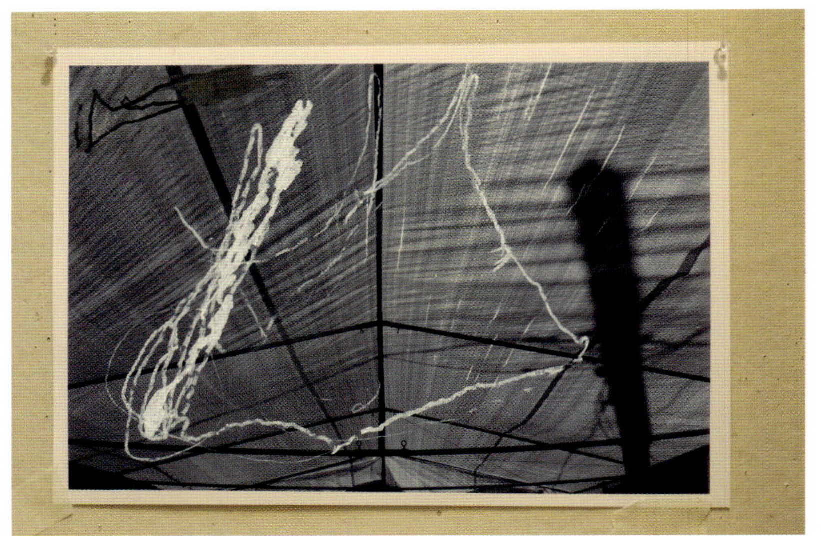

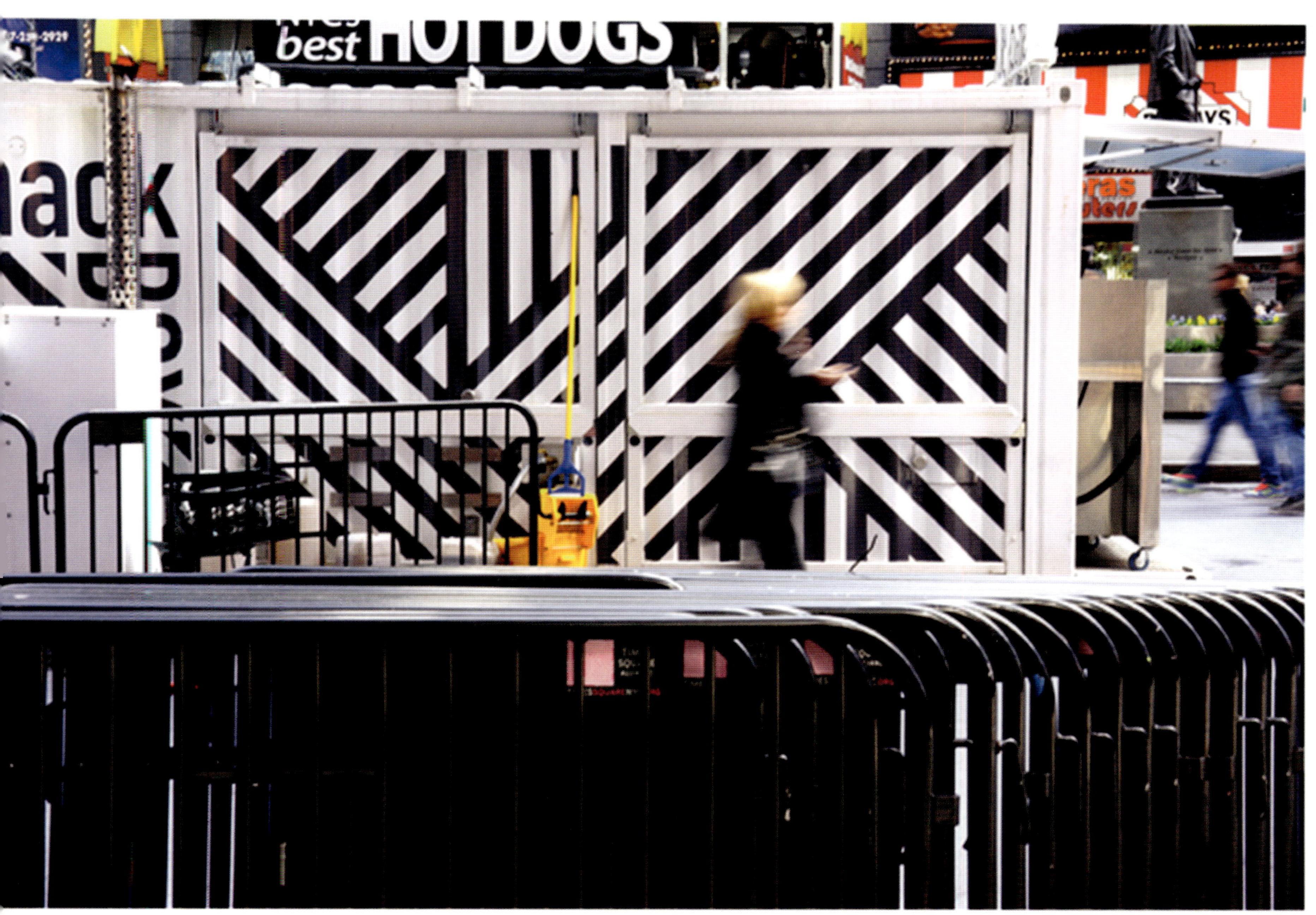
best HOT DOGS

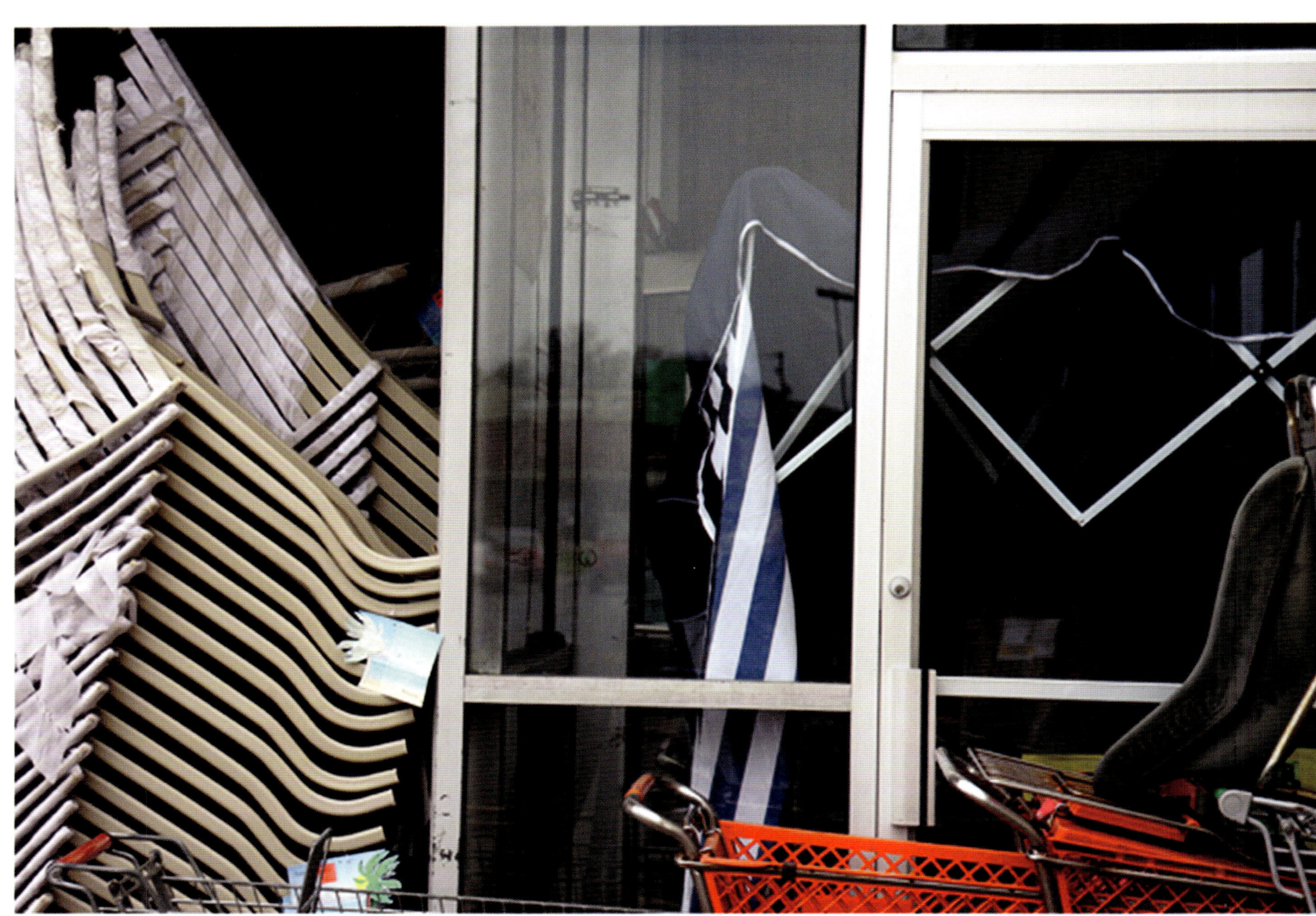

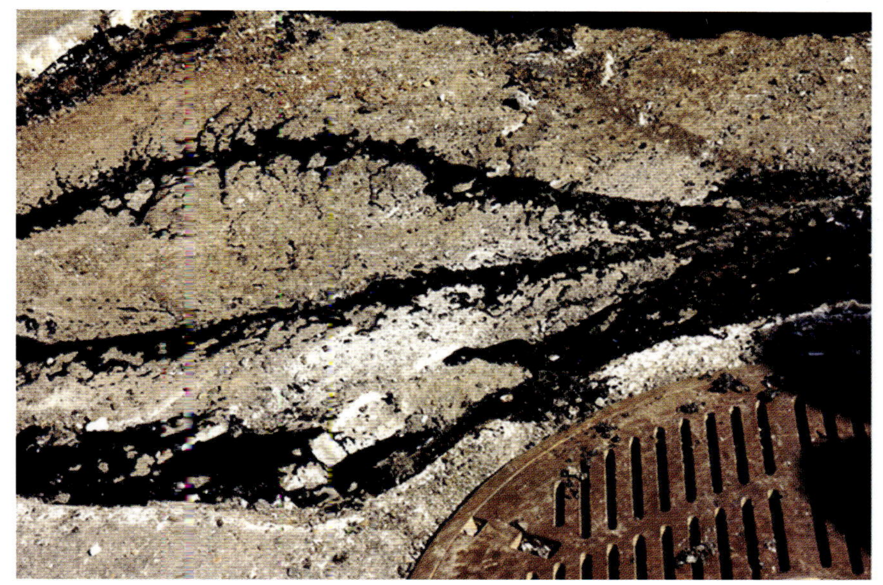

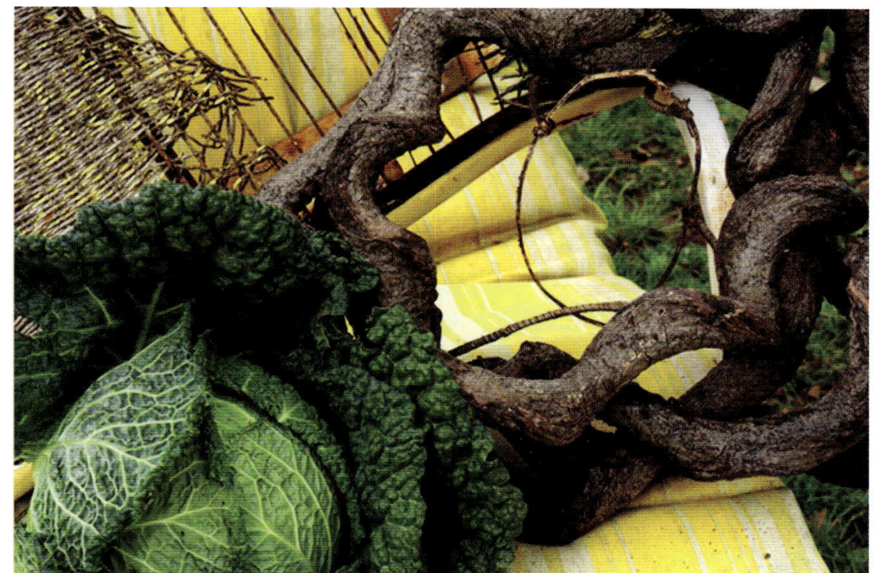

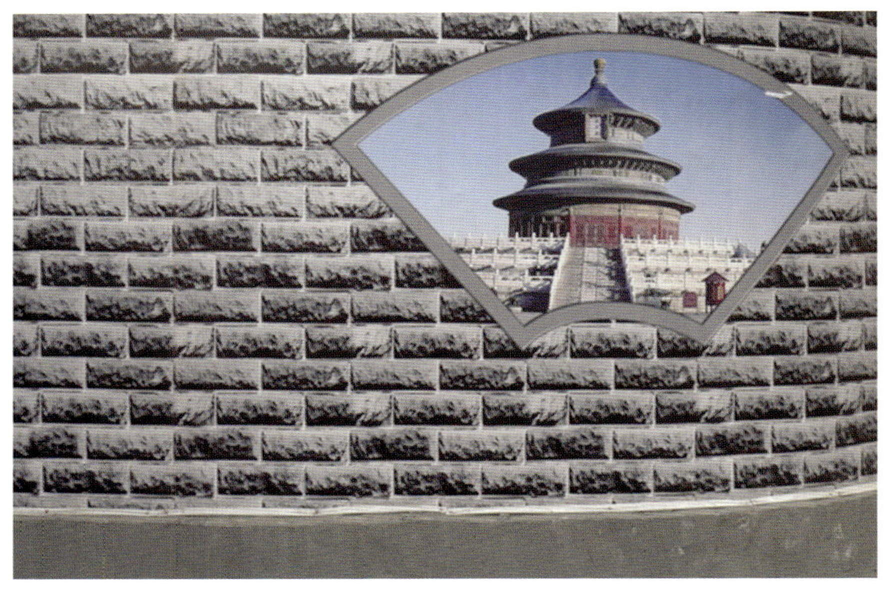

GOURMET
BURGERS

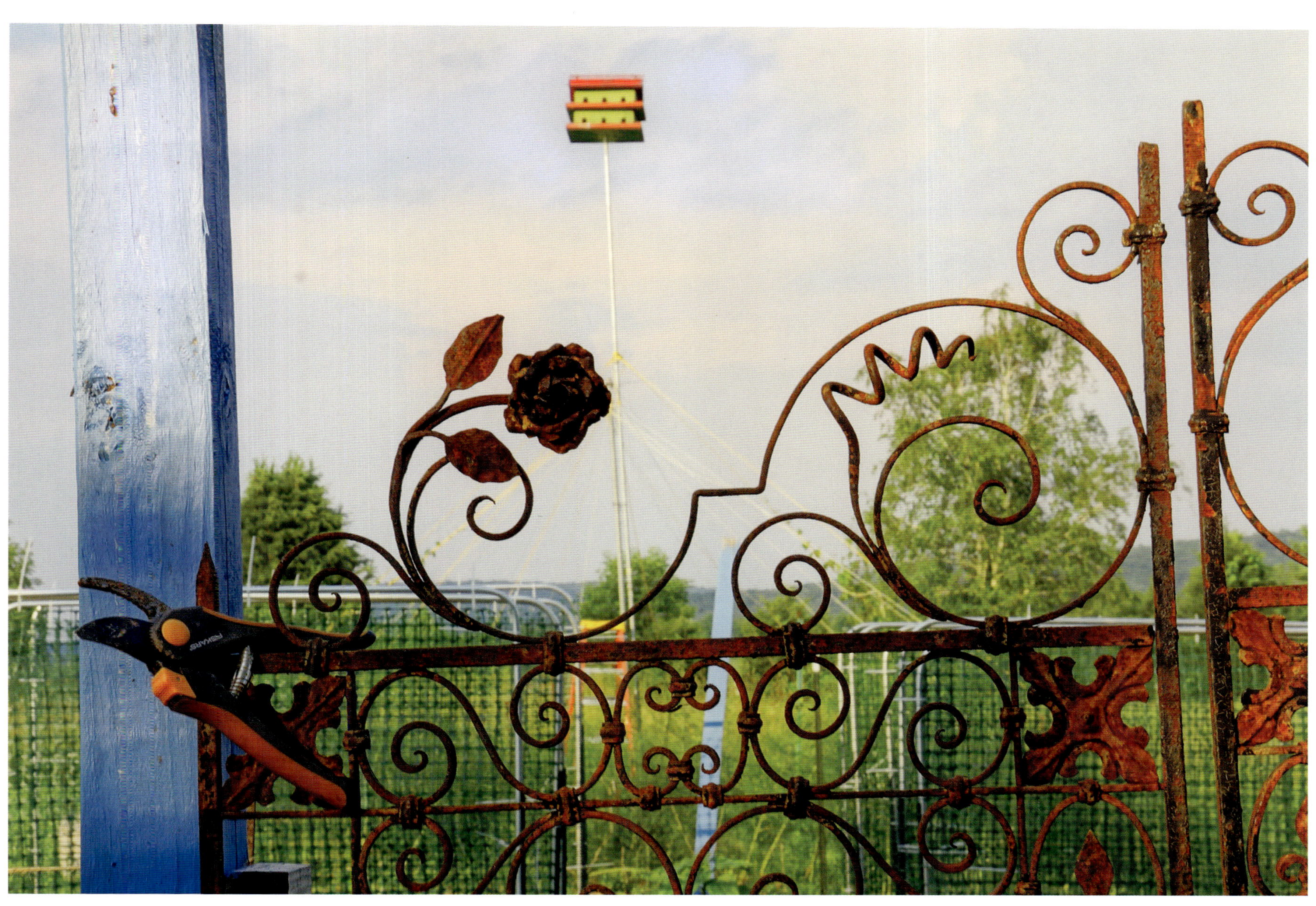

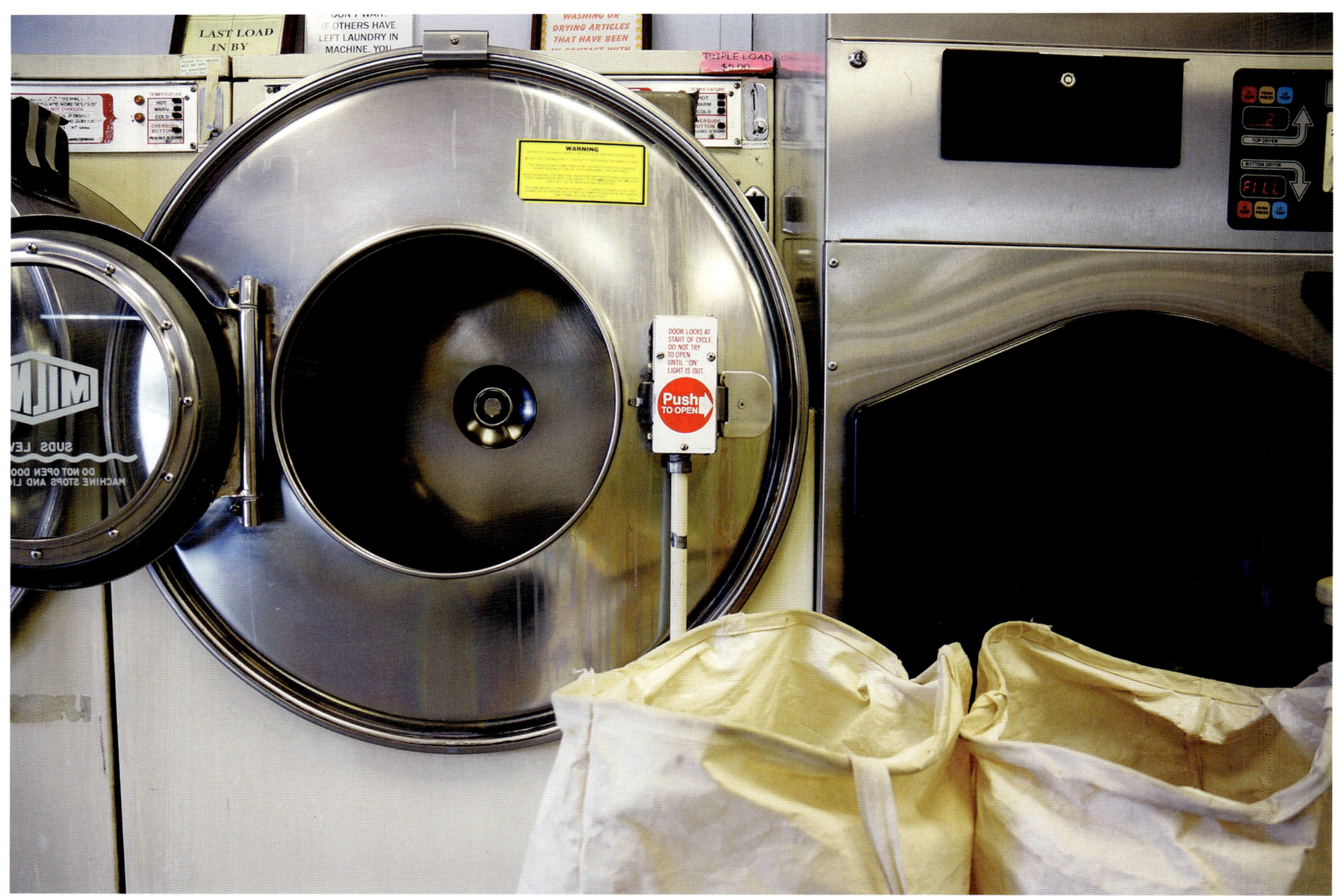
LAST LOAD
IN BY
IF OTHERS HAVE
LEFT LAUNDRY IN
DRYING ARTICLES
THAT HAVE BEEN
TRIPLE LOAD
WARNING
DOOR LOCKS AT
START OF CYCLE
DO NOT TRY
TO OPEN
UNTIL "ON"
LIGHT IS OUT
Push
TO OPEN
TOP DRYER
BOTTOM DRYER
FILL

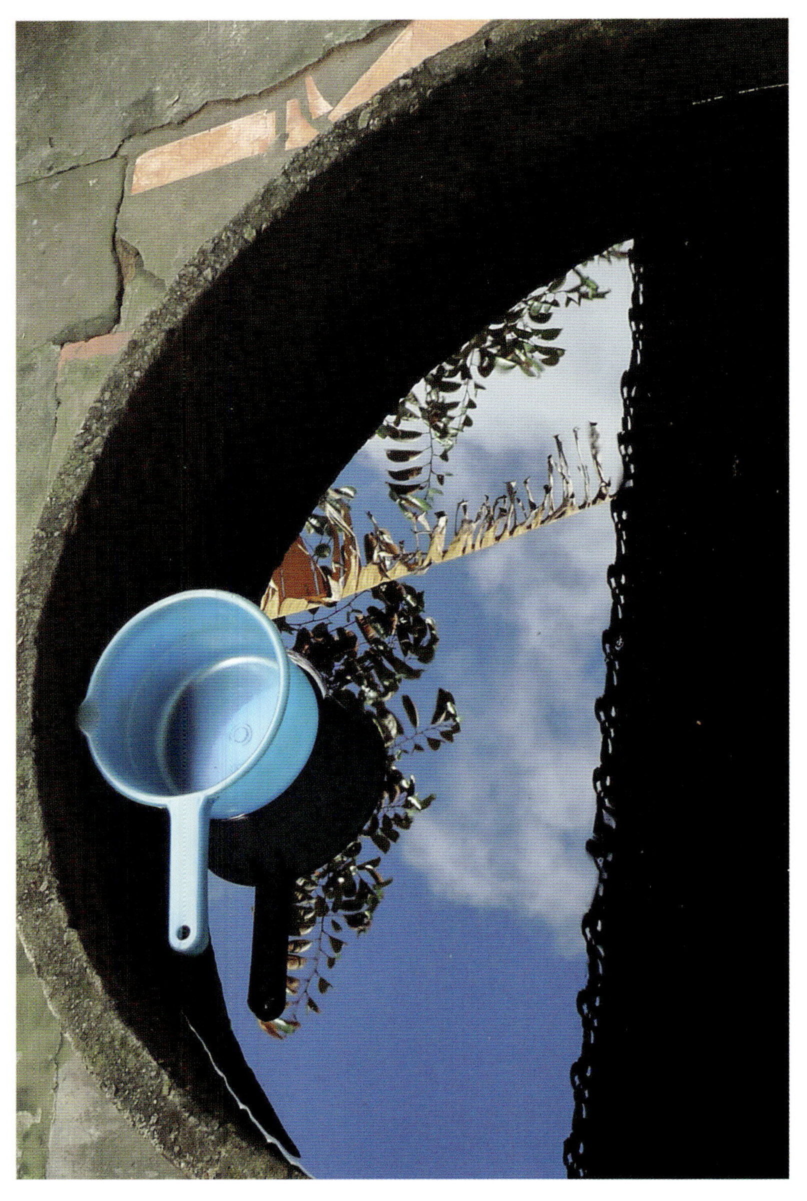

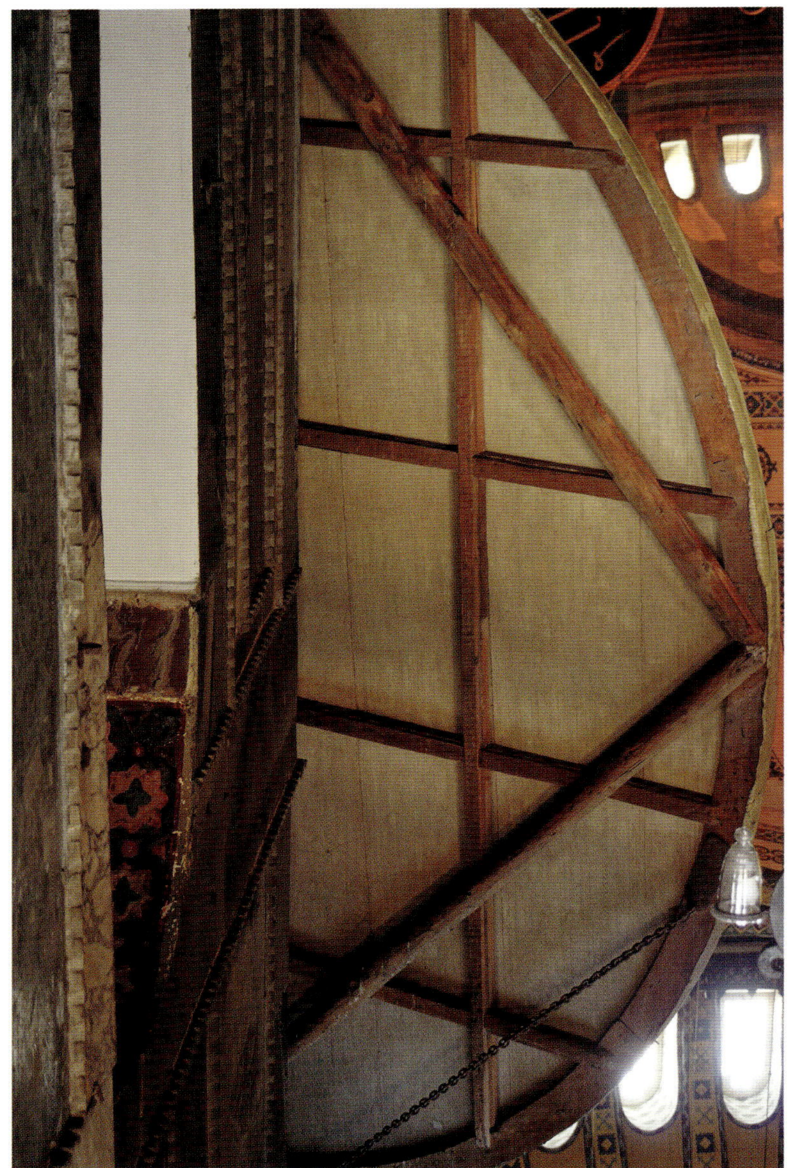

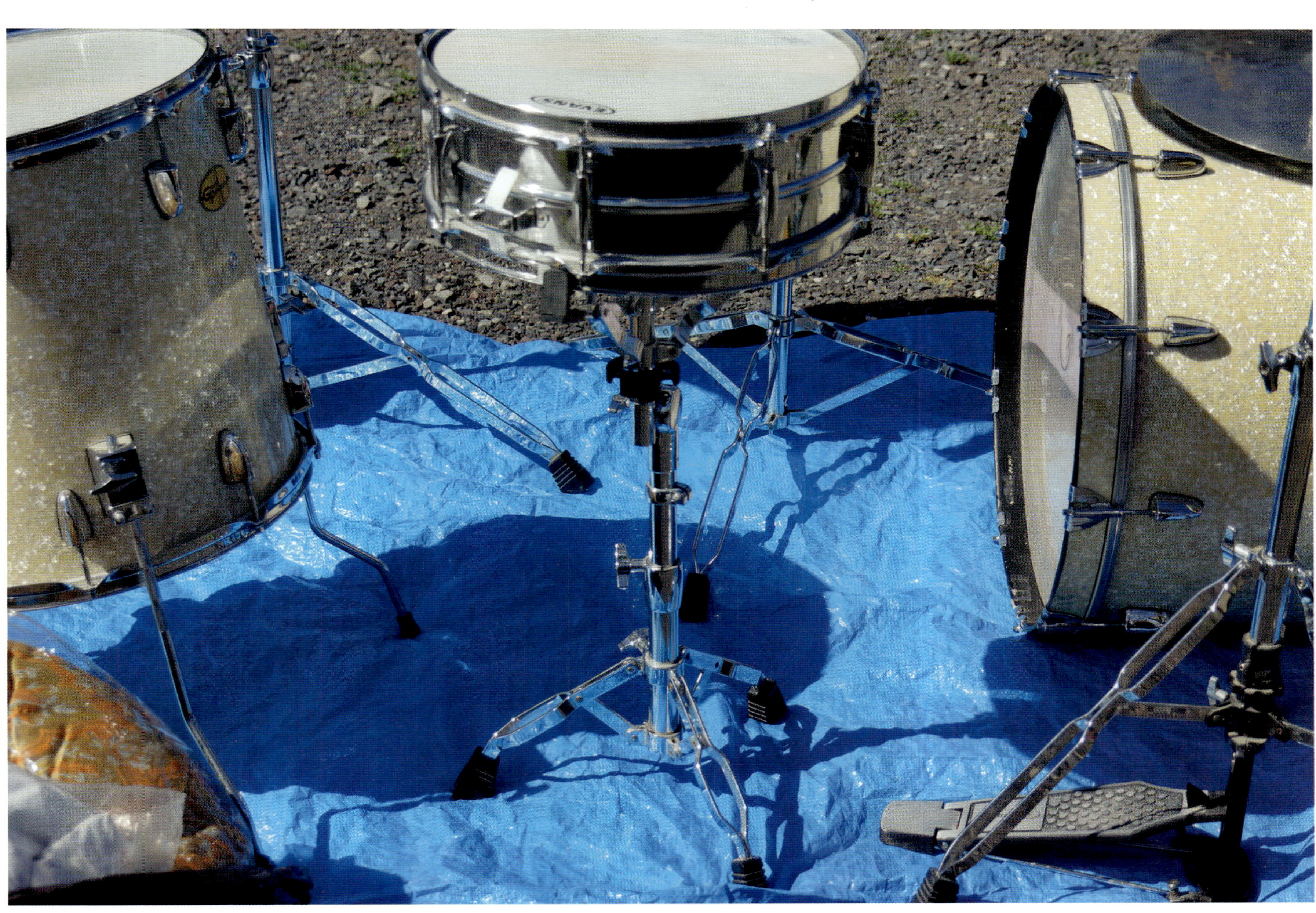
EVANS

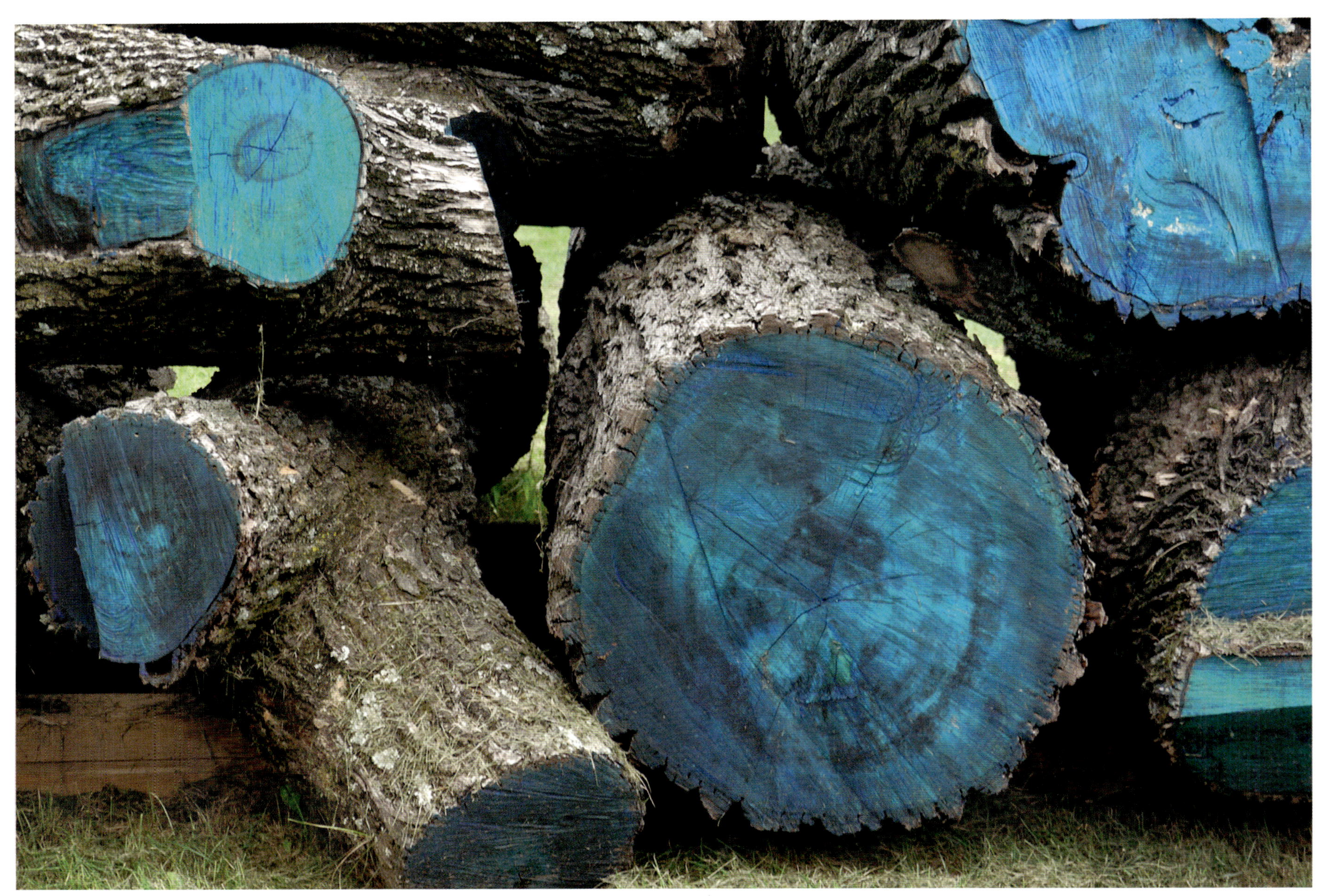

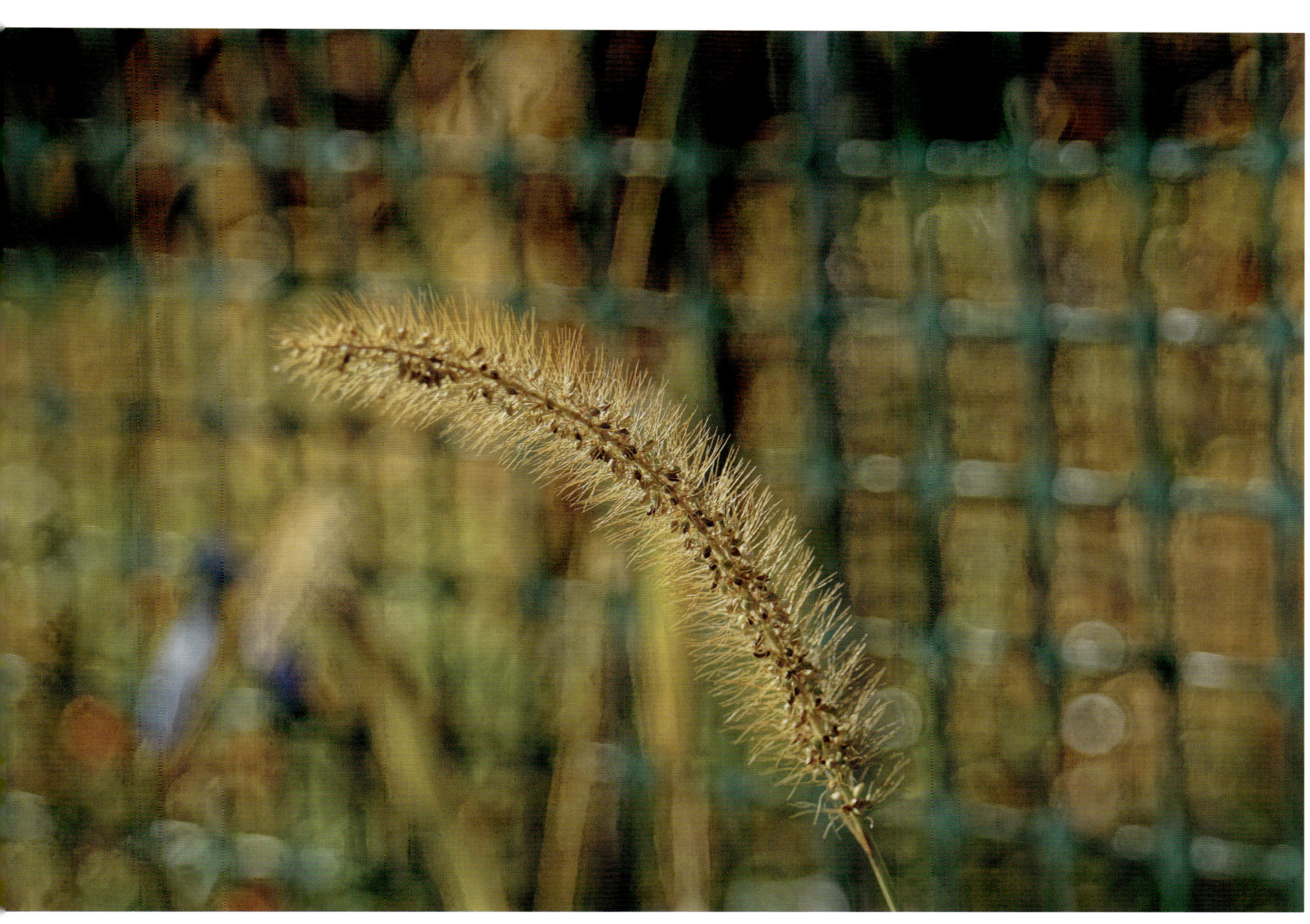

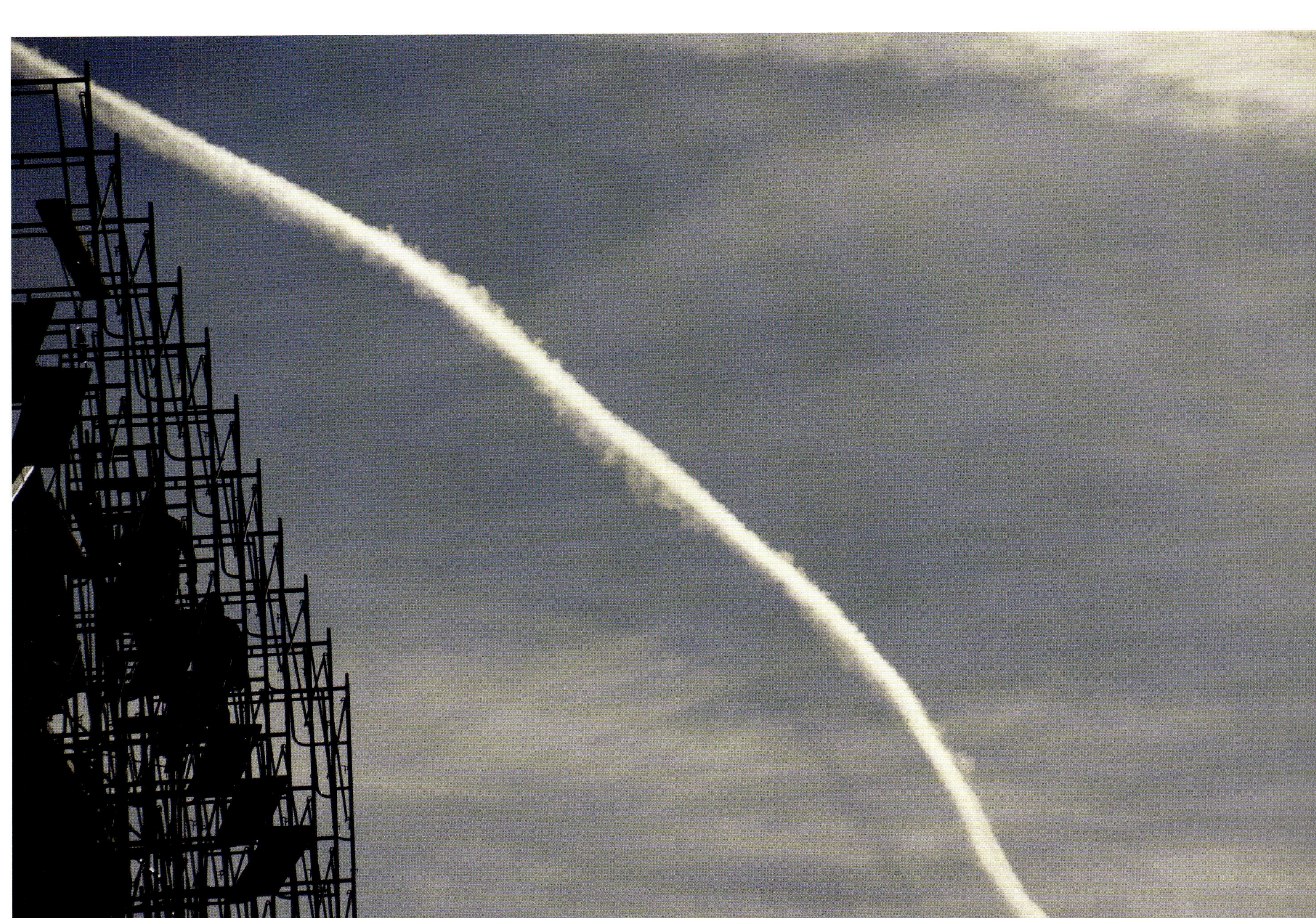

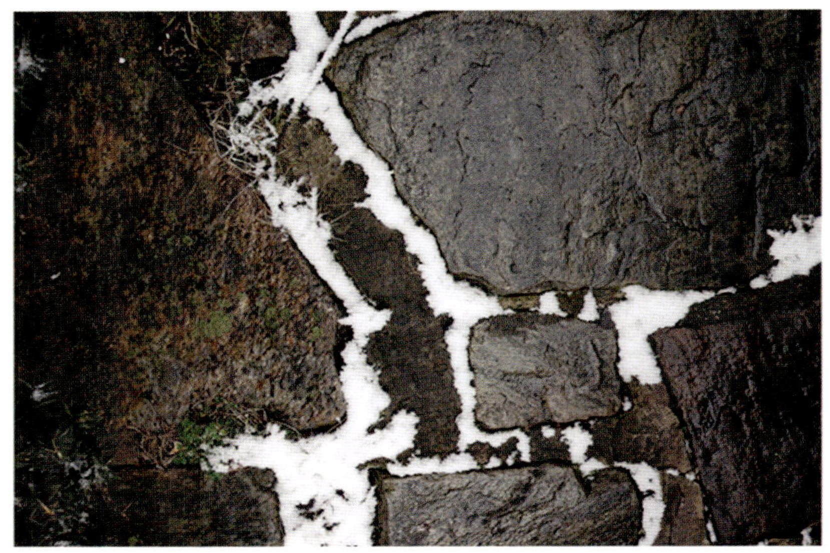

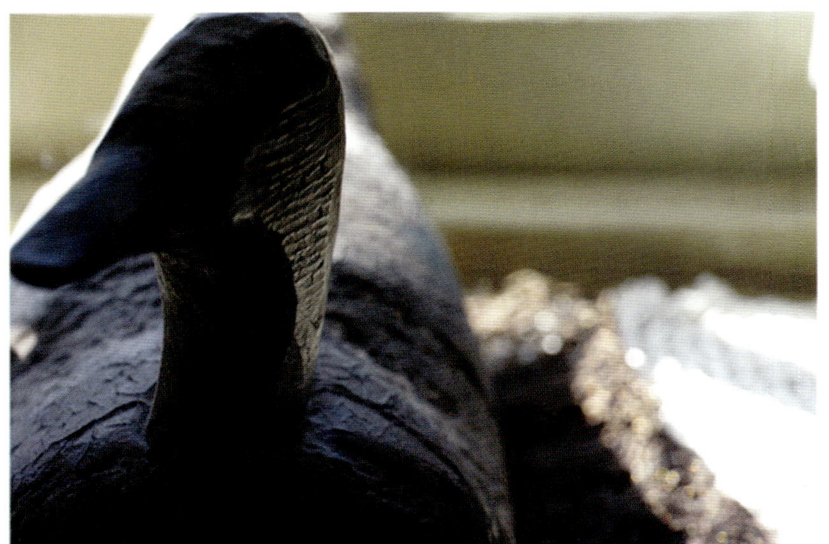

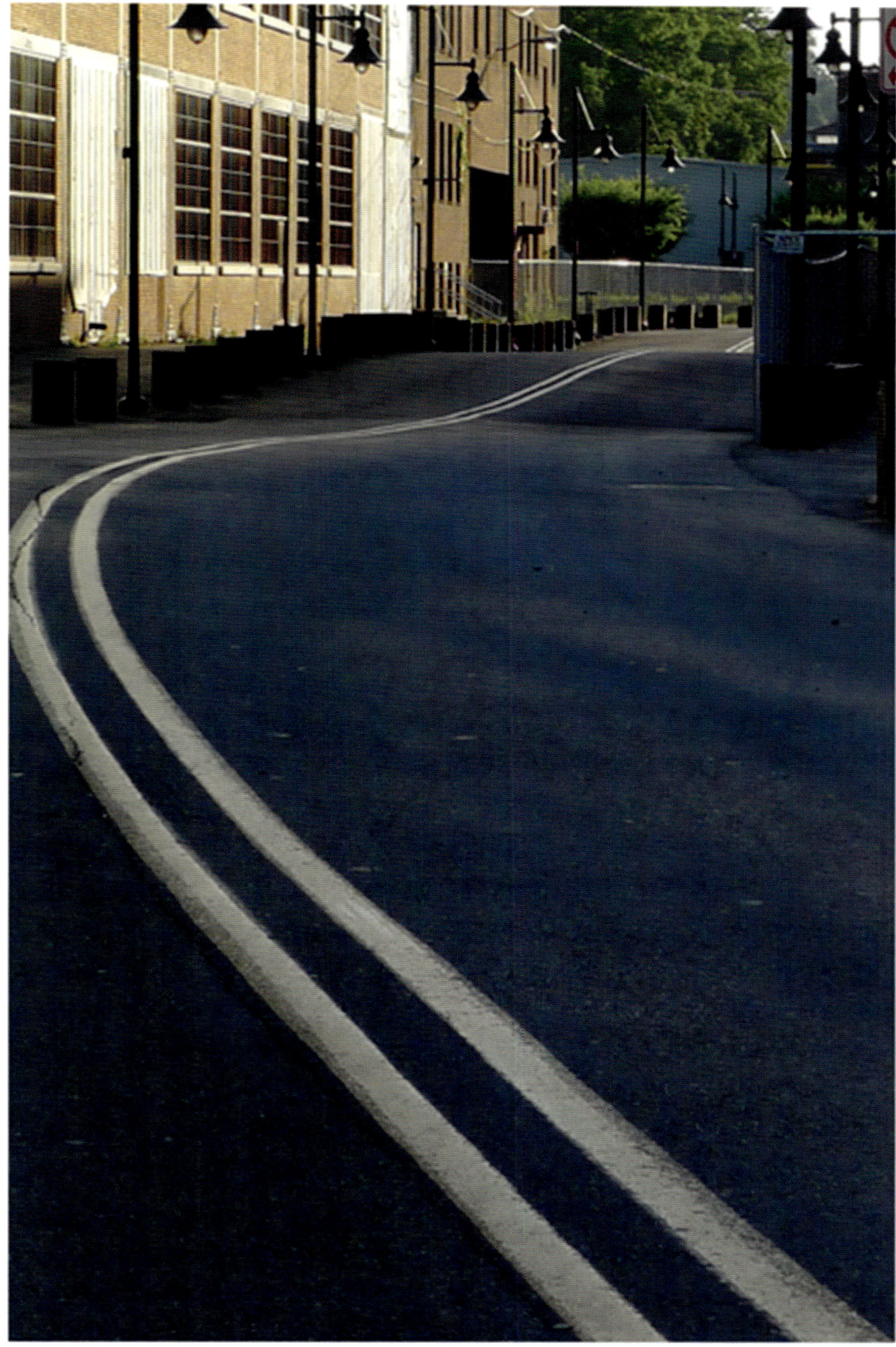

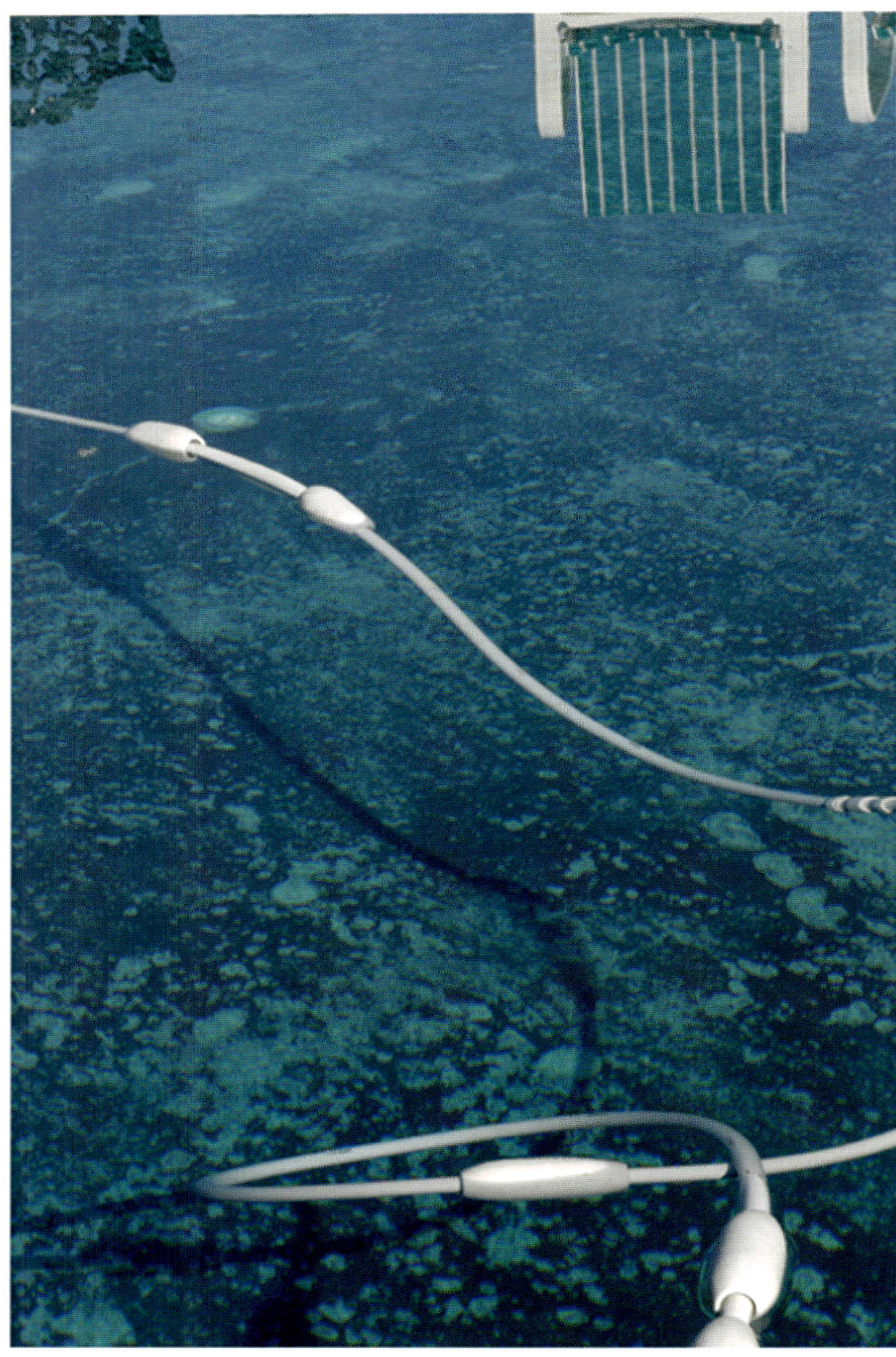

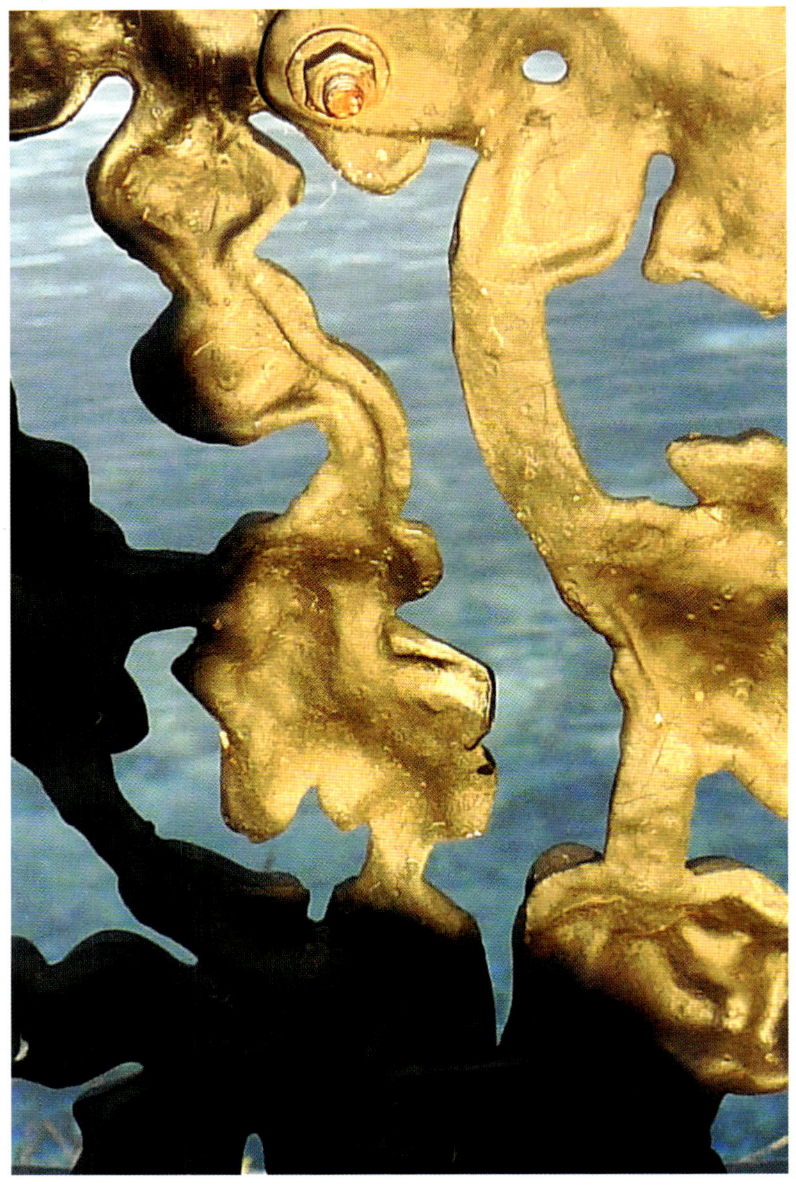

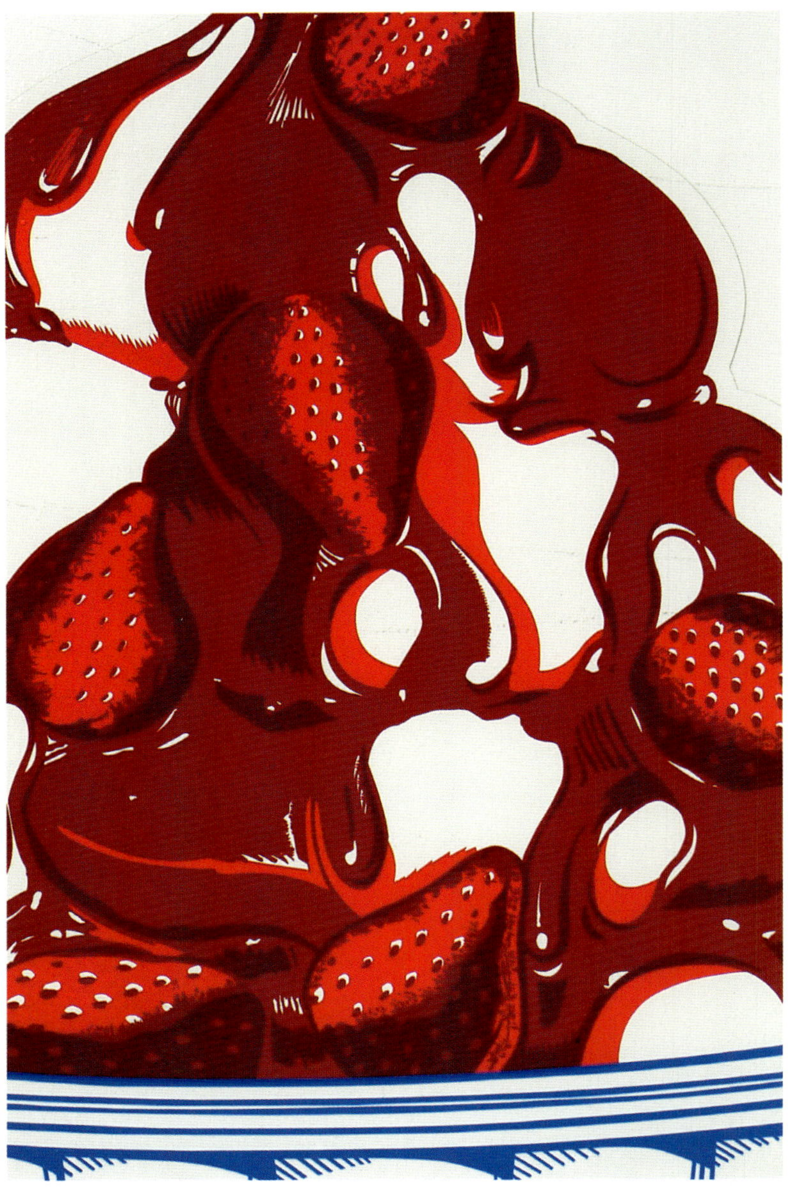

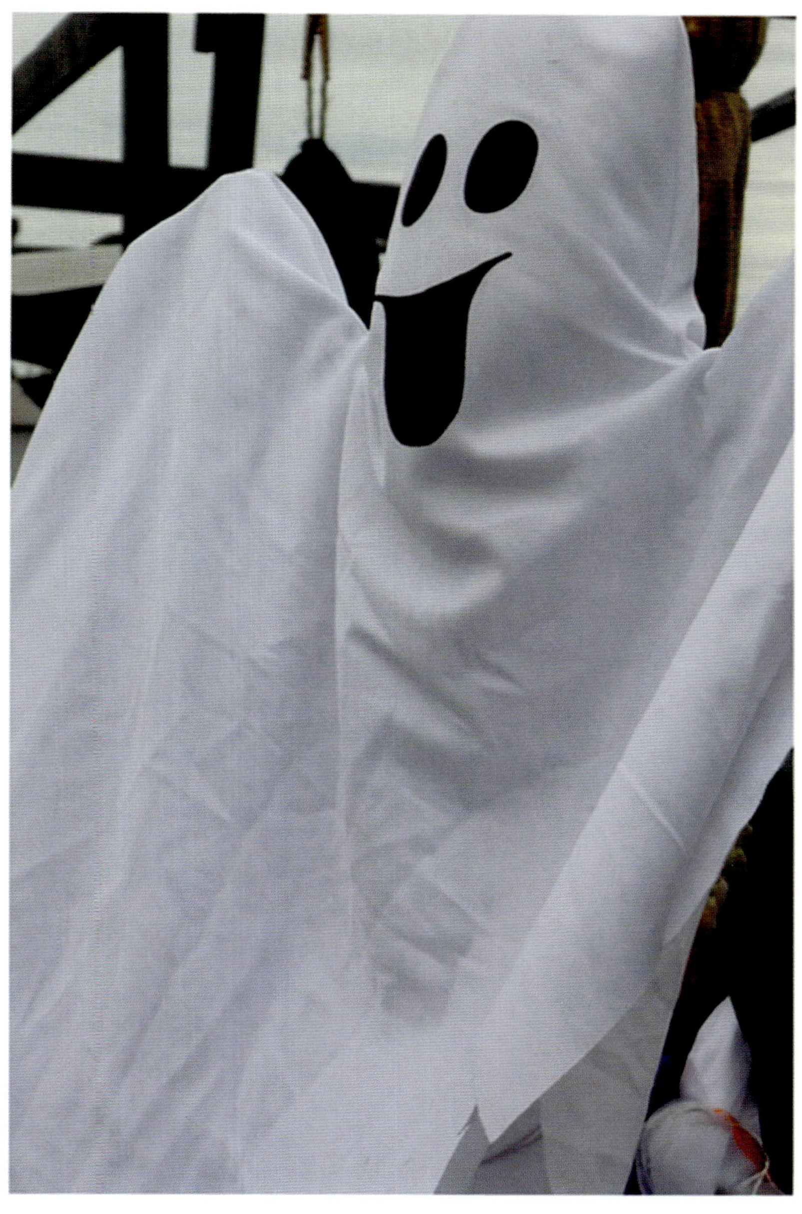

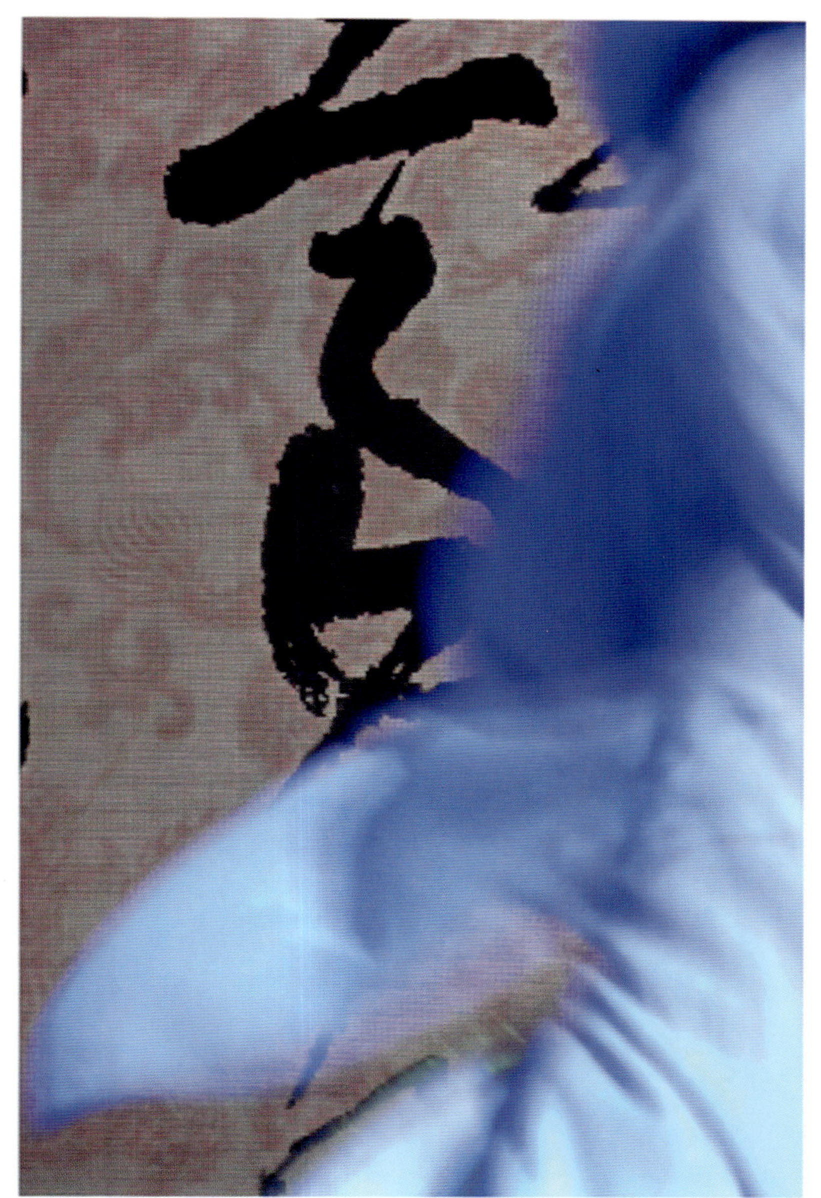

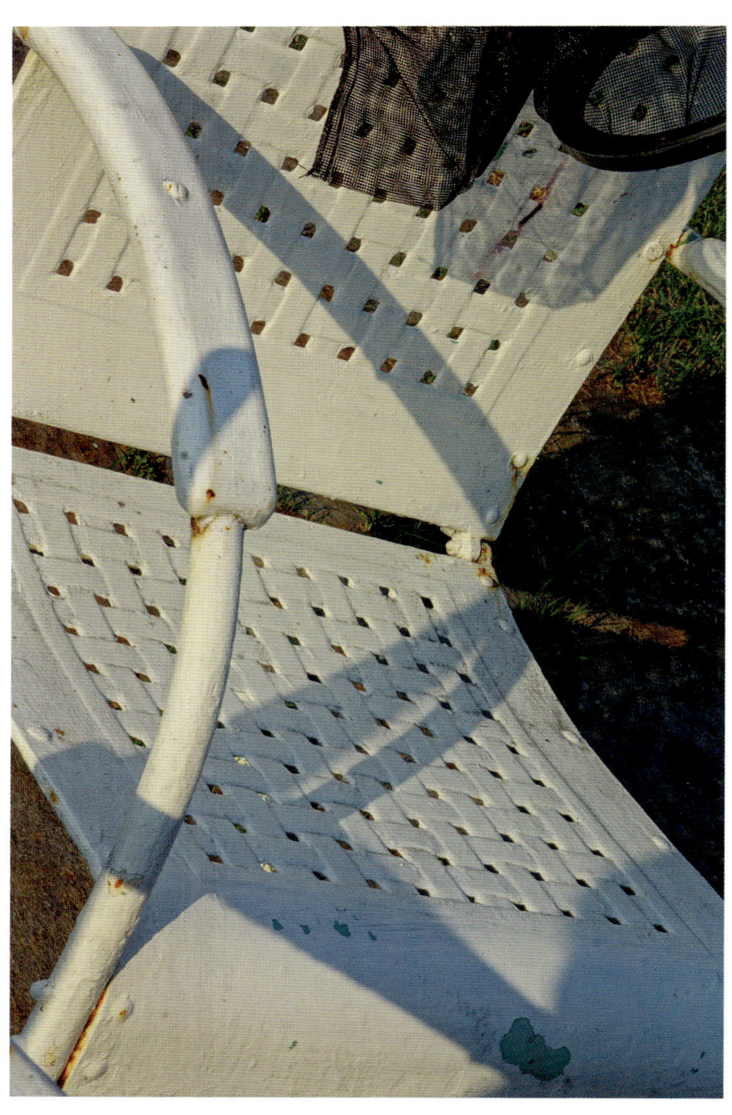

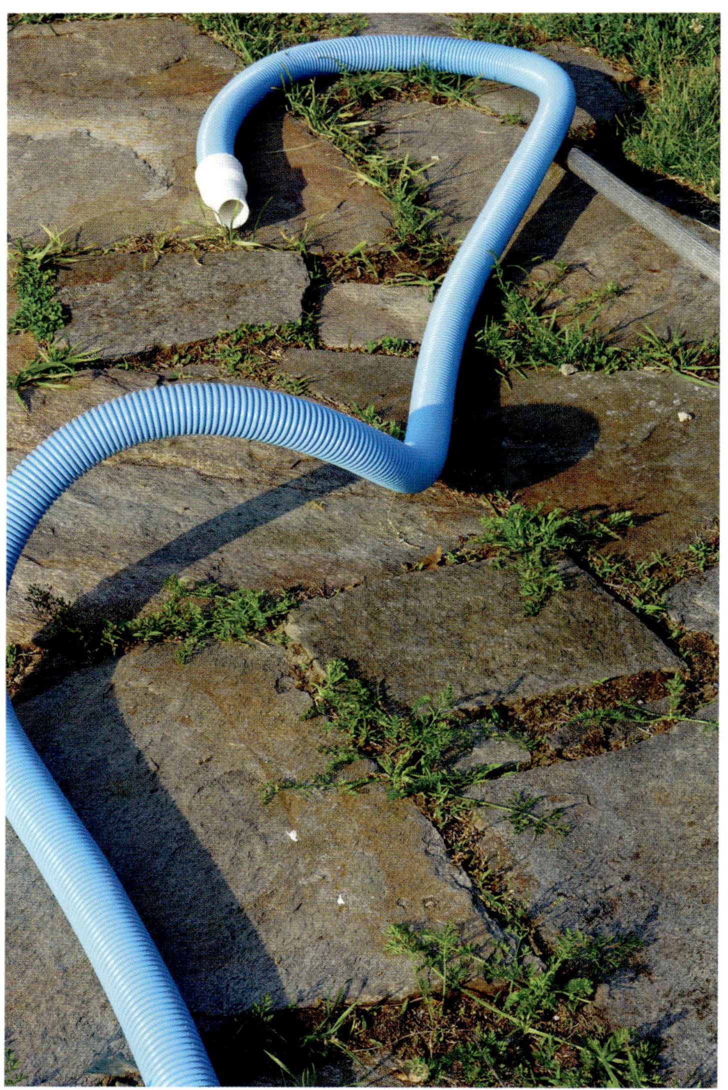

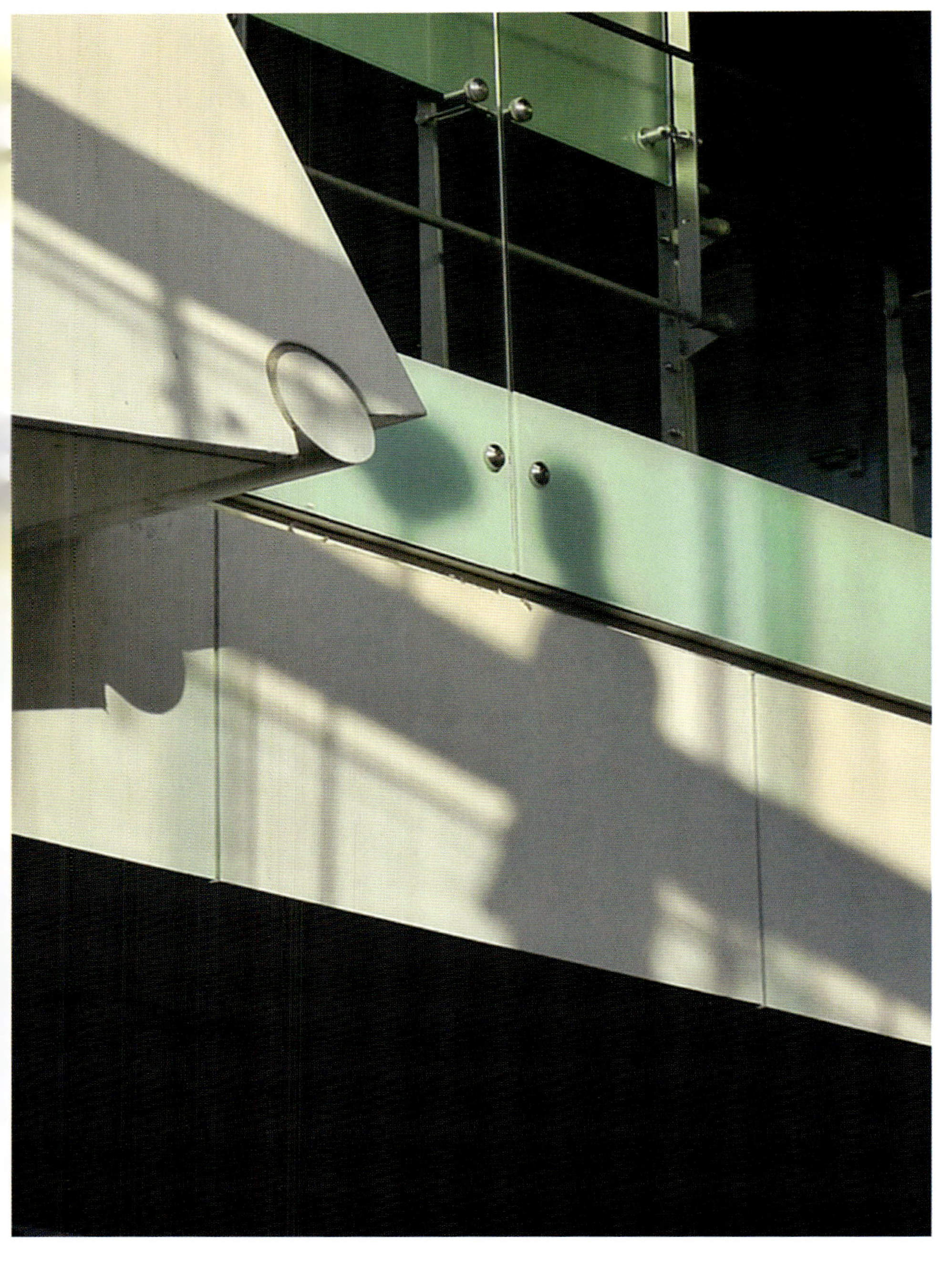

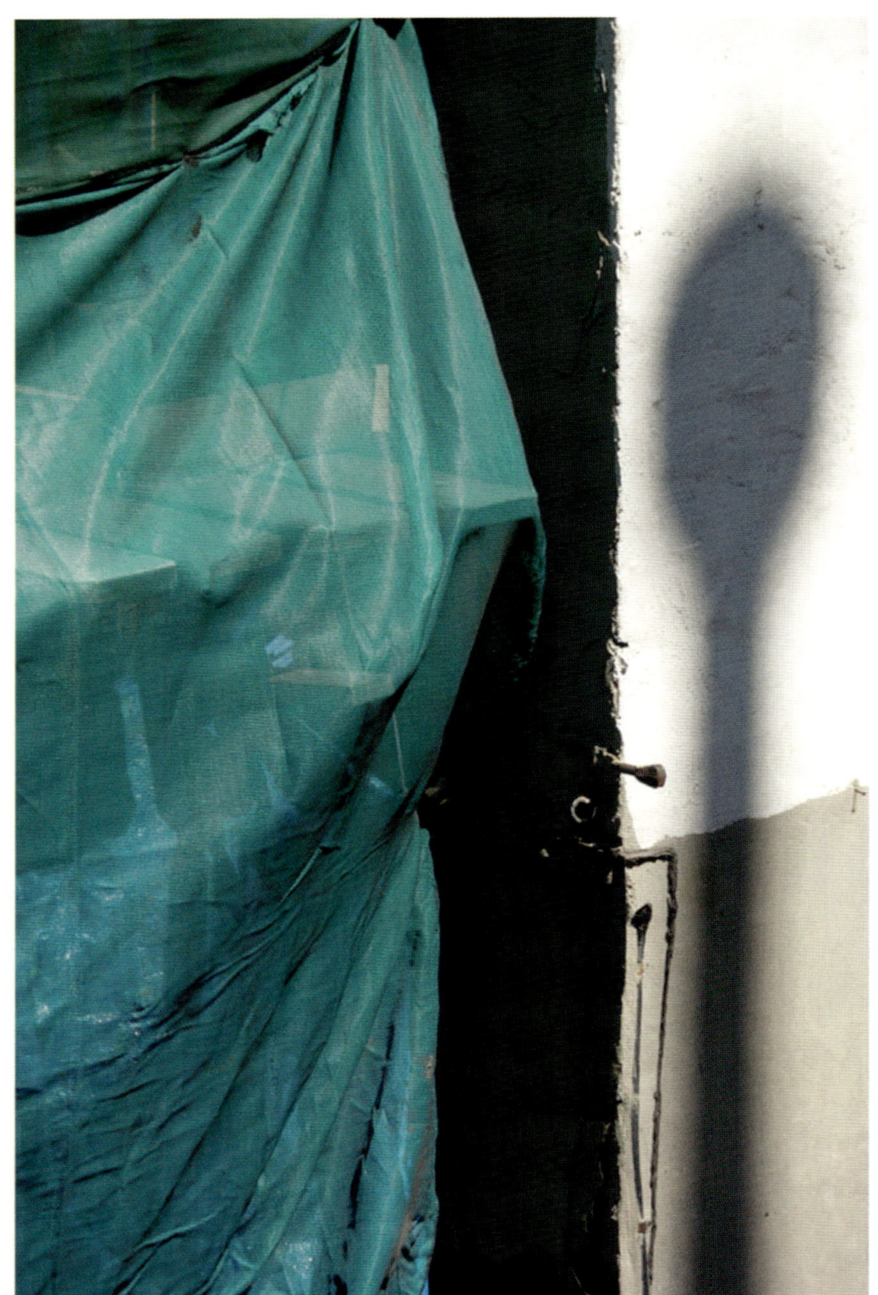

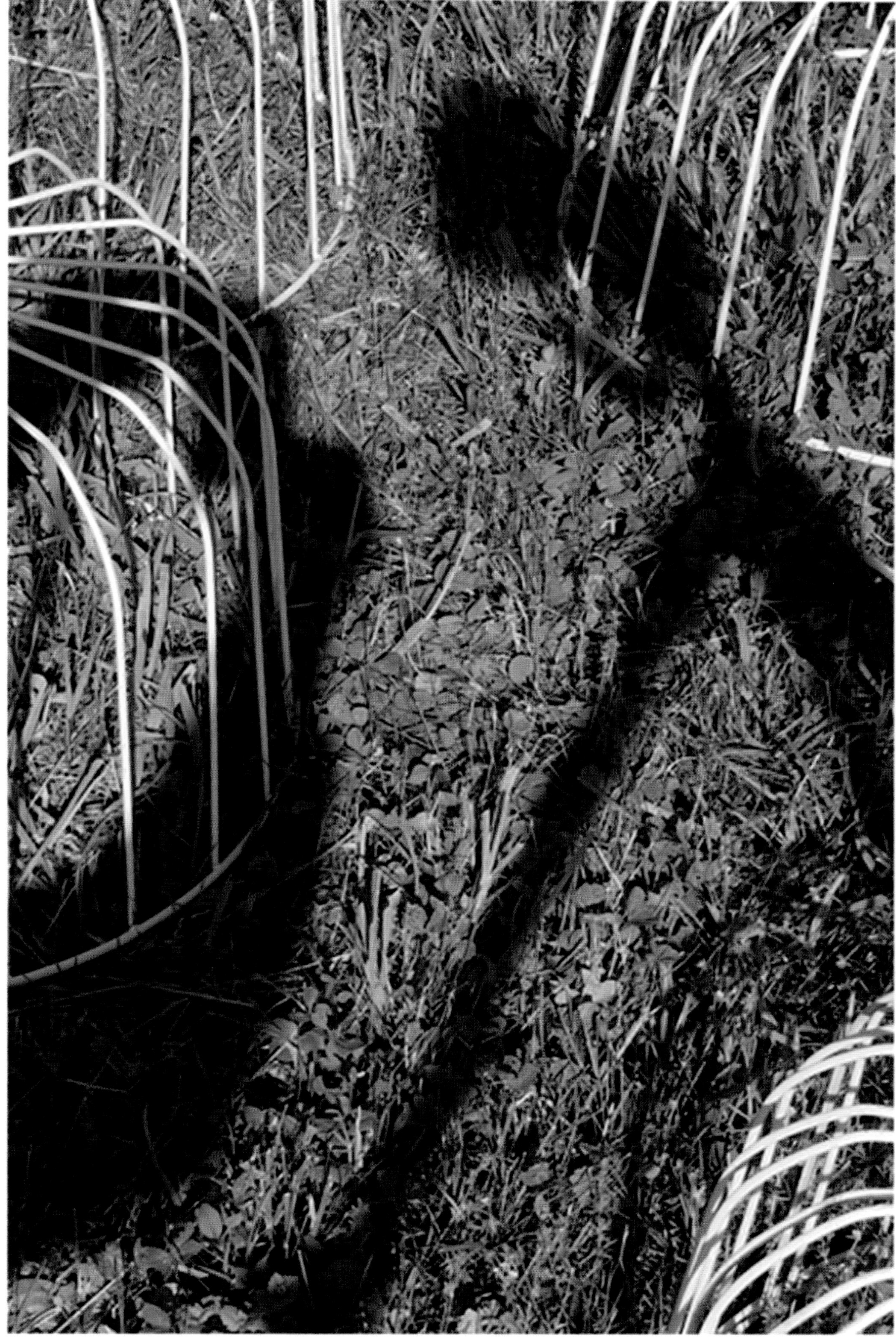

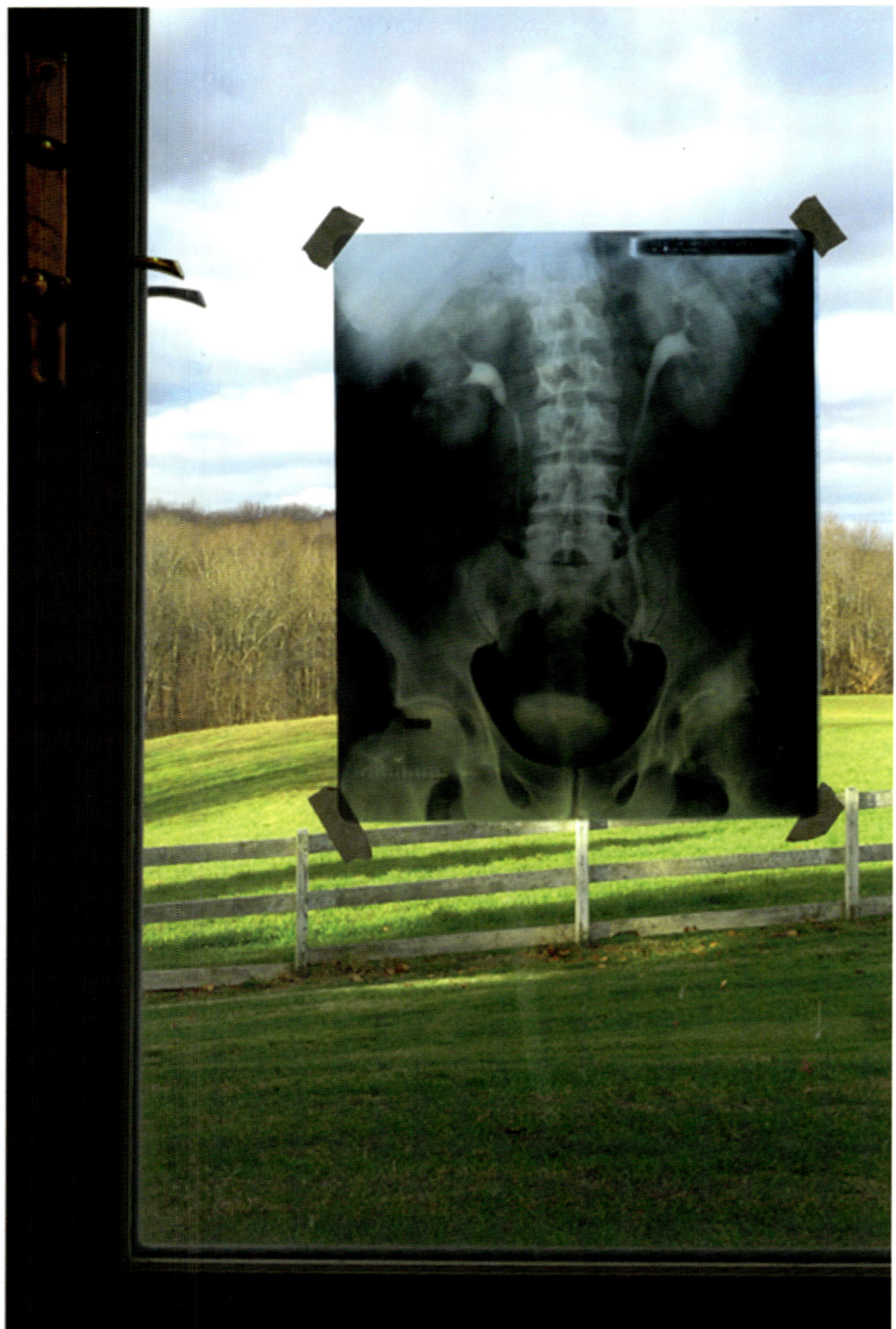

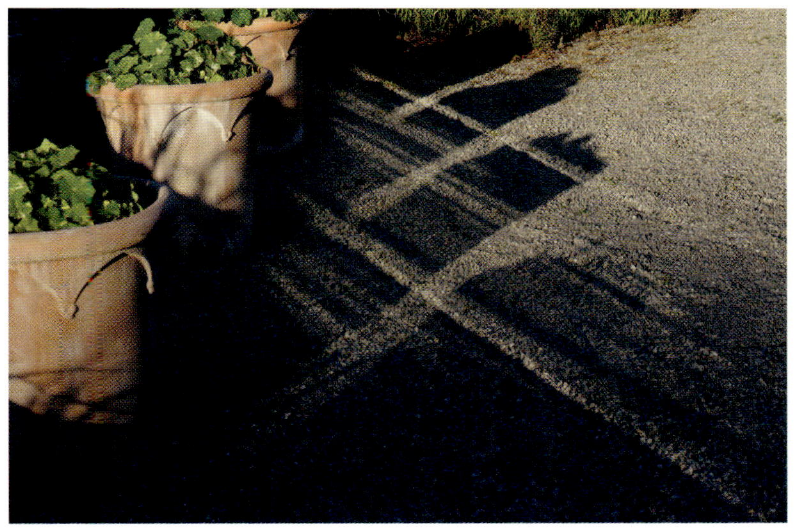

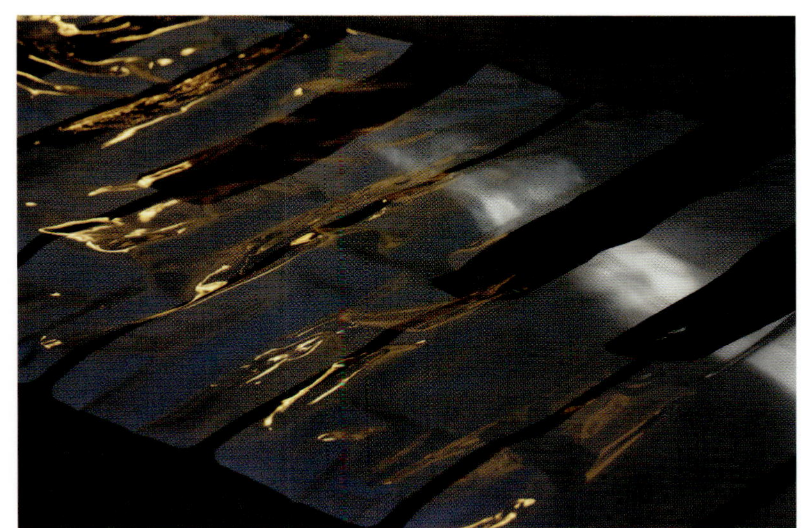

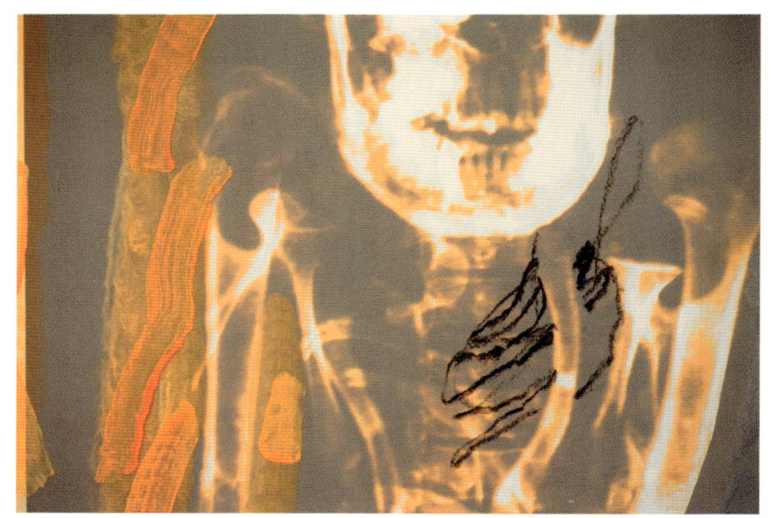

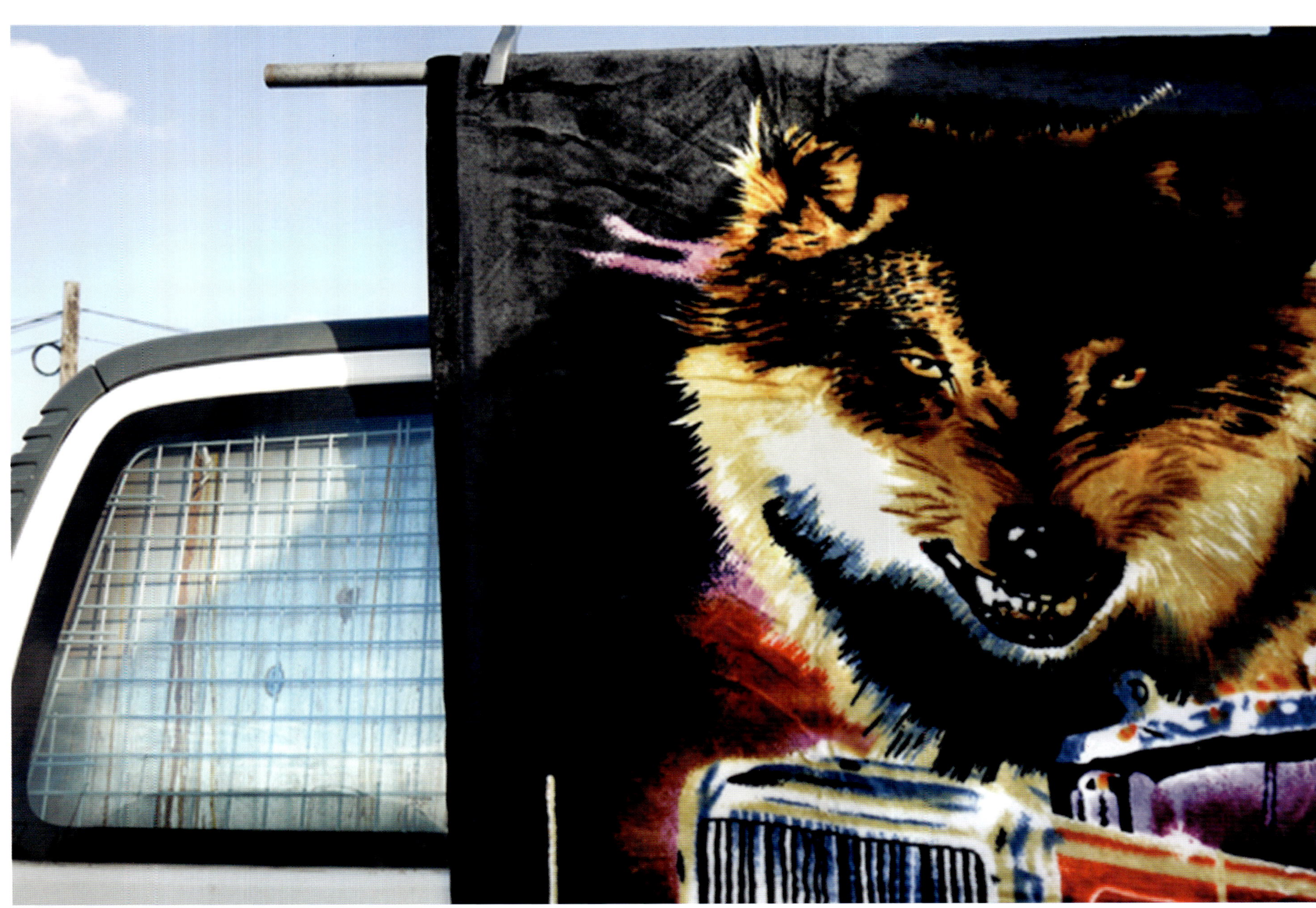

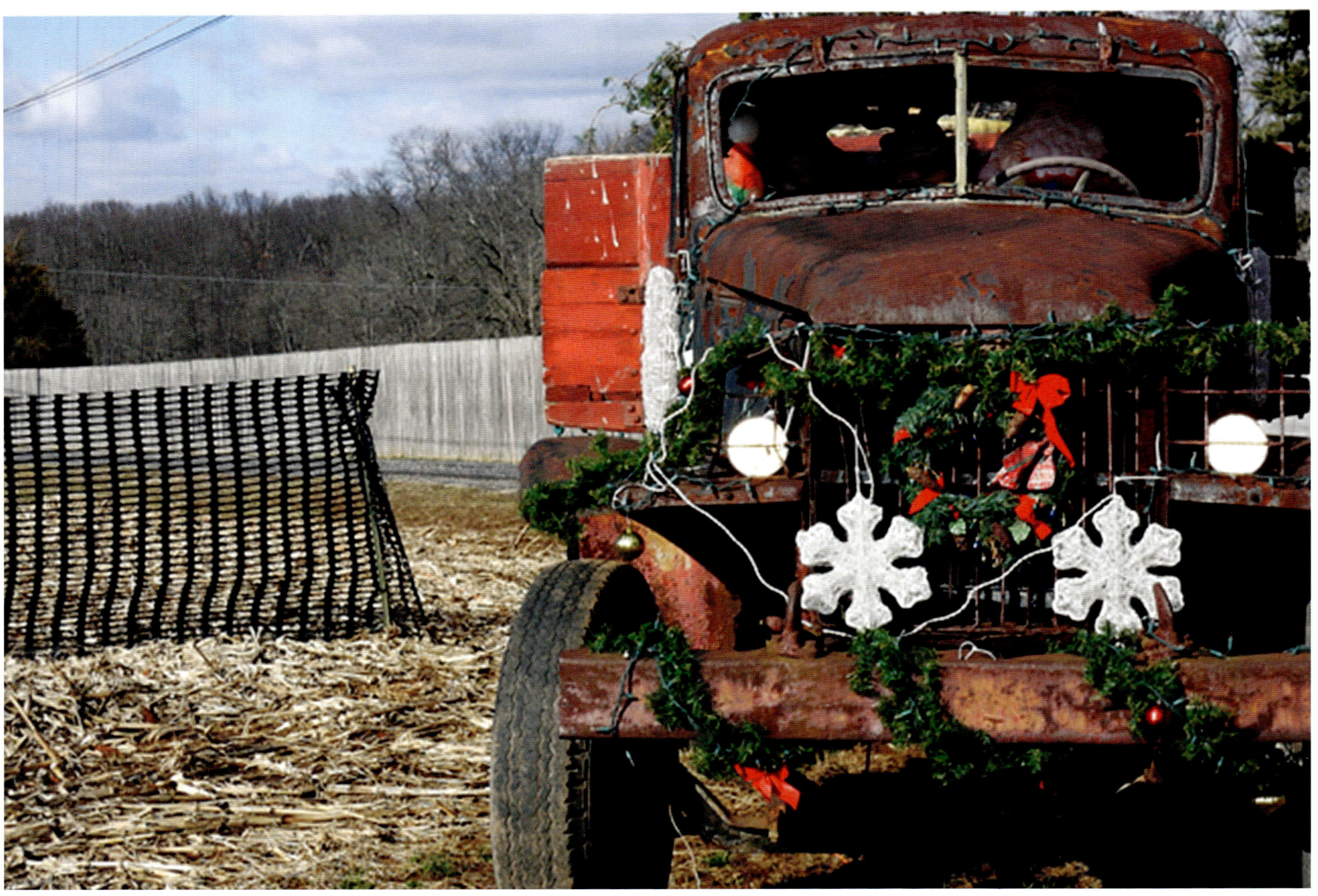

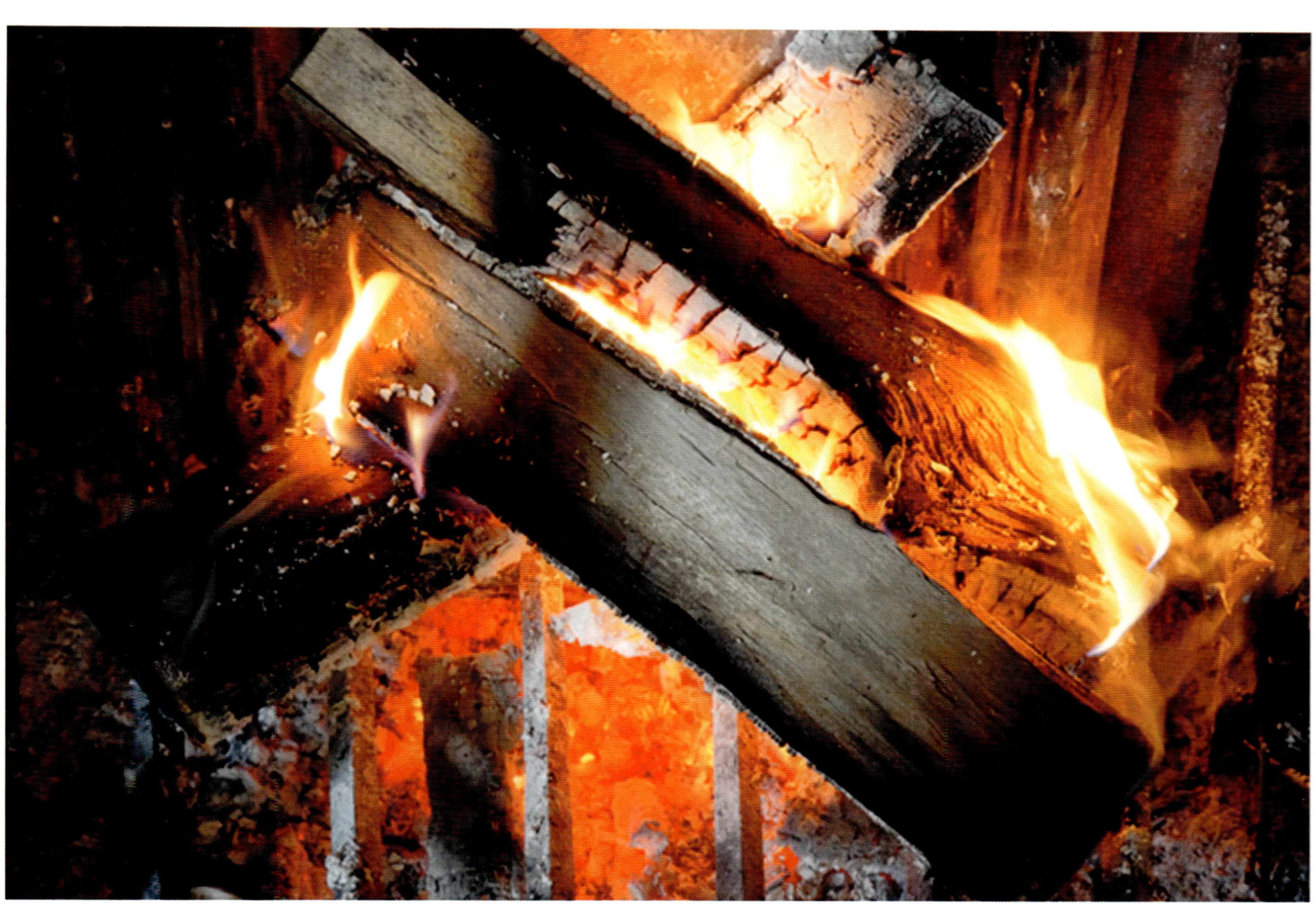

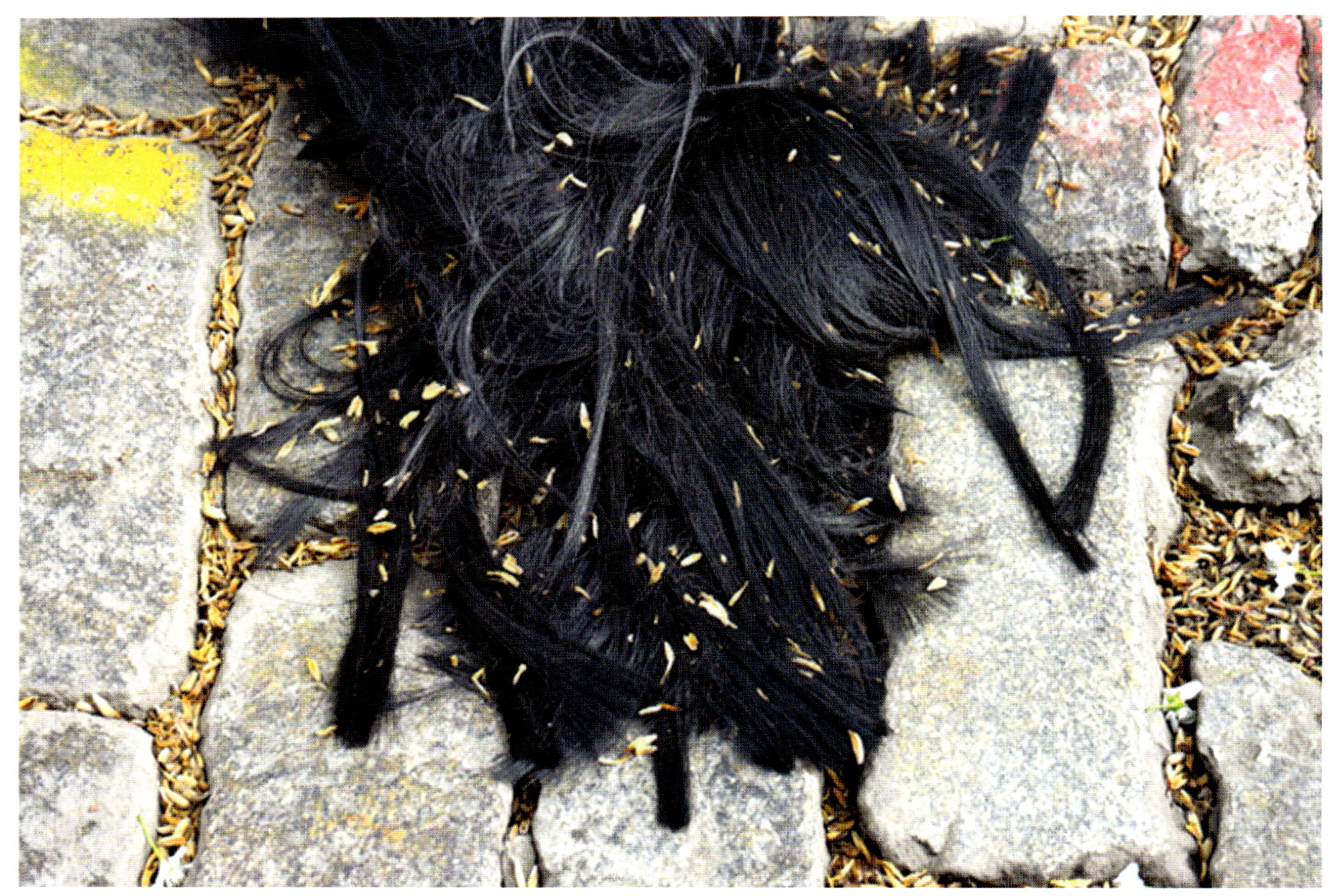

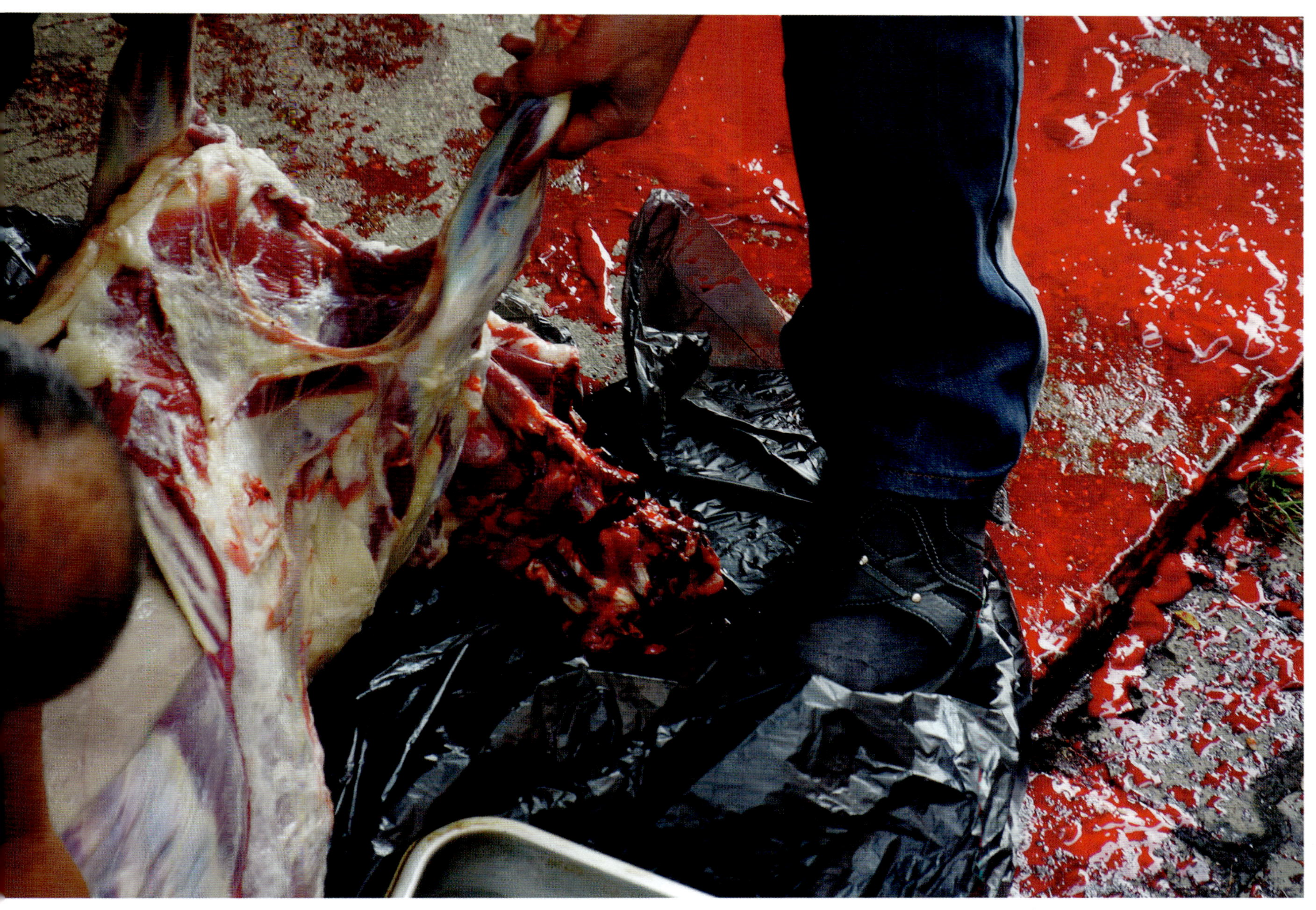

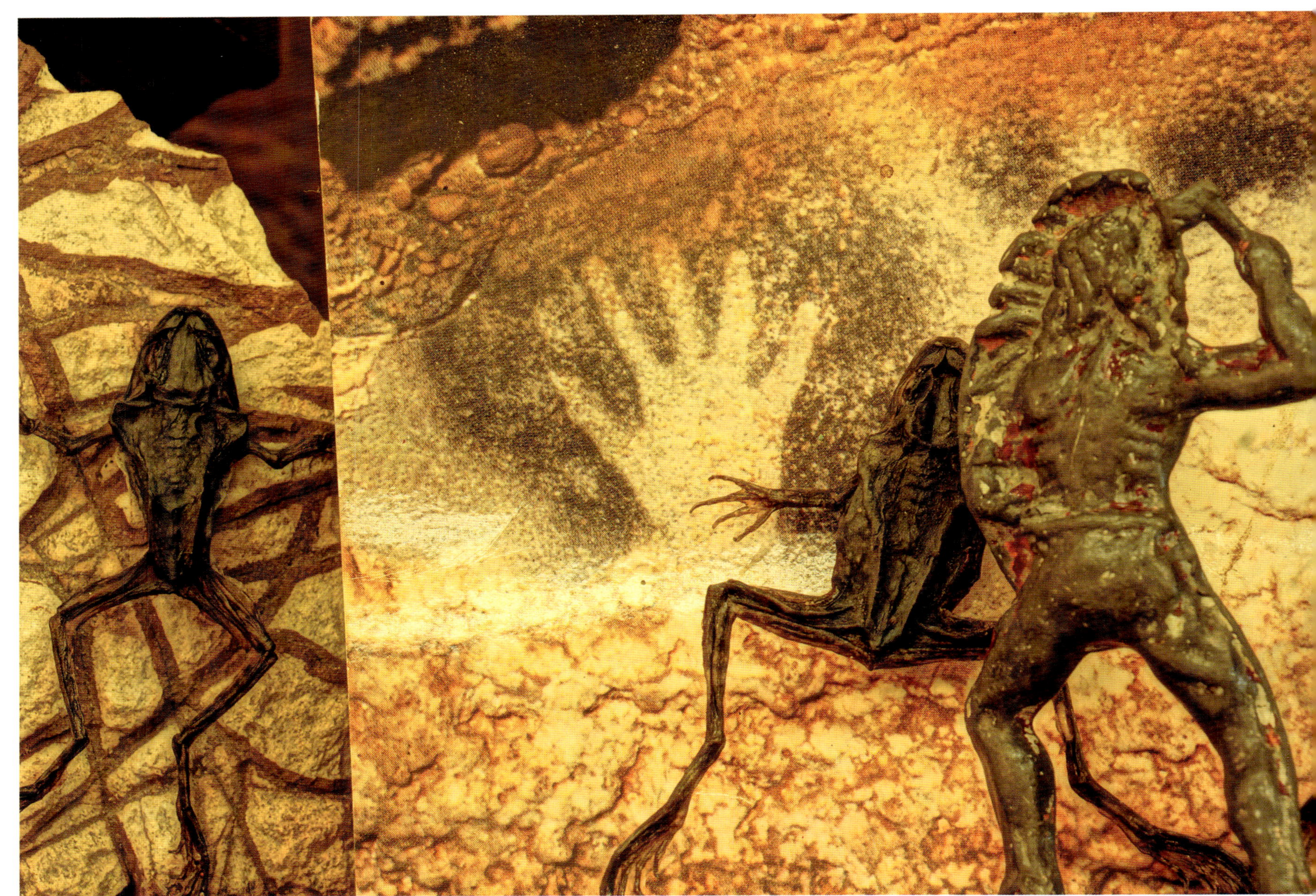

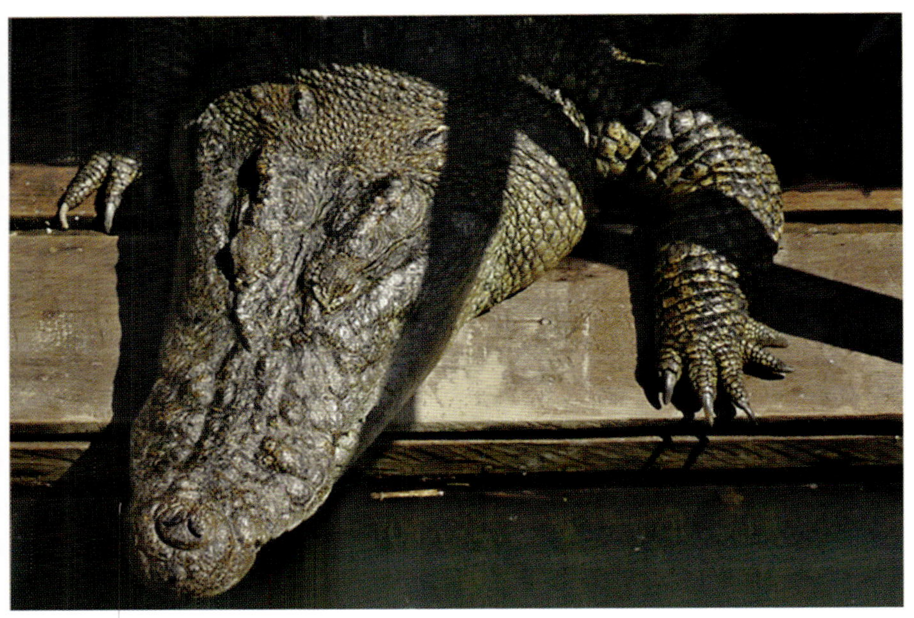

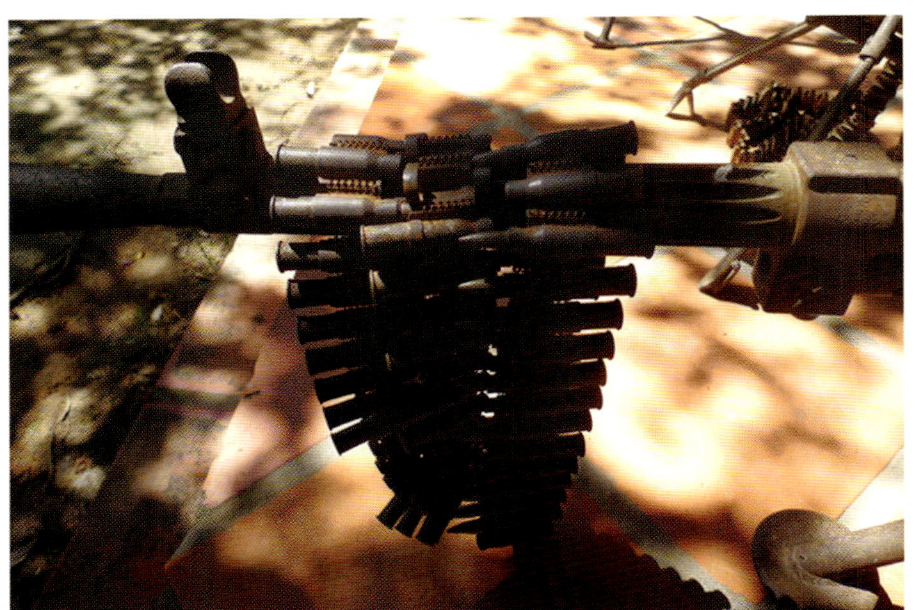

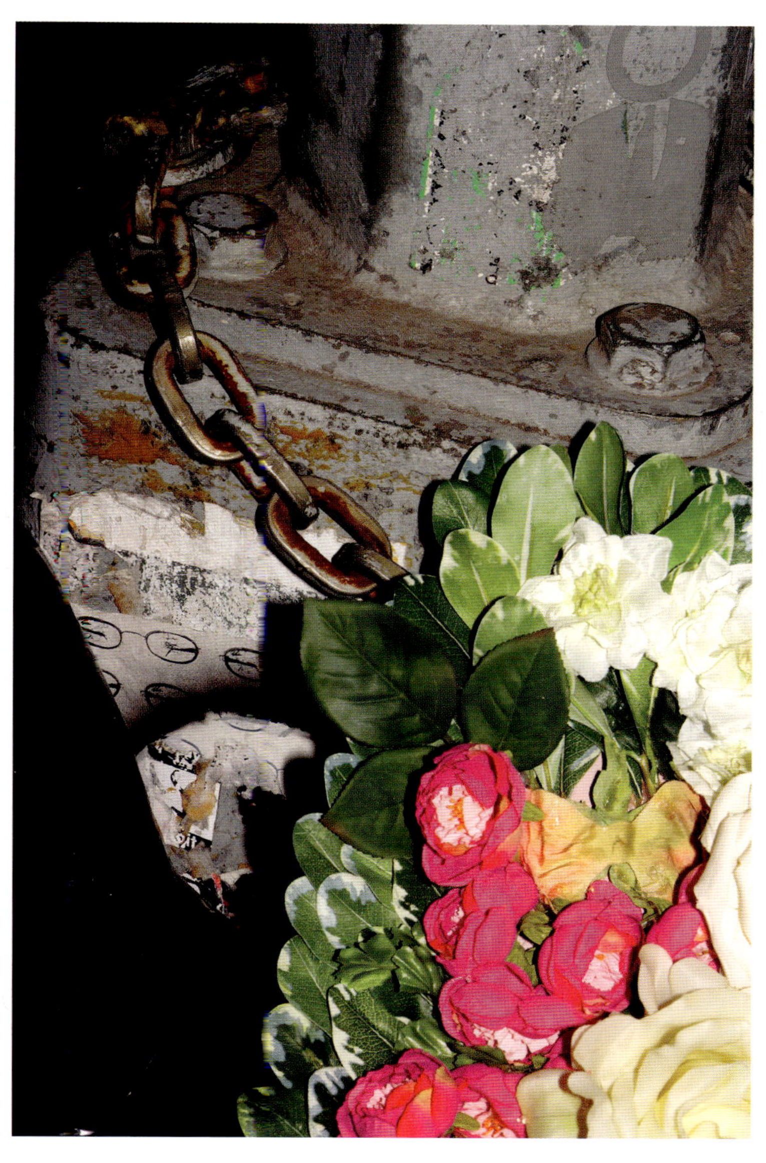

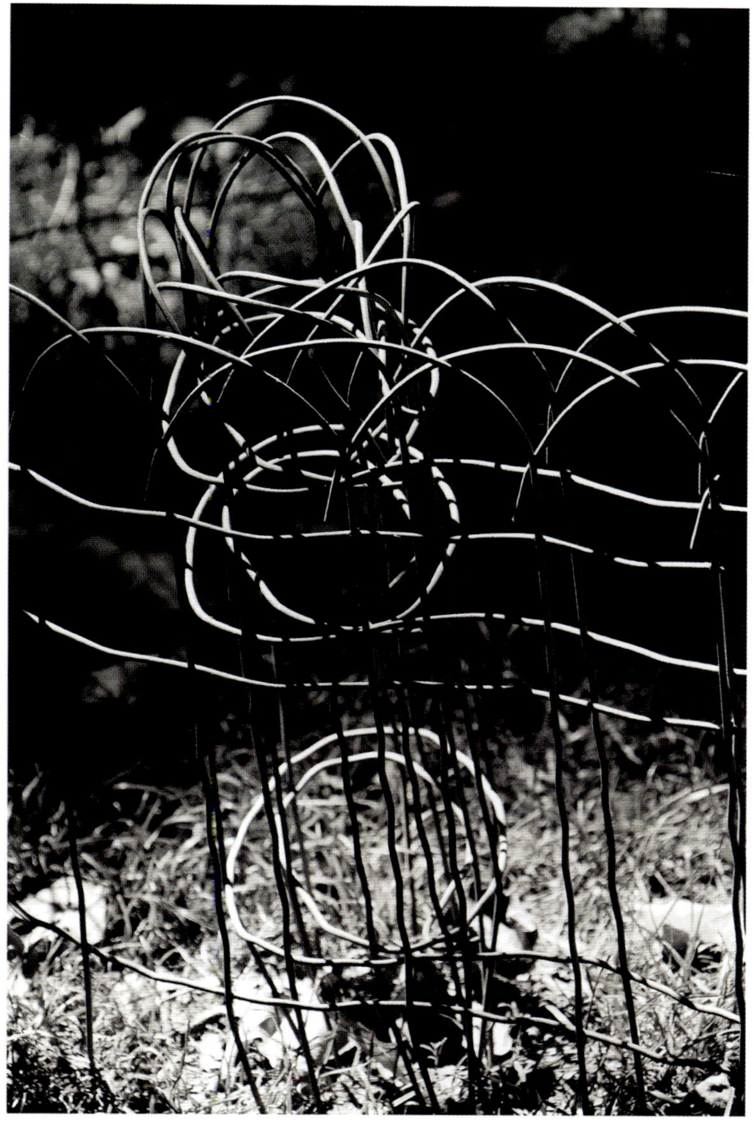

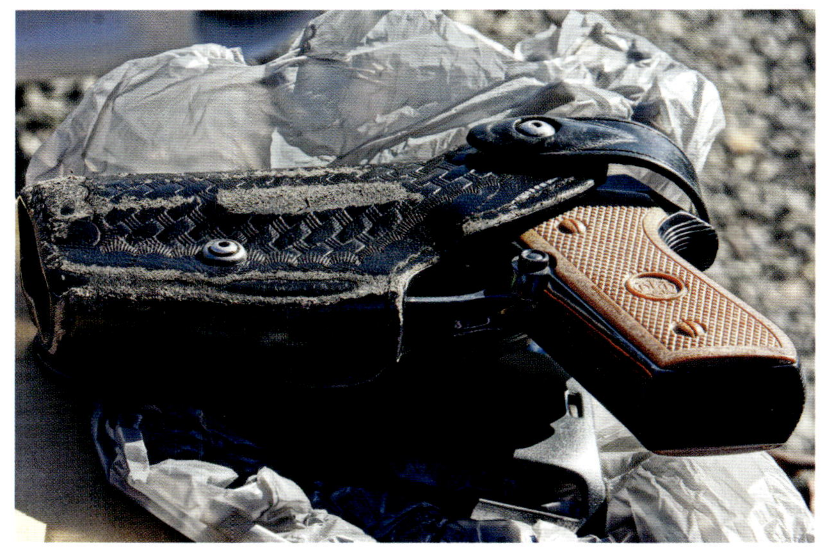

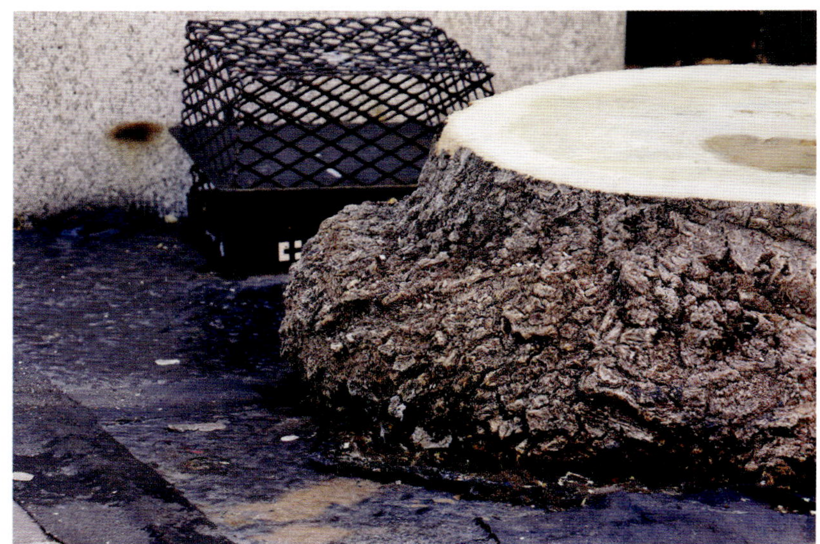

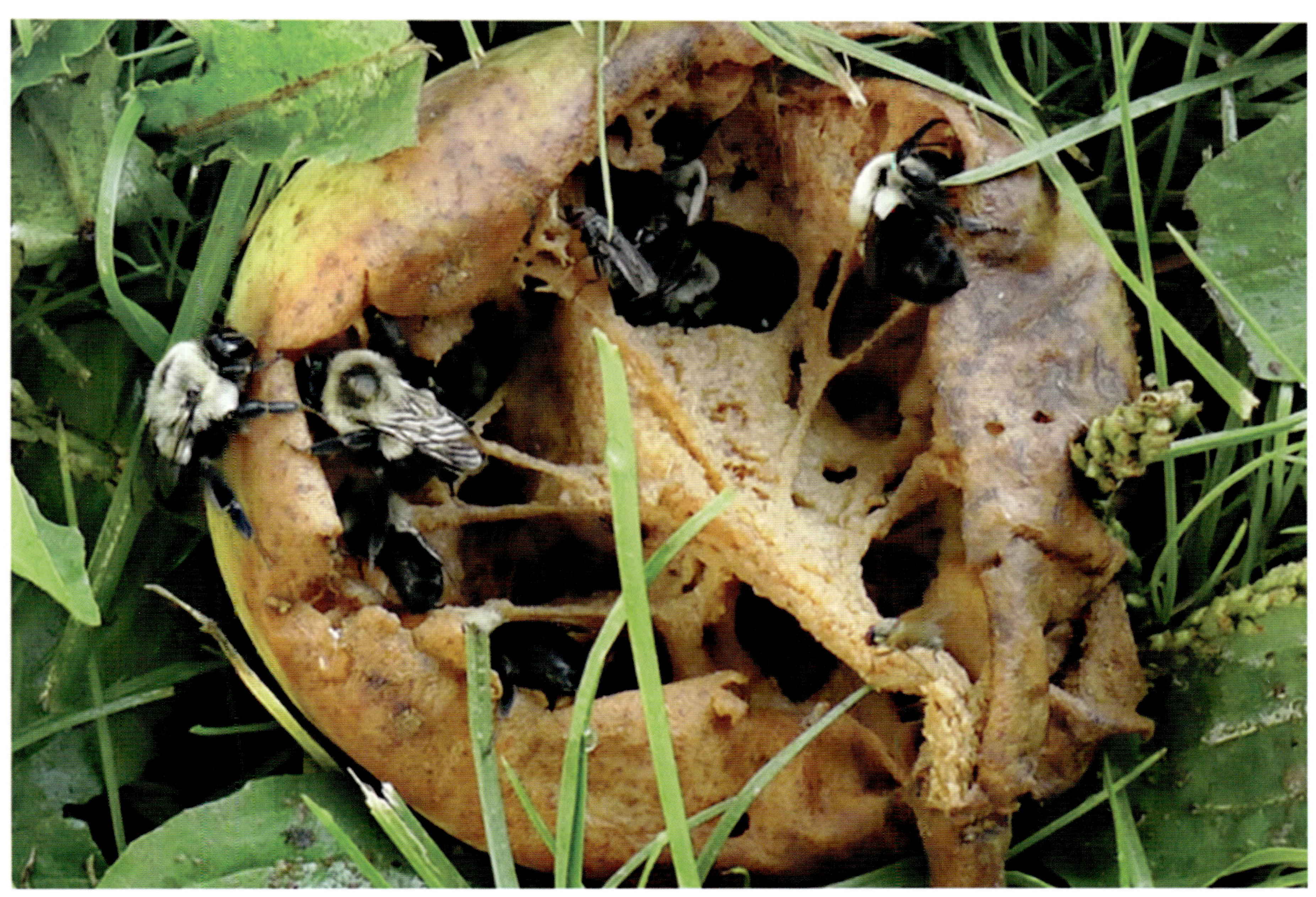

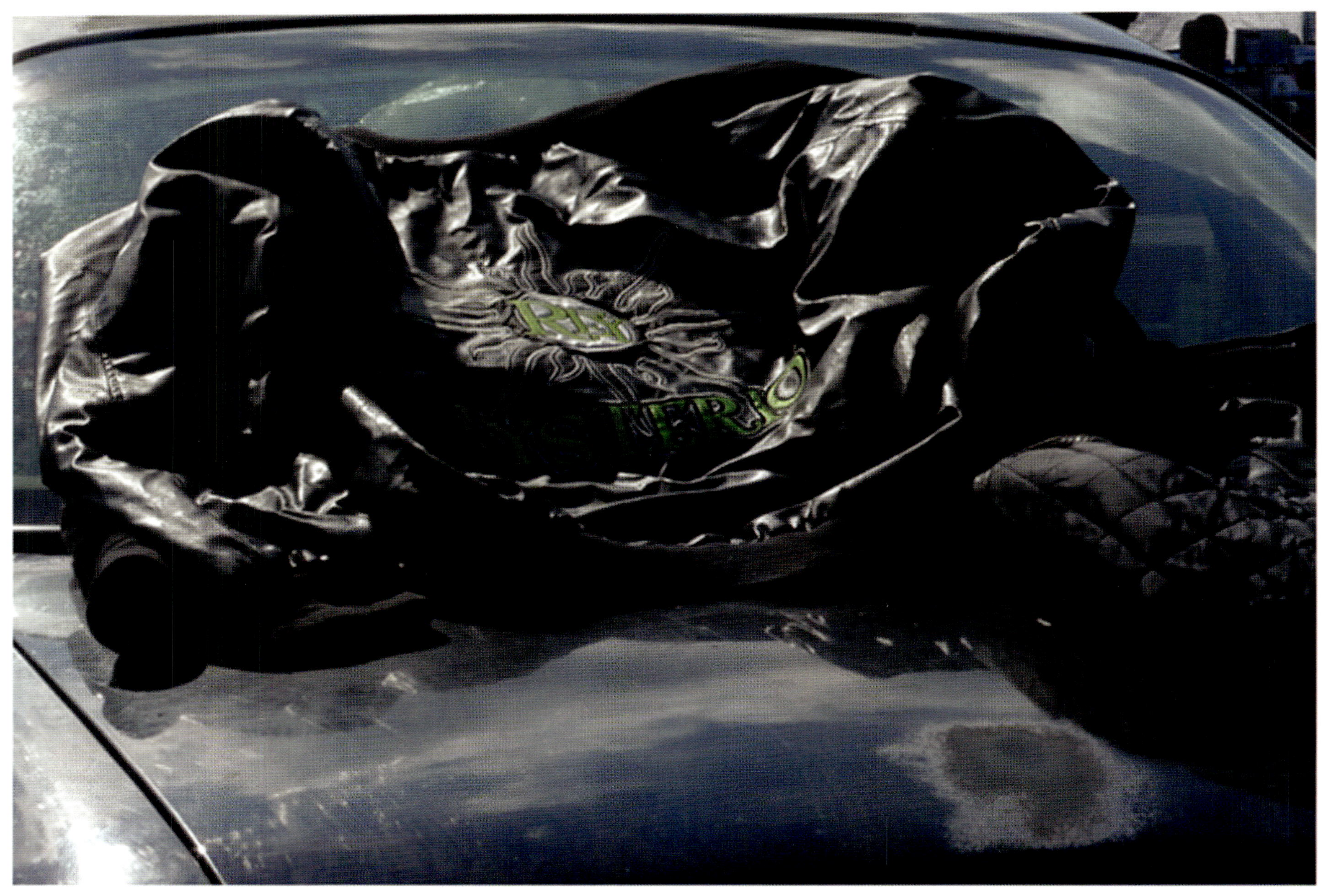

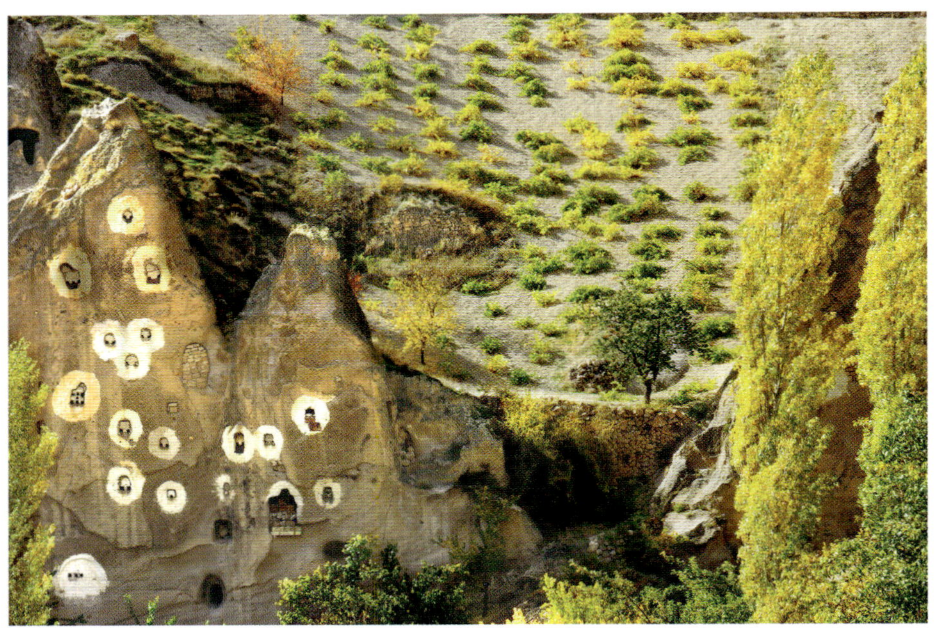

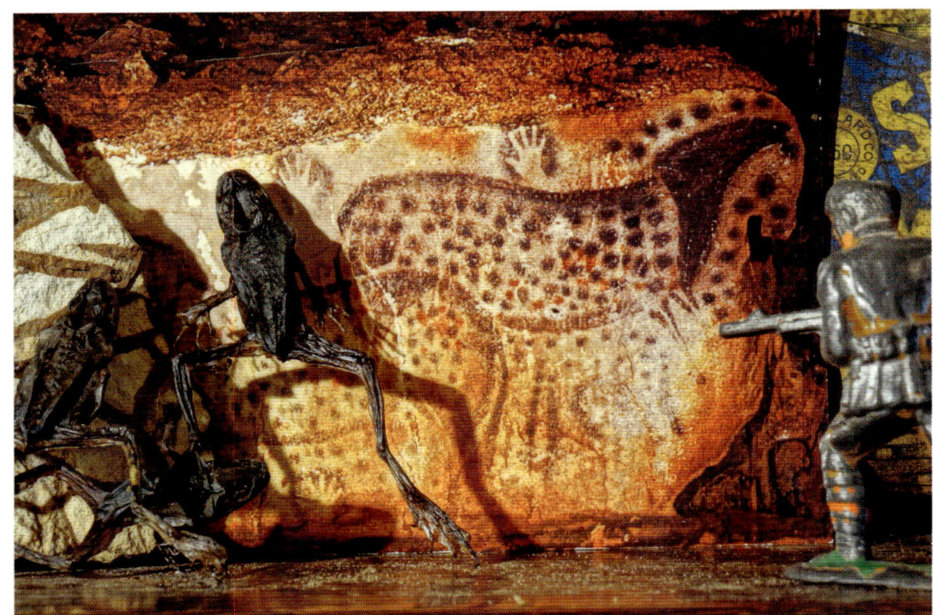

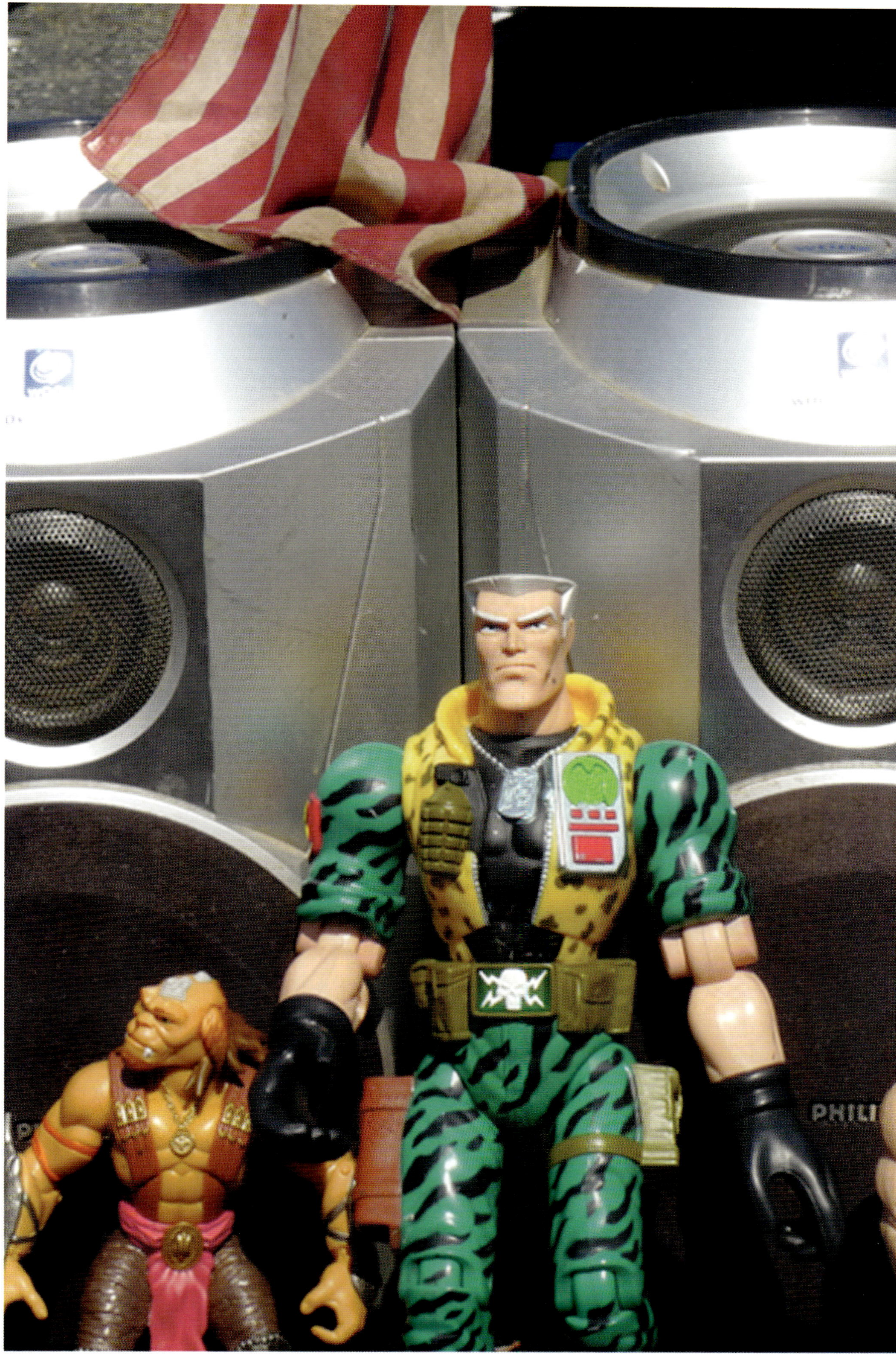

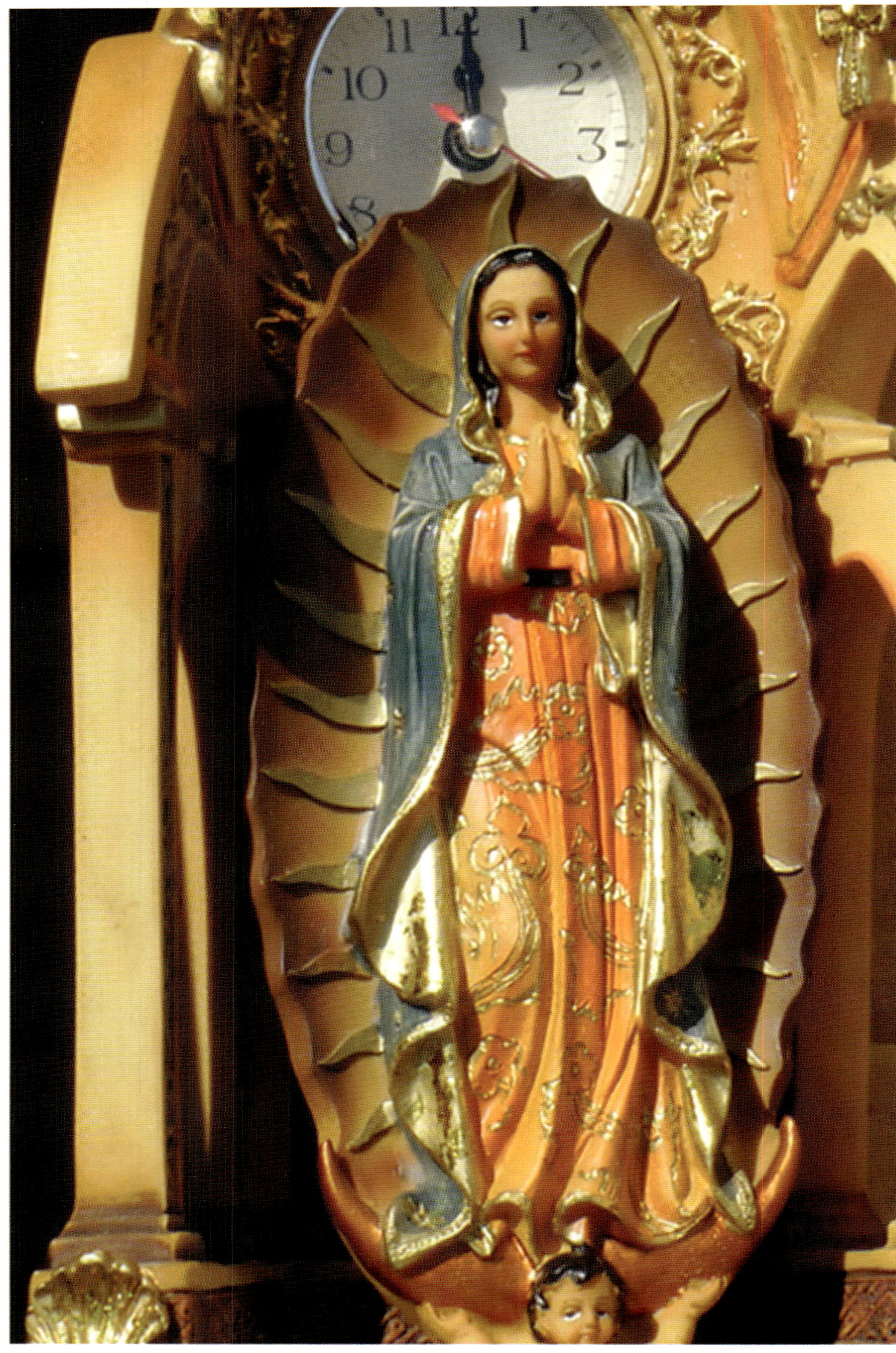

11
12
1
10
2
9
3
8

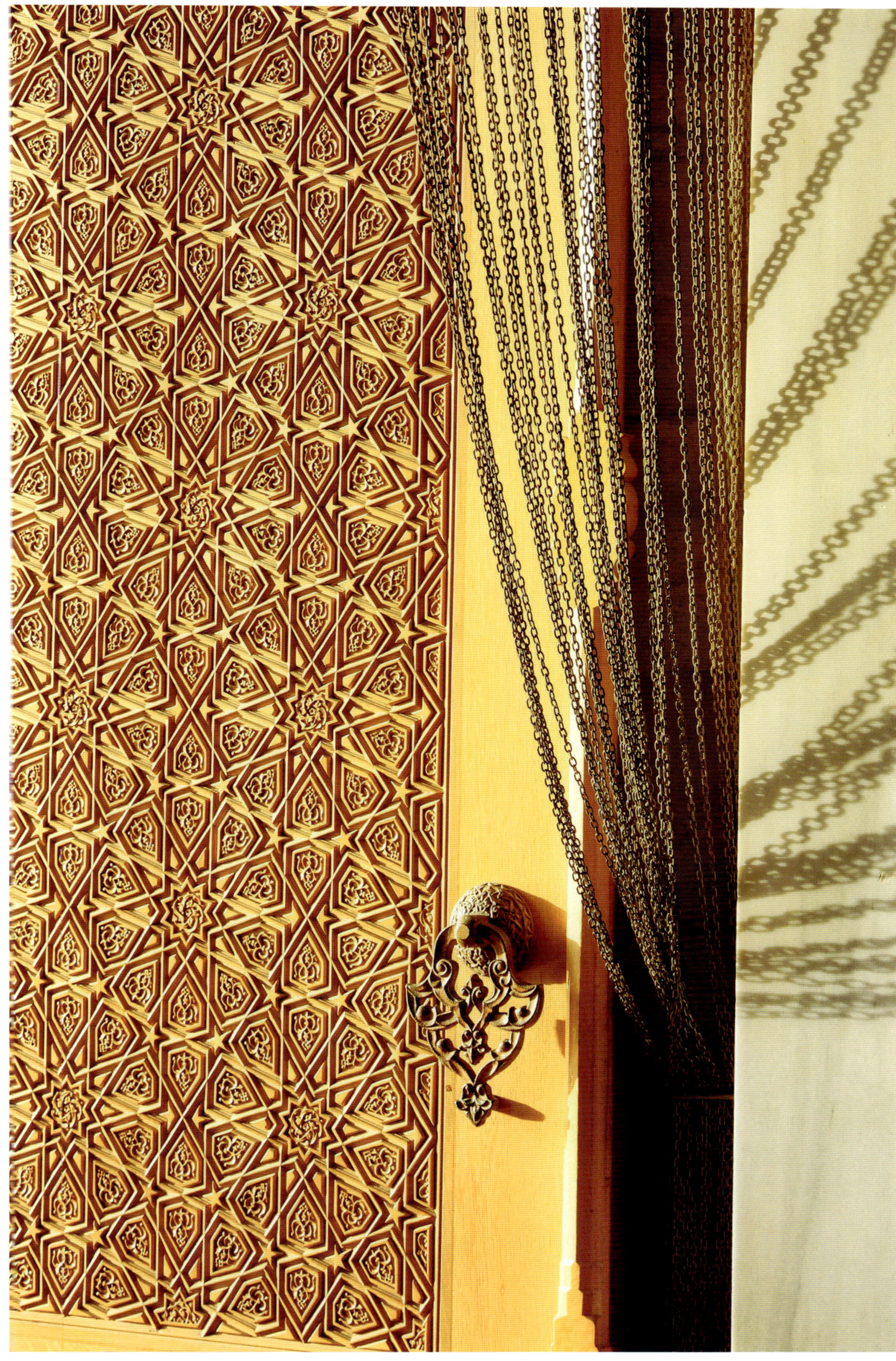

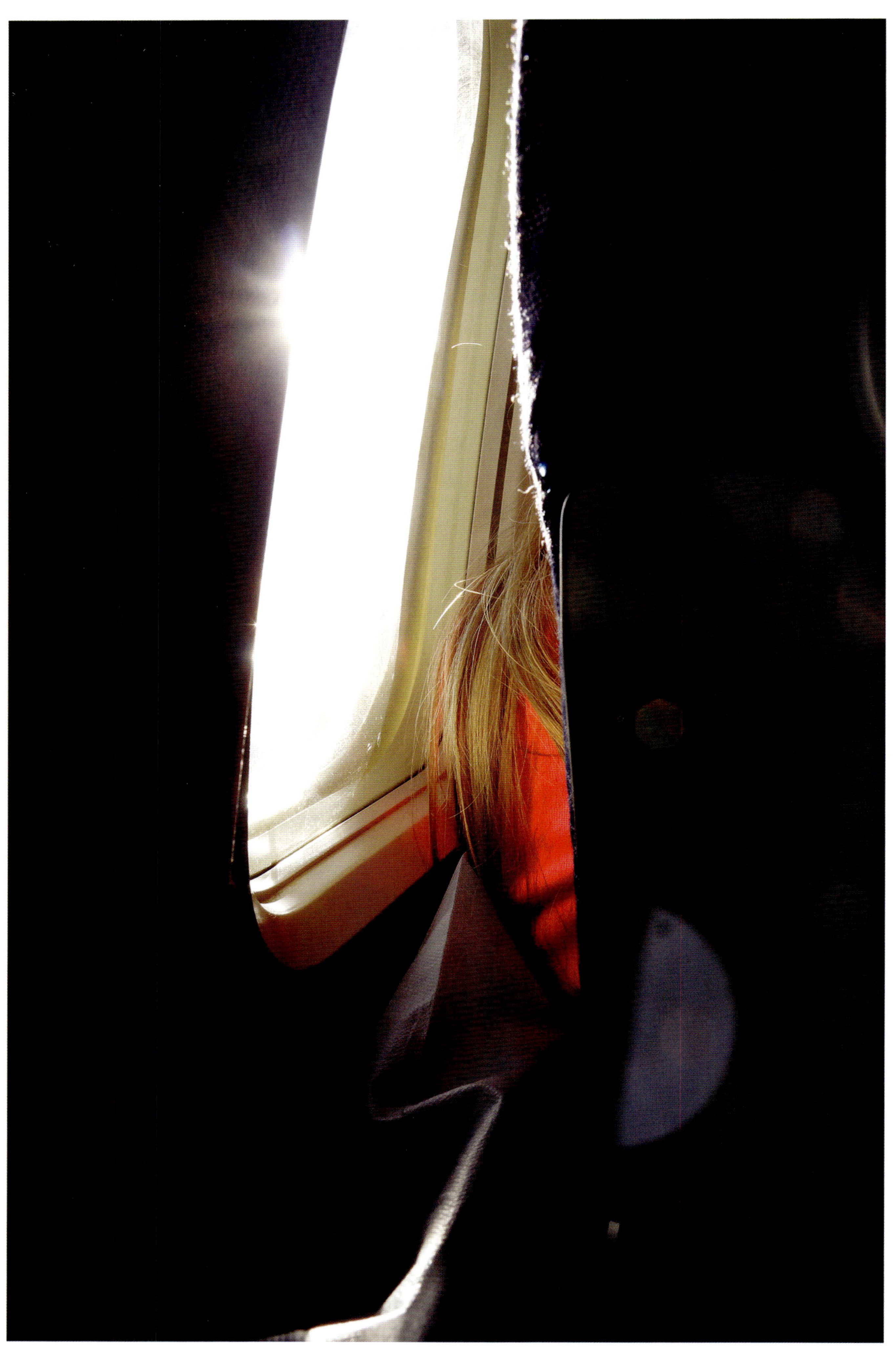

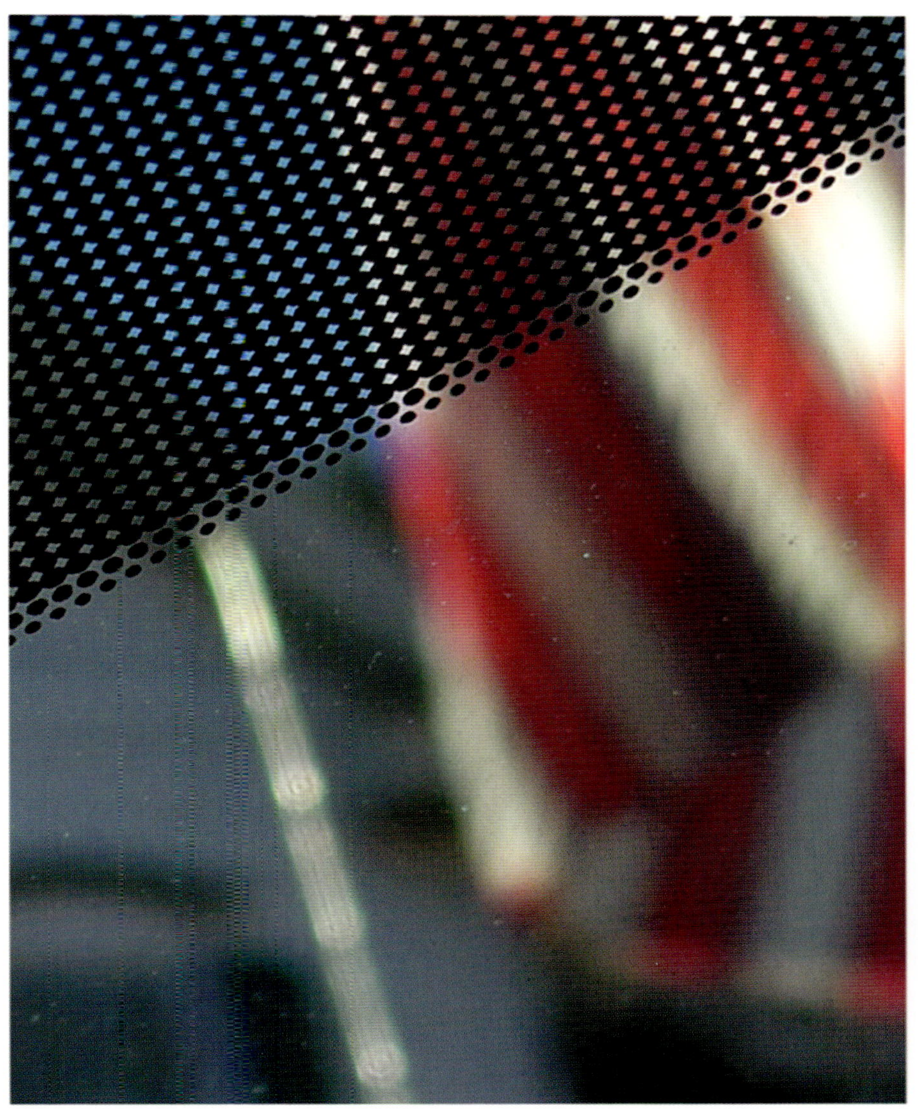

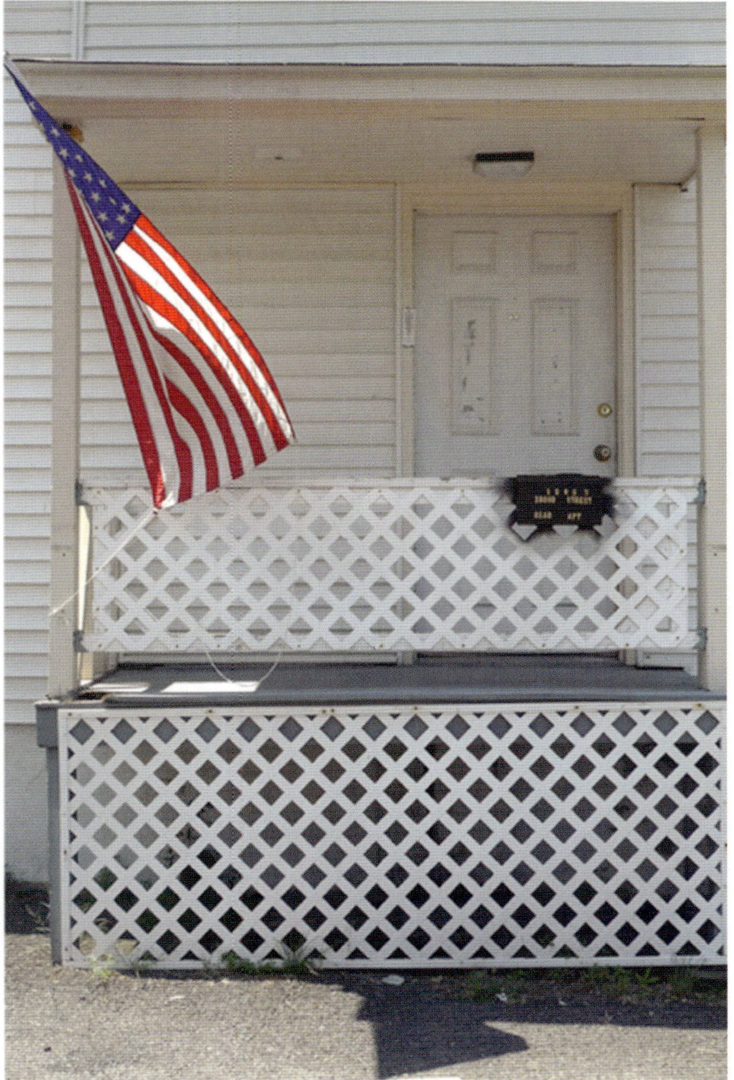

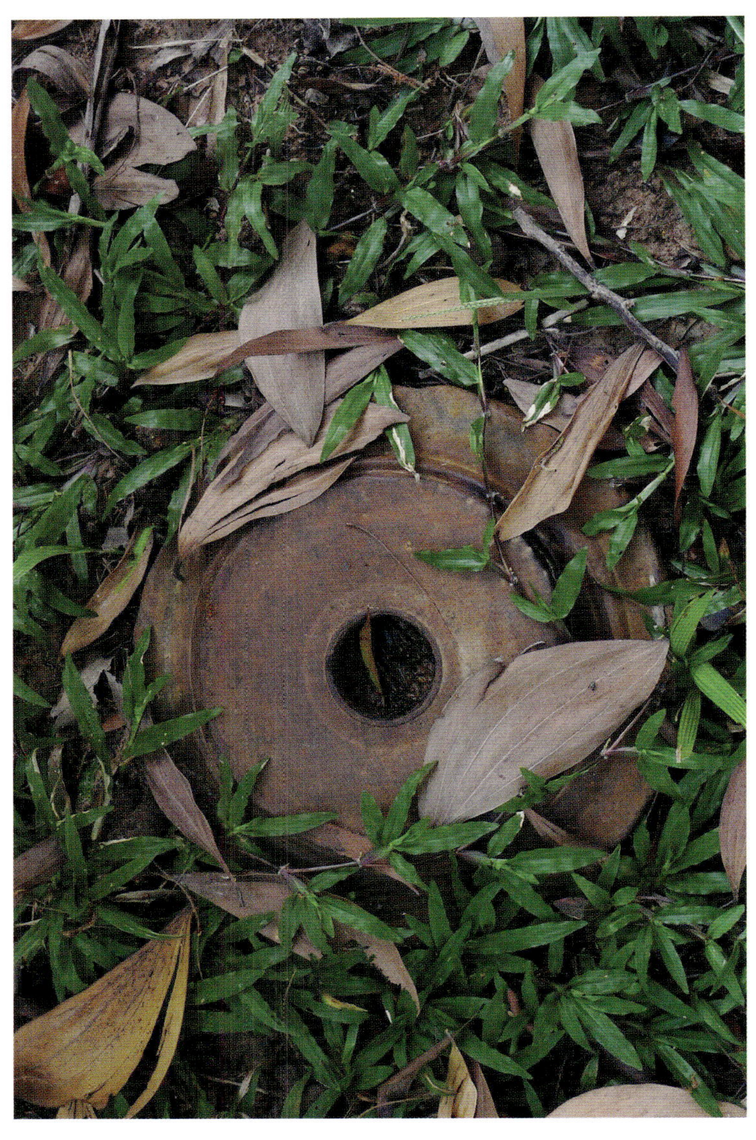

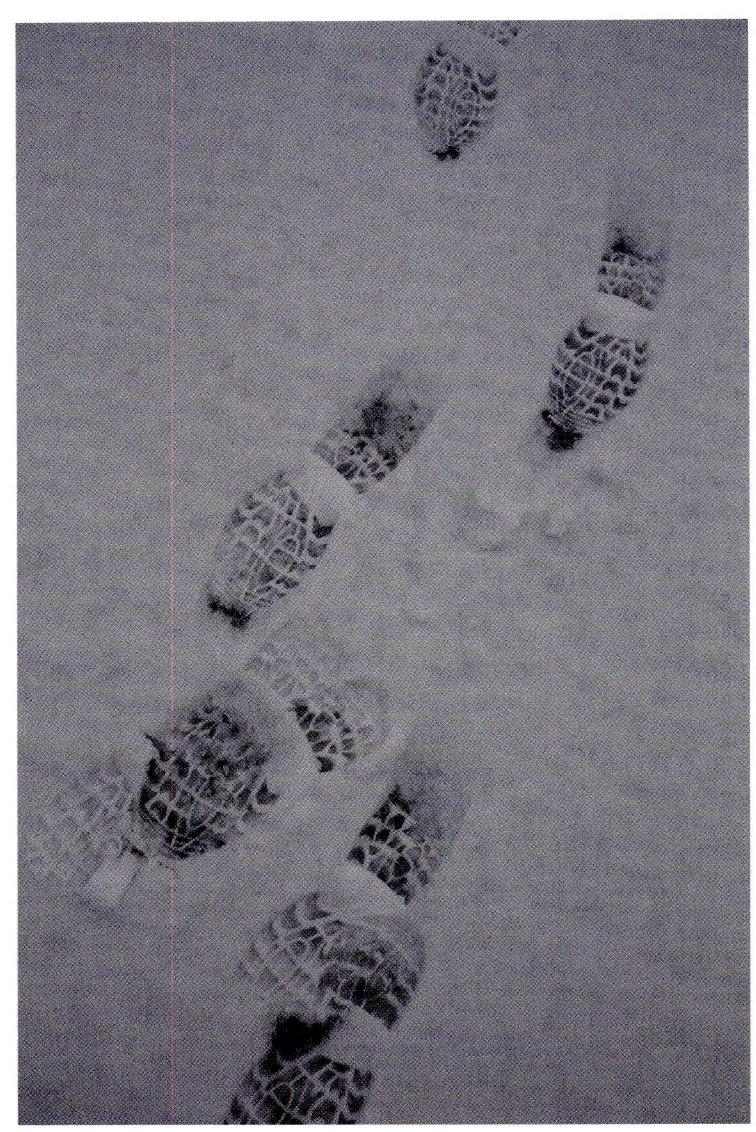

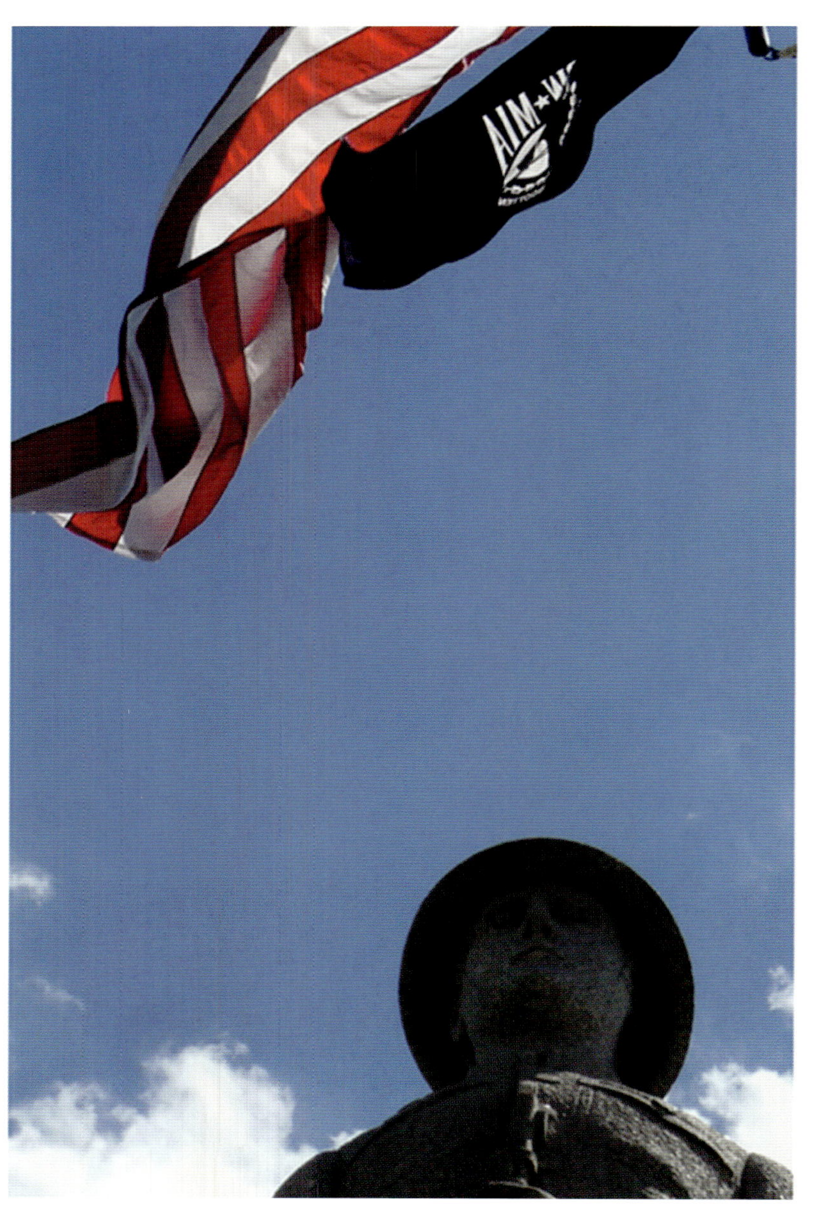

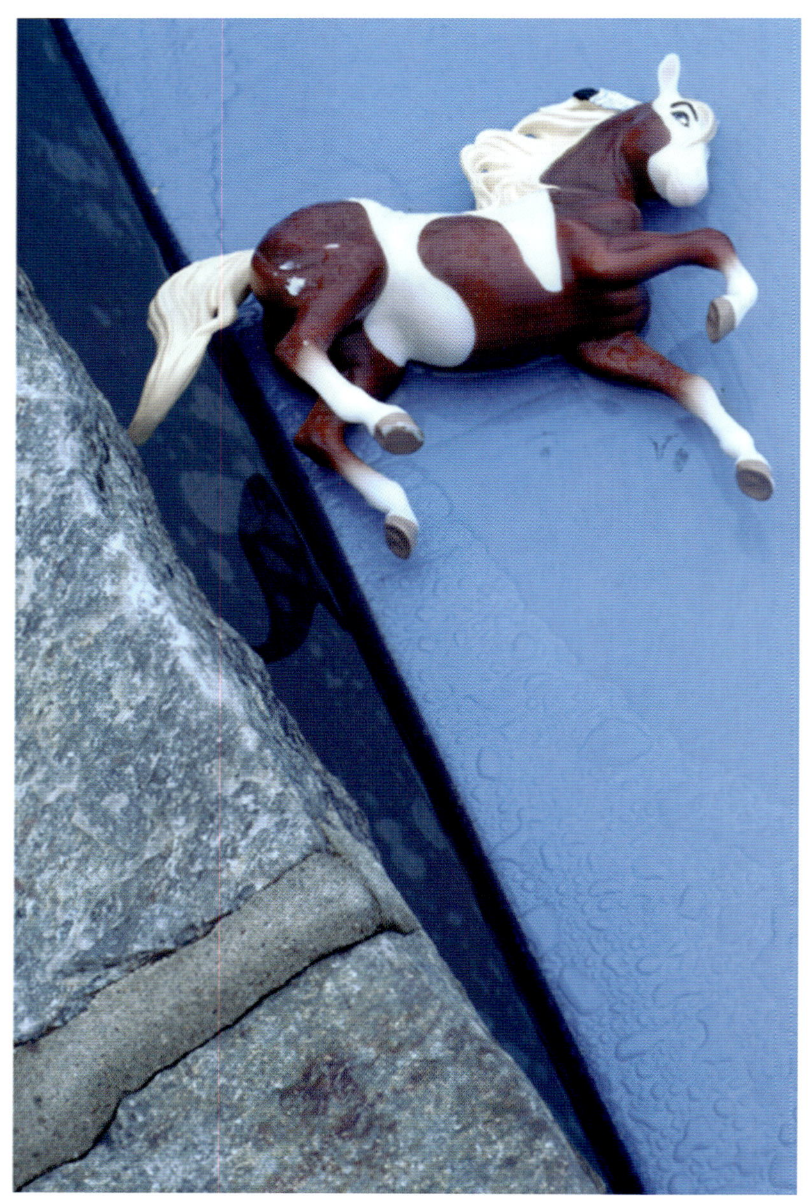

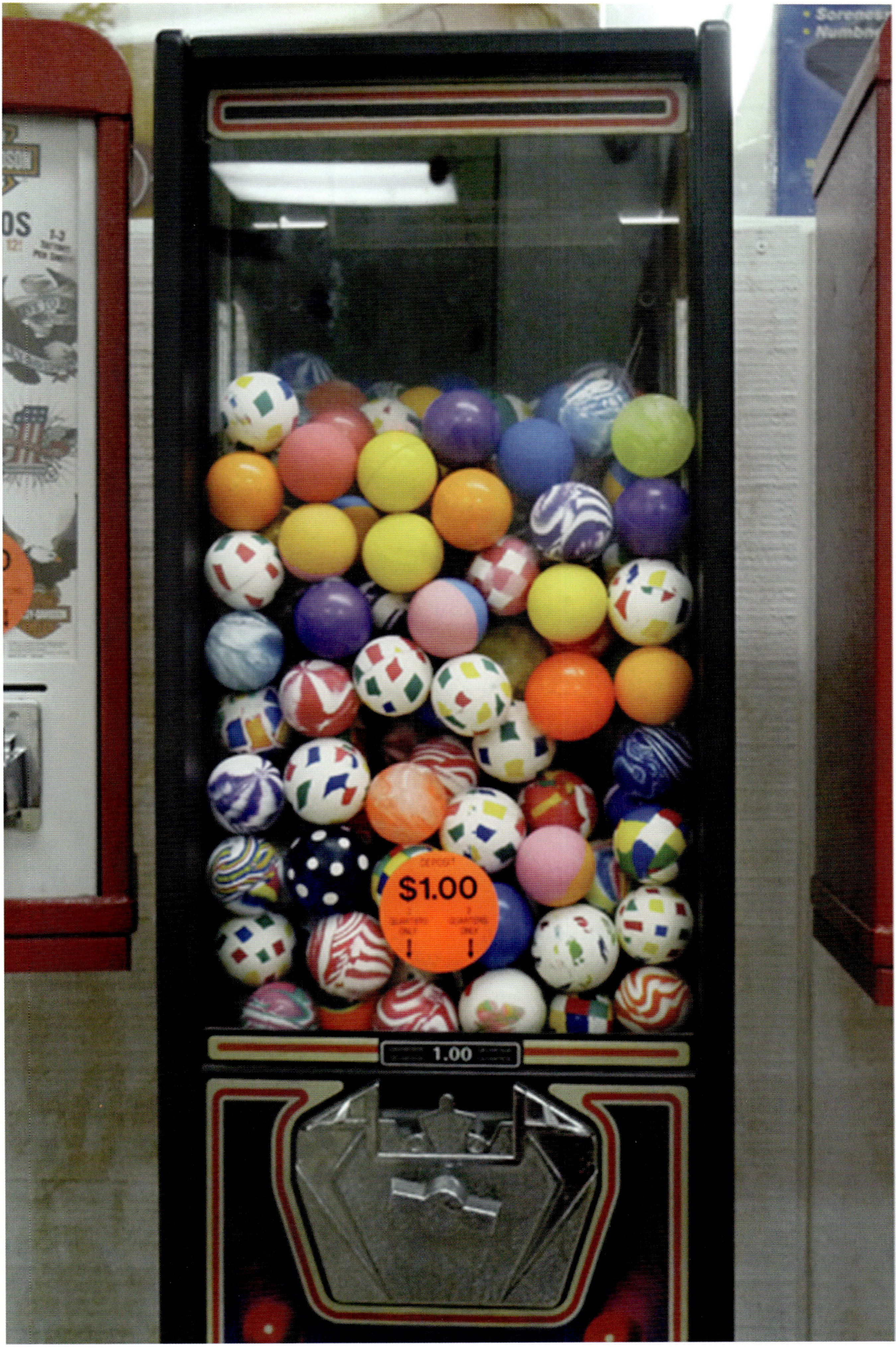
$1.00
1.00

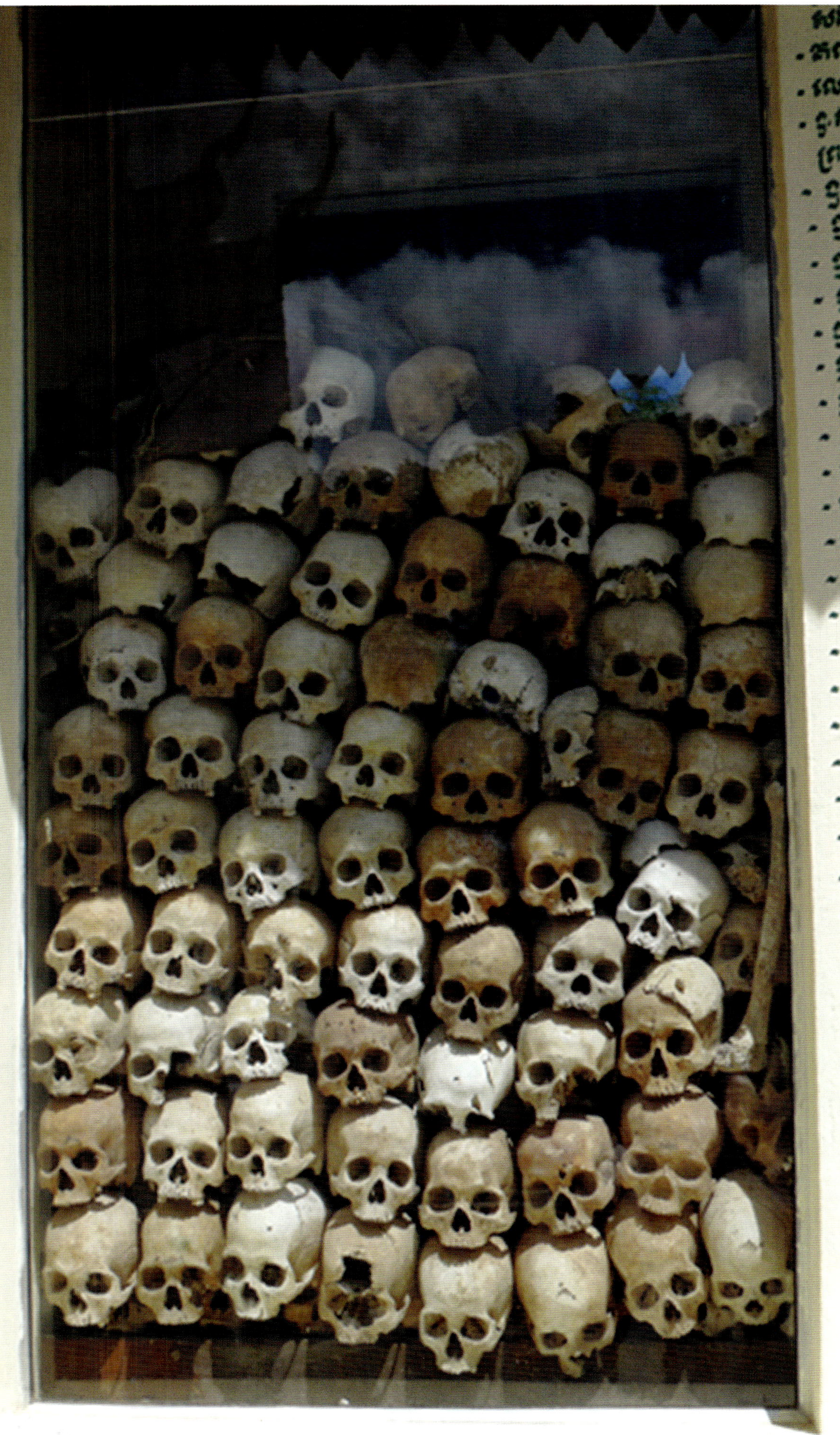

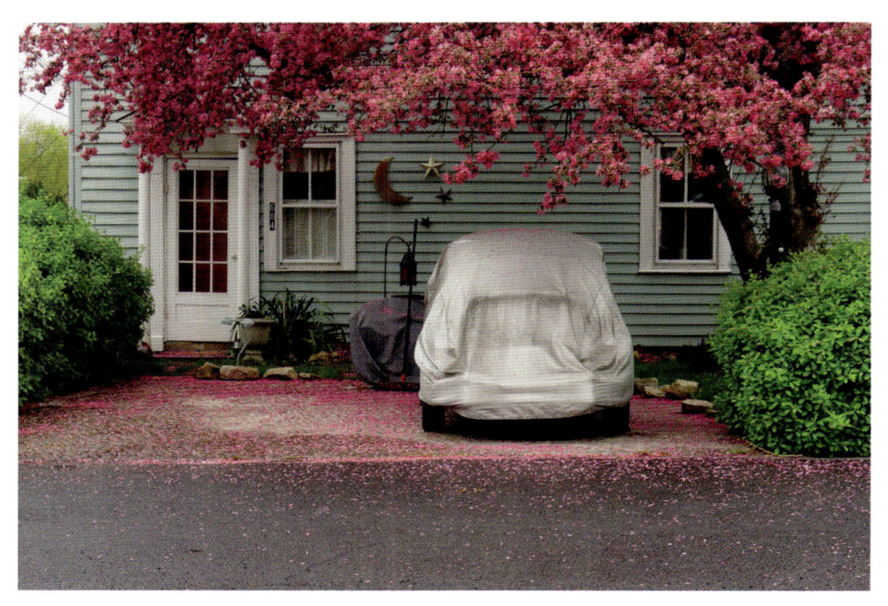

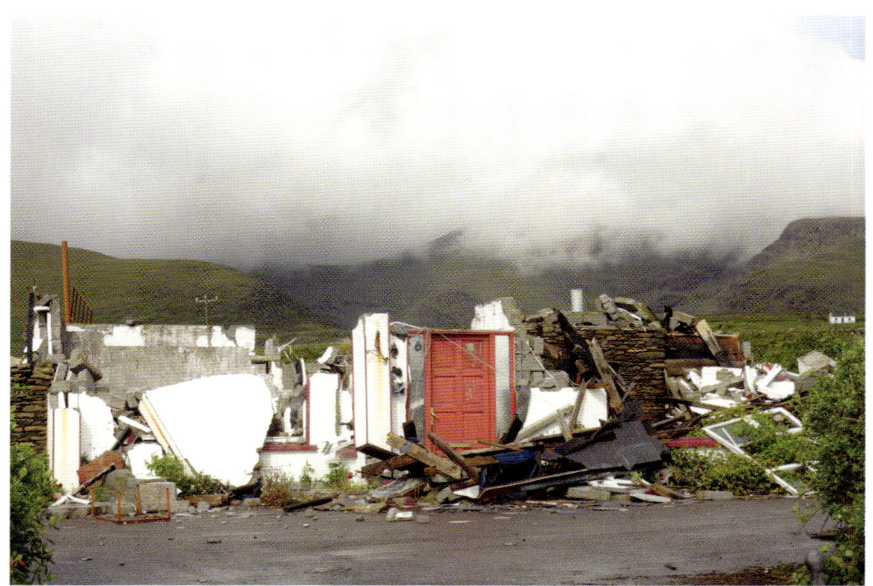

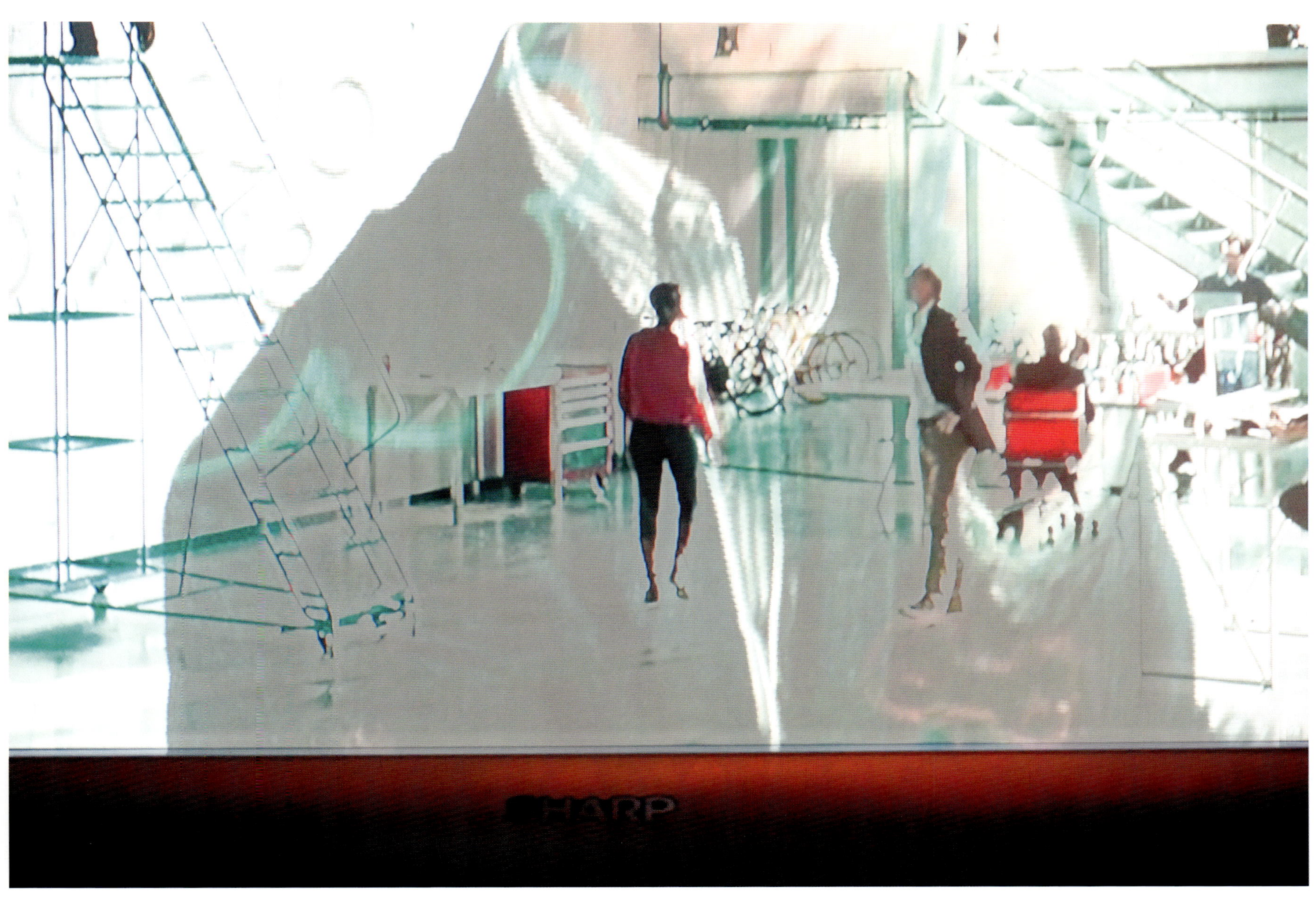

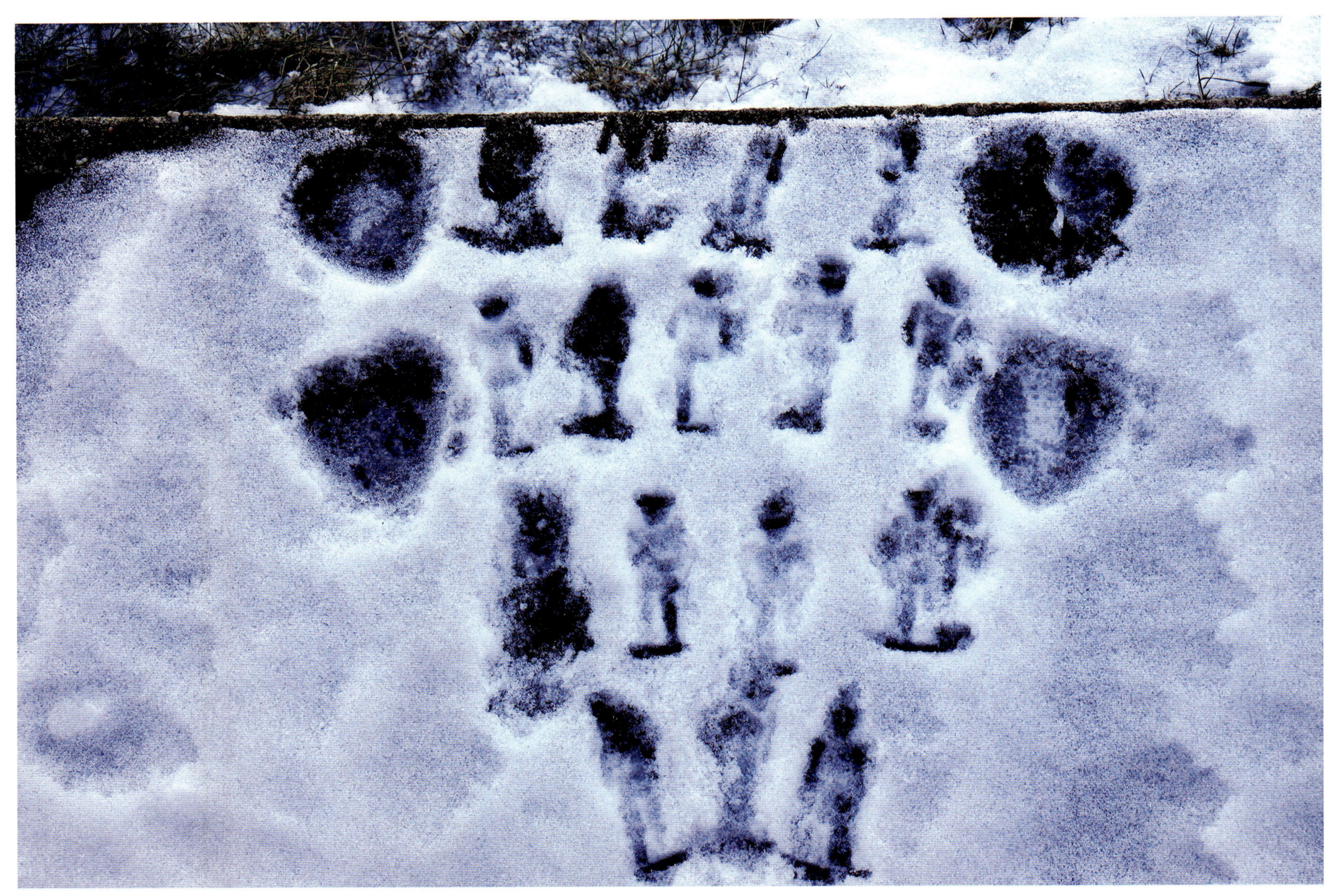

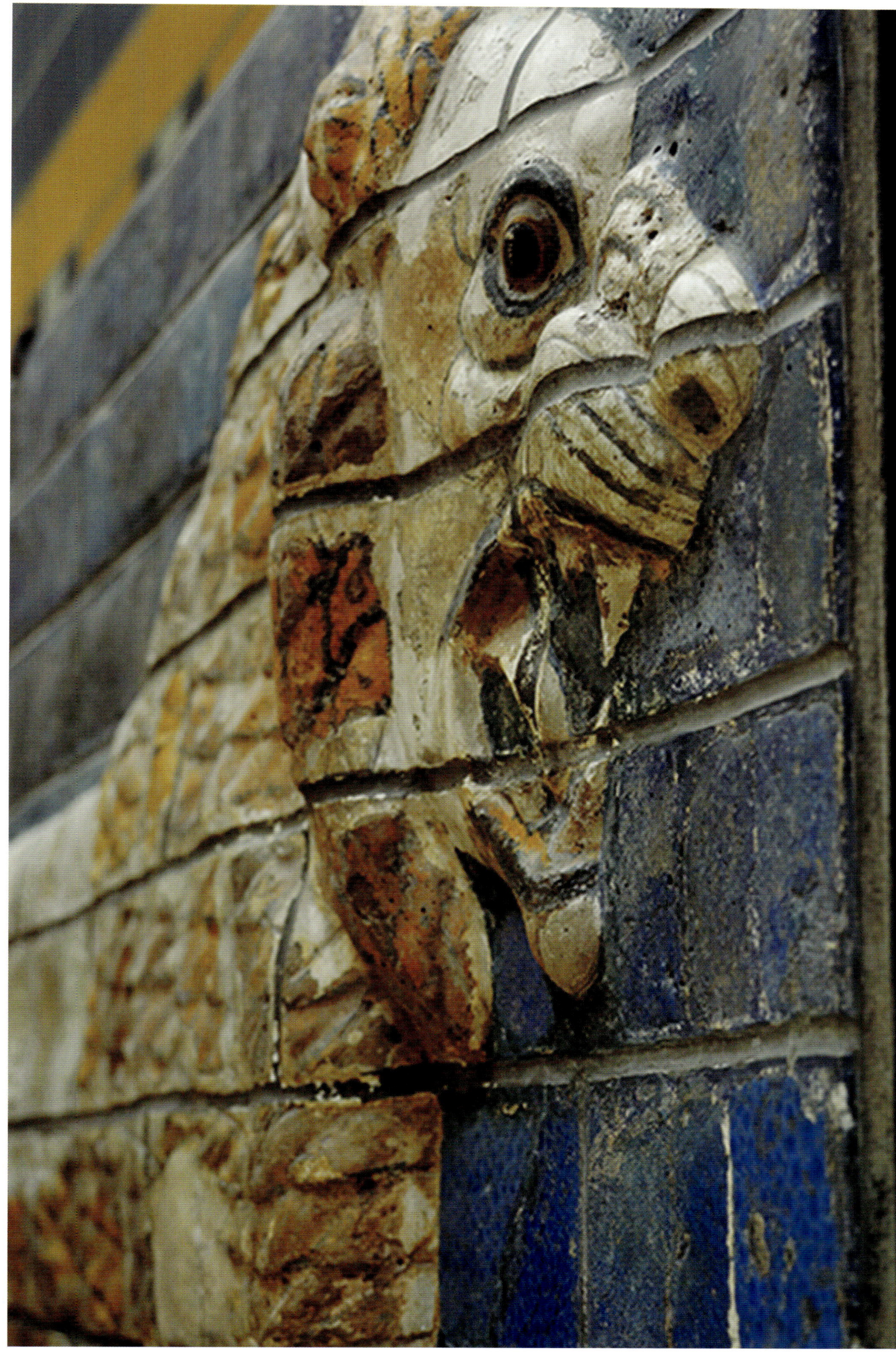

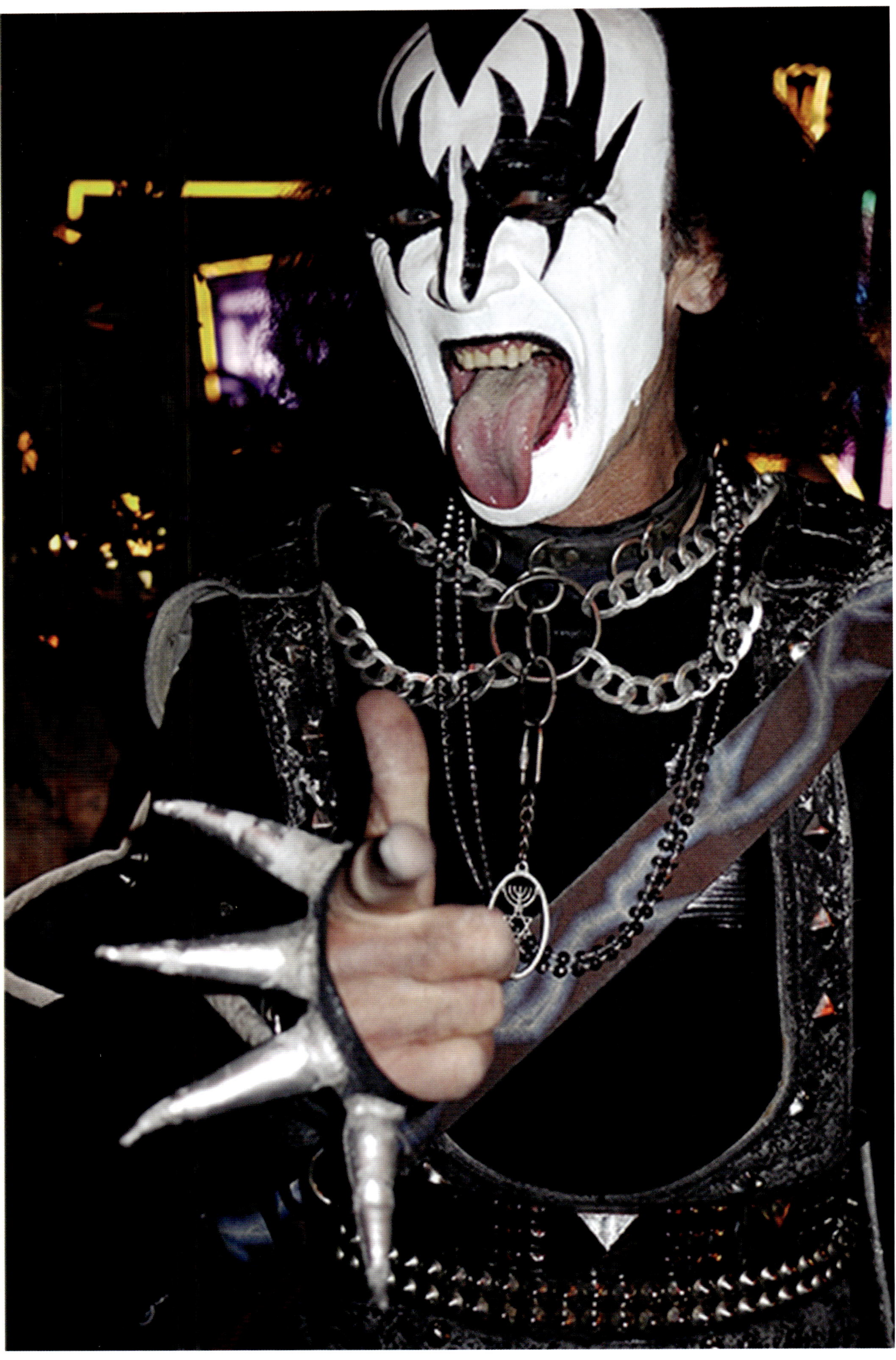

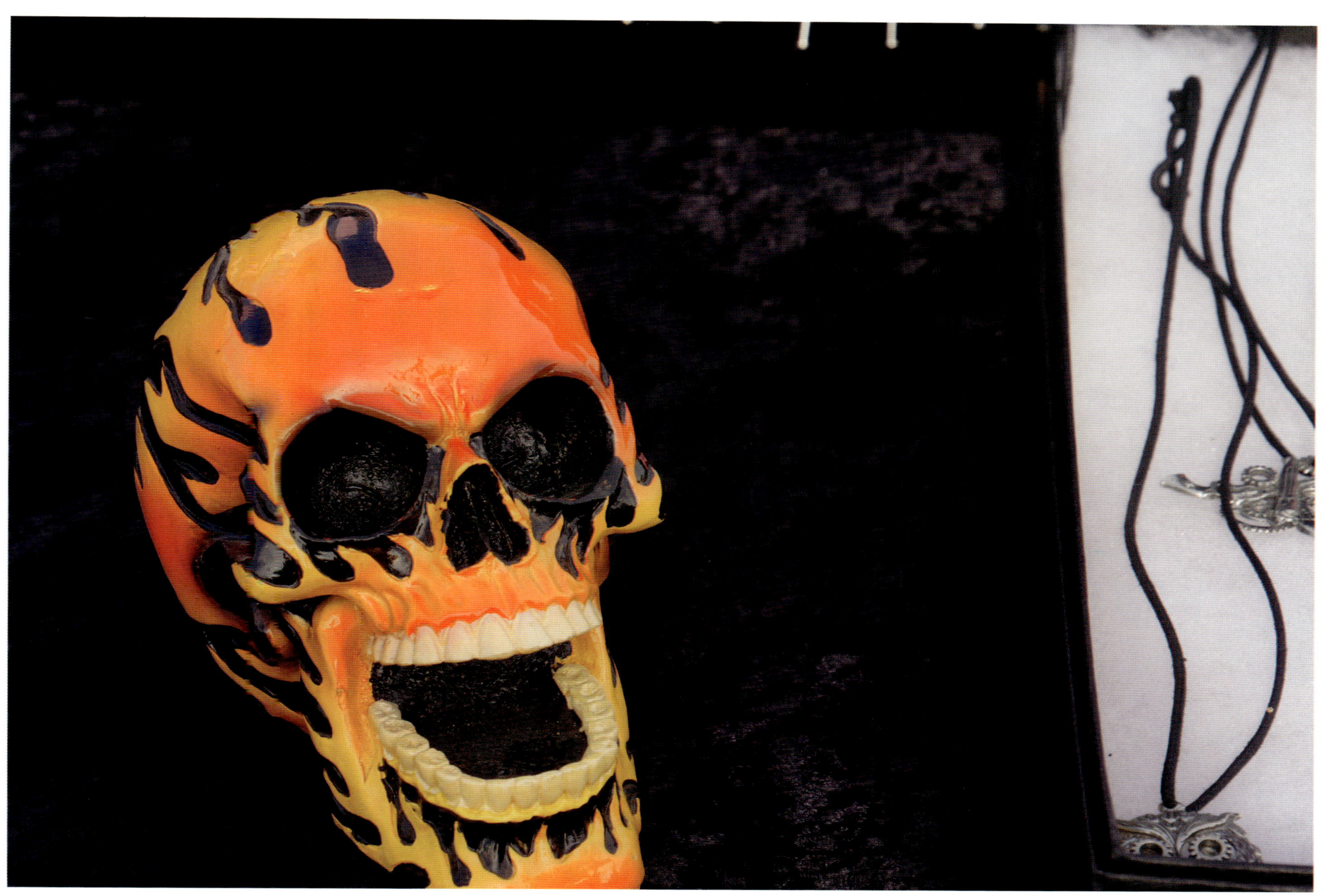

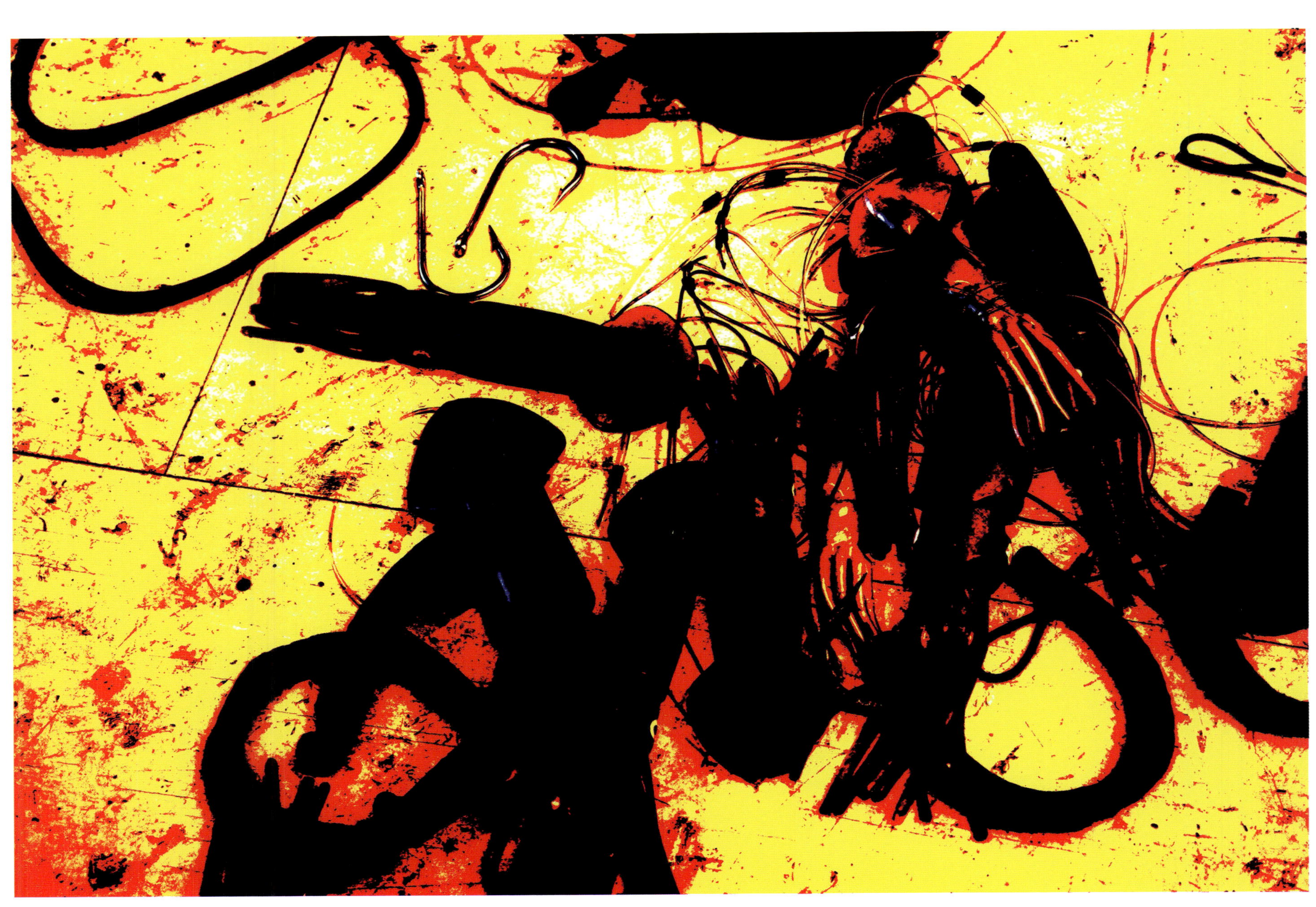

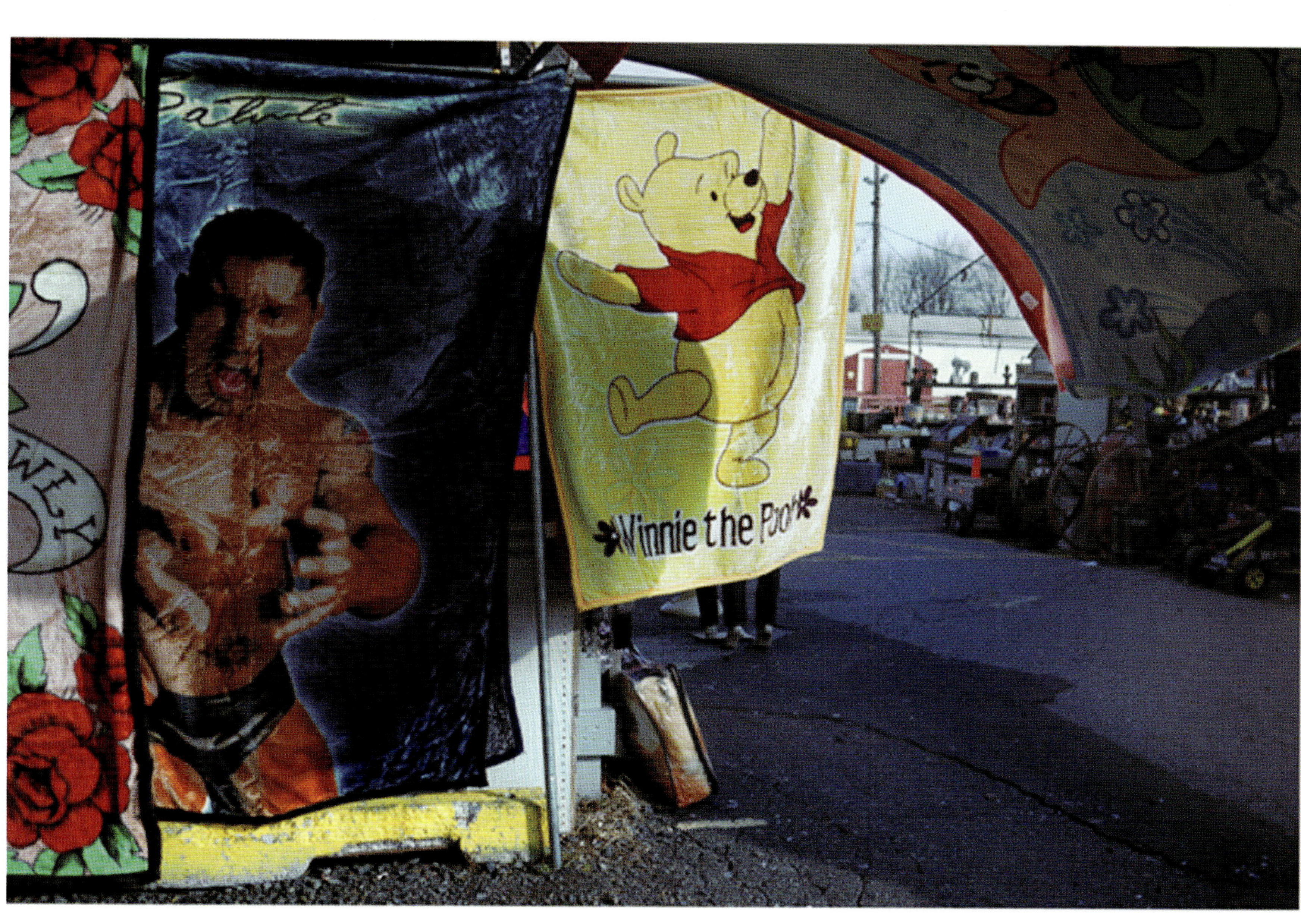
Winnie the Pooh

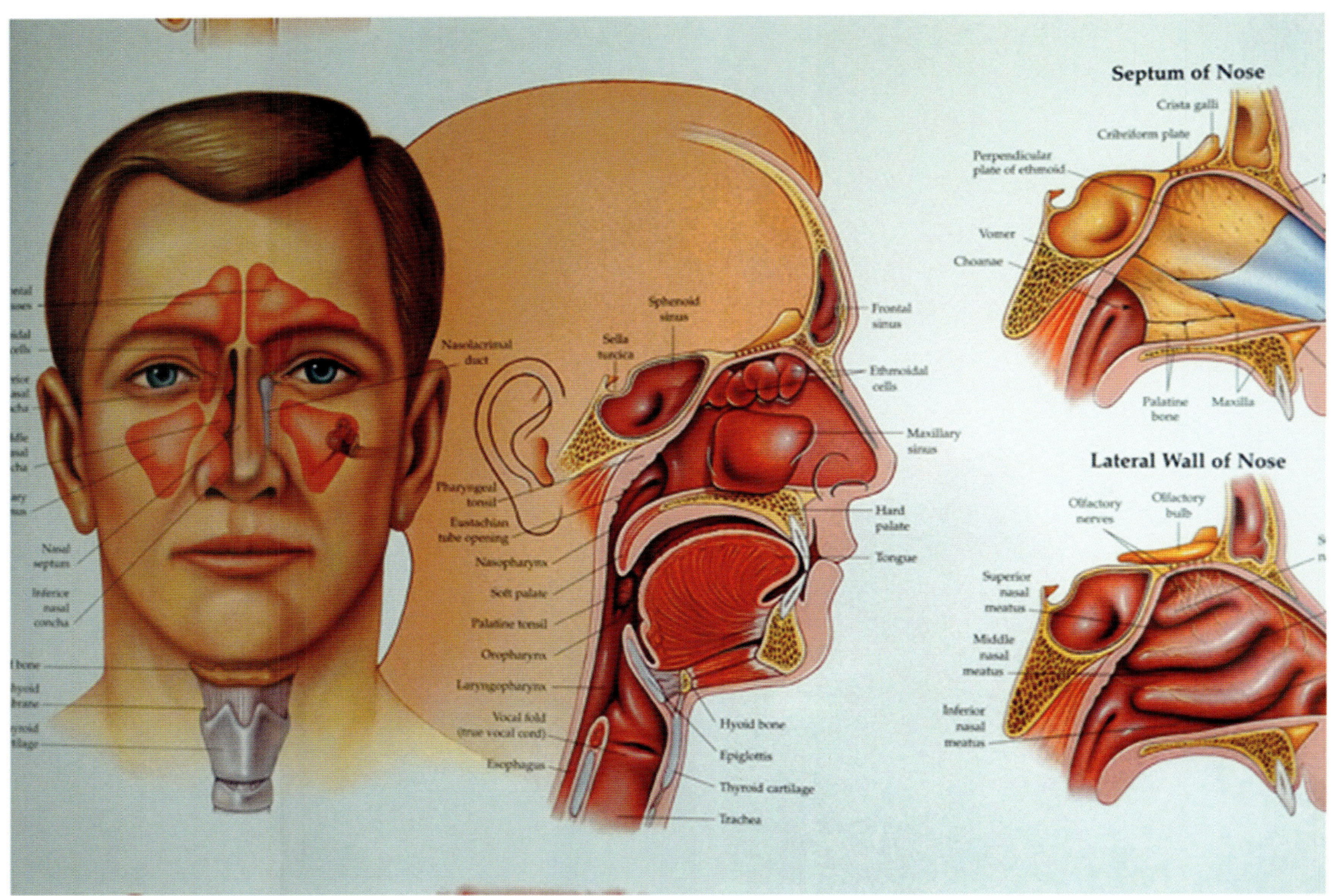

Nasal septum
Inferior nasal concha
Nasolacrimal duct
Sella turcica
Sphenoid sinus
Frontal sinus
Ethmoidal cells
Maxillary sinus
Pharyngeal tonsil
Eustachian tube opening
Hard palate
Tongue
Nasopharynx
Soft palate
Palatine tonsil
Oropharynx
Laryngopharynx
Vocal fold (true vocal cord)
Esophagus
Hyoid bone
Epiglottis
Thyroid cartilage
Trachea
Septum of Nose
Crista galli
Cribriform plate
Perpendicular plate of ethmoid
Vomer
Choanae
Palatine bone
Maxilla
Lateral Wall of Nose
Olfactory nerves
Olfactory bulb
Superior nasal meatus
Middle nasal meatus
Inferior nasal meatus

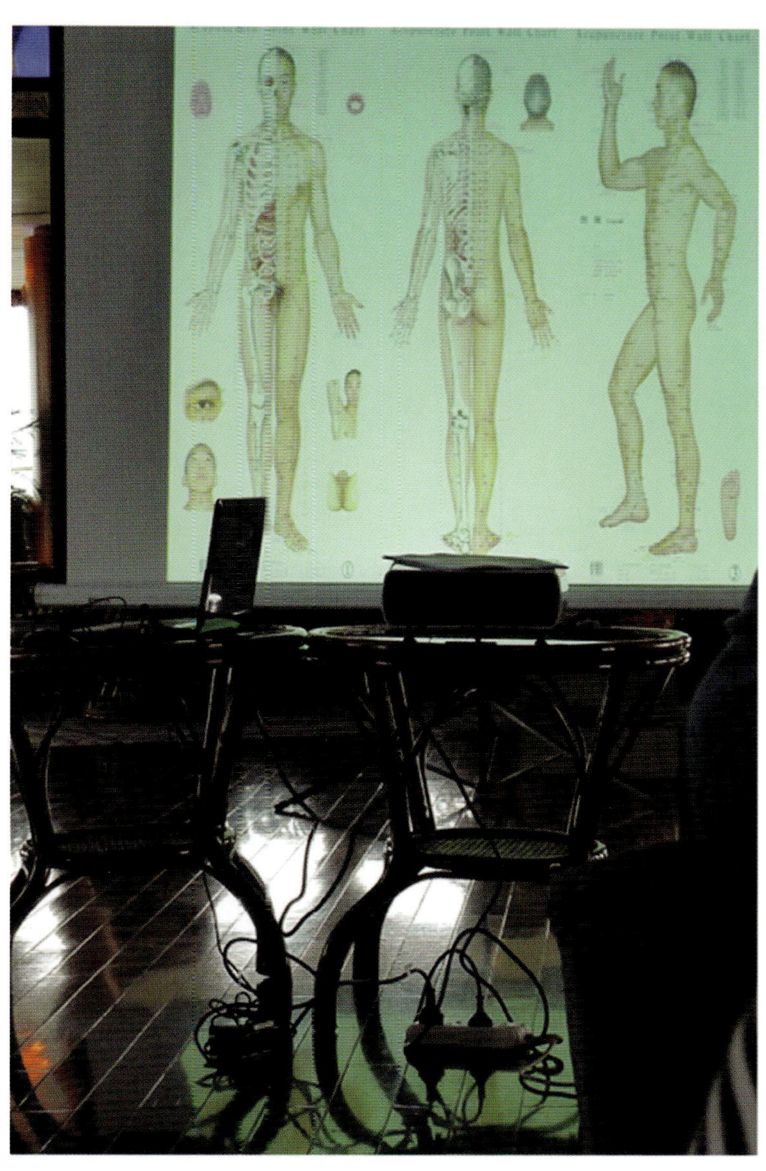

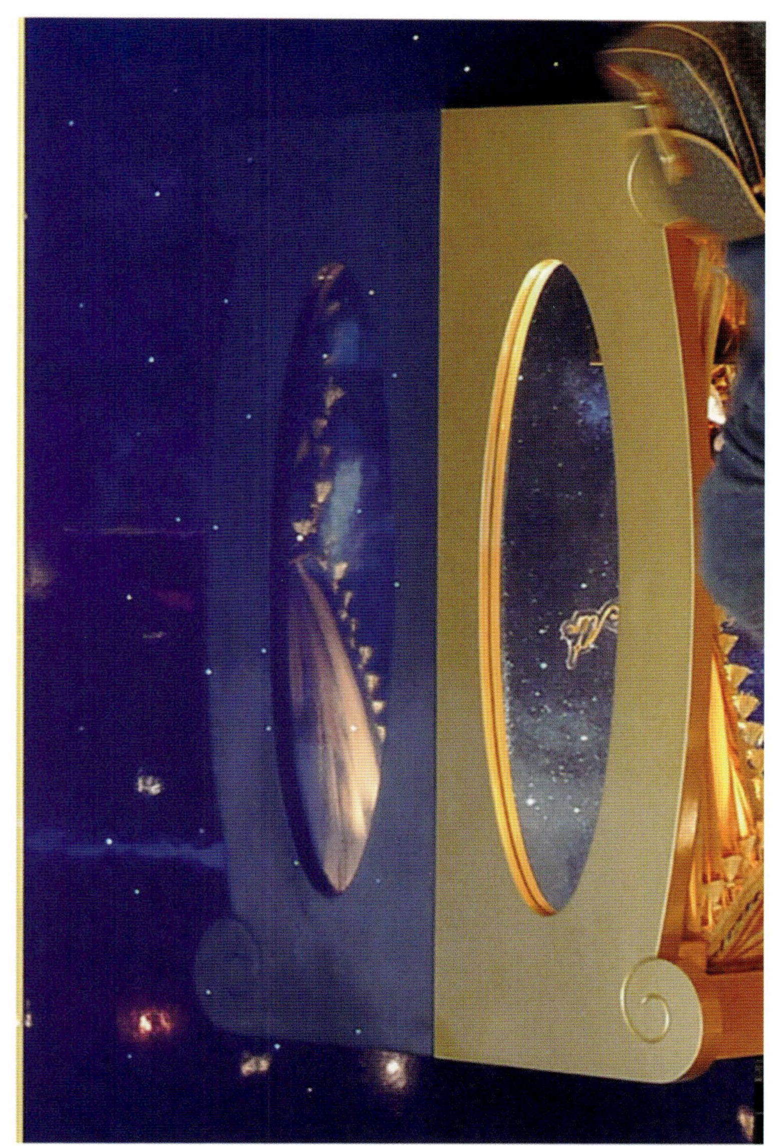

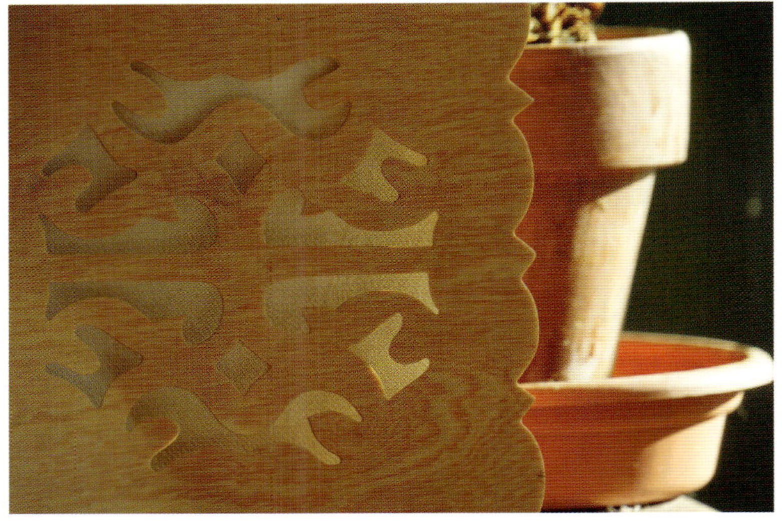

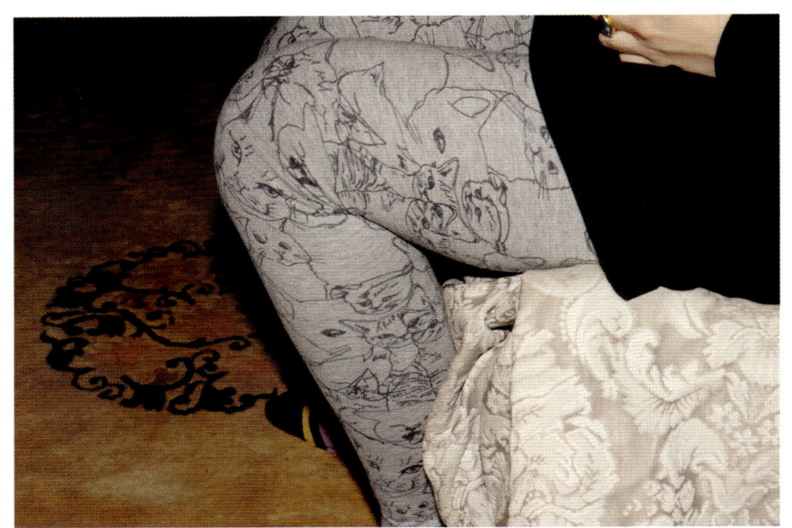

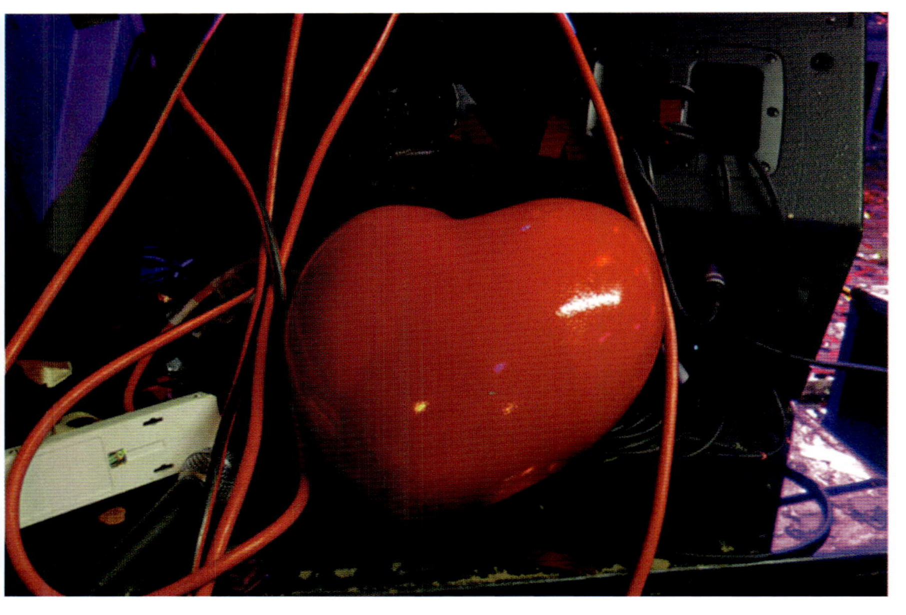

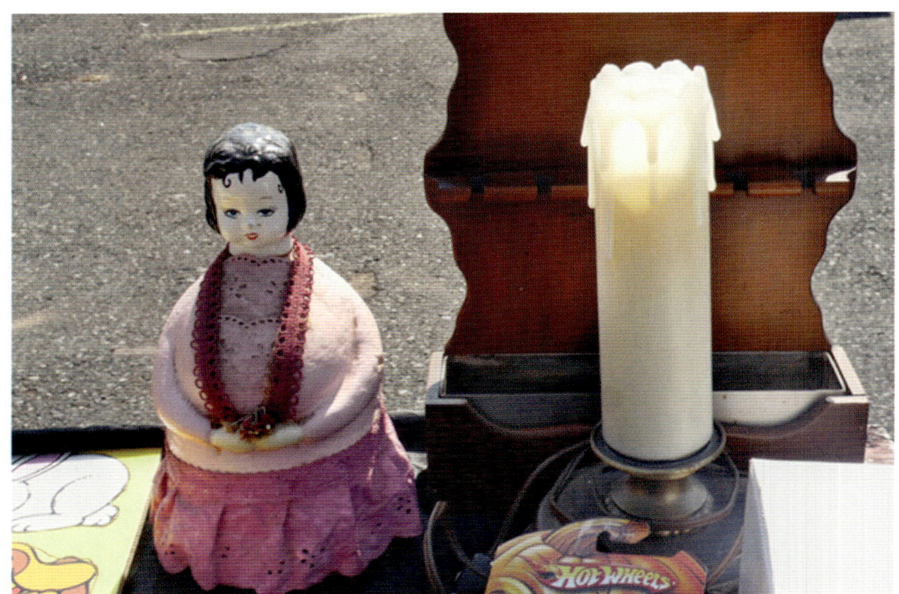
Hot Wheels

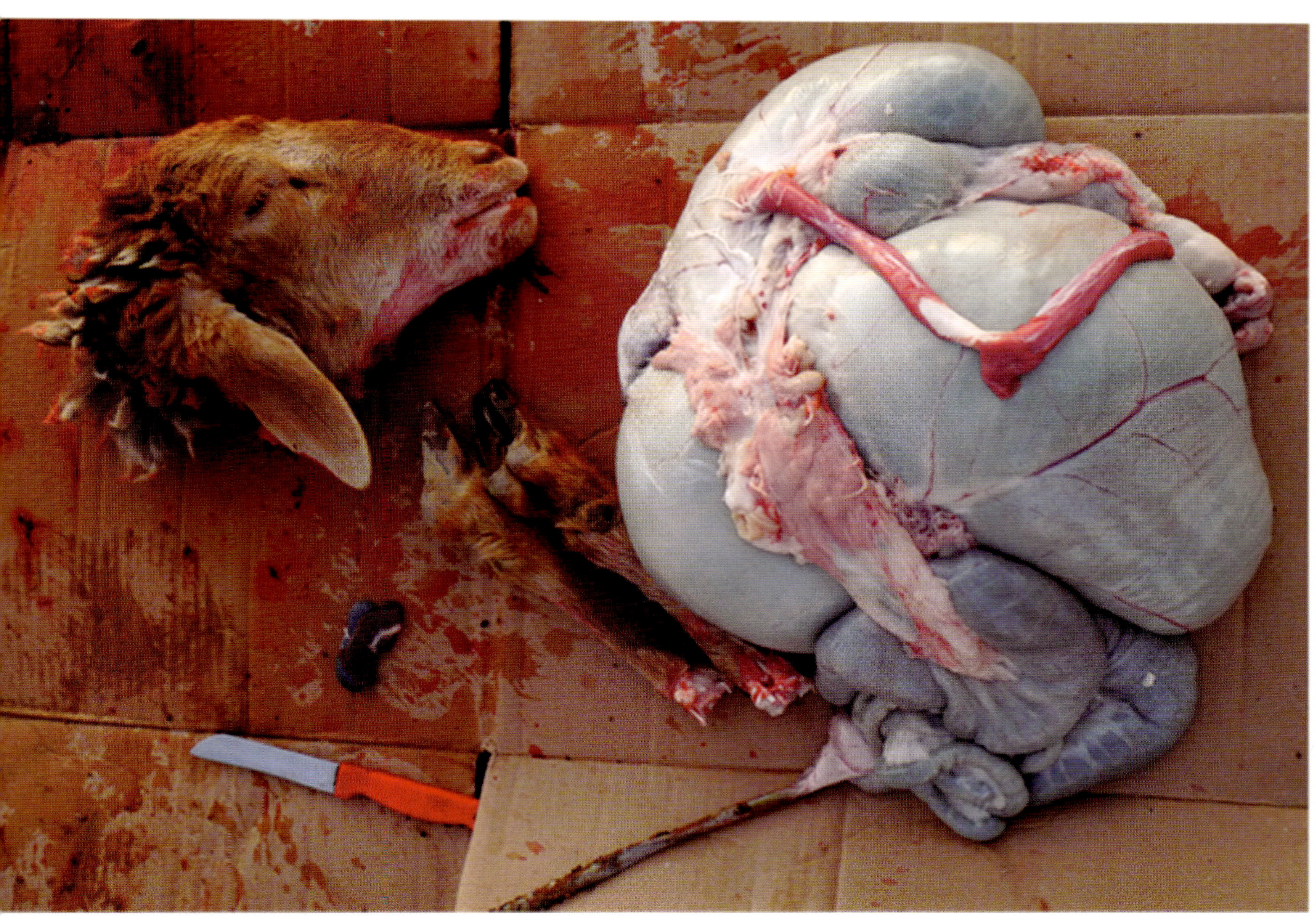

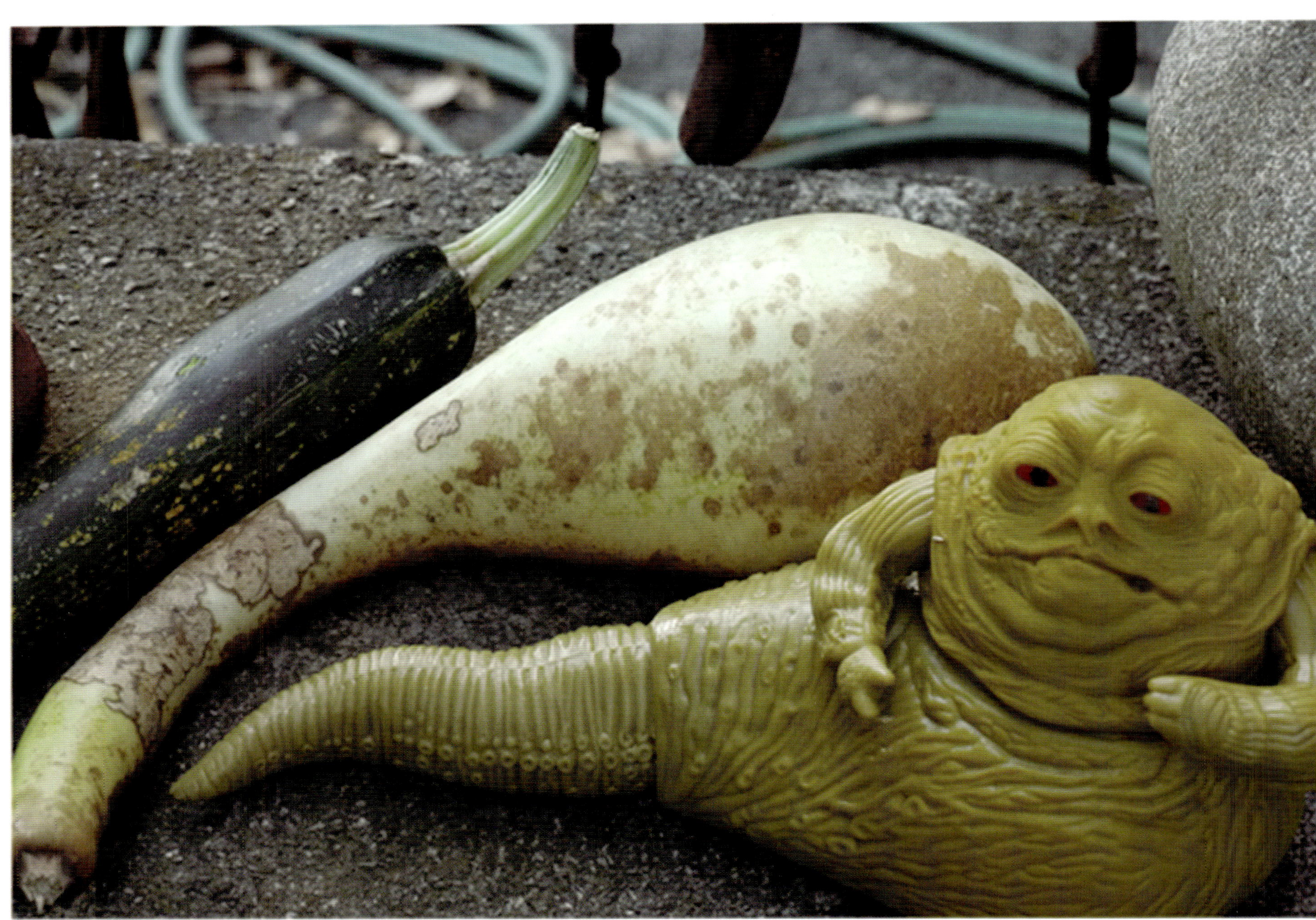

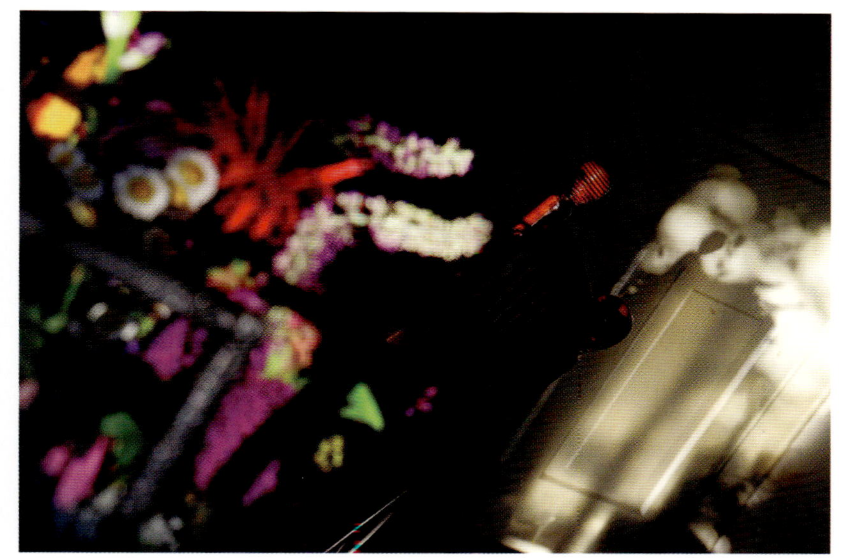

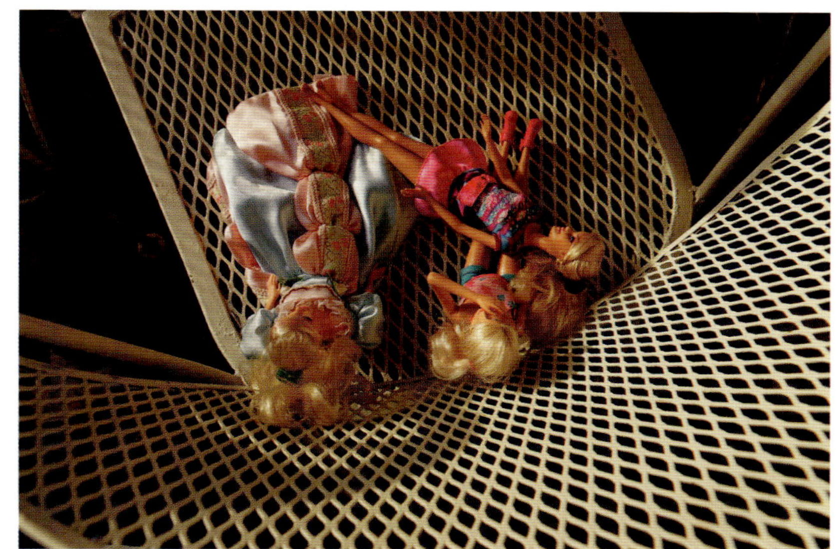

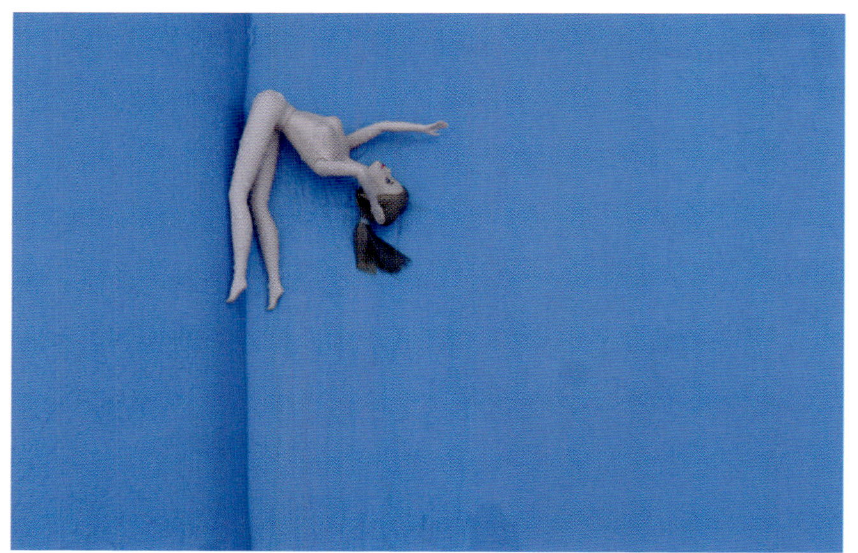

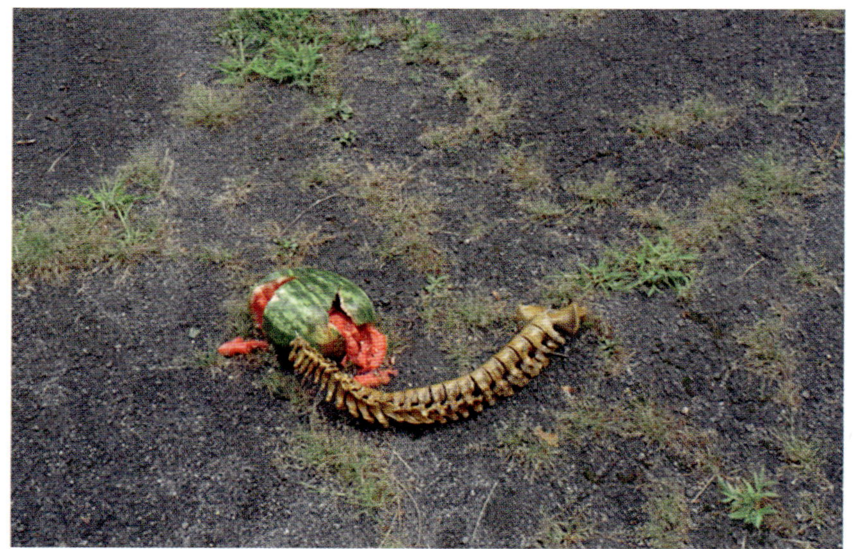

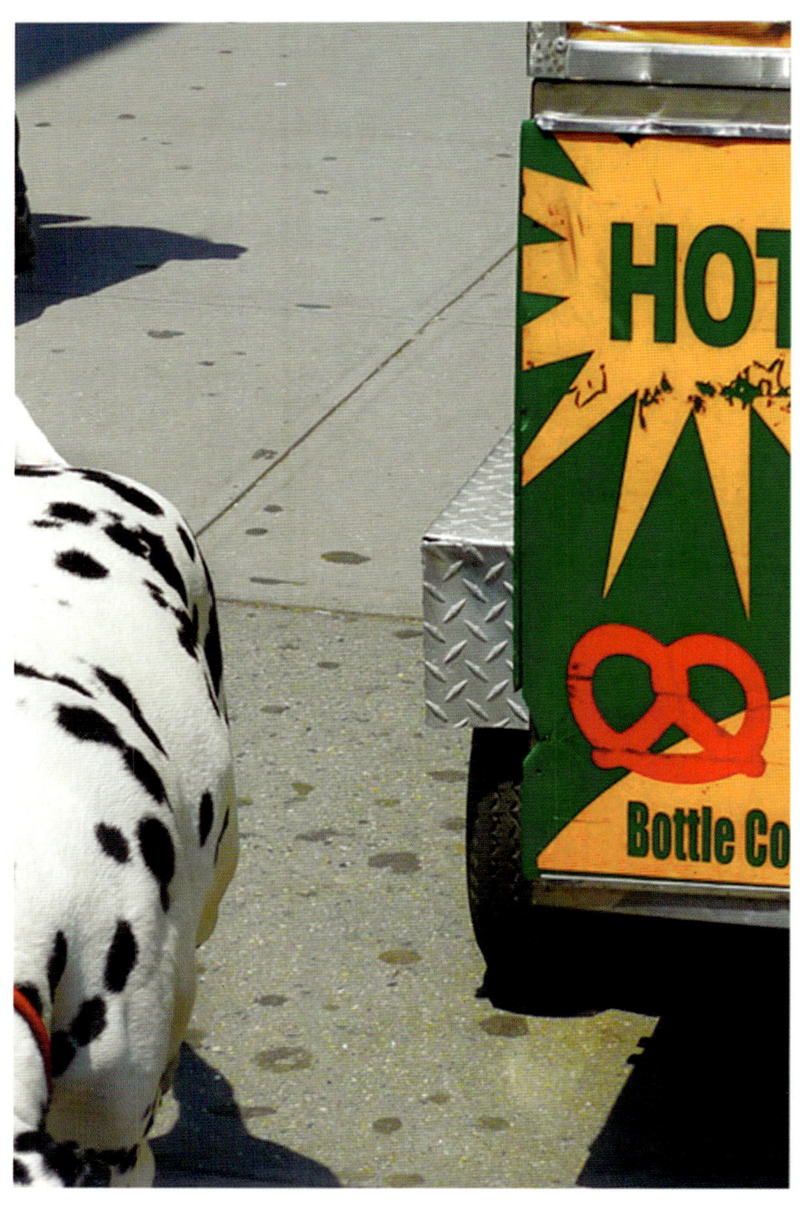
HOT
Bottle Co

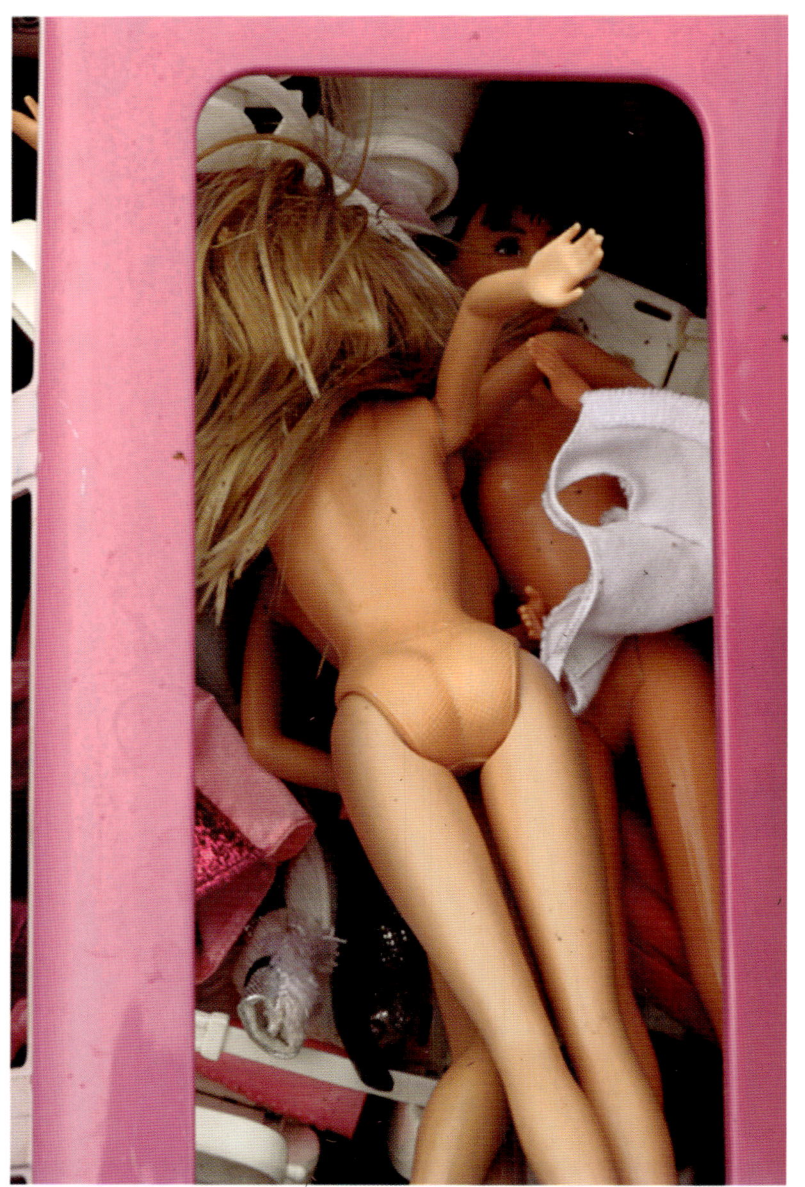

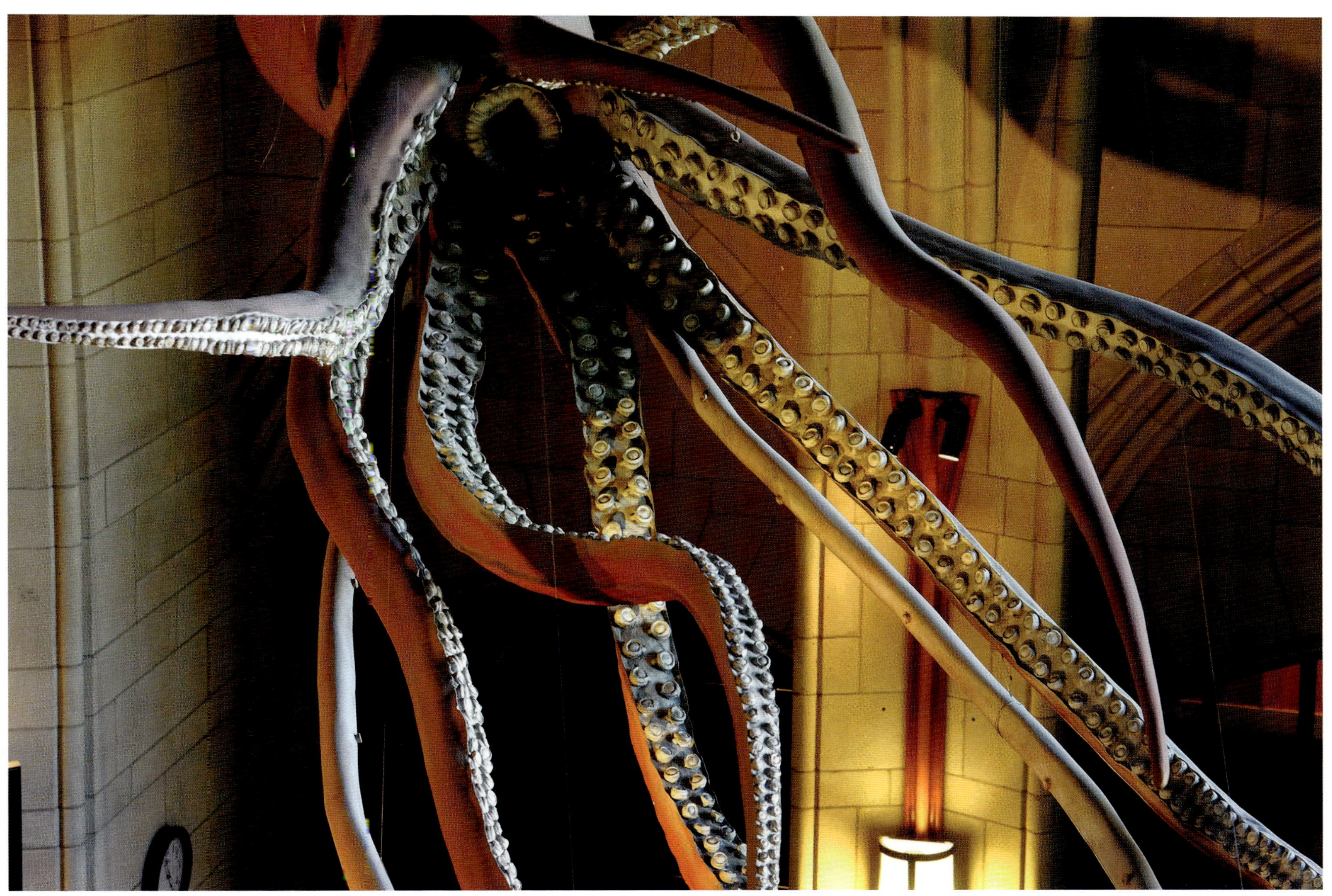

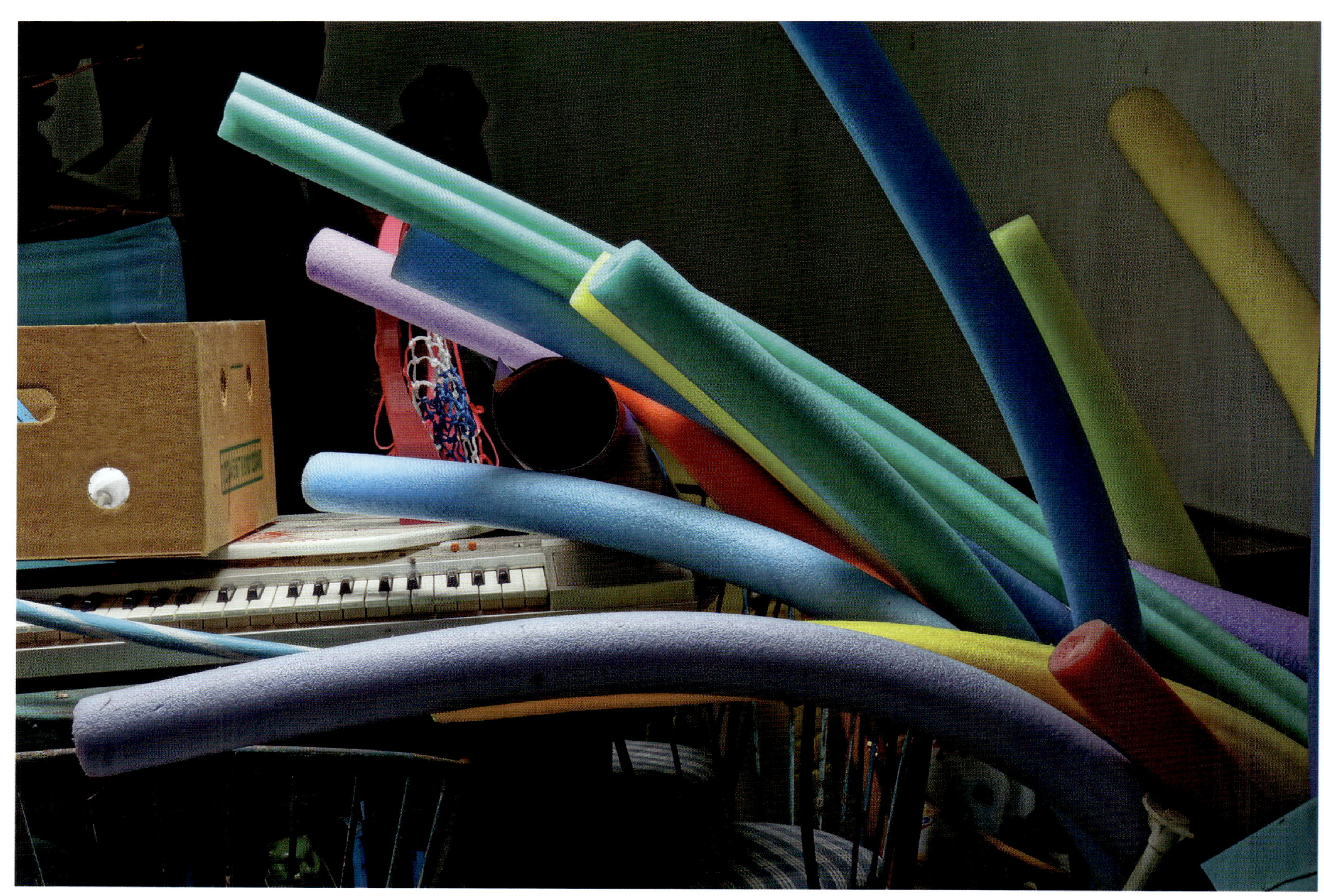

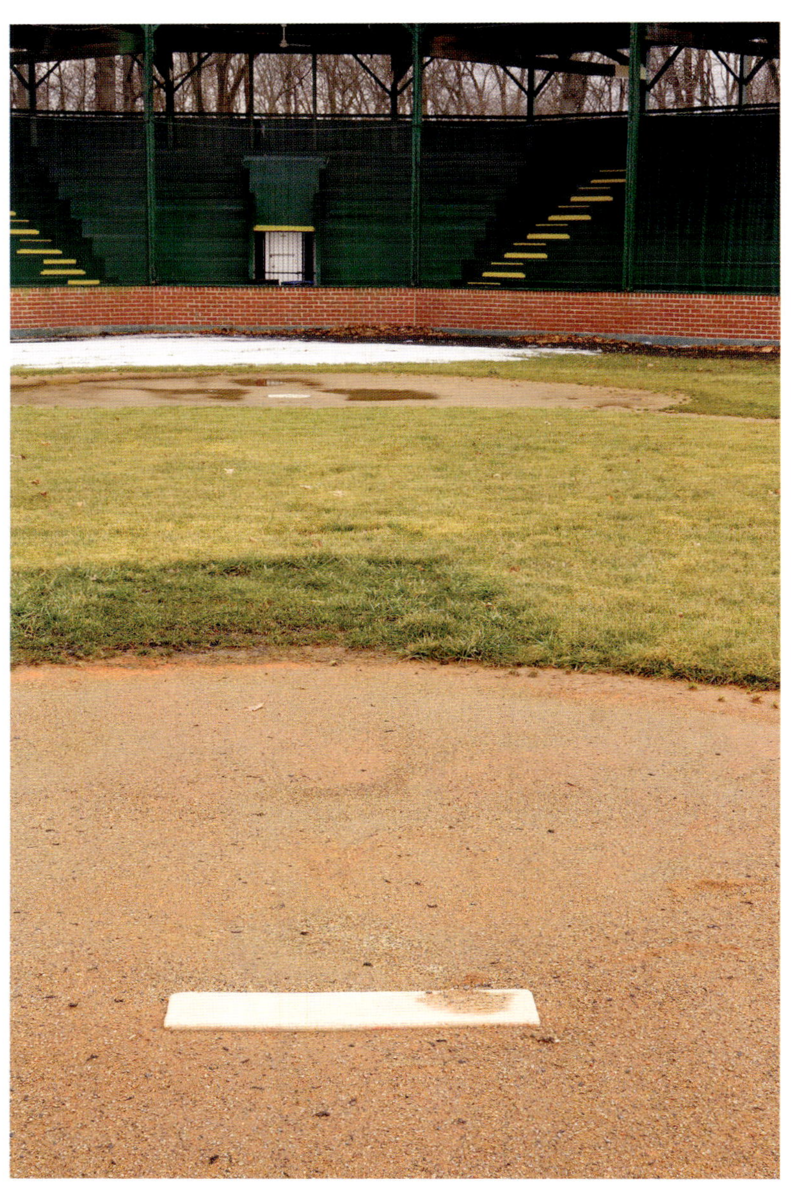

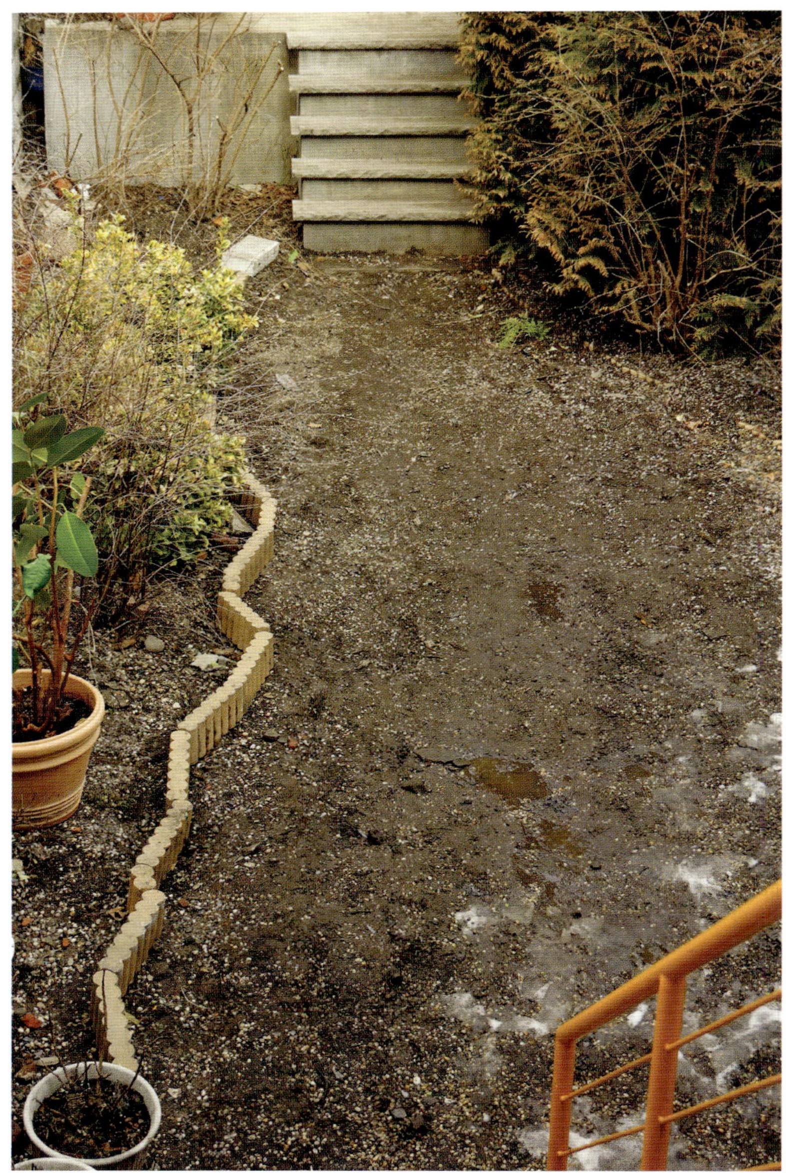

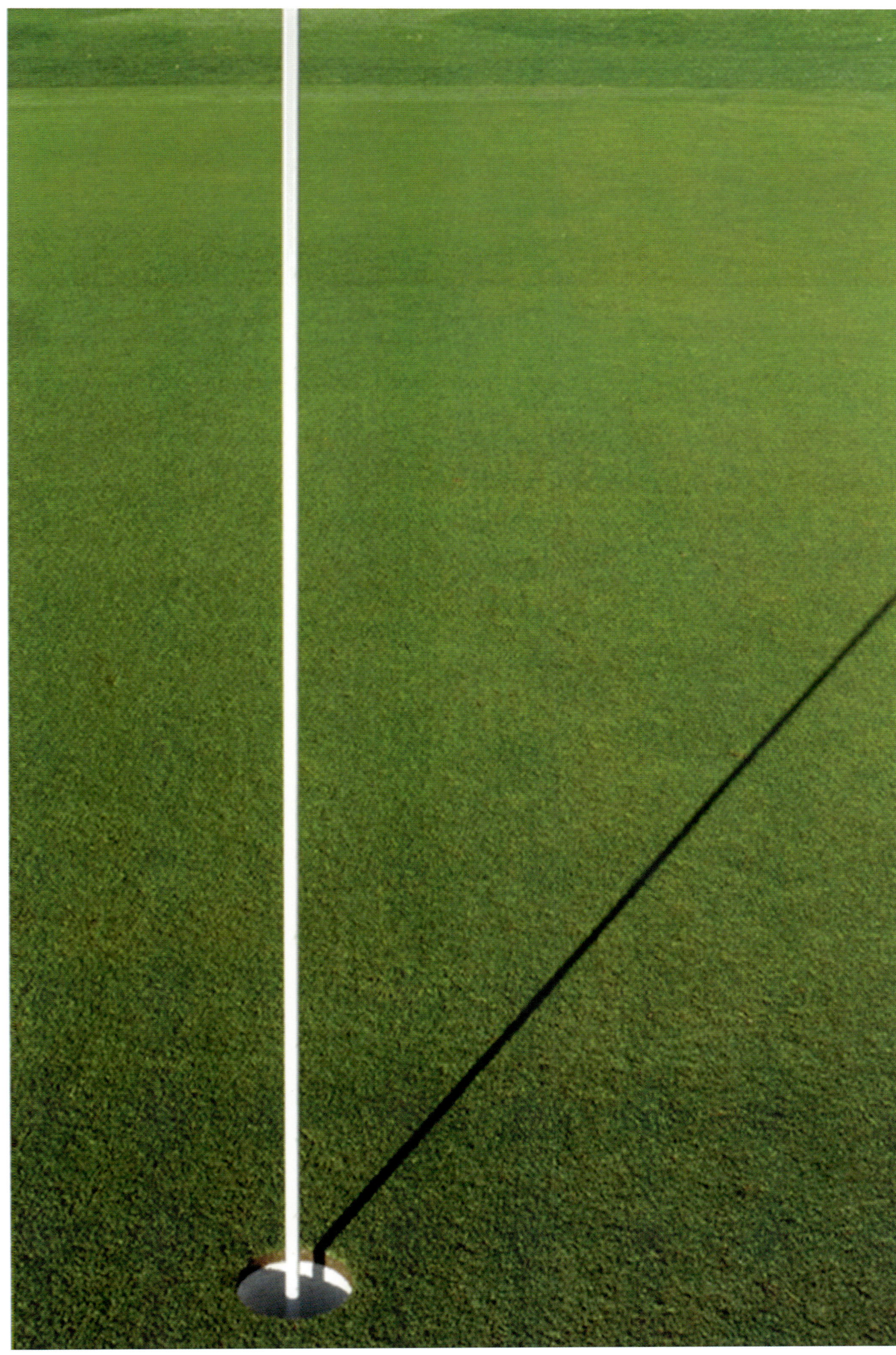

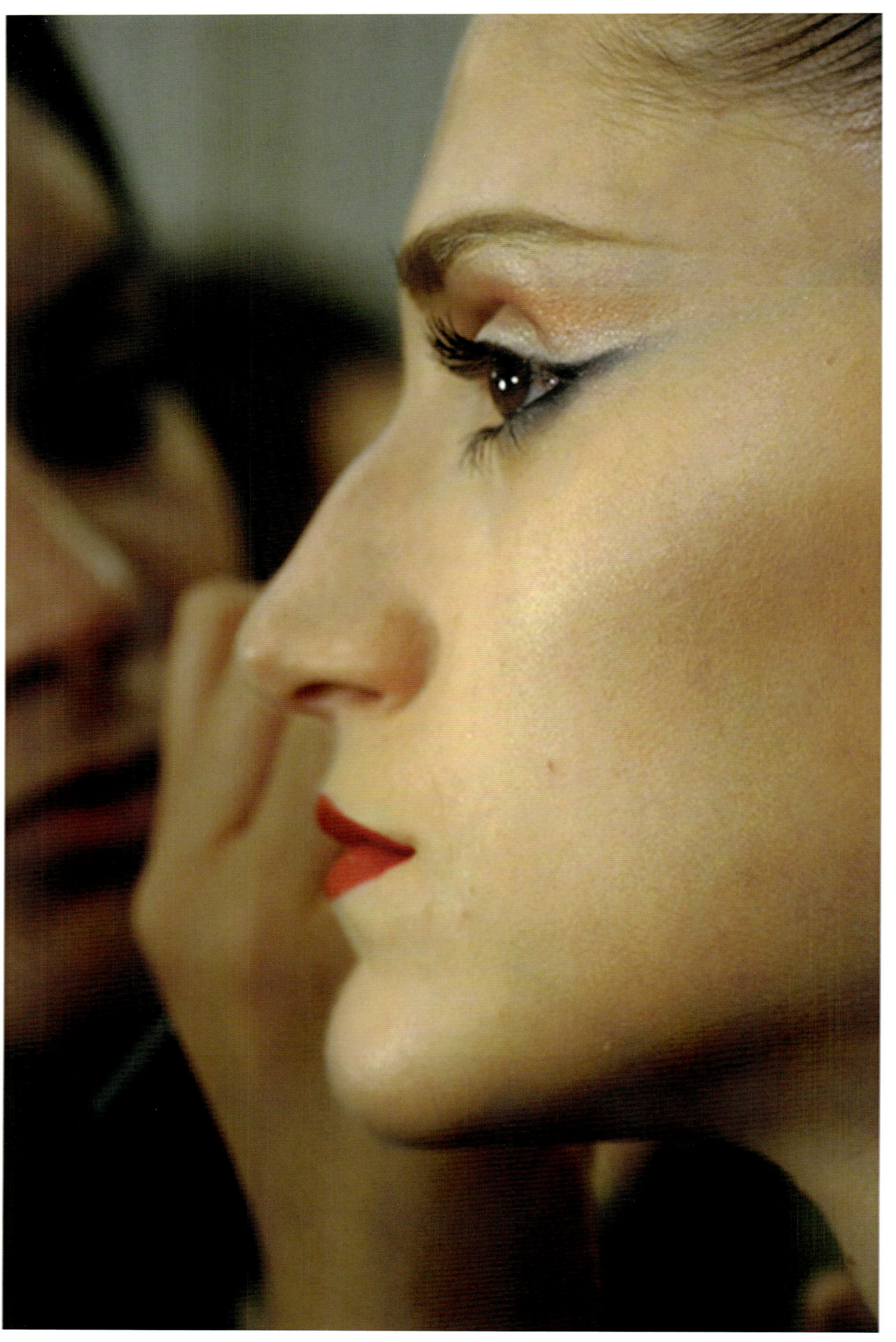

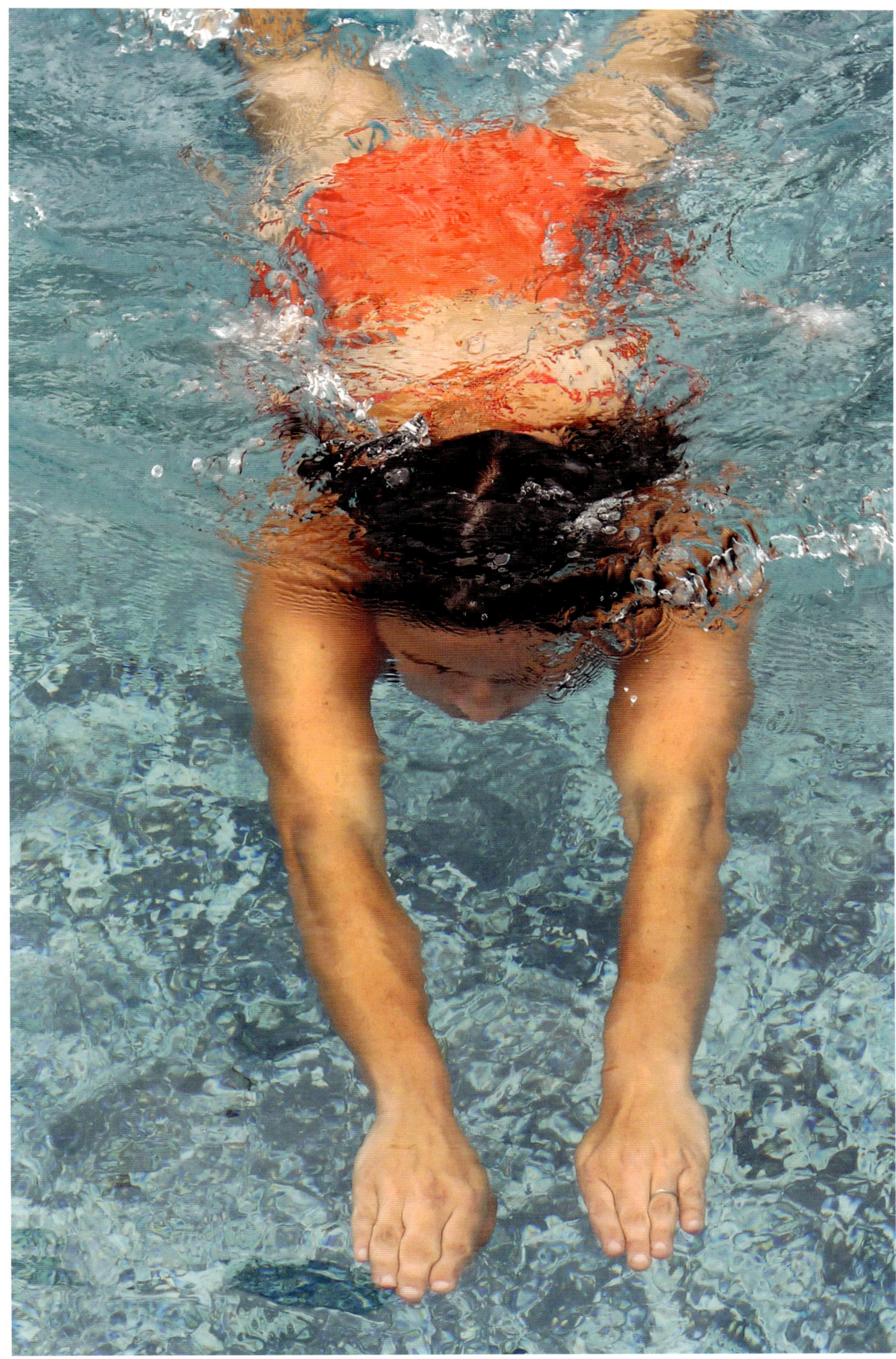

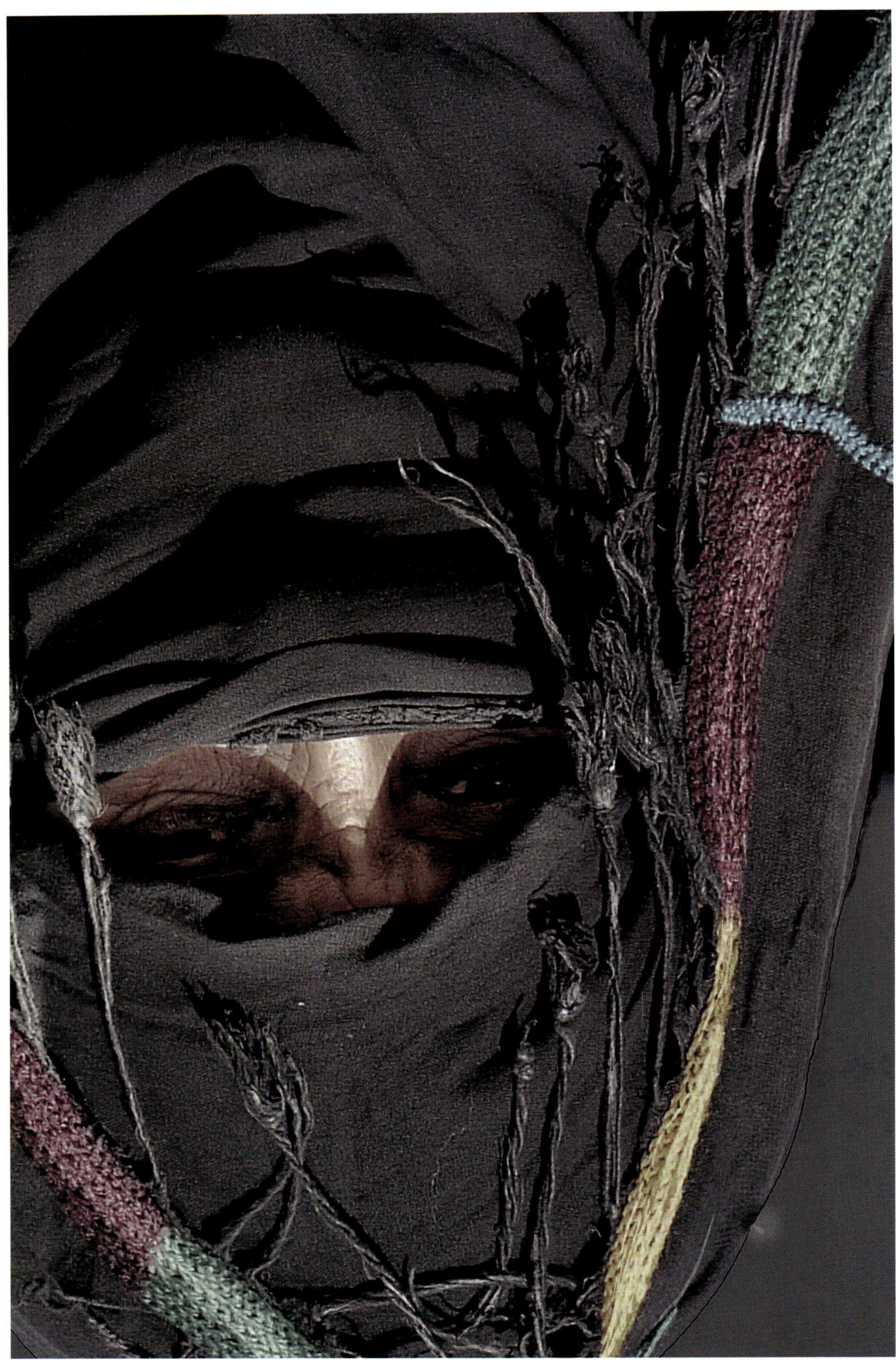

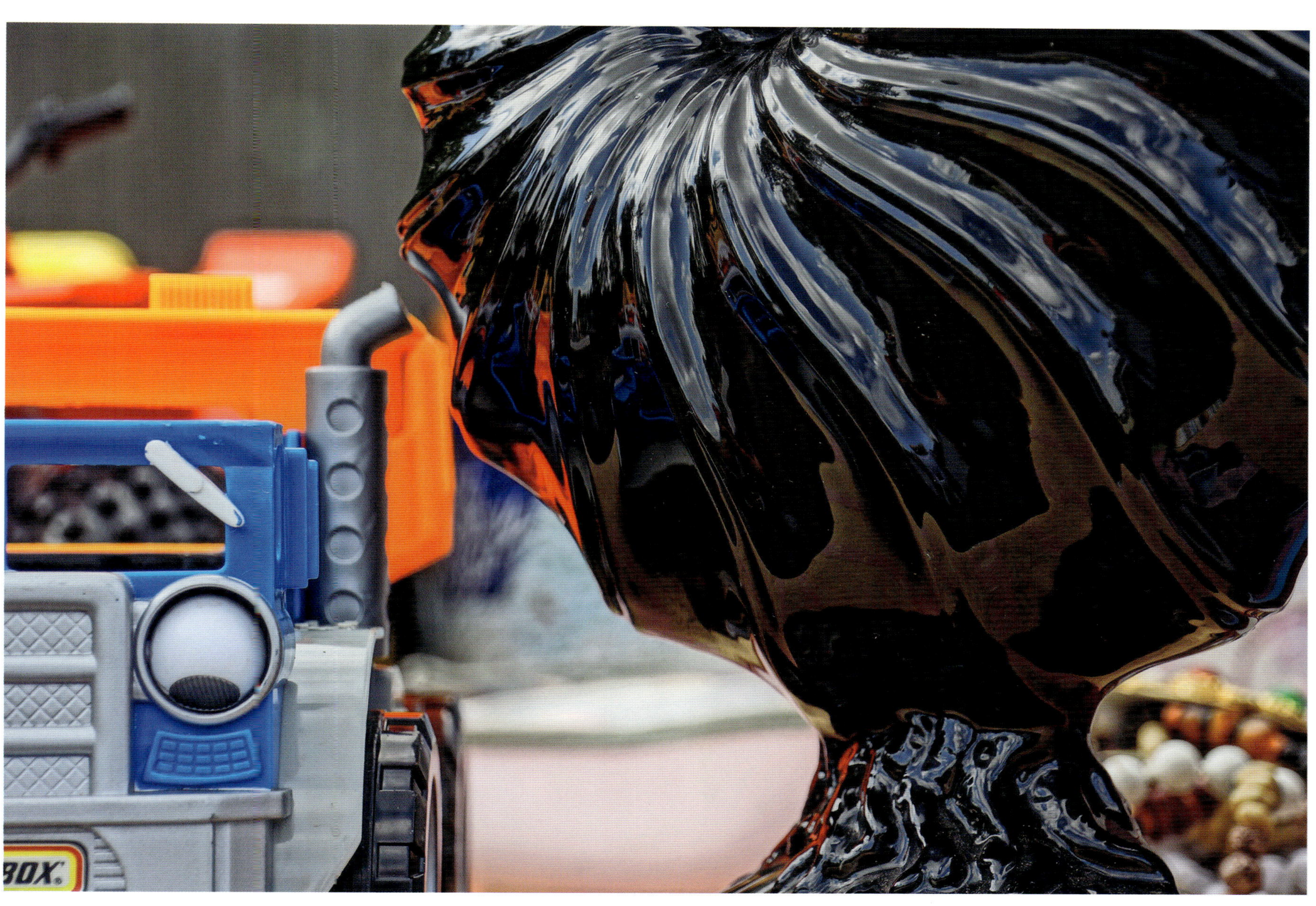

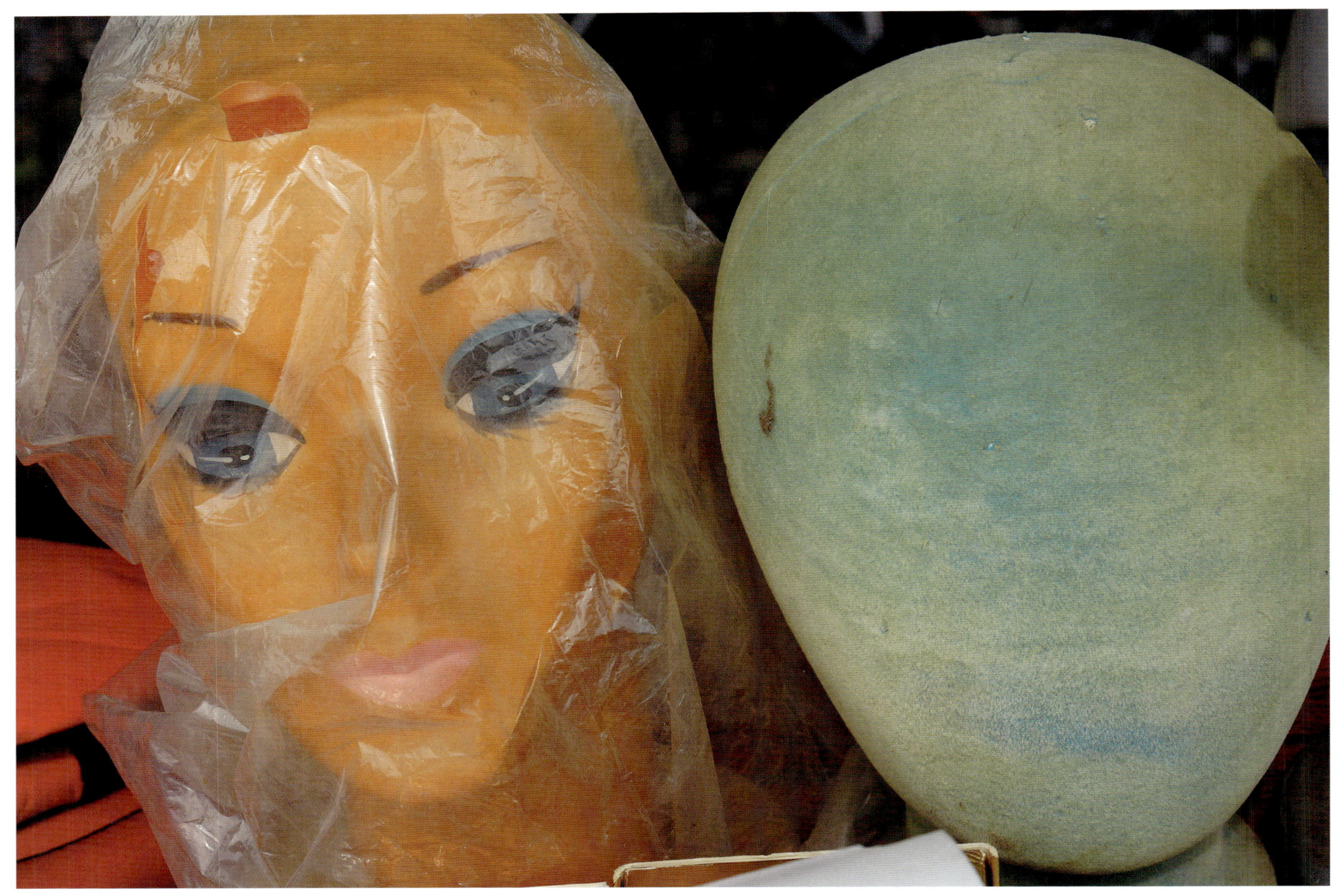

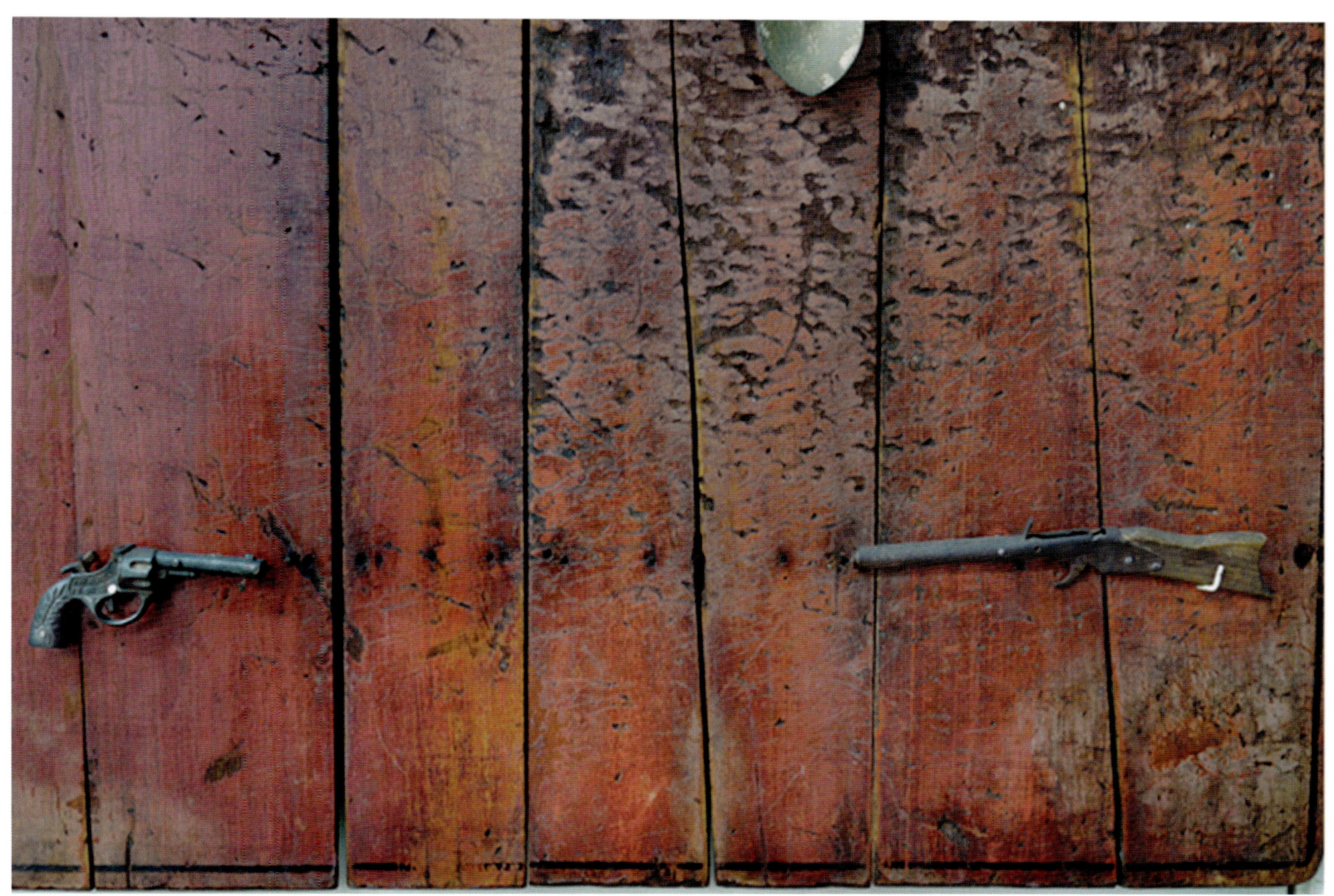

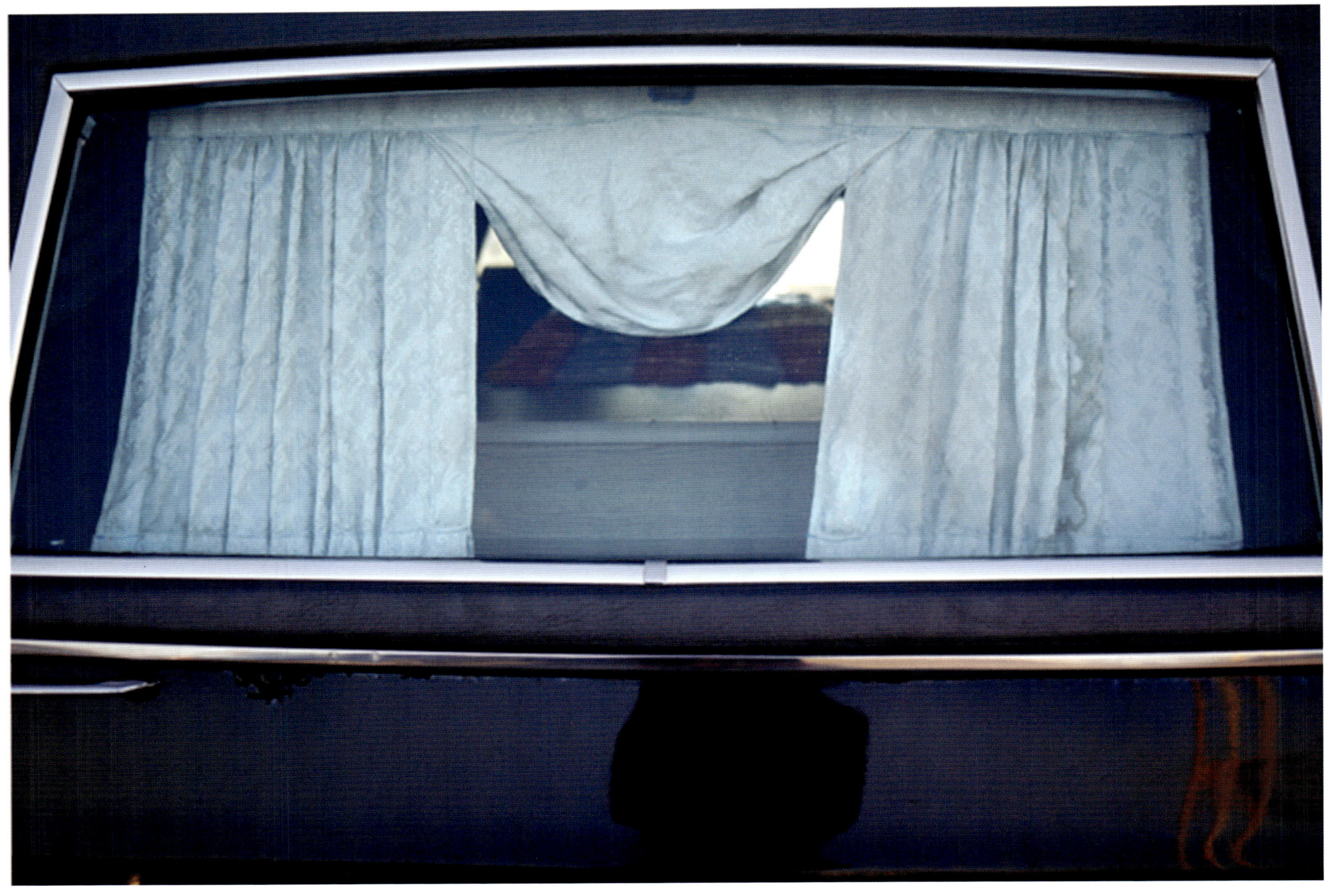

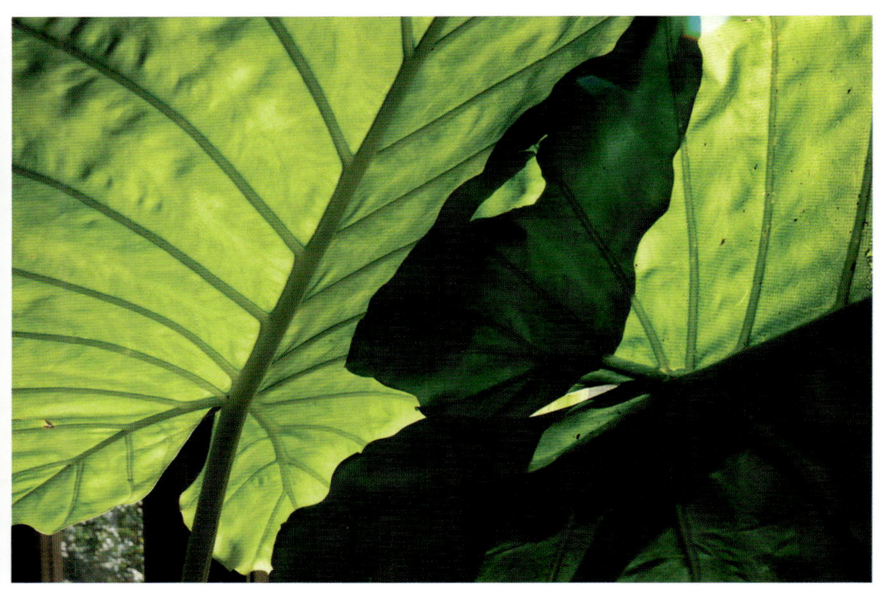

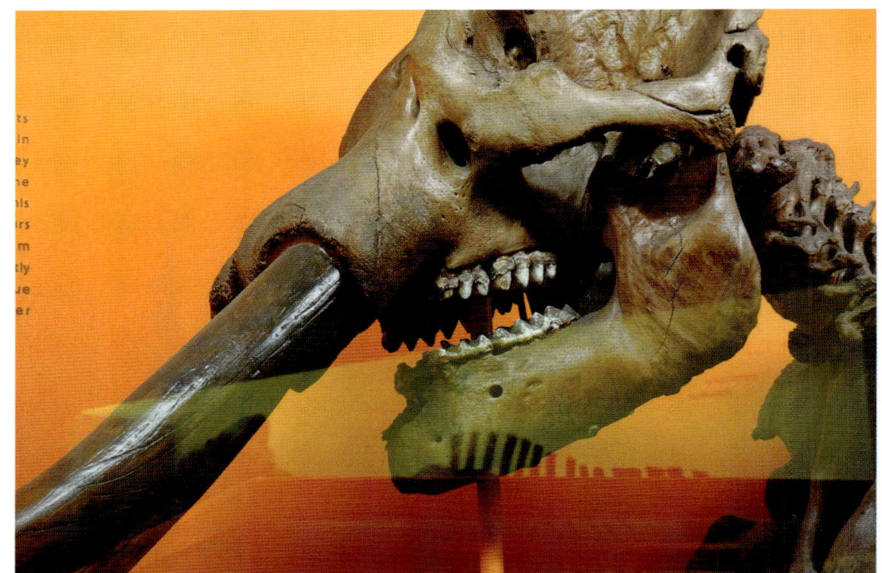

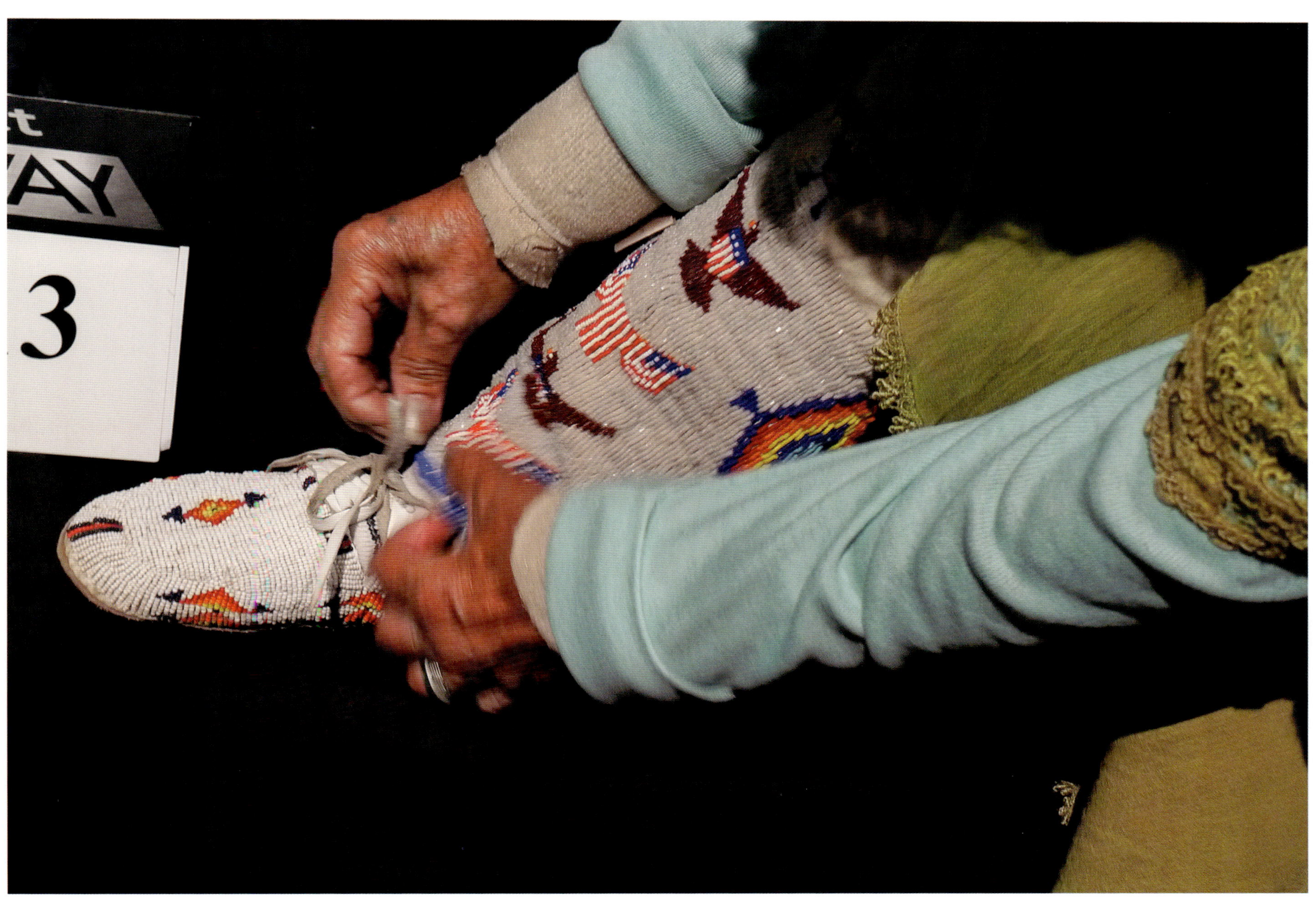

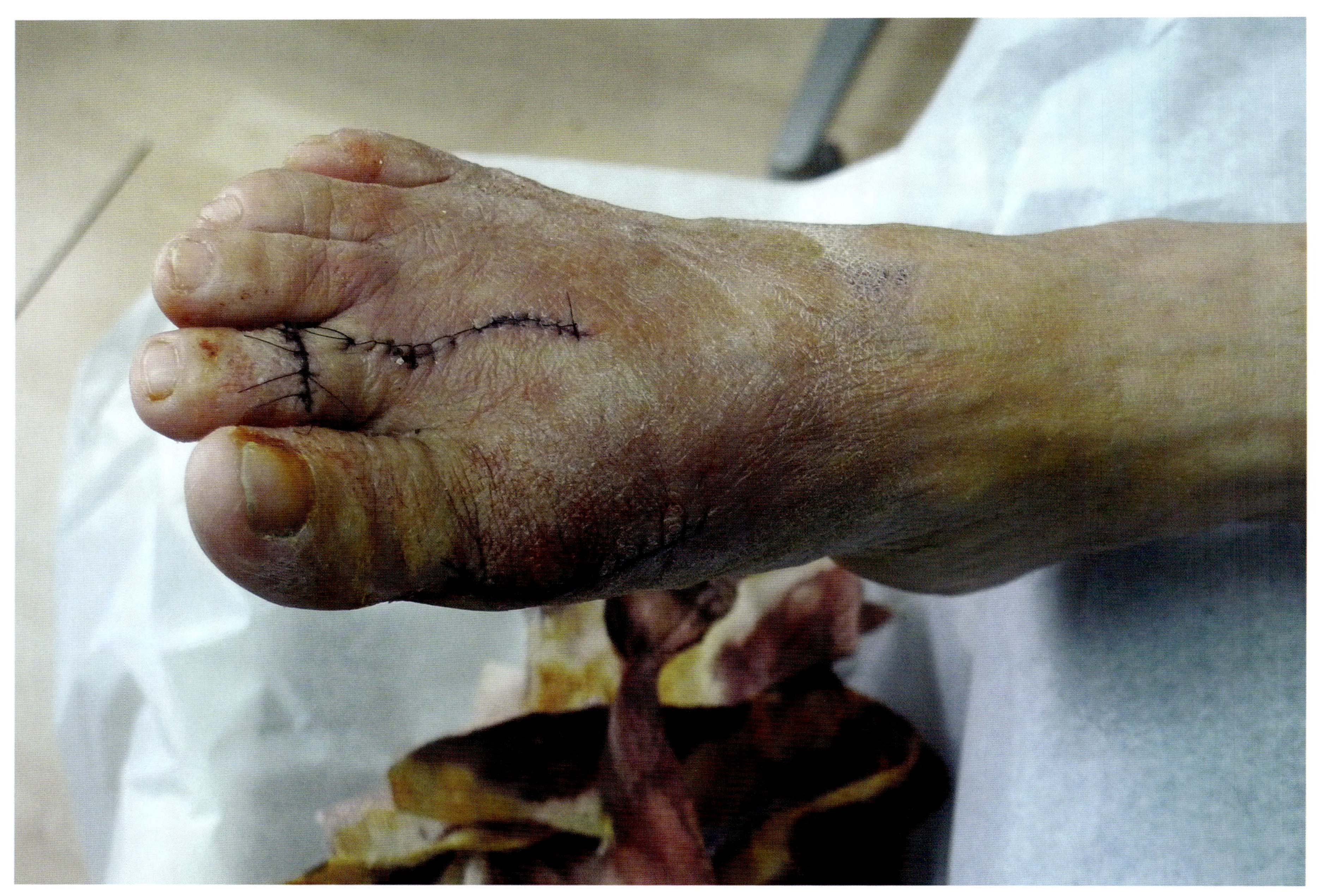

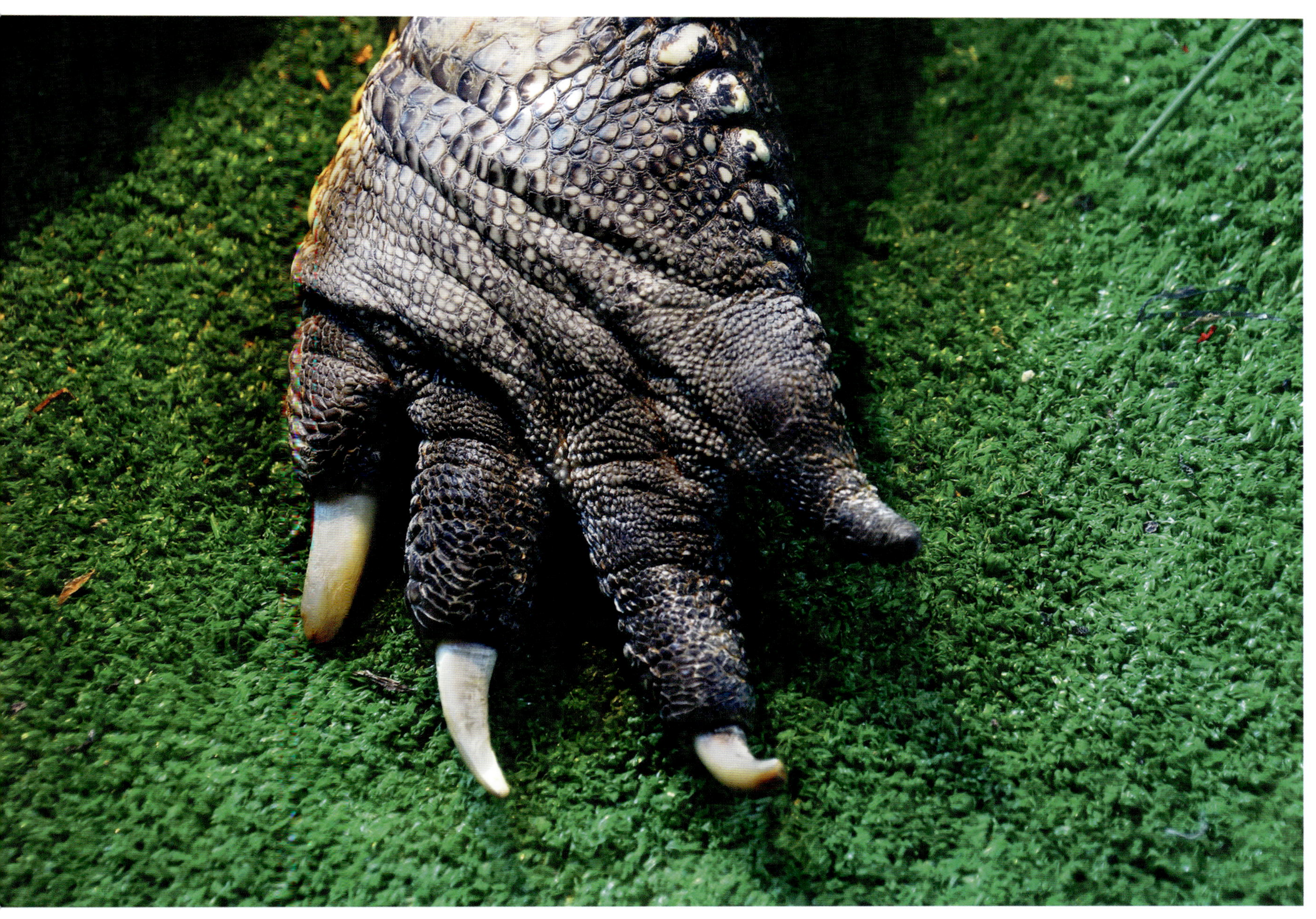

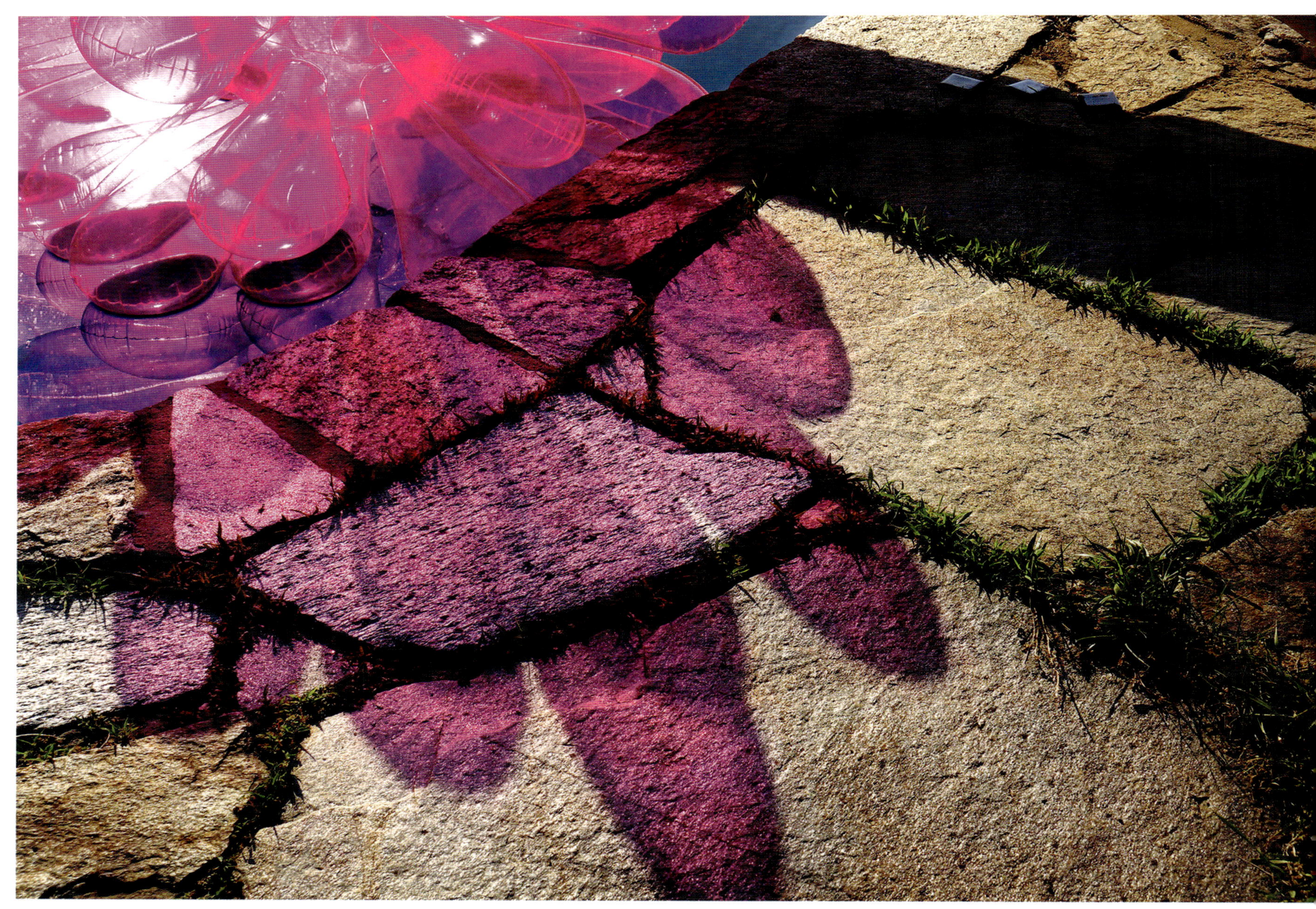

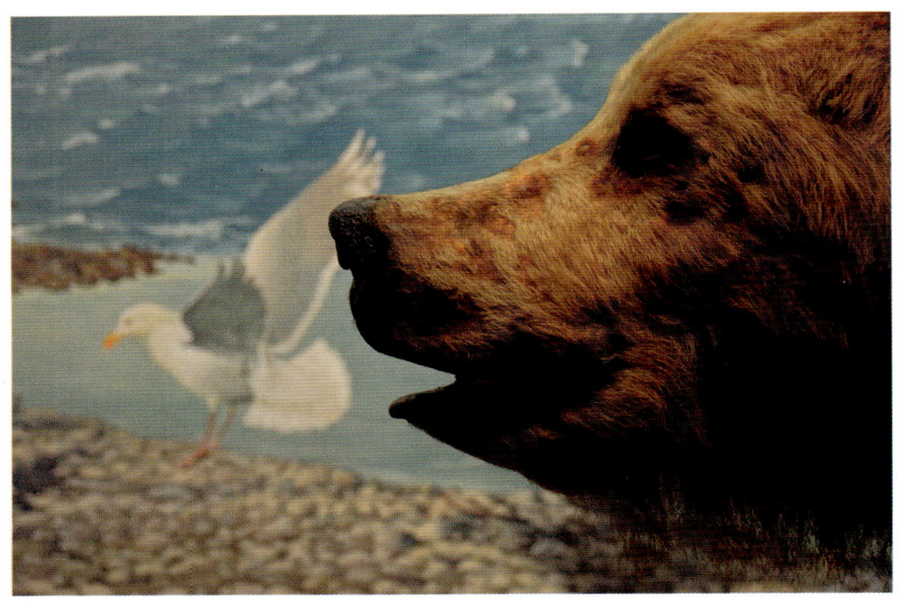

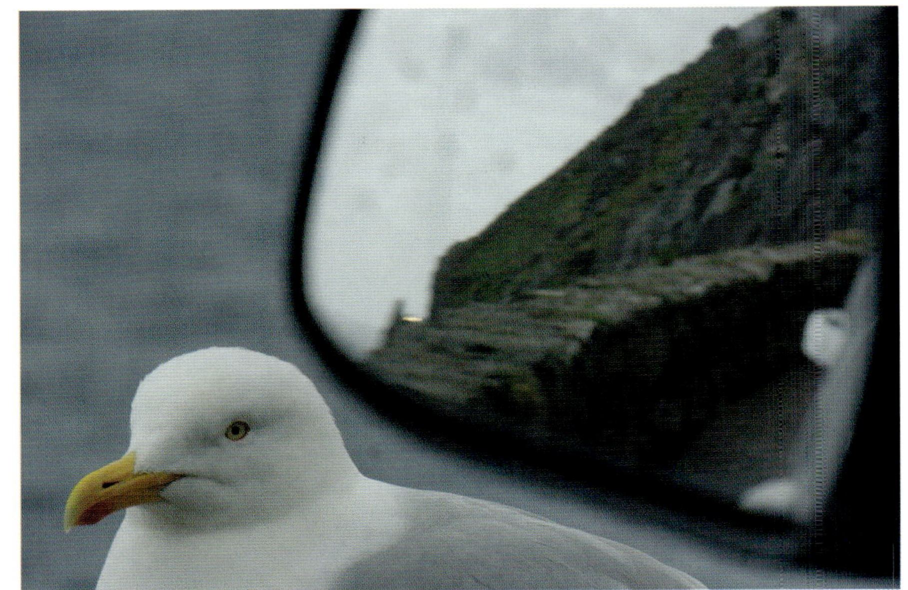

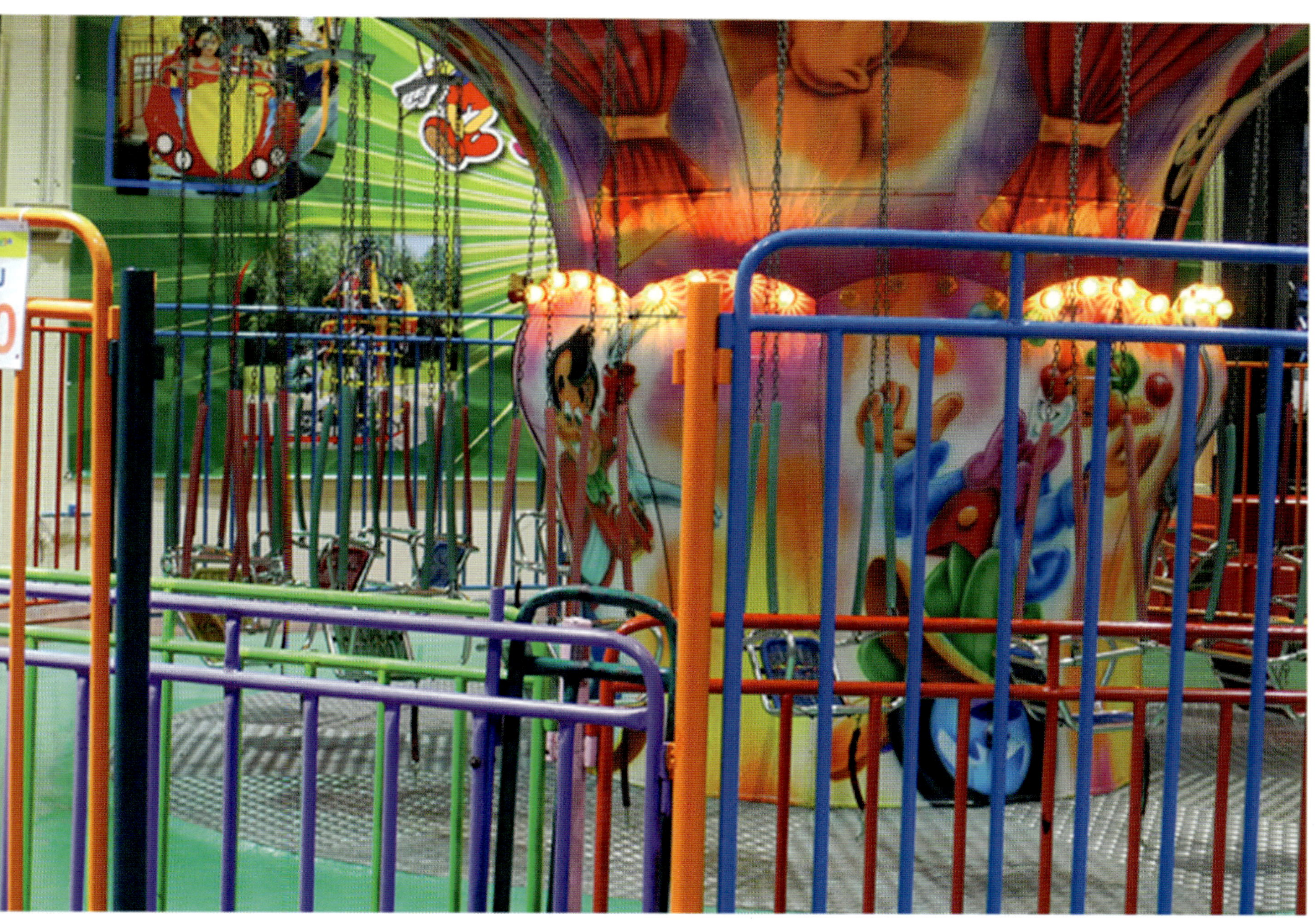

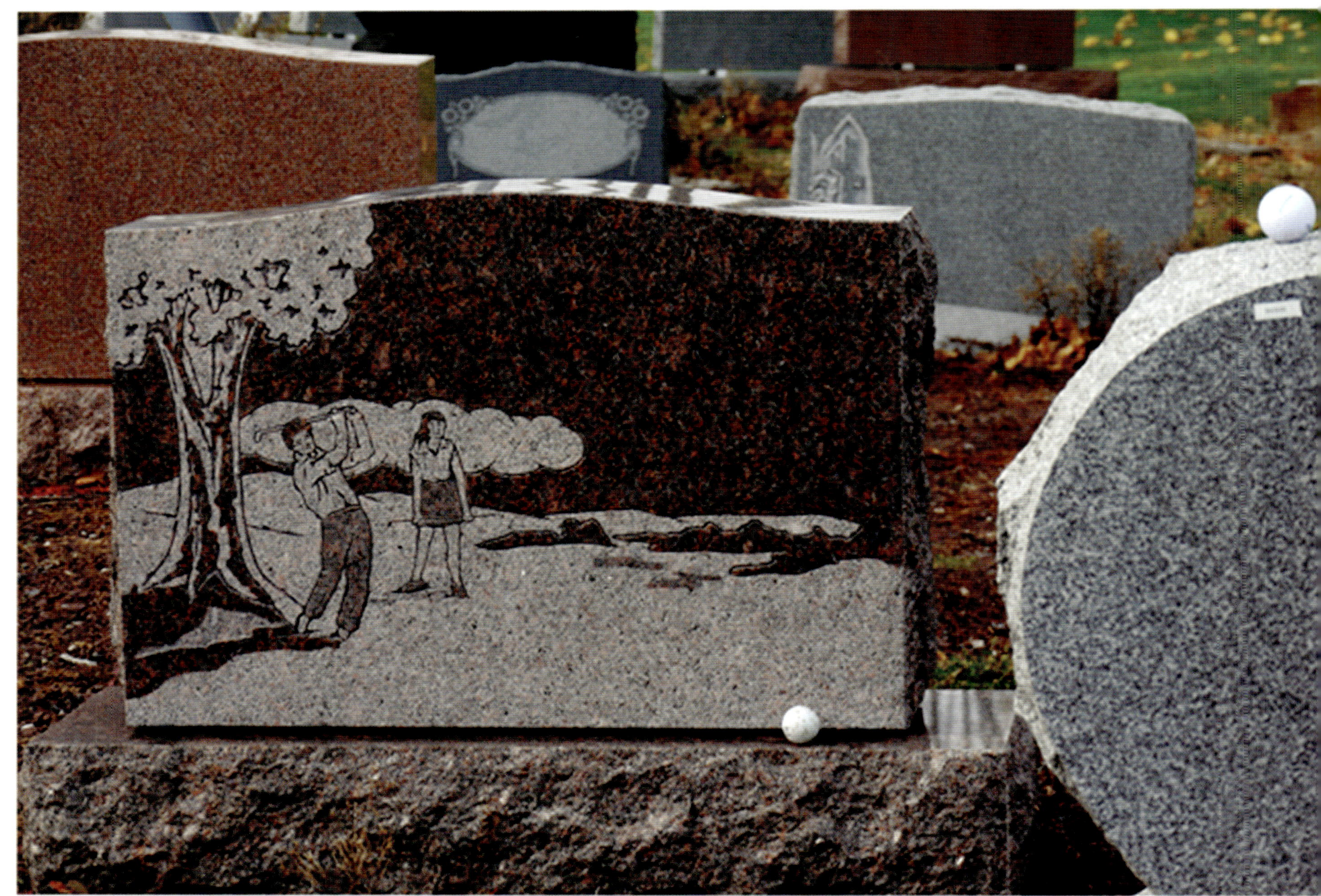

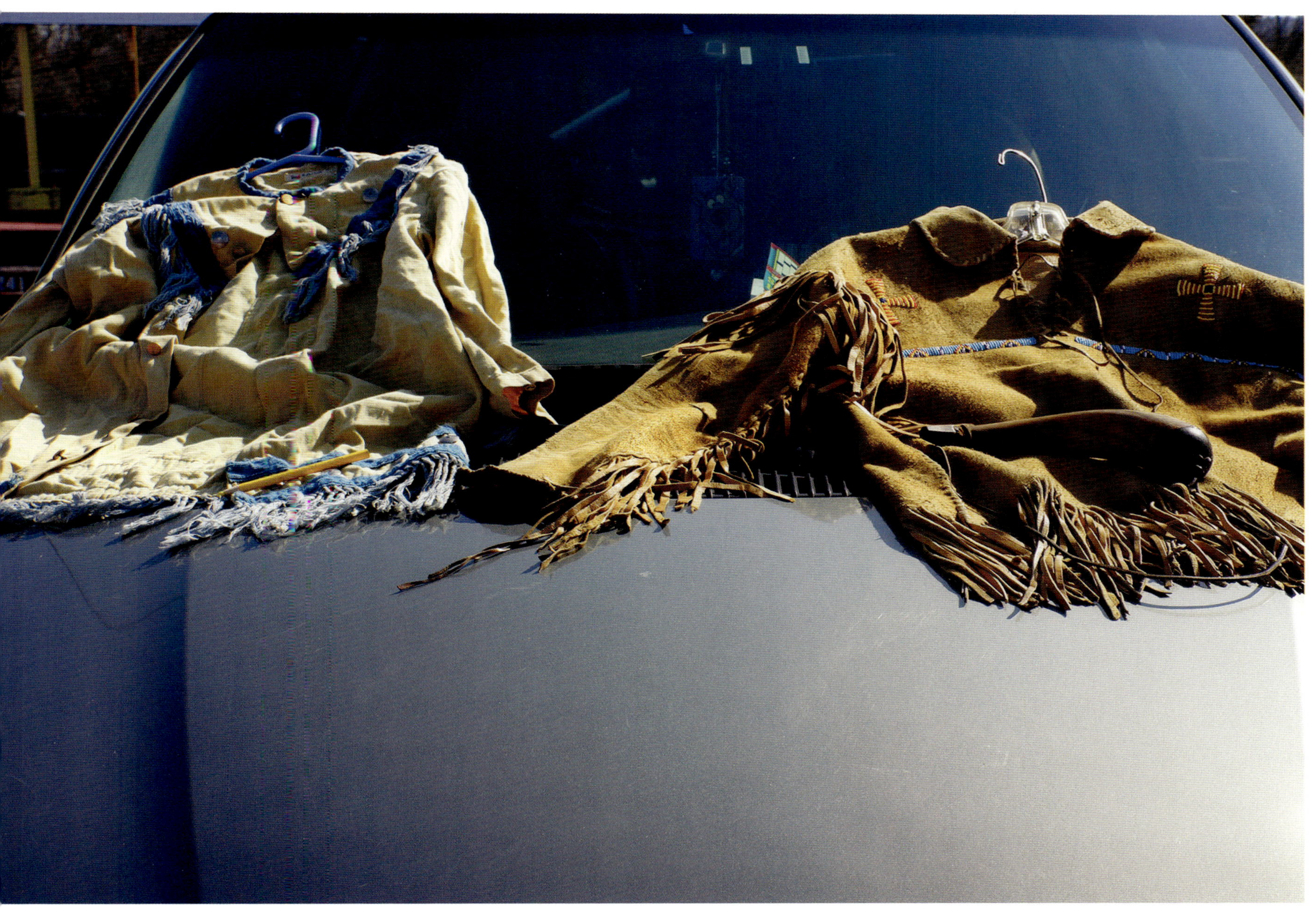

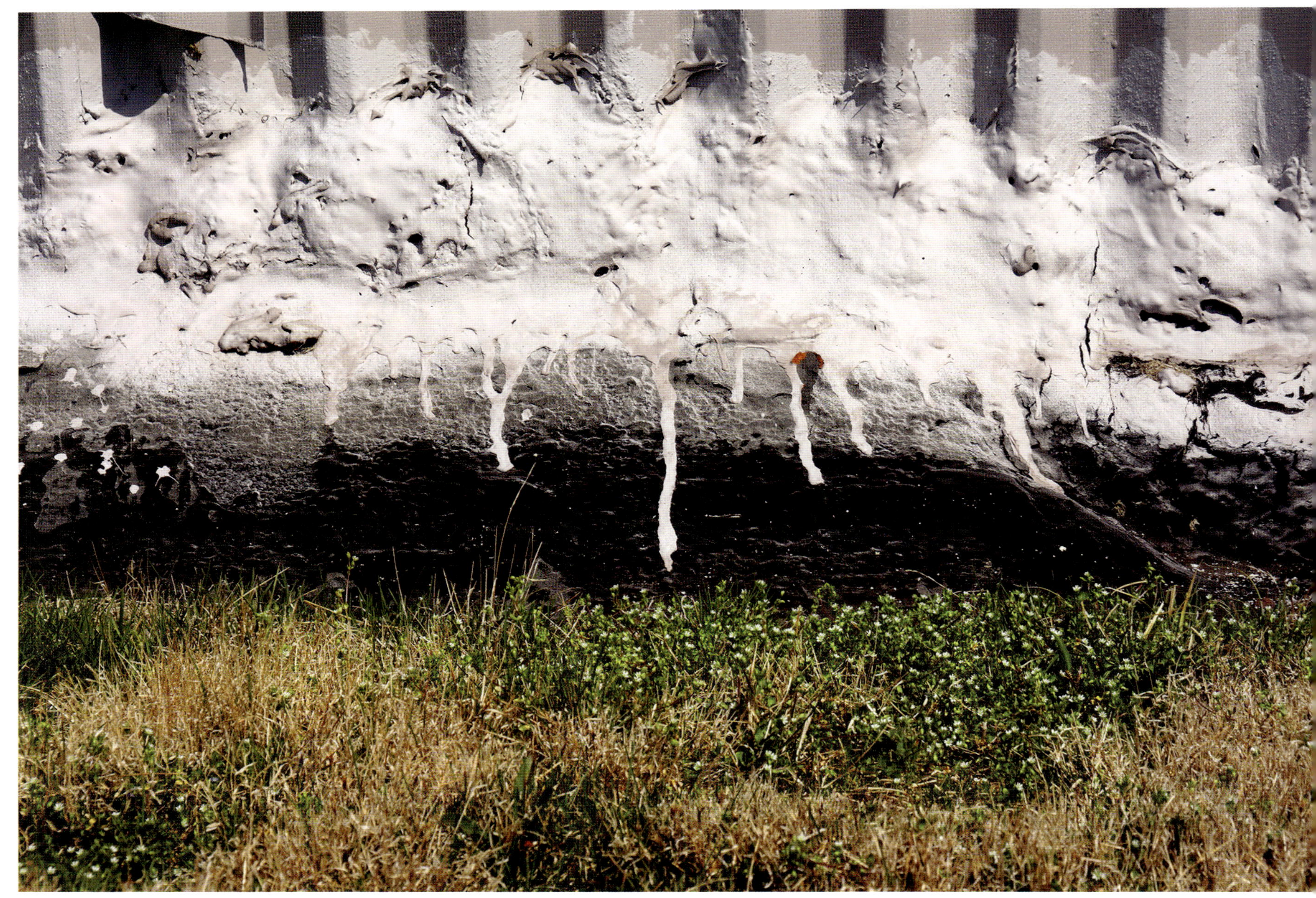

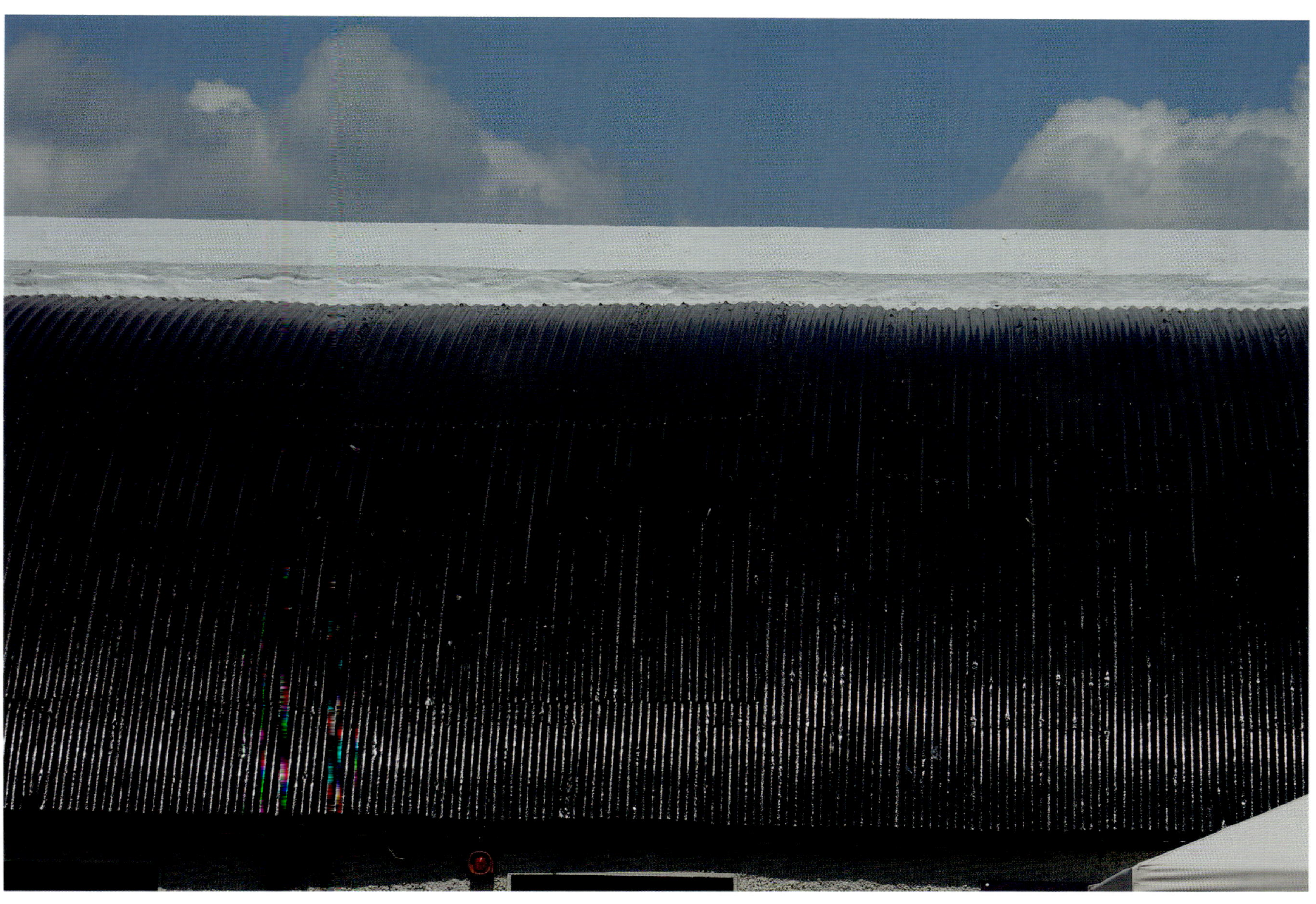

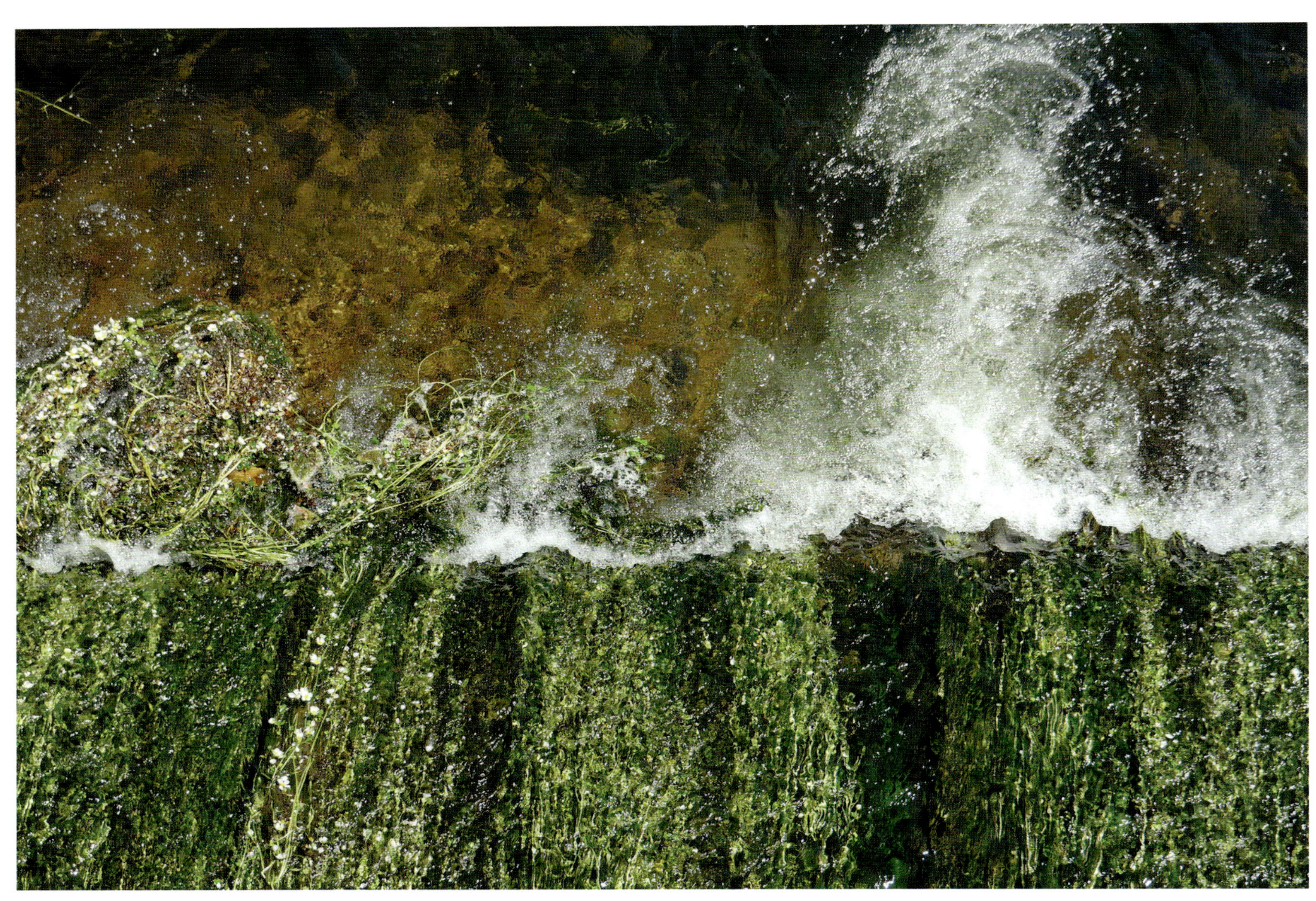

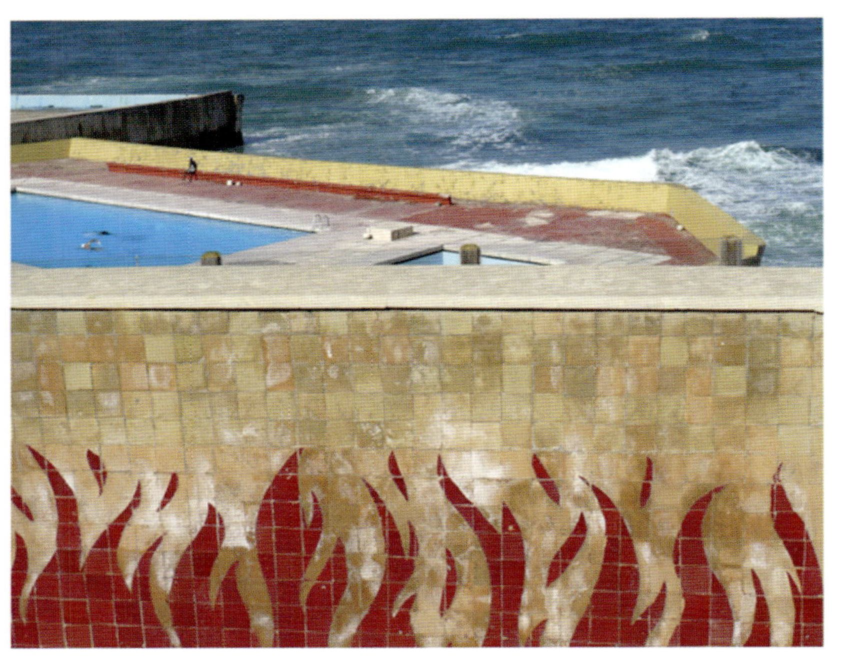

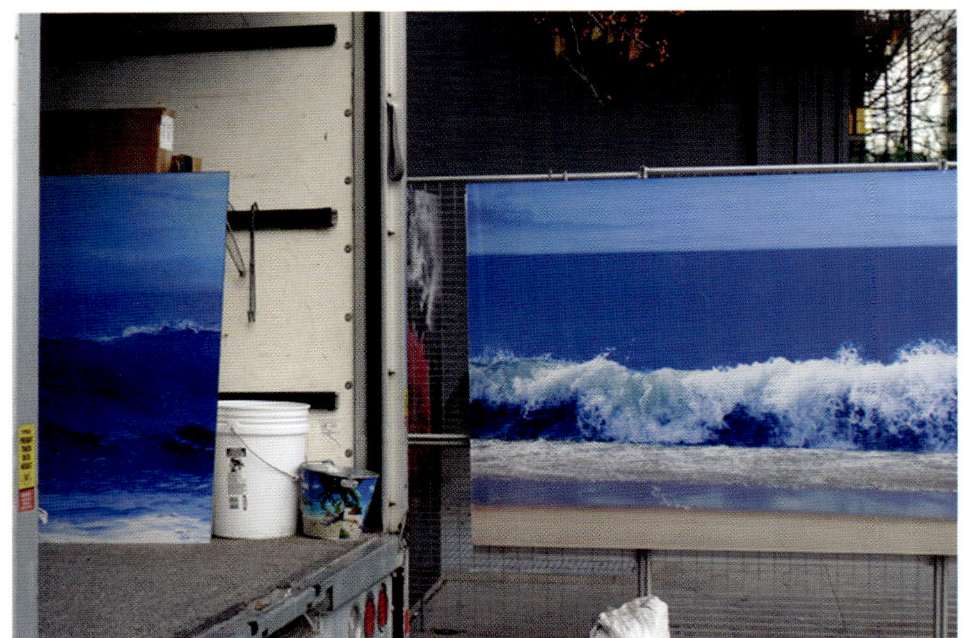

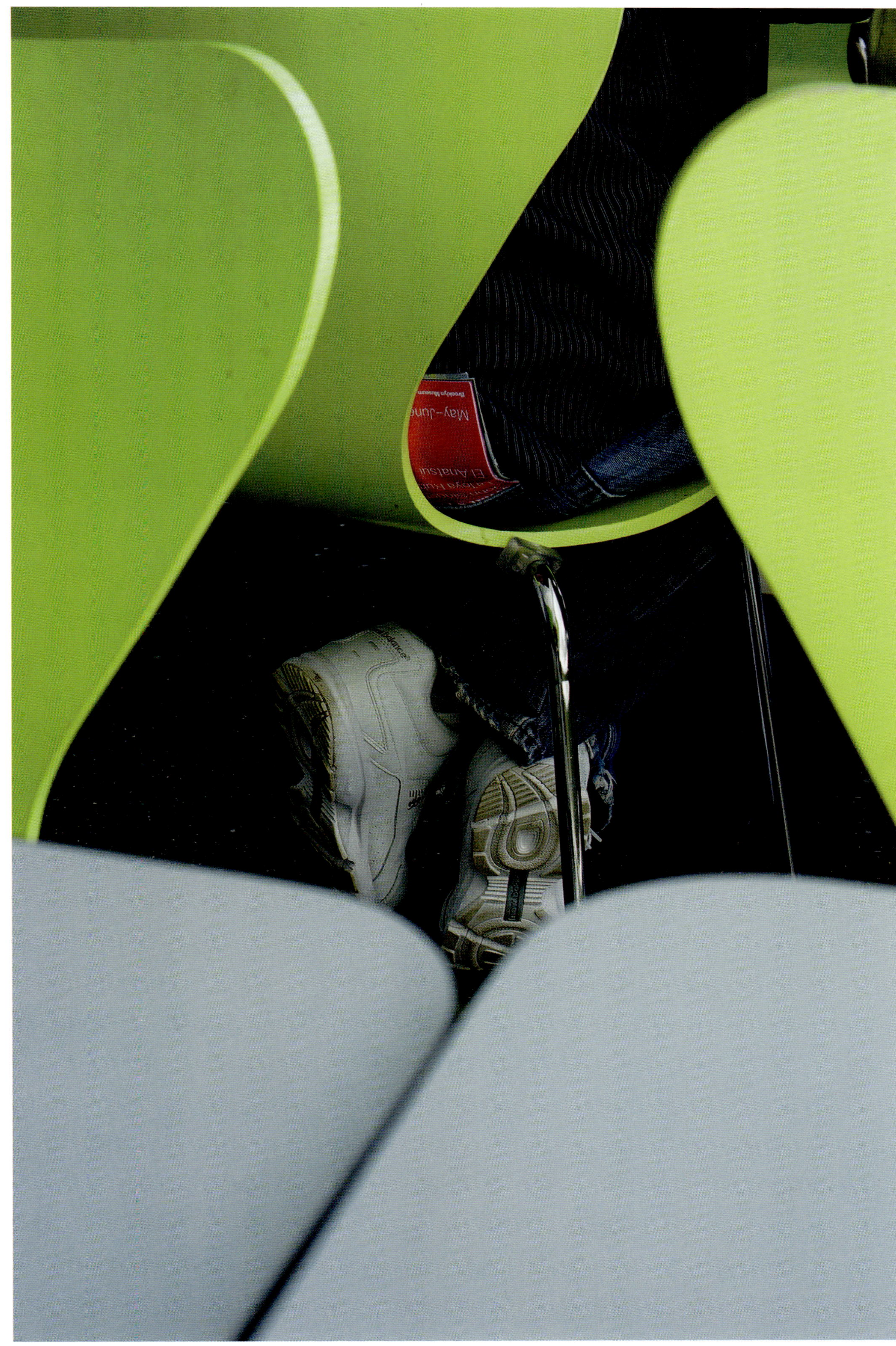
Brooklyn Museum
May–June

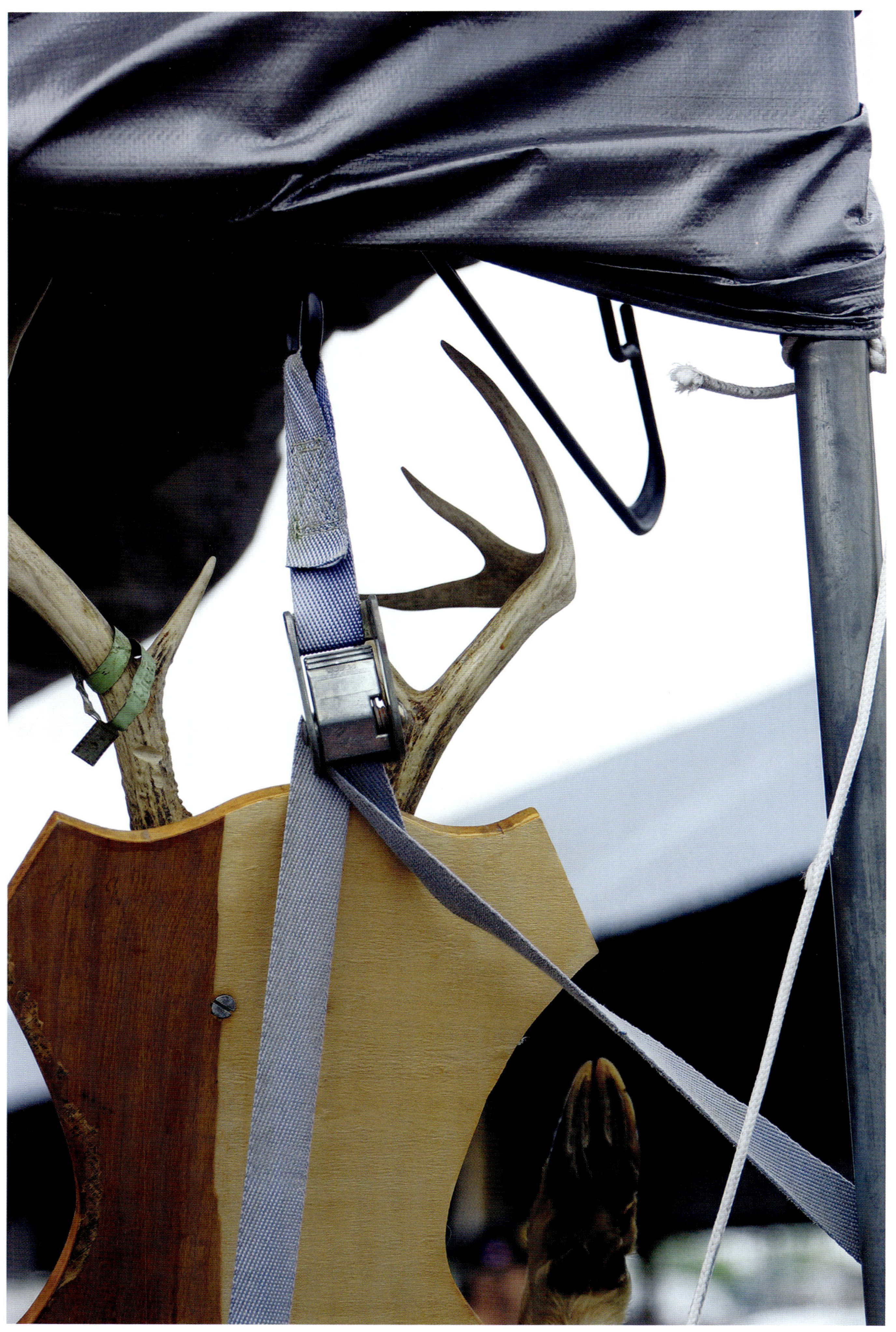

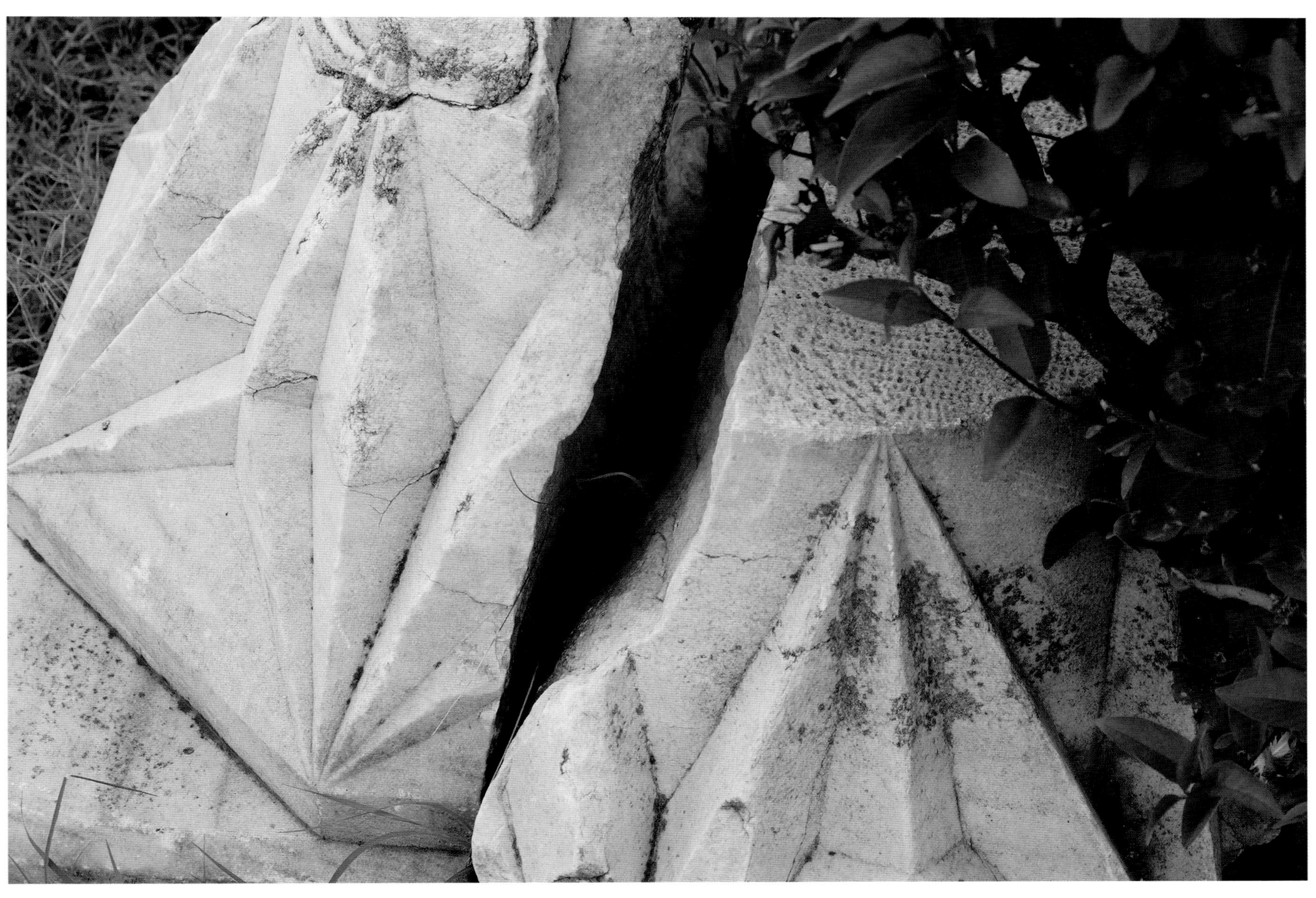

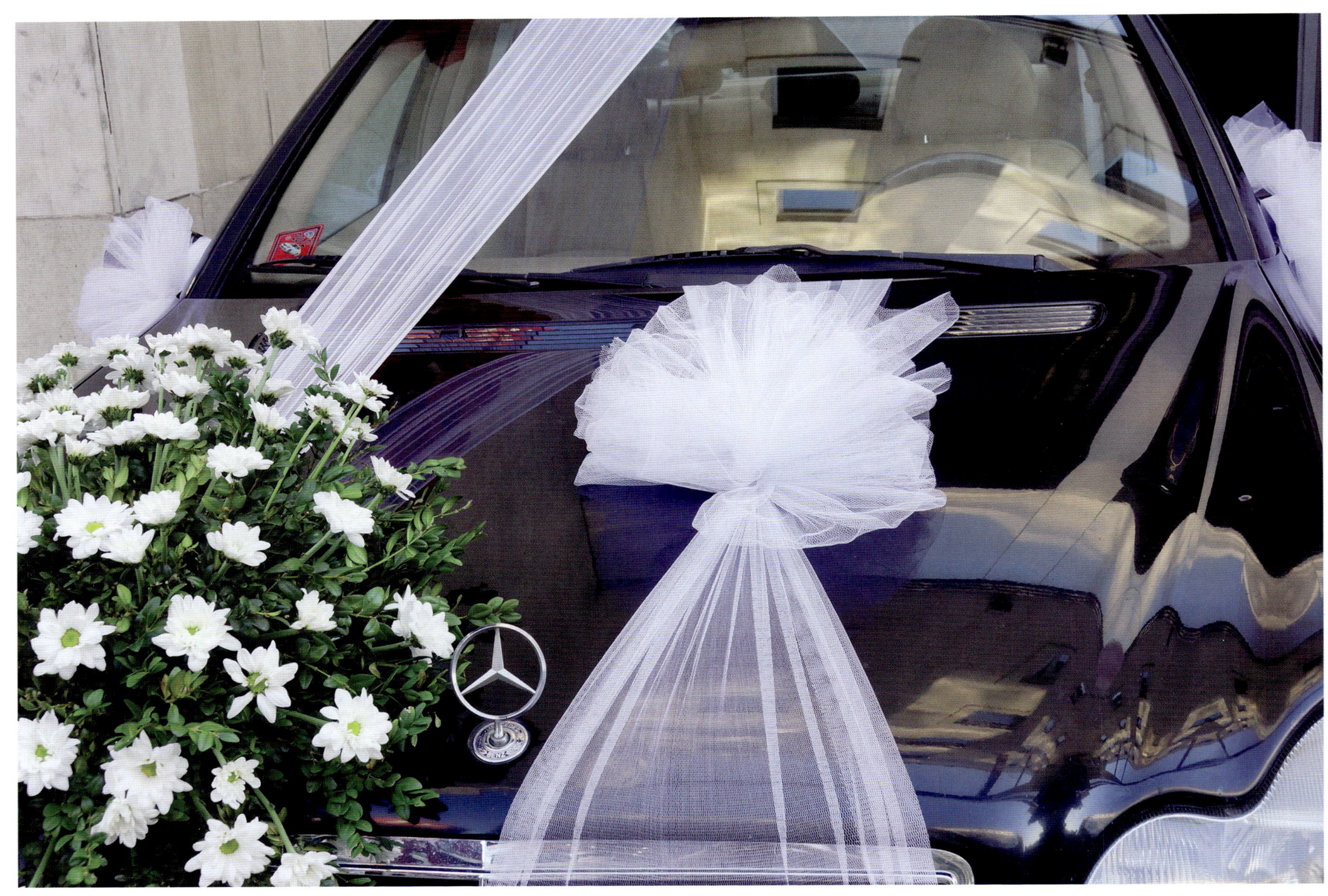

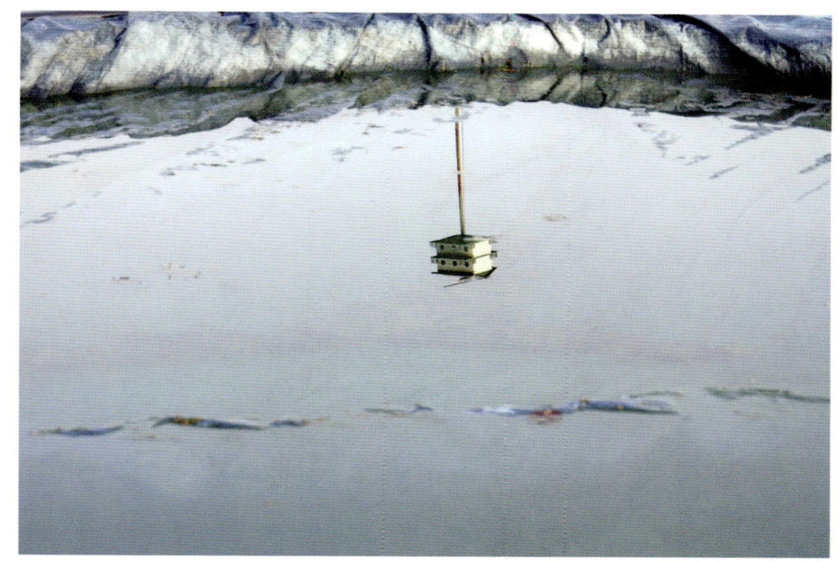

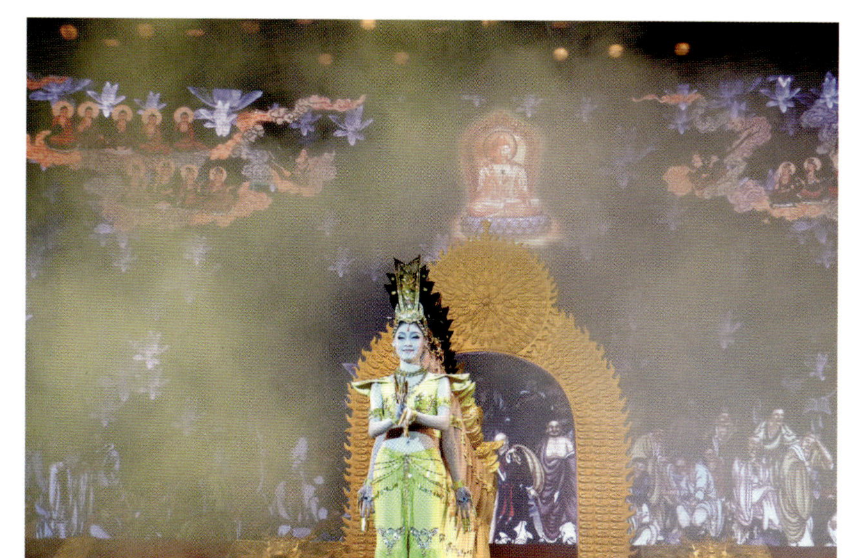

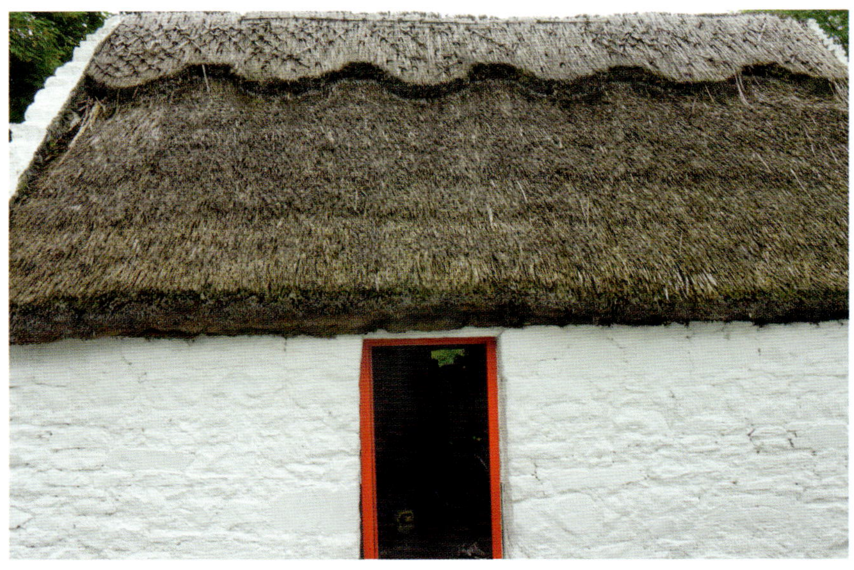

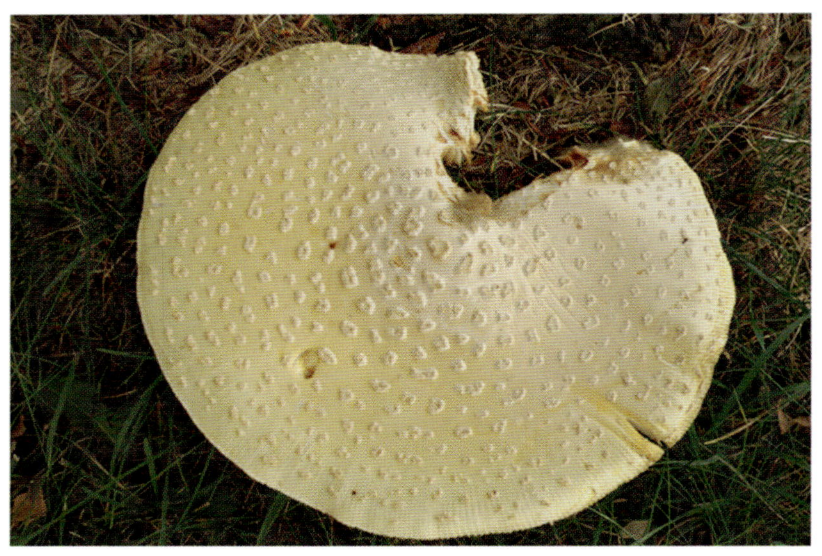

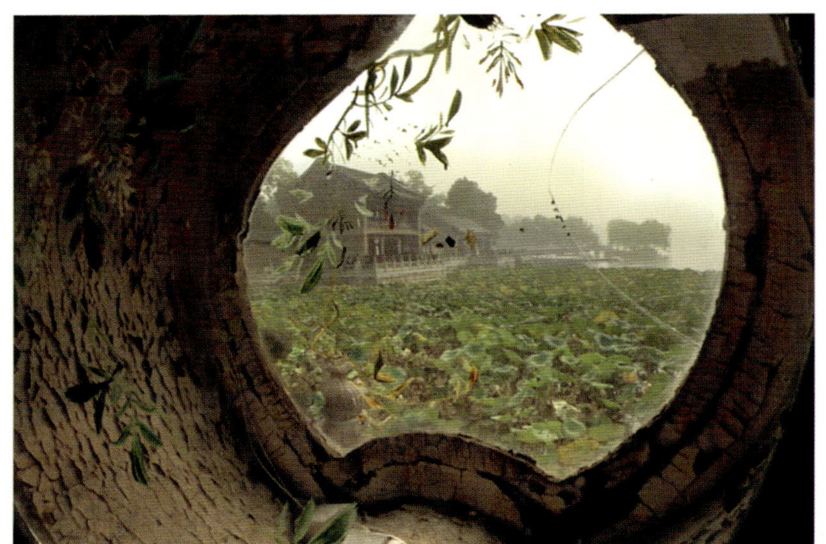

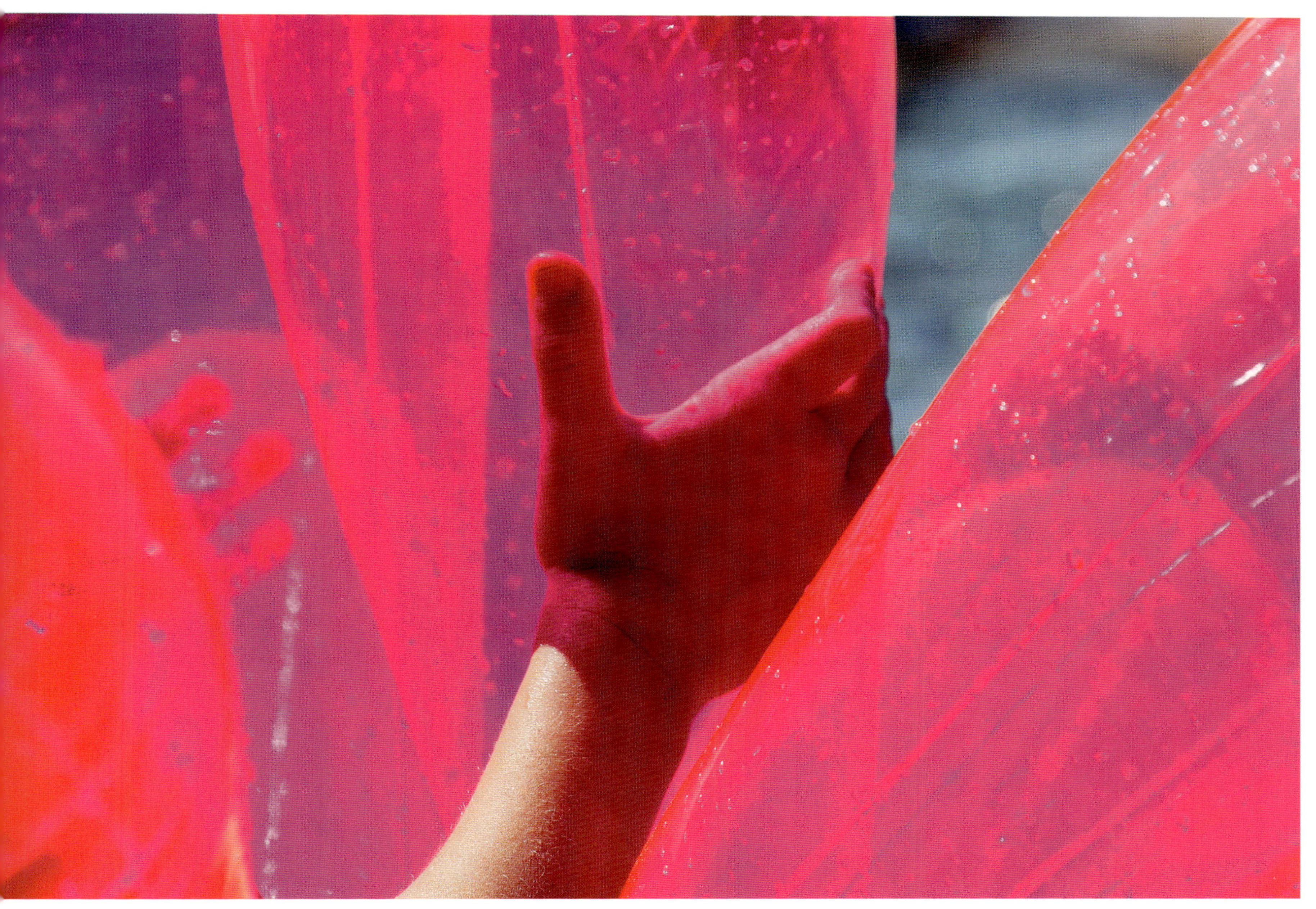

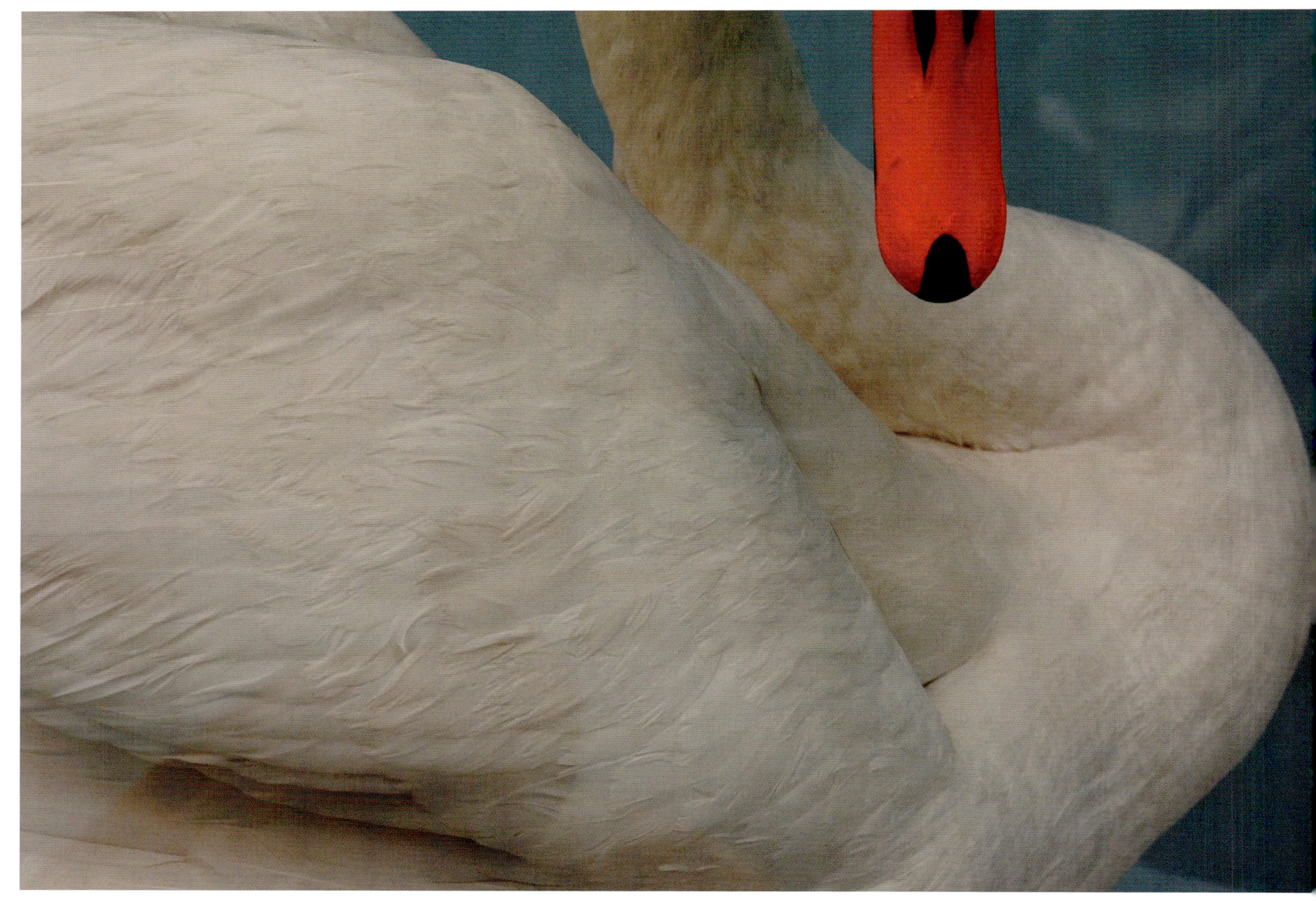

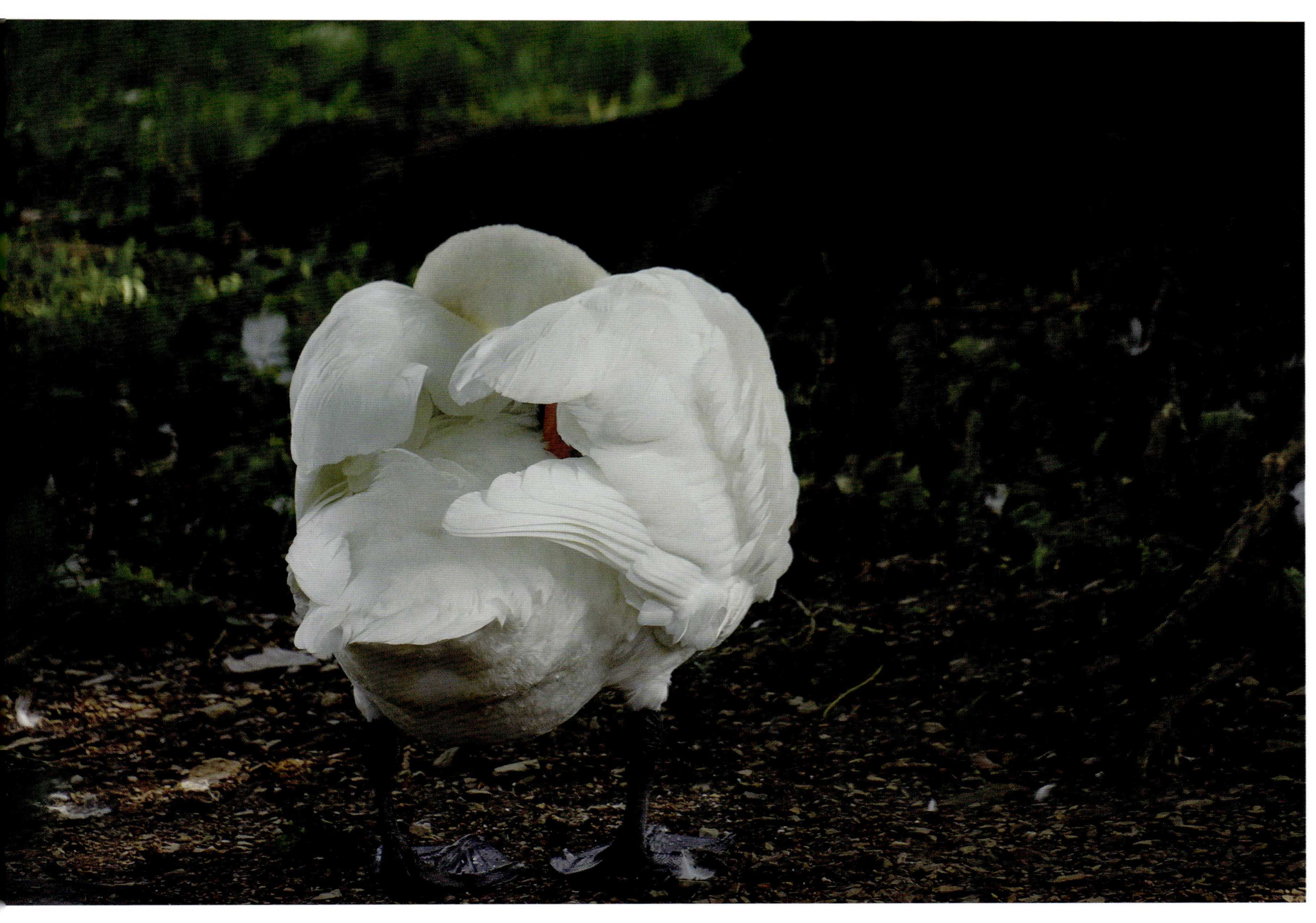

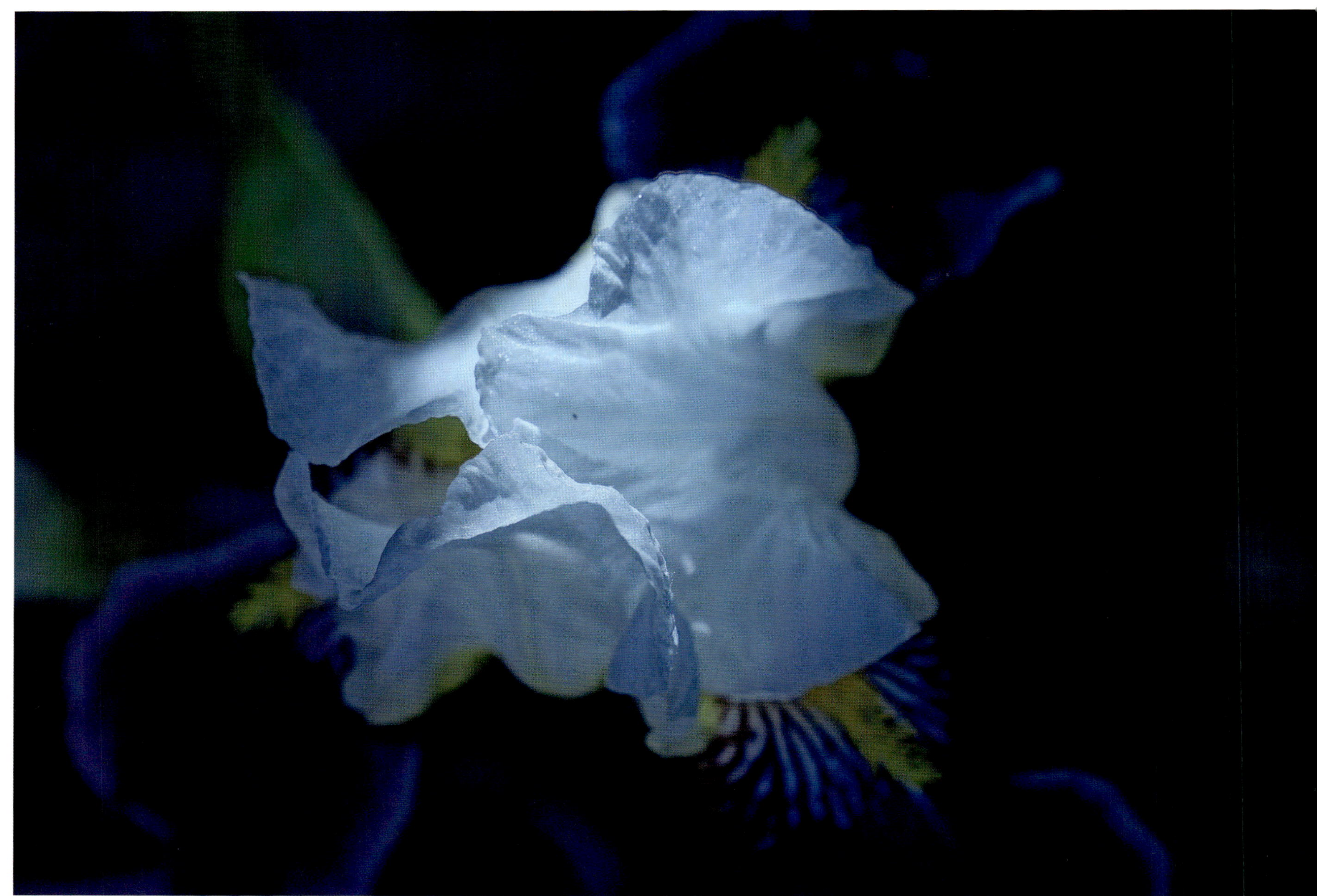

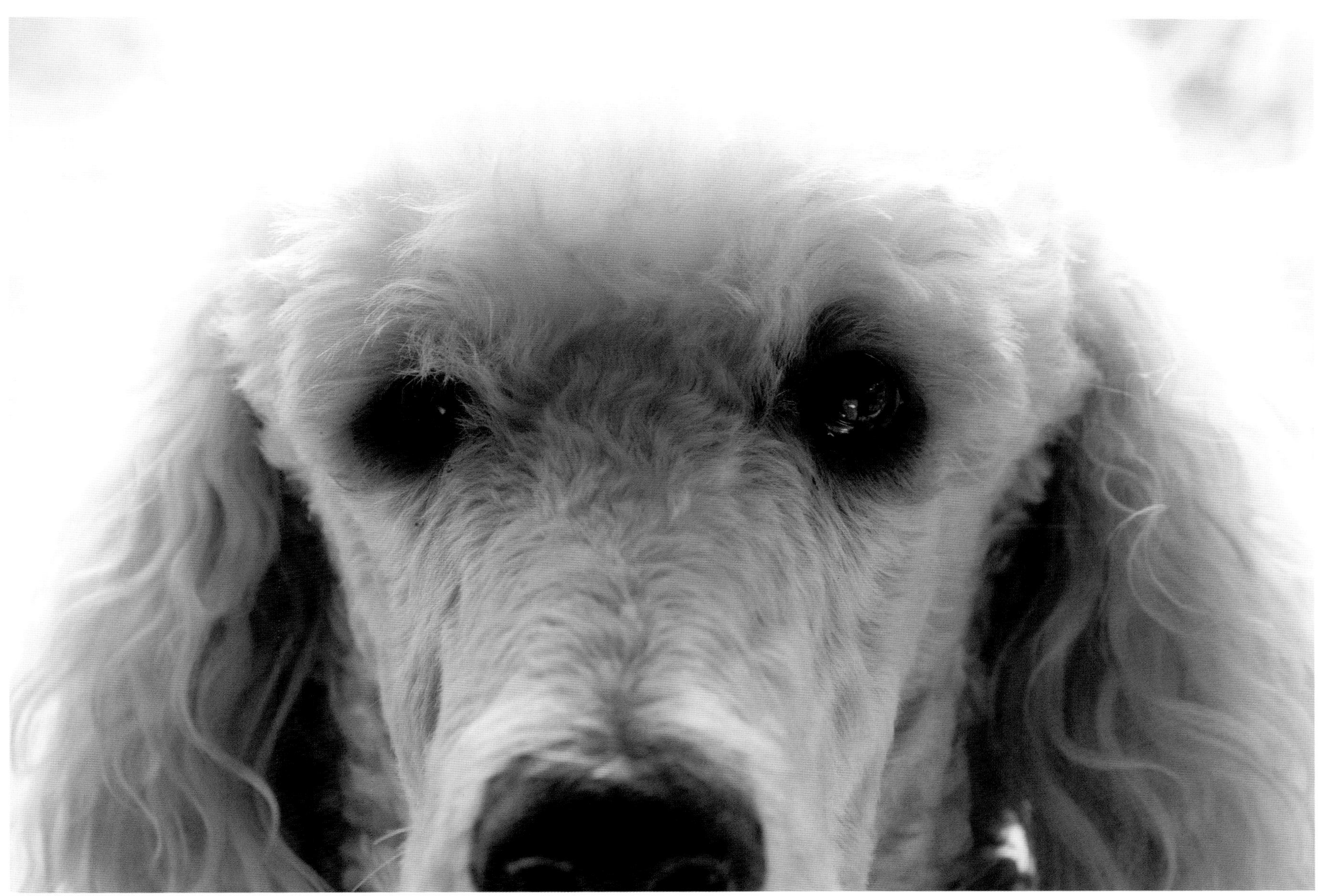

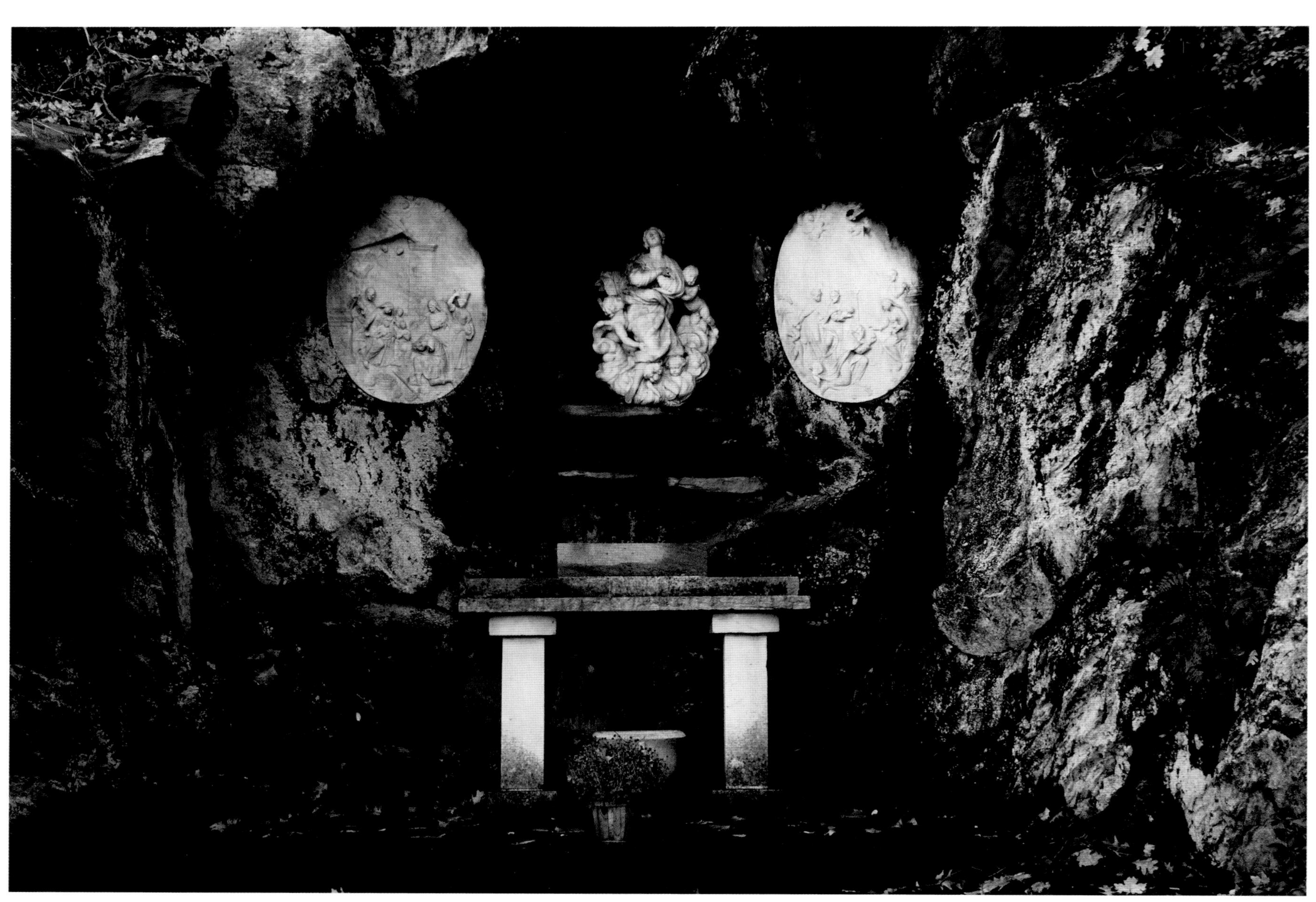

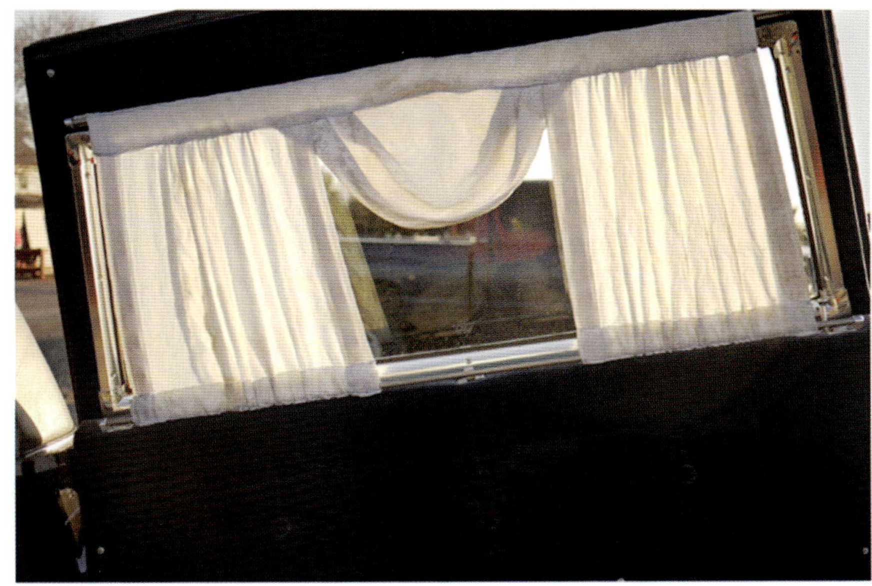

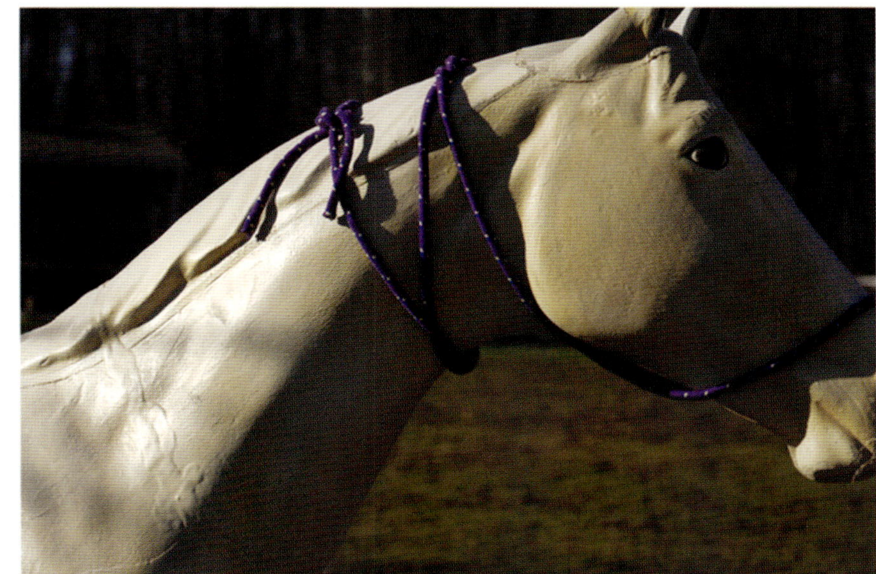

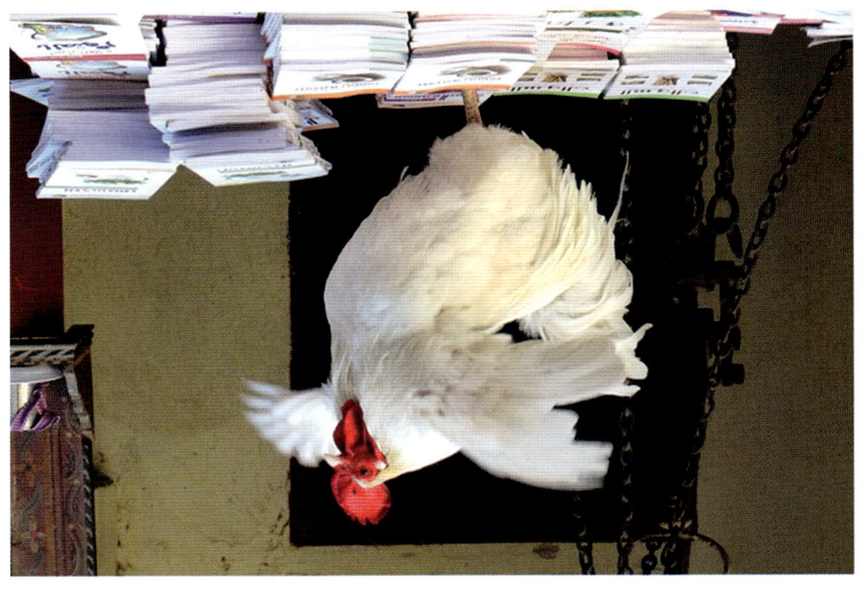

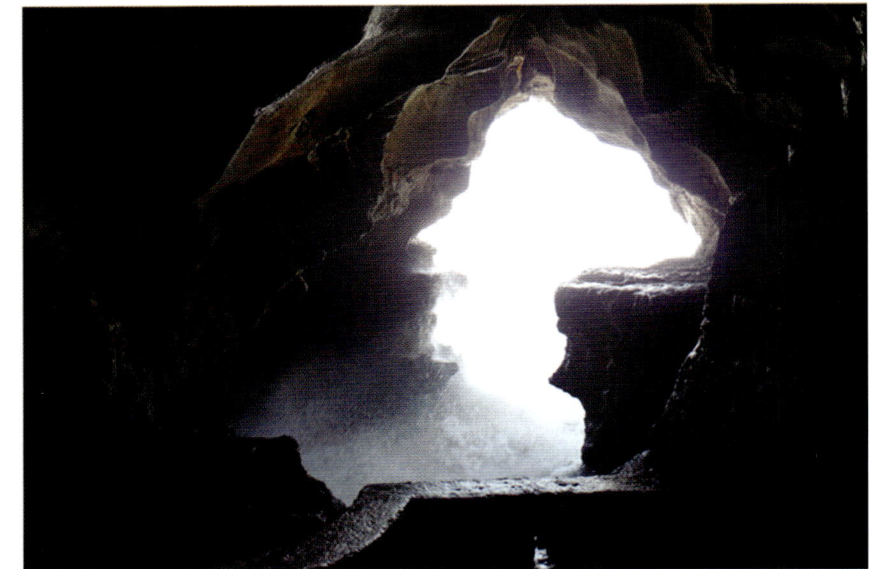

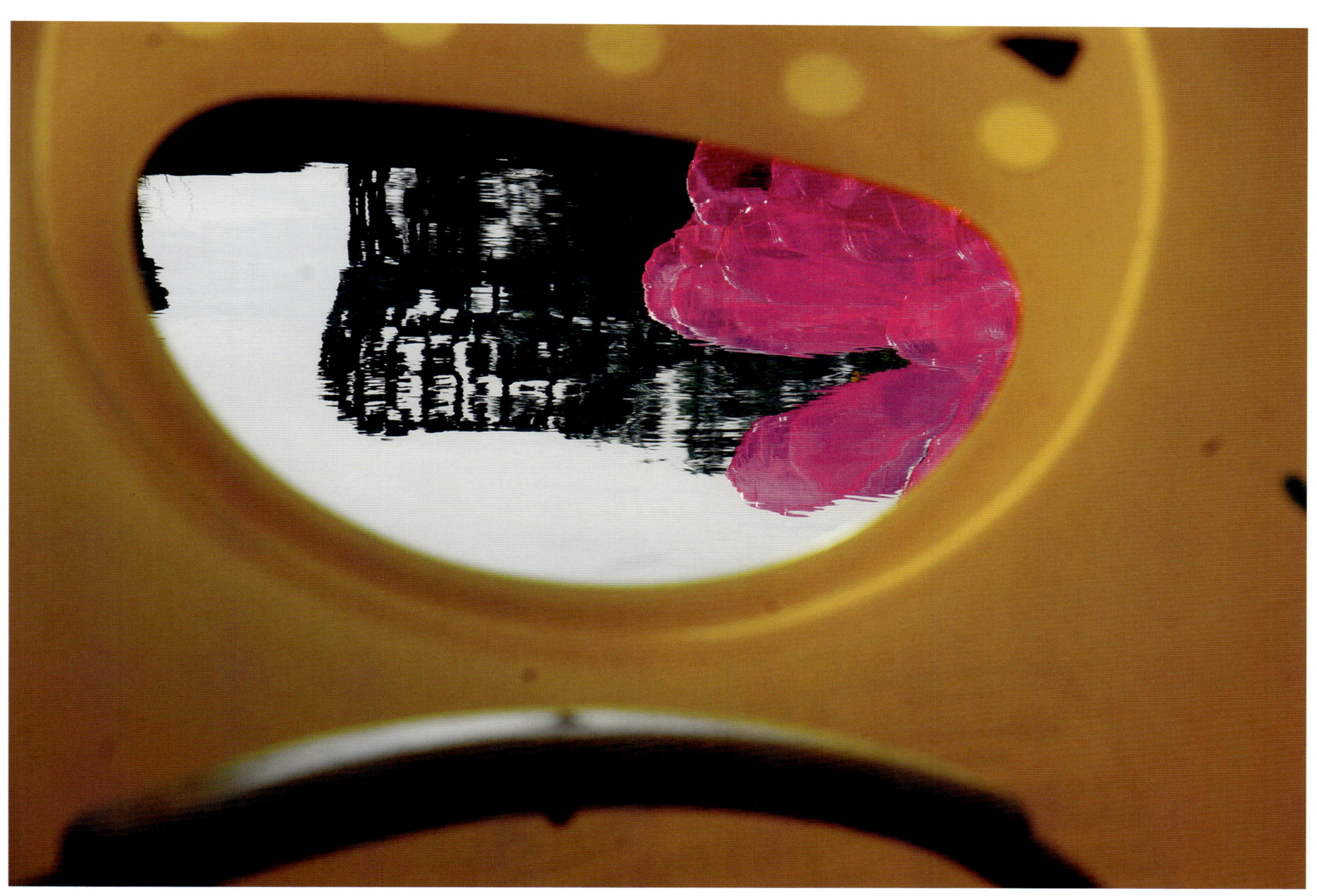

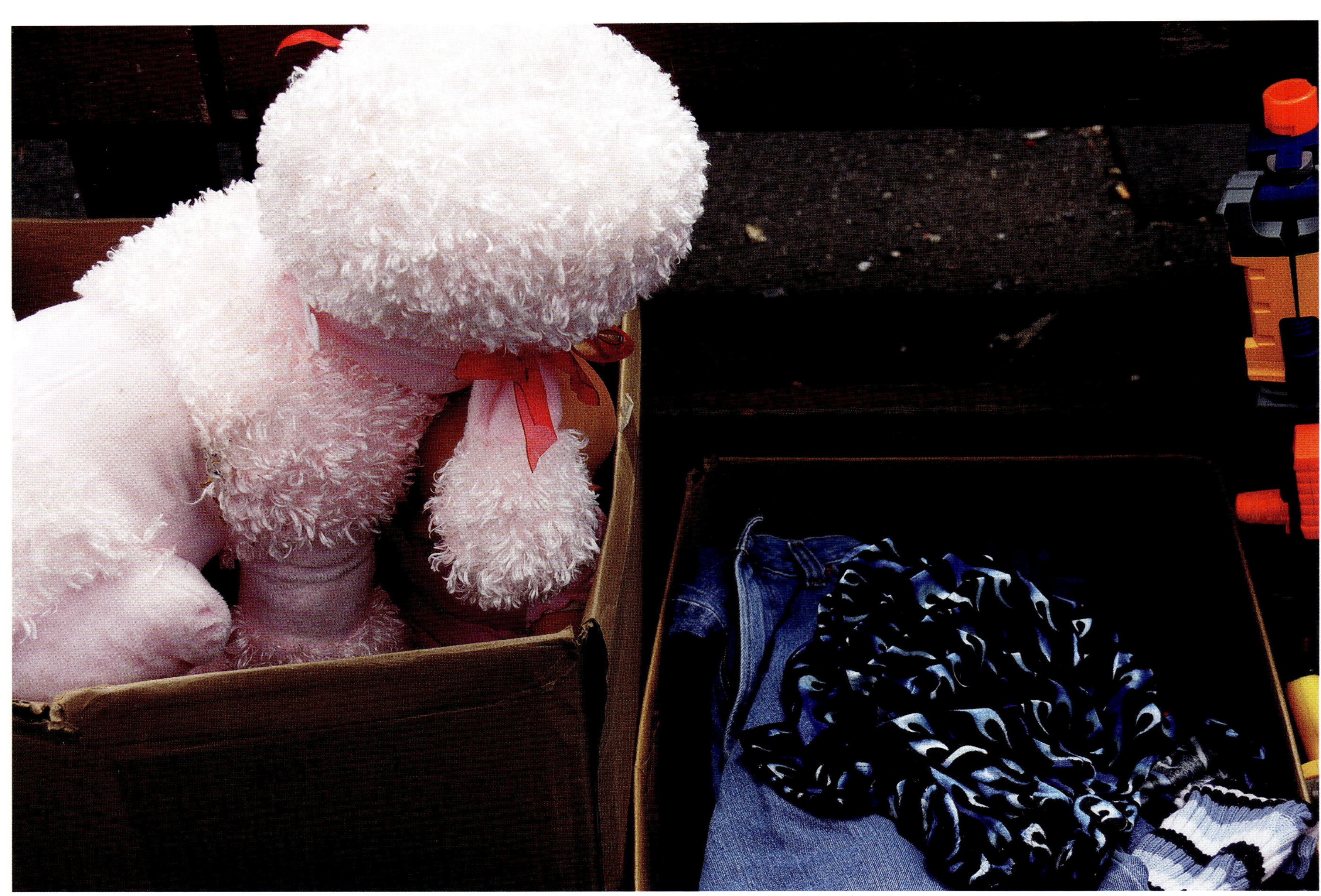

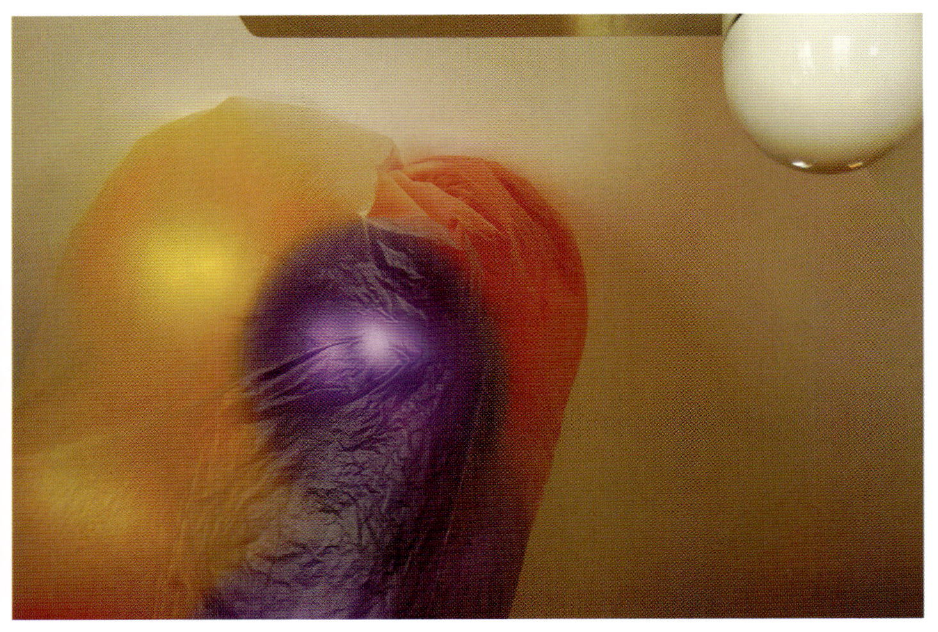

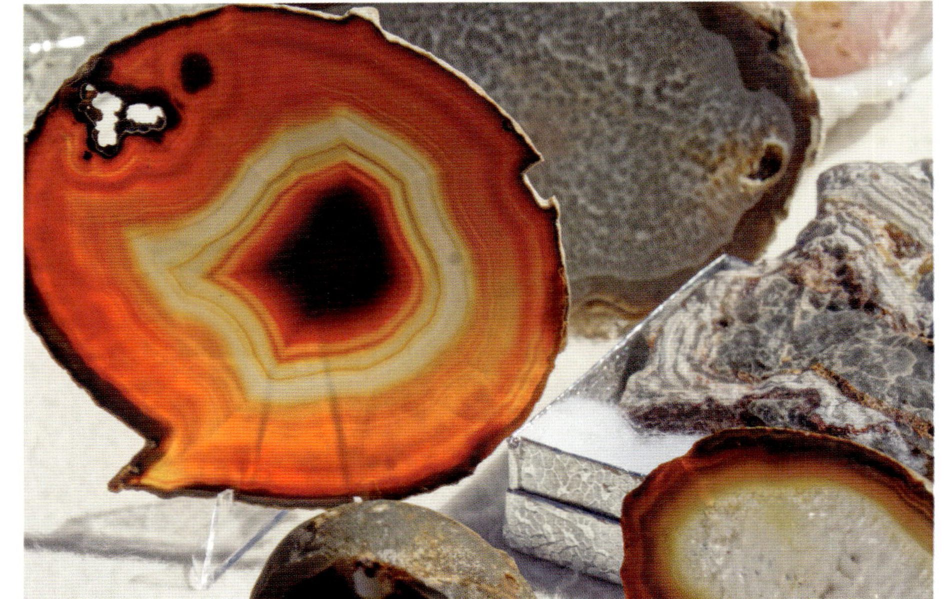

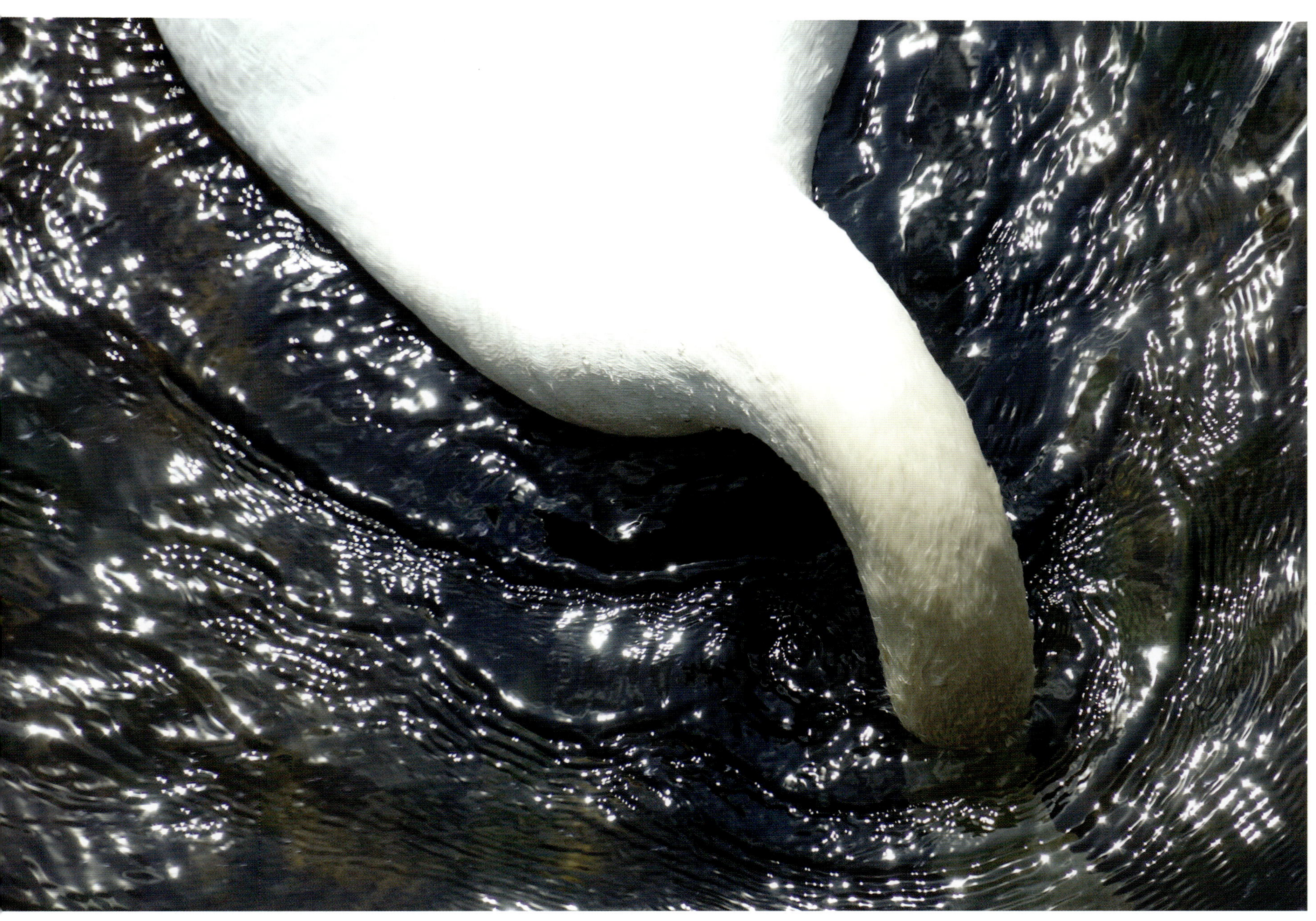

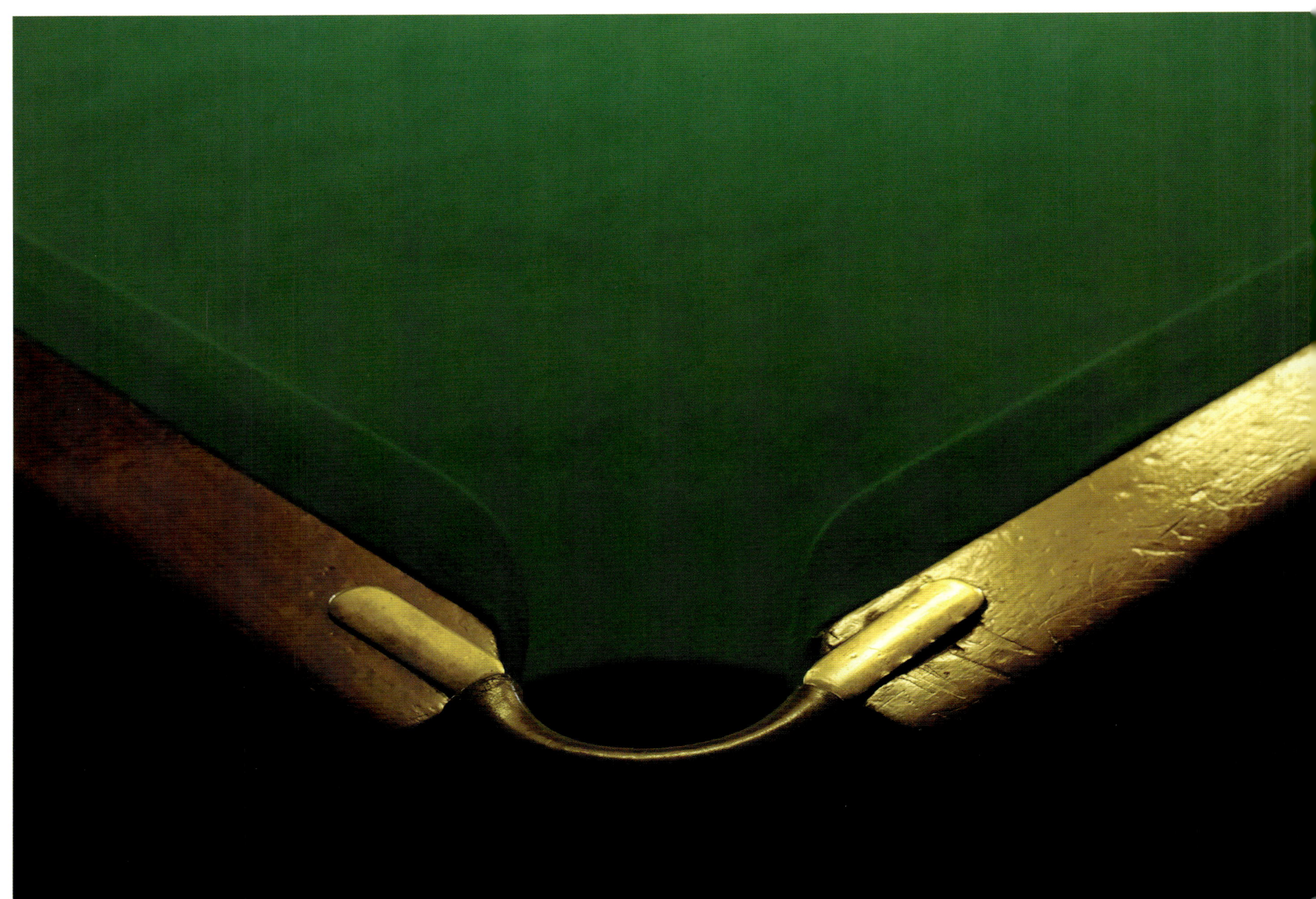

AFTERWORD:

TAKING INVENTORY

In organizing the sequence of images for this book, I sought a rhythmic feeling of fluidity. It can be read front to back or, if you choose, back to front. I present you with elliptical structures and not a linear narrative.

Walking with a camera is like shopping the aisles of culture. It slices the world into infinite variation and meaning, and suggestions for further adventure. Frequently I look for the detritus of urbanity loaded with history but isolated from its past context. In this process of isolating and cutting away from reality, the image acquires a new flexibility of meaning. I exploit this flexibility—to blur, soften, hone, formalize or further recontextualize an image already abstracted. I then combine two separate images into pairs derived in this manner using several strategies. My intent in pairing two photographs is to create a third and new possibility. More than any process I have worked with, photography offers exquisite decision-making, editing between like images or multiple variations of similar content. It is this editing process, first in the camera, then from my archive of photographs that is closest to drawing with the camera. This, coupled with pairing, is the place where my sensibility finds aesthetic satisfaction. Rather than manipulate images, I choose them. The seeing (the camera), storing (the computer), editing (selection) then repeats itself again and again.

HISTORY

My relationship to photography is somewhat circuitous. I am, and continue to be, a painter as well as a photographer. Indeed my painting practice has revolved around the ontology of photography for forty years. Simply put, I explore photography through a painter's eye. I do this in my paintings by using drawing and paint to move freely between a photograph's fictive space and its surface, including the white, iconic border.

This has enabled me to utilize a fresh approach to photography and led me to make the side-by-side images or "pairs" you see here. This was an intuitive choice derived by reviewing and looking for structural patterns, expressive equivalences, compositional choices, shared content and philosophy in disparate images, shot over a decade, including many from my travels to India, China, Cambodia,

"Any inventory of America is inevitably anti-scientific, a delirious 'abracadadabrant' confusion of objects, in which jukeboxes resemble coffins."

—Susan Sontag

From *On Photography*, referring to Jack Kerouac's introduction to Robert Franks' essay, "The Americans."

Turkey, Morocco and Ireland as well as closer to home, from the streets of New York City and the rural settings of Pennsylvania. This linkage between images provides surprising emotional resonance. I have no narrative intent, but engage in a thought process that creates an elliptical back and forth movement until a poetic occurrence makes itself known. I find this process to be self-revelatory. I am able to group and emphasize the weaving of my choices of imagery, revealing attitudes and fears about existence that I would have no other way of expressing.

In the selection process for this book I was able to discern several categories, not always nameable. They engage in varied ways: humor, violence, absurdity, war, dream, structure, chaos, stasis, history, pop culture, nature, theater and the urban existence. The components of the pair may belong to different categories, shifting back and forth, on into the other like consciousness itself. A pair of photos that satisfies me occurs when the content coincides with structure and a resulting third "place" of mind is proposed. Susan Sontag, who I find to be exceptionally insightful about the possibilities of photography, describes this third place:

> *Poetry's commitment to concreteness and to the autonomy of the poem's language parallels photography's commitment to pure seeing. Both imply discontinuity, disarticulated forms and compensatory unity: Wrenching things from their context (to see them in a fresh way), bringing things together elliptically, according to the imperious but often arbitrary demands of subjectivity.*

SELECTION OF THINGS AND PLACES TO PHOTOGRAPH

My approach to the magic of photography attempts to reveal the ideas that circulate just below the surface of our global culture. Even as I travel and photograph in other countries, I build a language of meaning that draws connections between architecture, art, religion, nature. As I join the photographs into pairs, connections are teased out through formal or content-driven means to pose questions. In order to be chosen, an image must survive rigorous ideological and moral scrutiny and provide me with significance beyond subject and beauty. I generally prefer objects—either manmade or natural—rather than human representations as signifiers. I would note that this book contains very few representations of humans, all of whom are masked or sightless, or reduced in scale.

I spend a lot of time trolling in rural flea markets. Again, Susan Sontag, from *On Photography:*

> *Recall that it was Breton and other Surrealists who invented the secondhand store as a temple of vanguard taste and upgraded visits to flea markets into a mode of aesthetic pilgrimage. The surrealist rag pickers acuity was directed to finding beautiful what other people found ugly or without interest or relevance—bric-a-brac, naïve or pop-objects, urban debris.*

Moving from table to table is a discontinuous way of seeing and photographing. I select details that tease at the whole or are pieces of a bigger reference or context. The flea market is a microcosm of this bigger context. It is a place where the extras, the old, broken, unwanted, odd, and rusted reside, waiting to be repurposed. I find content there because over time I have recognized rhythms: products in relation to the state of the economy, to the trade of the seller, to the varied sizes of pocketbooks and all manner of needs and desires. There are less and less old, collectible items. Instead many things are newly minted in China. There is food (past its freshness date), watches, jewelry, stationery and tools that have become obsolete because of new technology. Table after table, aisle upon aisle presented cinematically, for individual frames. It is outdoors in all weather and roofless. There are regular vendors and those who are selling a family estate on one day only. There is every kind of reason to be selling. Product display can be haphazard or set with precision. I never know what I am going to find to buy or acquire with my camera.

When I travel or am in the street or in nature I maintain the same mindset. There is always something, I invent as I click the shutter. There is always light and formalism to interpret and further ponder.

The time it takes for a viewer to recognize or associate with an image is important to me. I wish for the viewer to linger and for the image to reveal itself or its potential to move beyond its monocular information perhaps offering a trigger to memory. I am both the outside observer and then the subjective presenter. All emotions are open to me, and often I will use them in opposition to one another. In saving and storing my photos on the computer, I think of them as an atlas from which to select, elevate, hold and muse over. I surf the images in my computer over and over, and it is not a dissimilar process from how I take pictures themselves. In using the camera I most often will take five to ten images of the same thing, as many nuanced variations as I think useful. I have no set agenda when I see. I let my mind wander and wonder. I try to make distinctions between vision that is both abstract and literal, at times both. In both my selective processes (shooting and editing) content or congruence comes to me. I savor these moments of freshness when a presence makes itself known in a way that I have never seen or compels me to make it known. Put another way, a pair of photos is satisfying when their content coincides with structure and a third "silent presence" is proposed to the viewer.

This reordering of the world takes pieces of ideas suggested in photographic information and forces them to communicate with unrelated imagery, differing in time, space and content. One aspect of an image may provide the complimentary content to another, revealing a truth that only exists in the space between the two selected images. I selectively and subjectively juxtapose photographic information and propose a new reality.

—Stephen Posen
New York City

INDEX

OF ARTWORKS

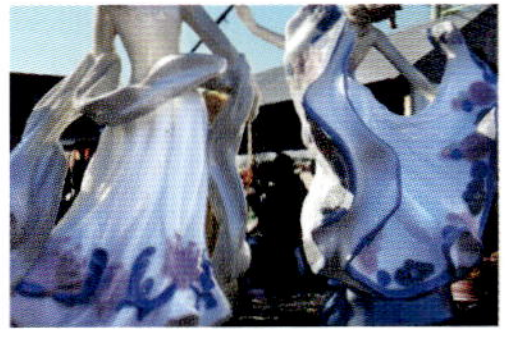
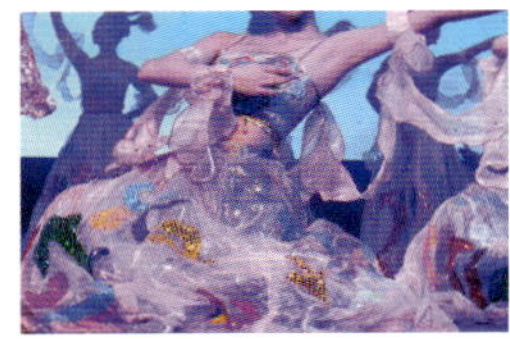

Flea Market, Quakertown, Pennsylvania, January 2012; *Beijing Opera,* Beijing, China, October 2011

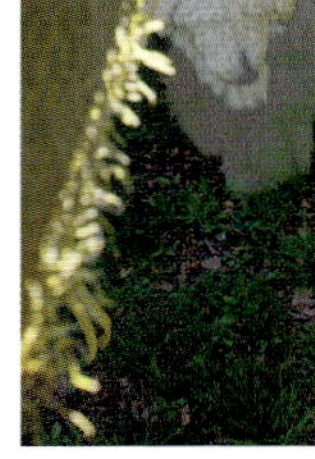
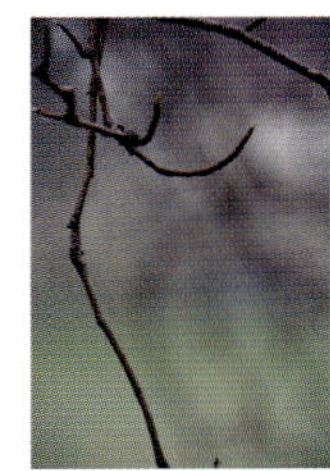

Puppy on grass, Pleasant Valley, Pennsylvania, March 2012; *Sticks and spider web,* Pleasant Valley, Pennsylvania, March 2012

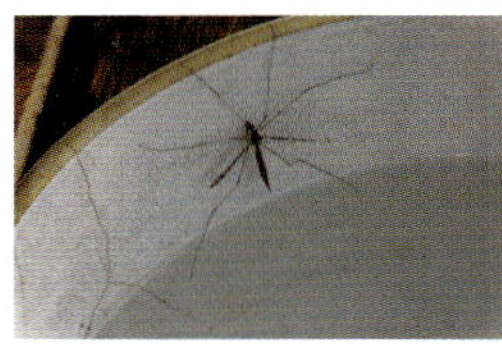
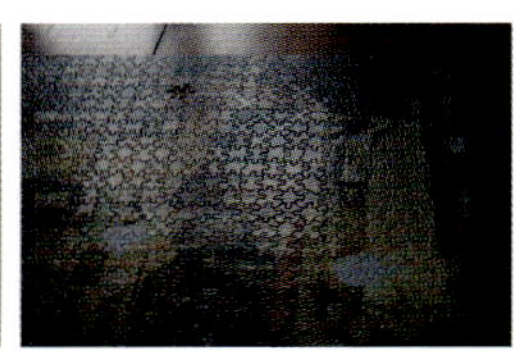

Insect on bowl, Pleasant Valley, Pennsylvania, August 2013; *Jigsaw puzzle,* Lismore Castle, Ireland, June 2013

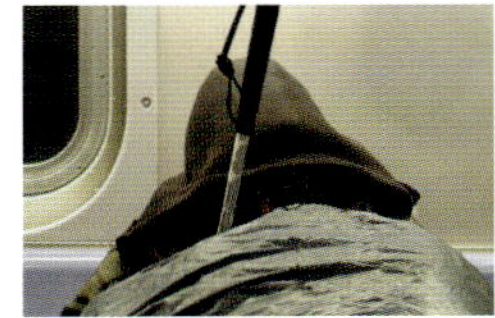
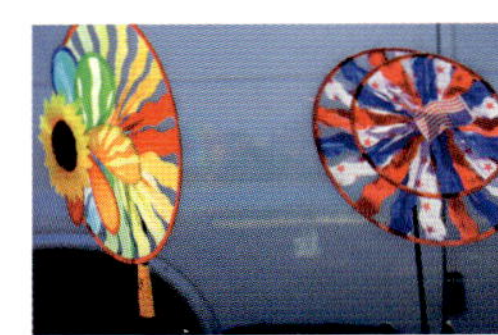

Blind person on subway car, New York, New York, April 2010; *Whirligigs at flea market,* Quakertown, Pennsylvania, March 2013

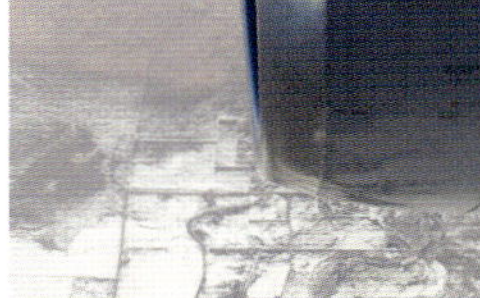
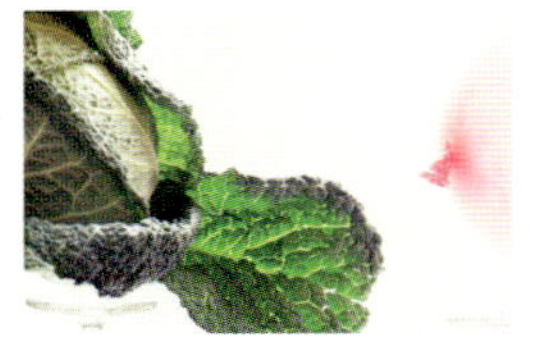

Airplane window over Colorado, January 2012; *Still life with cabbage and balloon,* Pleasant Valley, Pennsylvania, February 2012

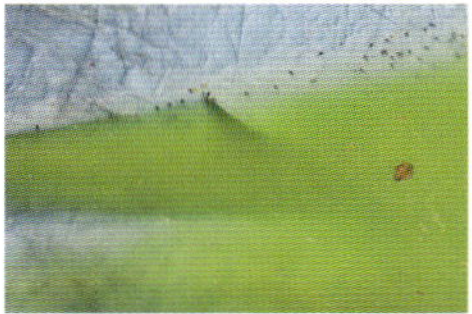

Tadpoles, Cherry Hill Farm, Pennsylvania, May 2012; *Still life with banana and marble,* New York, New York, June 2012

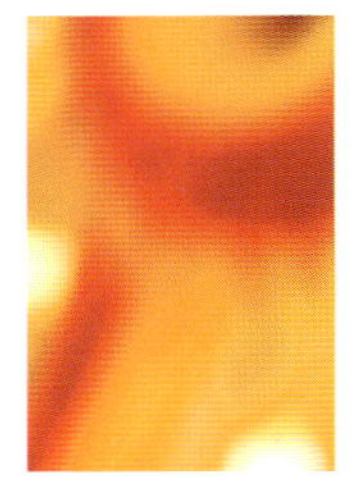
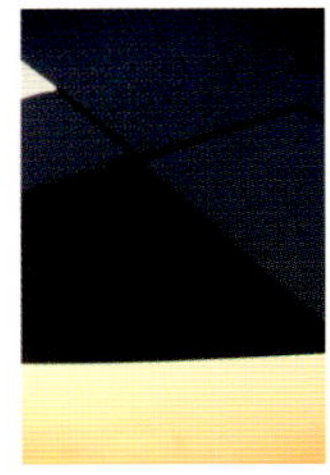

Neon sign, Las Vegas, Nevada, January 2012; *Airplane wing and engine,* over Rockies, Colorado, June 2013

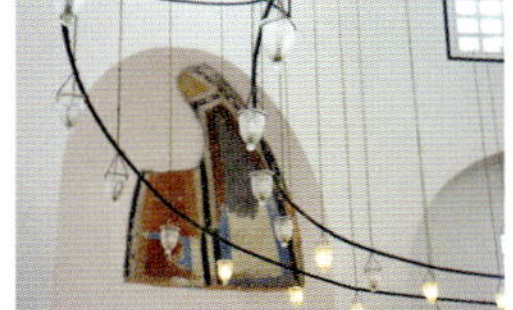
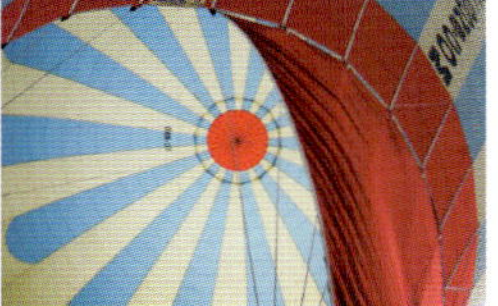

Mosque ceiling, Istanbul, Turkey, November 2012; *Hot air balloon interior,* Cappadocia, Turkey, October 2012

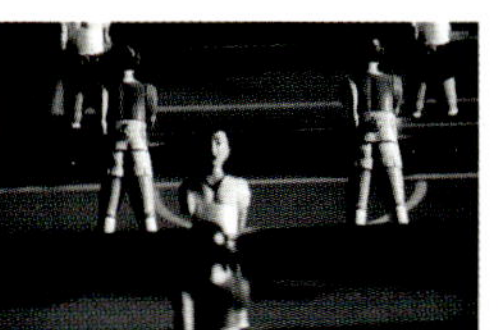
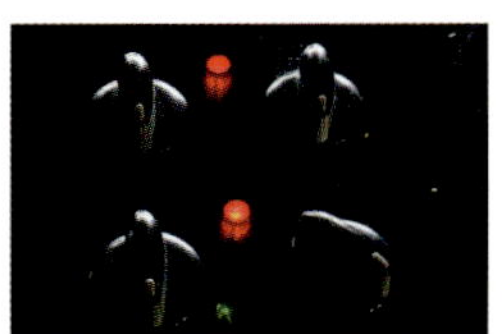

Table hockey, Lismore, Ireland, June 2013; *Electric stove top,* Cherry Hill Farm, Pennsylvania, February 2013

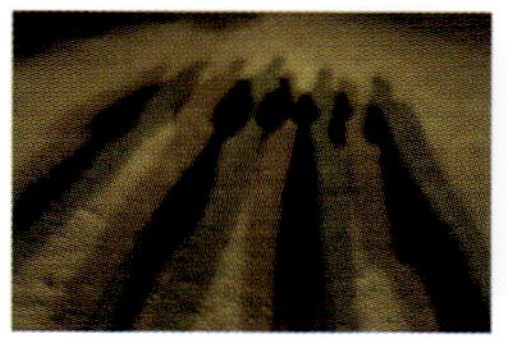
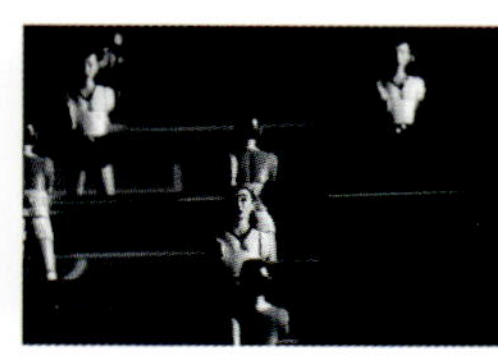

Shadows, Lismore, Ireland, June 2013; *Table hockey,* Lismore, Ireland, June 2013

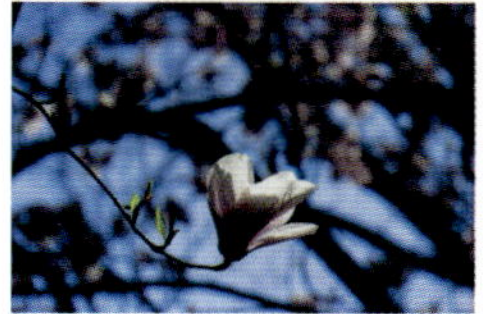
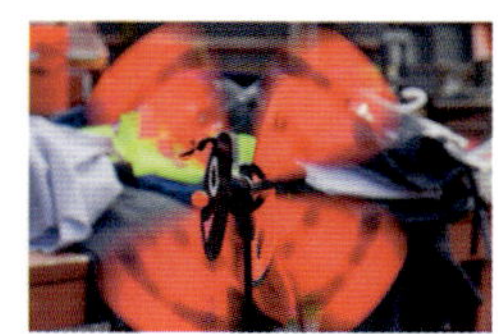

Magnolia blossom, Cherry Hill Farm, Pennsylvania, May 2013; *Whirligig,* Quakertown, Pennsylvania, April 2013

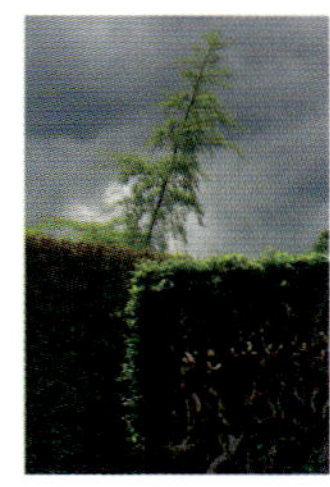
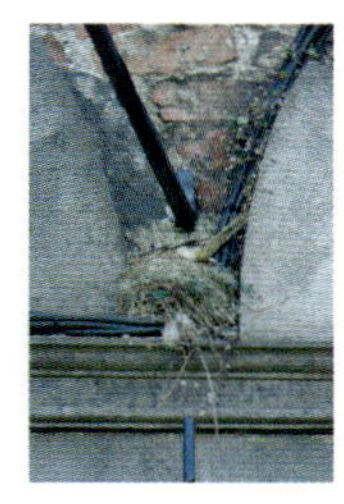

Hedge, Lismore, Ireland, June 2013; *Wall,* Kilkenny, Ireland, June 2013

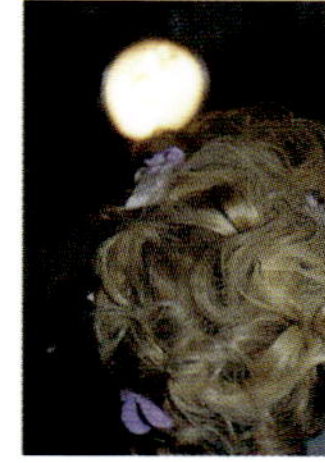

Styled hair, New York, New York, September 2013; *Cornice,* New York, New York, September 2013

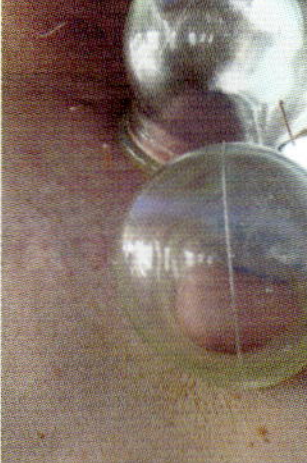
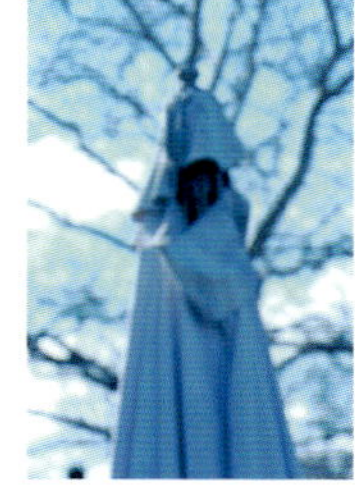

Acupuncture and cupping, Yangtze River, China, October 2011; *Pool umbrella with tree,* Cherry Hill Farm, Pennsylvania, December 2011

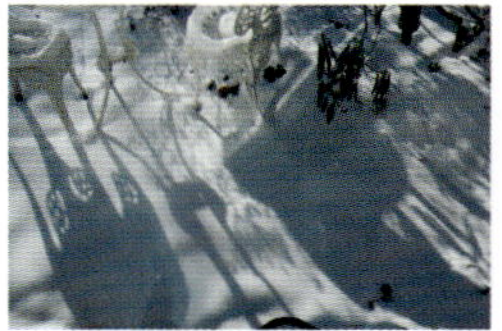
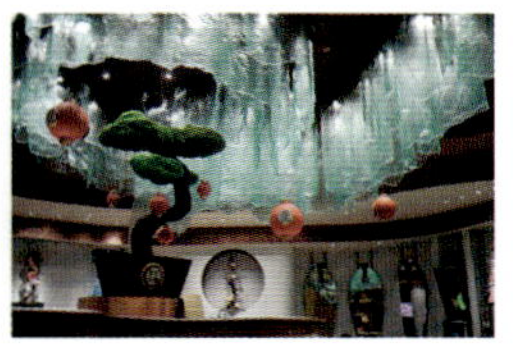

Snow shadows, Pleasant Valley, Pennsylvania, January 2012; *Bar,* Las Vegas, January 2012

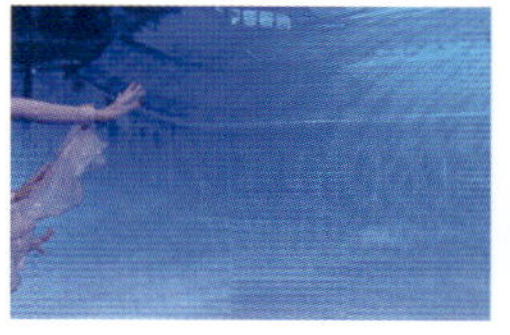
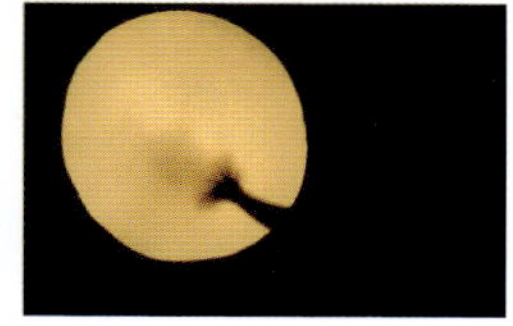

Dancer, Beijing Opera, China, October 2011; *Shadow Puppet Theater,* Beijing, China, October 2011

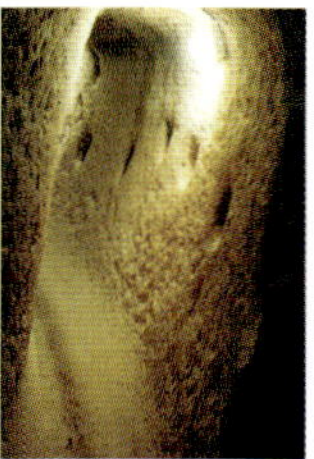
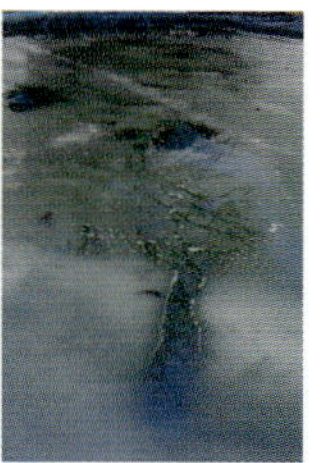

Interior passageway, Cappadocia, Turkey, November 2012; *Ice reflection on swimming pool,* Pleasant Valley, Pennsylvania, January 2013

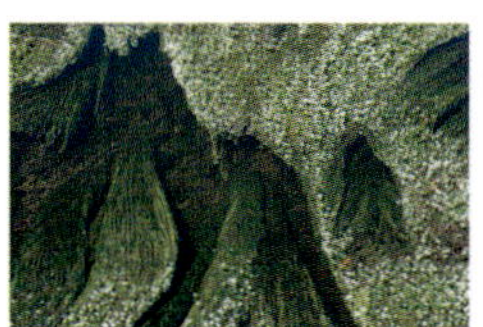
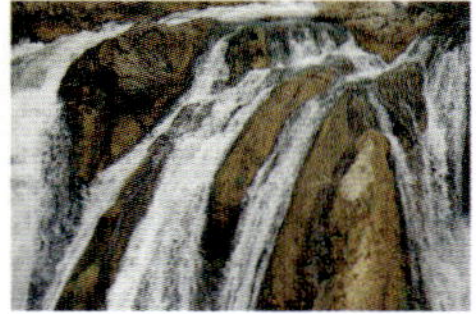

River Blackwater, County Cork, Ireland, June 2013; *Muradiye waterfalls,* Kars, Turkey, October 2012

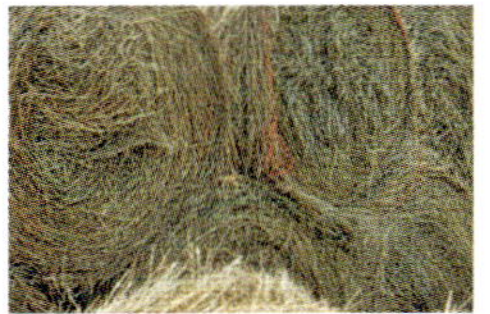
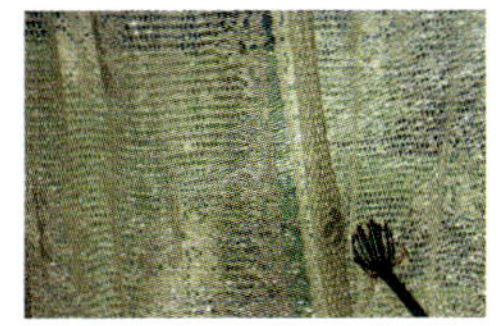

Straw bales, Hottle Farm, Pennsylvania, July 2013; *Window with Clivia bud,* Pleasant Valley, Pennsylvania, June 2012

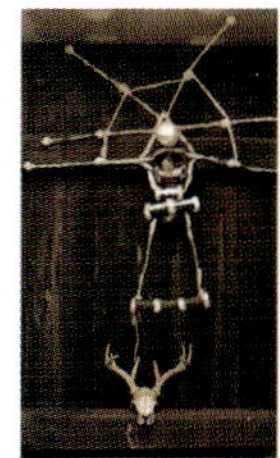
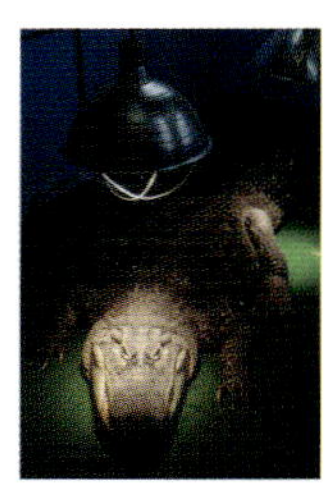

Mask with deer skull, Cherry Hill Farm, Pennsylvania, November 2010; *Wally, the alligator, at Farmers' Market,* Quakertown, Pennsylvania, June 2011

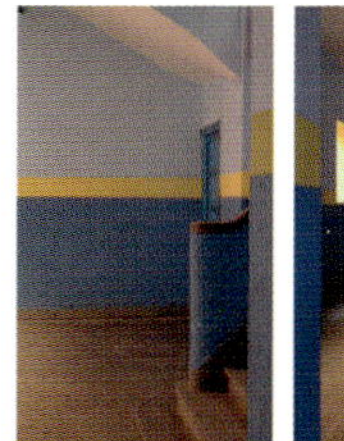
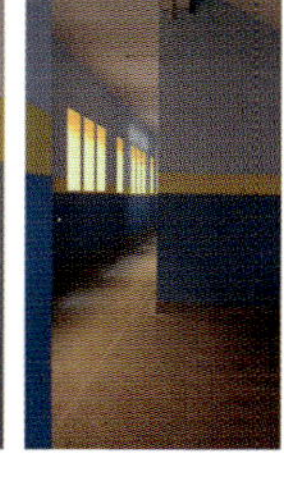

High school hallway, Marrakesh, Morocco, February 2011

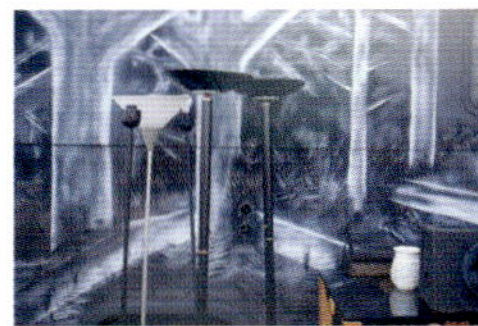
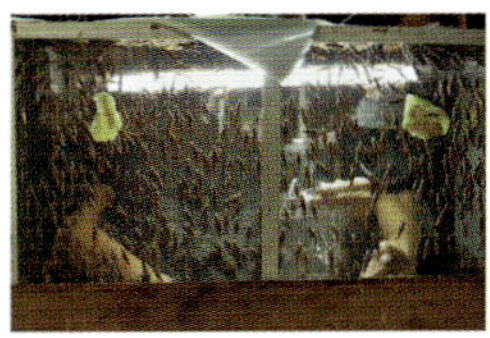

Flea market lamps and painted recreational vehicle, Quakertown, Pennsylvania, September 2011; *Harvesting crickets at bird market,* Hong Kong, China, October 2011

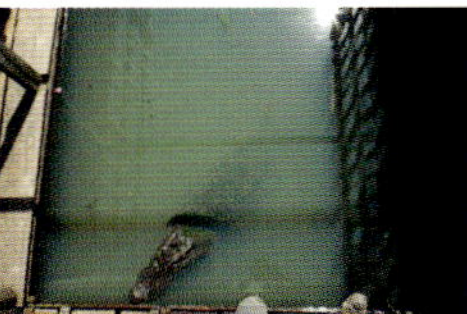
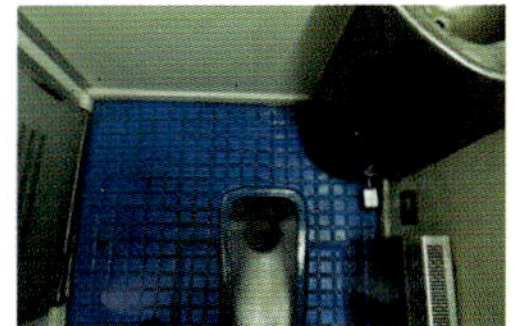

Crocodile pit at floating village, Tonlé Sap Lake, Cambodia, October 2011; *Toilet on Chinese train,* en route to Xi'an, China, October 2011

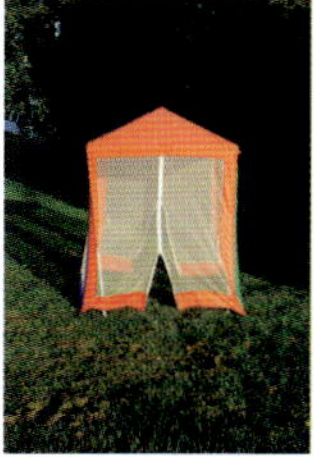
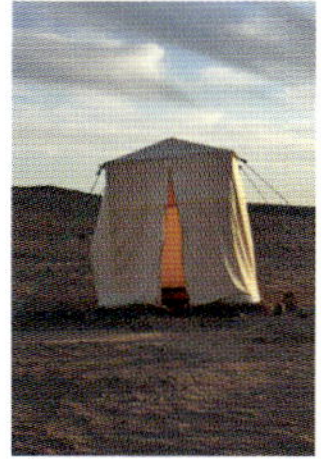

Tent at Cherry Hill Farm, Pennsylvania, September 2009; *Tent in desert,* Merzouga, Morocco, February 2011

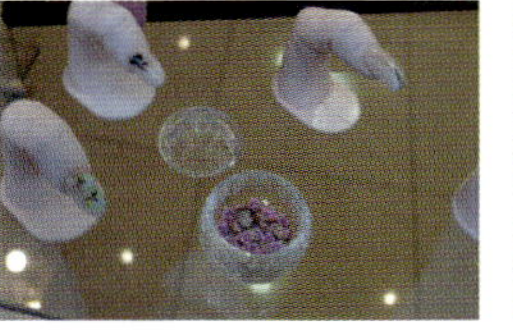
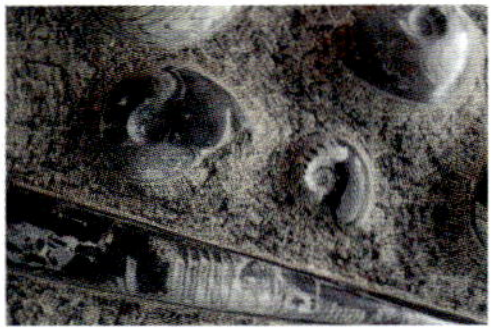

Window display of manicures, Paris, France, September 2010; *Wall of fossils,* Ouarzazate, Morocco, February 2011

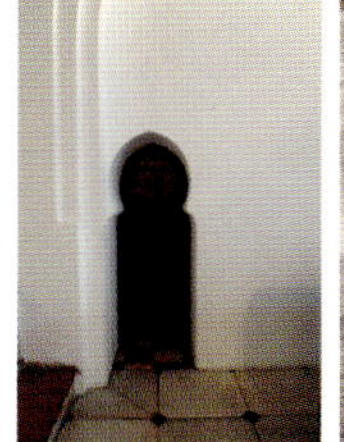
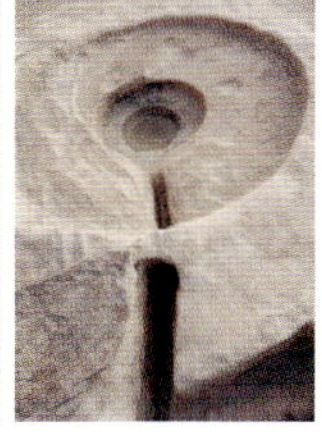

Entrance to apse, English Church, Tangier, Morocco, February 2011; *Sacrificial font,* Petra, Jordan, February 2011

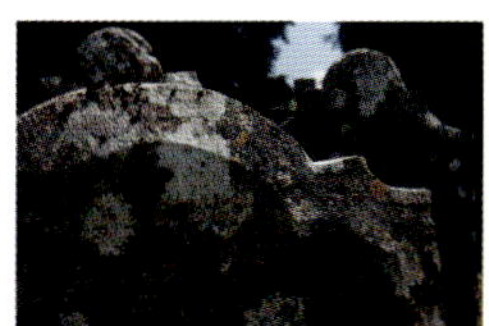
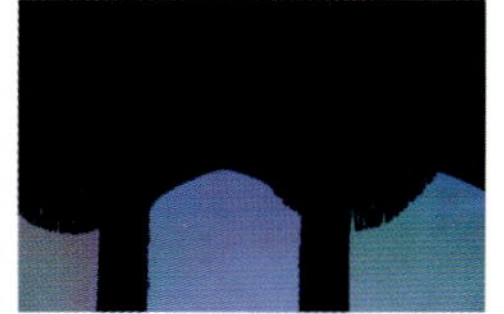

Tombstones, Conna, County Cork, Ireland, June 2013; *Curtains,* Lismore Castle, Lismore, Ireland, June 2013

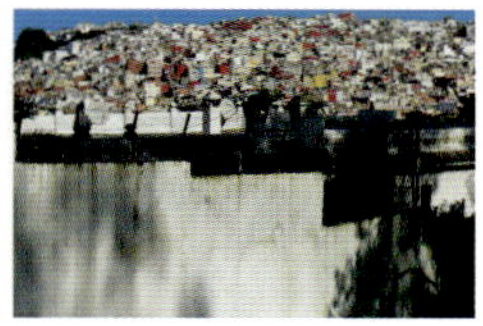

Electrical repair box with snow, New York, New York, December 2010; *View of Tangier with fortress wall,* Tangier, Morocco, February 2011

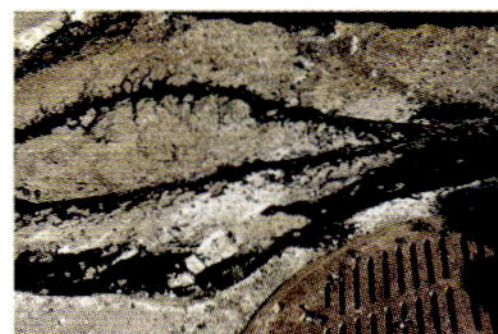
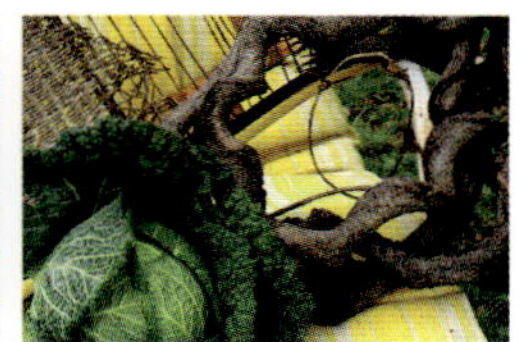

Street paving, Soho, New York, March 2012; *Vines with cabbage,* Cherry Hill Farm, April 2012

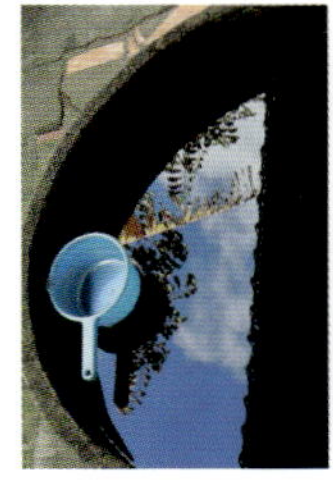
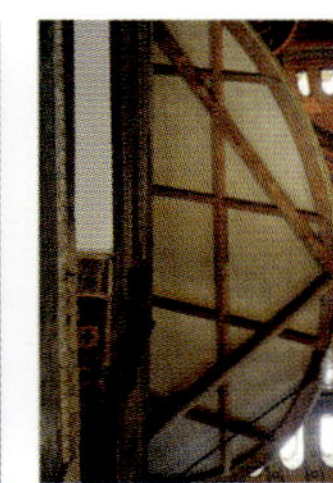

Cup on well, Tibet, China, October 2011; *Hagia Sophia,* Istanbul, Turkey, October 2012

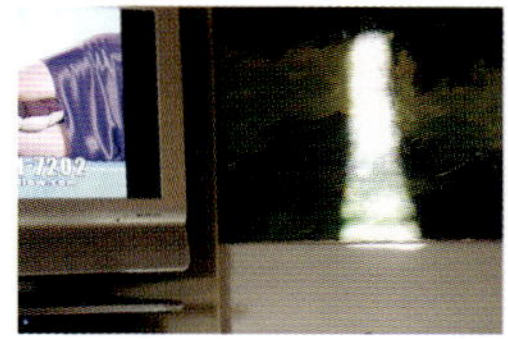
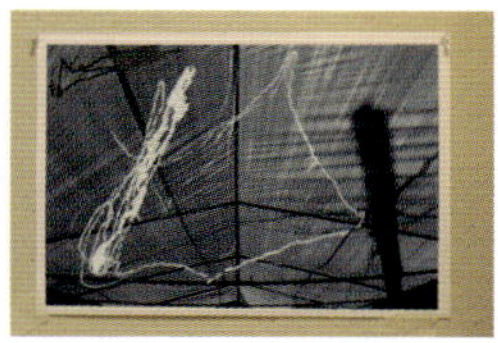

TV screen with sunspot on painting by Stephen Posen, Cherry Hill Farm, Pennsylvania, March 2011; *Photo of artwork by Stephen Posen,* September 2010

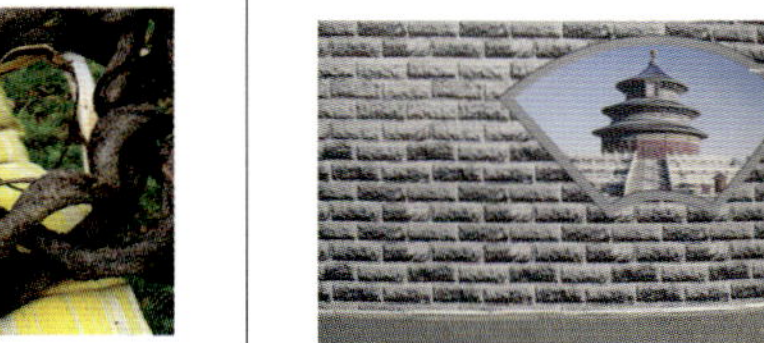
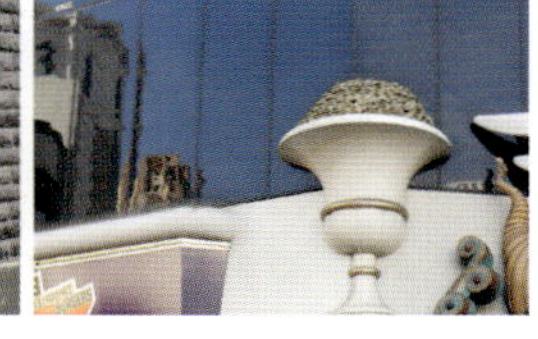

Trompe l'oeil wall, Beijing, China, October 2011; *Decorative cornice,* Las Vegas, Nevada, January 2012

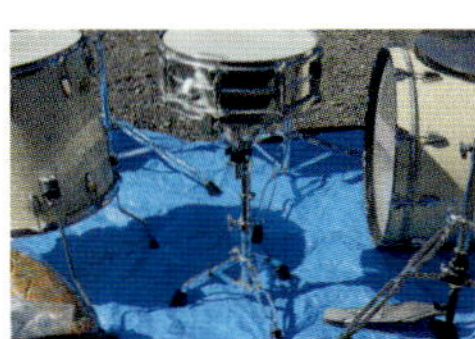
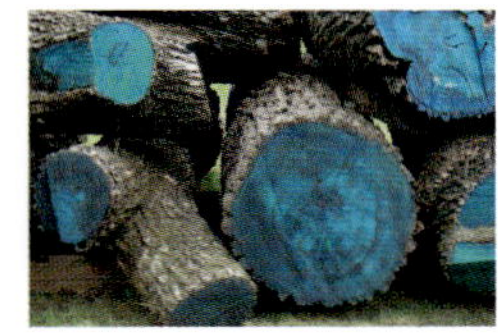

Drum set at flea market, Quakertown, Pennsylvania, May 2013; *Logs,* Riegelsville, Pennsylvania, July 2013

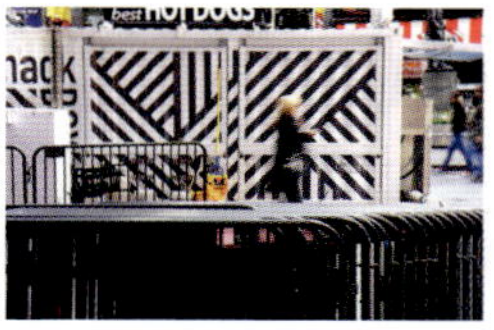
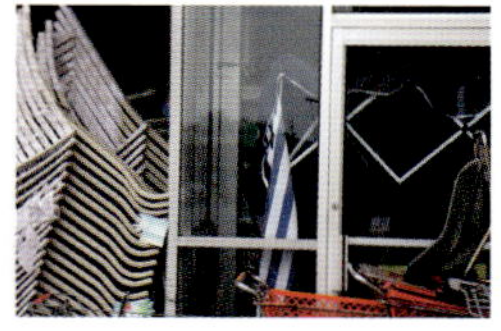

Food stand, Times Square, New York, March 2013; *Stacked chairs at mall,* Quakertown, Pennsylvania, March 2012

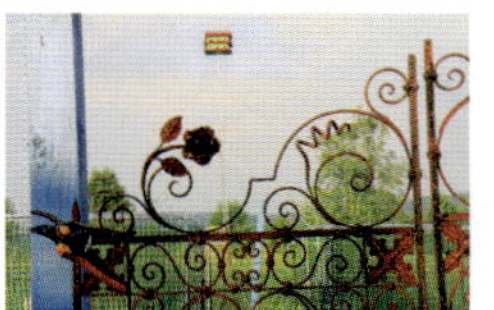
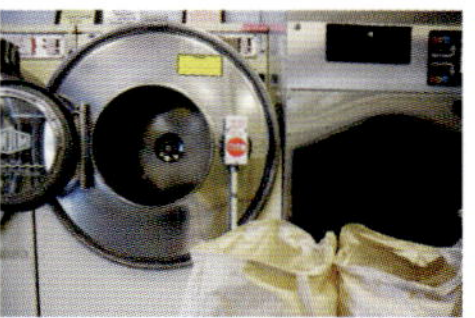

Garden gate at Cherry Hill Farm, Pennsylvania, June 2012; *Launderette,* Coopersburg, Pennsylvania, July 2012

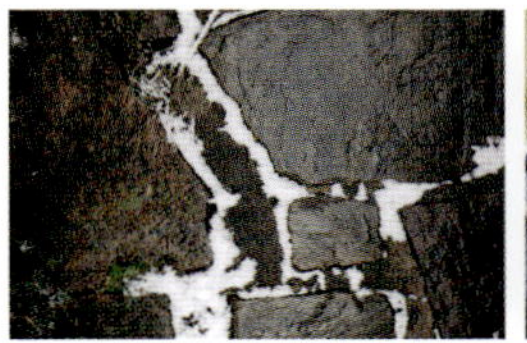
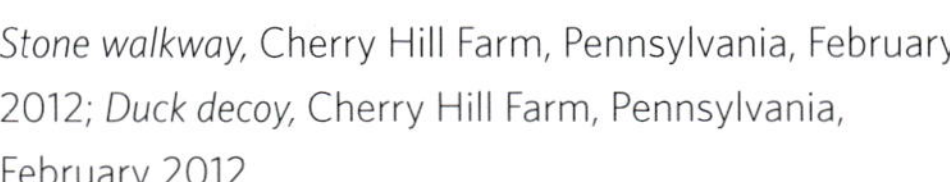

Stone walkway, Cherry Hill Farm, Pennsylvania, February 2012; *Duck decoy,* Cherry Hill Farm, Pennsylvania, February 2012

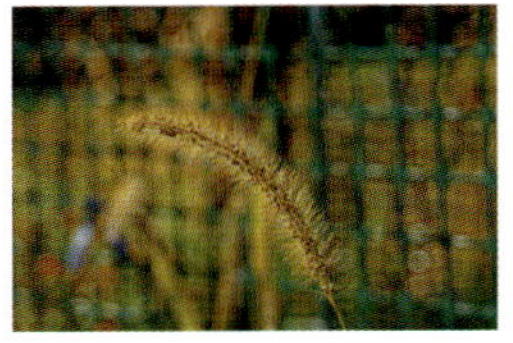
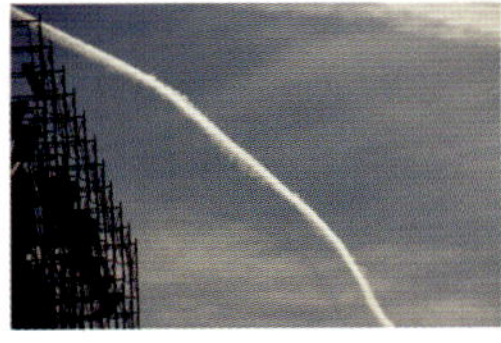

Weed, Cherry Hill Farm, Pennsylvania, Autumn 2012; *Skywriting over Soho,* New York, New York, March 2014

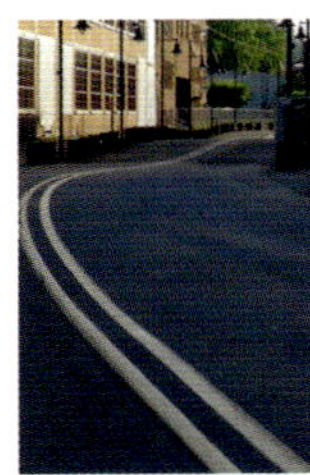
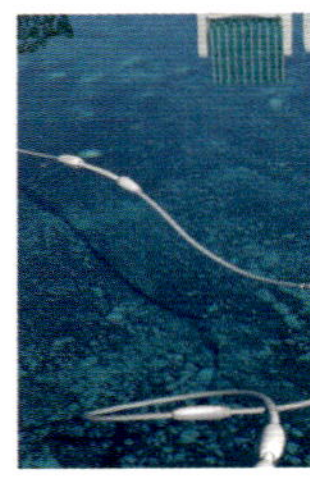

Road through Bethlehem Steel yards, Pennsylvania, July 2011; *Swimming pool hose,* Cherry Hill Farm, Pennsylvania, July 2011

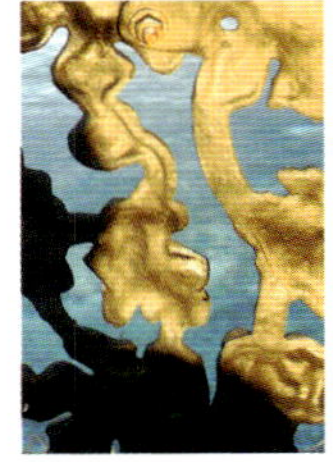
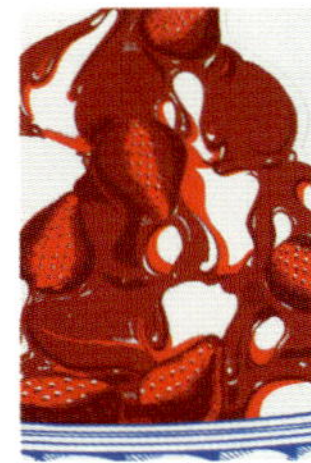

Garden bench at sunset, Cherry Hill Farm, Pennsylvania, September 2011; *Advertisement on ice cream truck,* New York, New York, April 2012

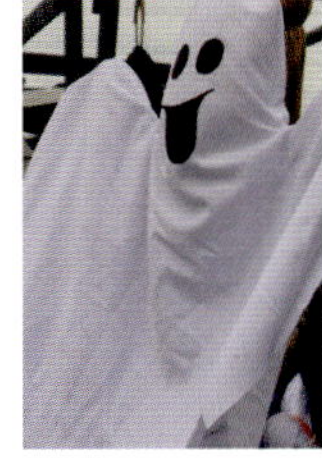
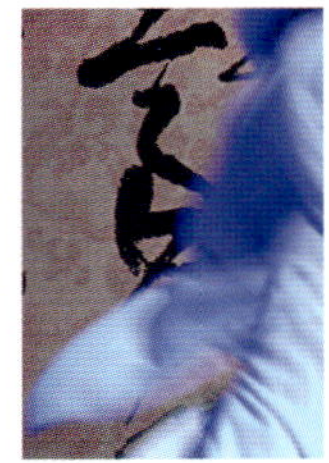

Halloween costume at flea market, Quakertown, Pennsylvania, September 2011; *Calligraphy behind dancer,* Chengdu, China, October 2011

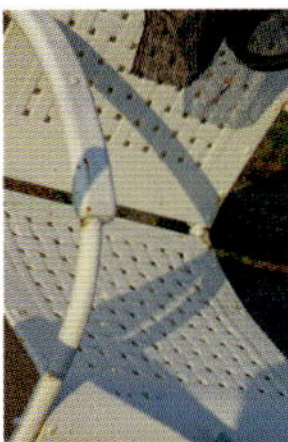
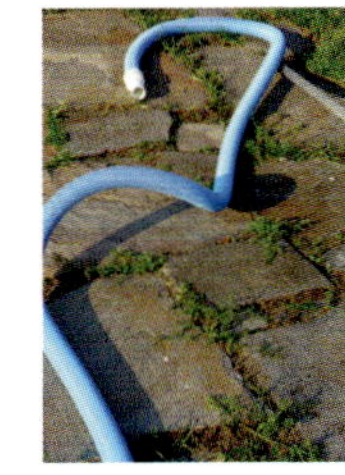

Chair; vacuum hose, both at Cherry Hill Farm, Pennsylvania, June 2012

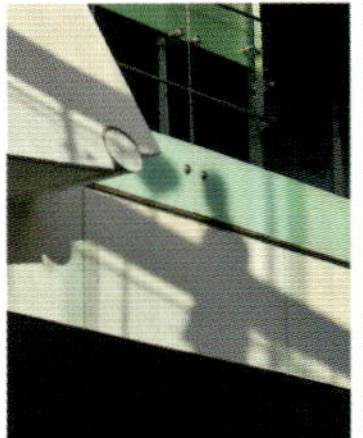
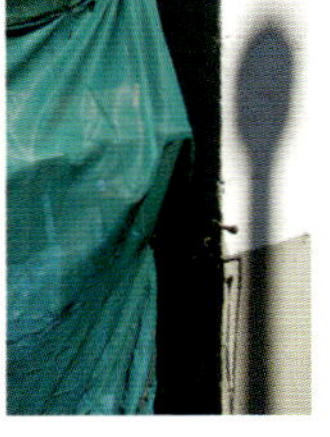

Hayden Planetarium, New York, New York, April 2011; *Scaffolding,* New York, New York, March 2011

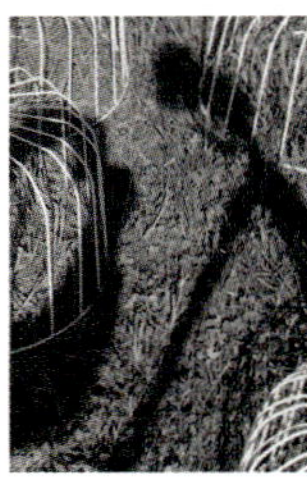
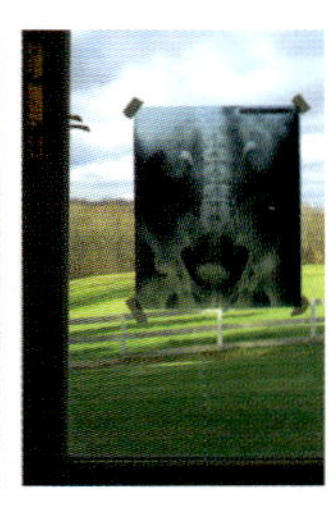

Asparagus patch at Cherry Hill Farm, Pennsylvania, October 2012; *X-ray on door at Cherry Hill Farm,* Pennsylvania, October 2010

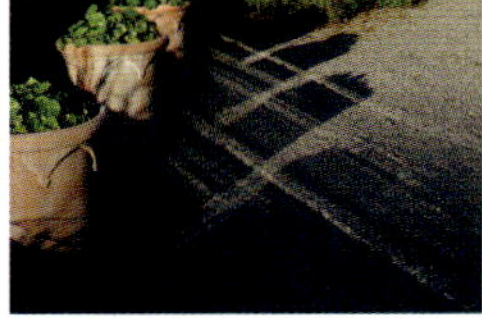
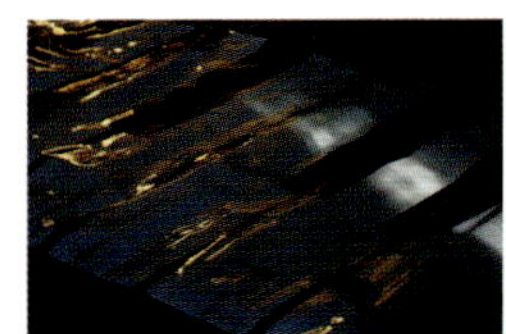

Garden shadows, Lismore Castle, Lismore, June 2013; *Toy keyboard,* Cherry Hill Farm, Pennsylvania, December 2013

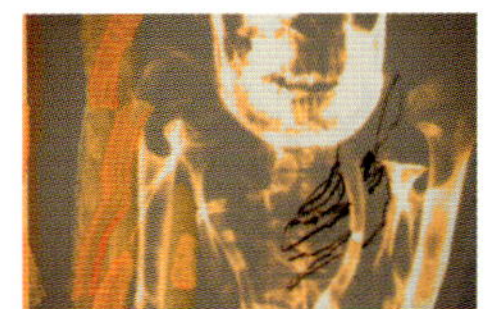

Spot, Soho, New York, February 2013; *Studio drawing on inkjet,* New York, New York, February 2013

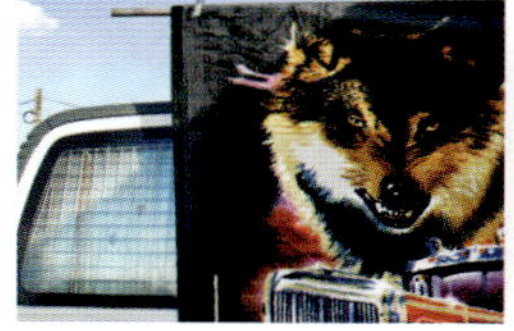
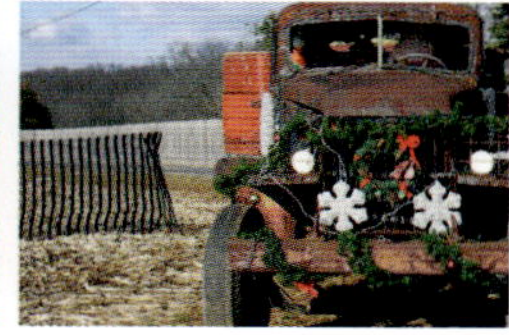

Hanging blanket at flea market, Quakertown, Pennsylvania, August 2011; *Truck in cornfield,* Richlandtown, Pennsylvania, December 2011

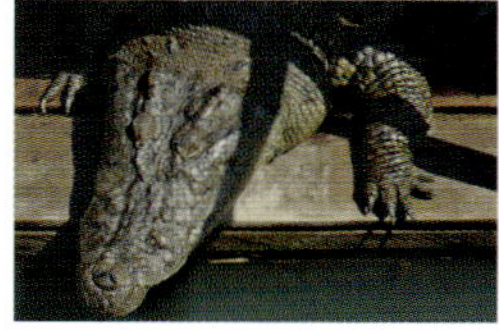
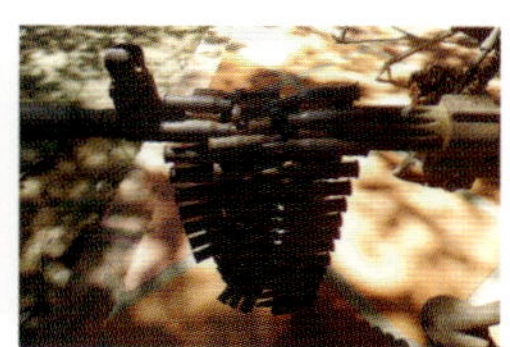

Crocodile pit, Tonlé Sap Lake, Cambodia, October 2011; *Machine gun at War Museum,* Siem Reap, Cambodia, October 2011

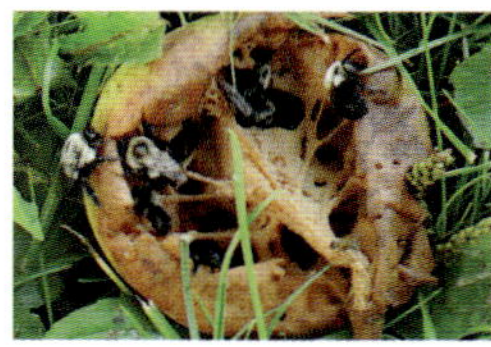
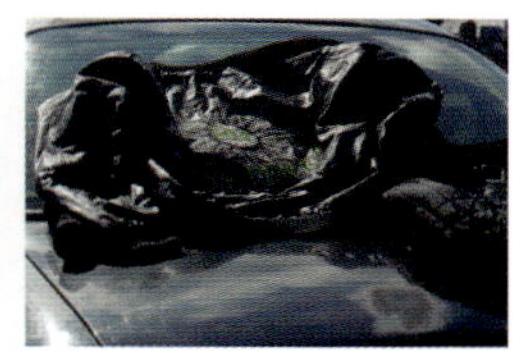

Bees eating pear, Cherry Hill Farm, Pennsylvania, August 2011; *Leather jacket on car at flea market,* Quakertown, Pennsylvania, August 2011

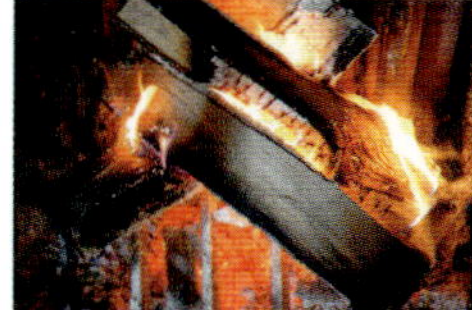
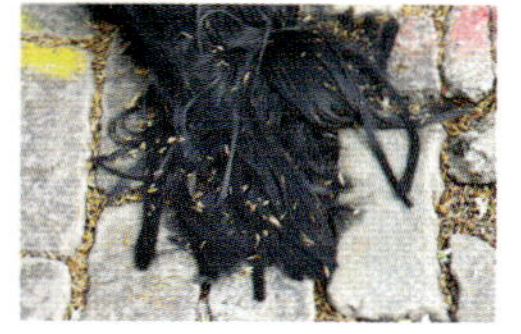

Burning logs at Cherry Hill Farm, Pennsylvania, March 2012; *Lost wig on street,* New York, New York, March 2012

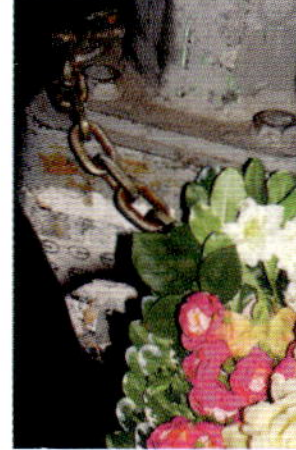

Discarded flowers, New York, New York, April 2013; *Garden fence,* Cherry Hill Farm, Pennsylvania, August 2012

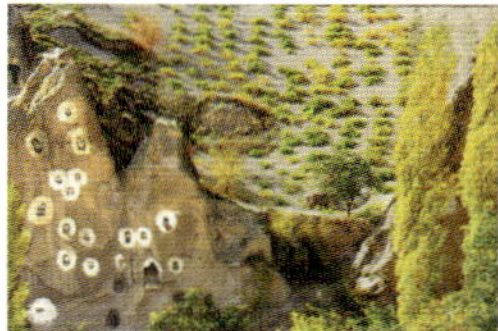
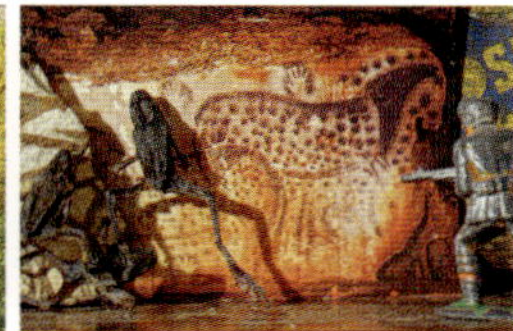

Landscape with white pigeon cotes, Cappadocia, Turkey, October 2012; *Still life, lead soldier, dried frogs and postcard,* Pech Merle, France, December 2012

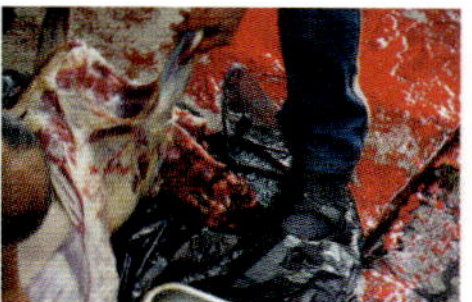
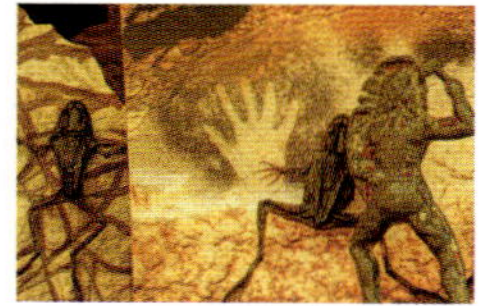

Feast of the Sacrifice, Kars, Turkey, October 2012; *Lead soldier, dried frog and postcard,* Pech Merle, France, September 2012

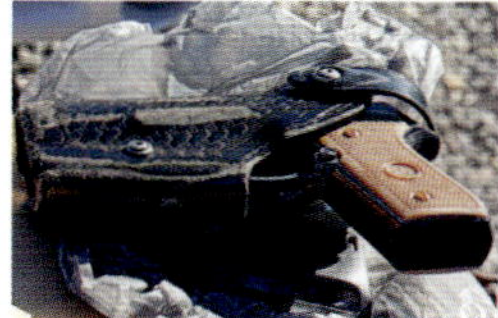
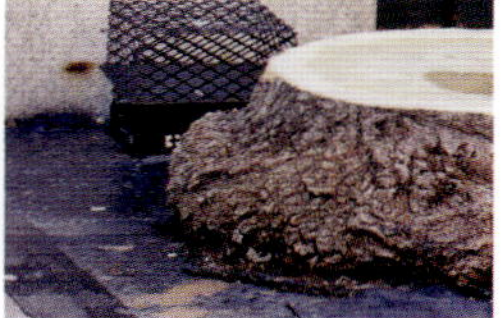

Pistol for sale at flea market, Quakertown, Pennsylvania, March 2013; *Tree stump,* Soho, New York, New York, February 2013

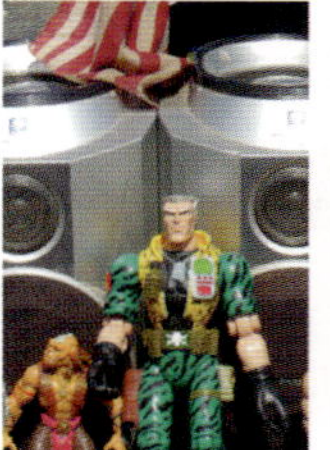
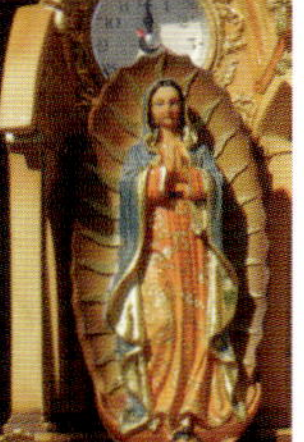

Hero figures with stereo and flag at flea market, Quakertown, Pennsylvania, July 2011; *Madonna figure with clock at flea market,* Quakertown, Pennsylvania, July 2011

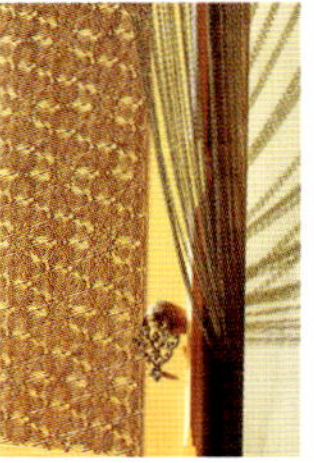
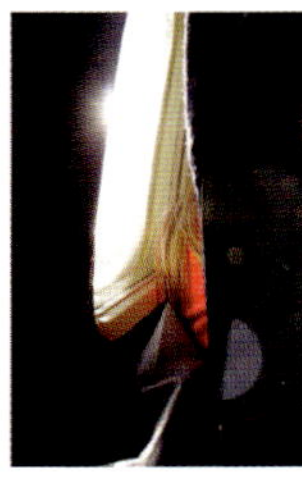

Mosque door with curtain, Adana, Turkey, November 2012; *Airplane window,* Atlantic Ocean, June 2013

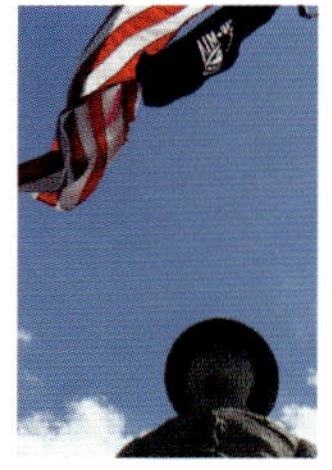
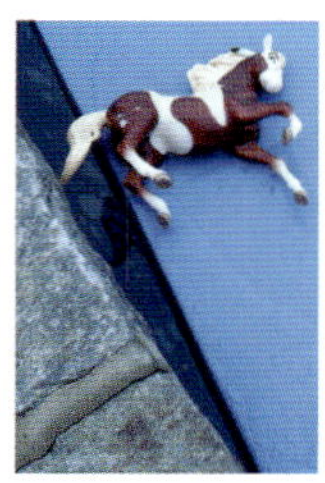

War monument at Memorial Park in Quakertown, Pennsylvania, May 2011; *Toy horse on pool float,* Cherry Hill Farm, Pennsylvania, June 2011

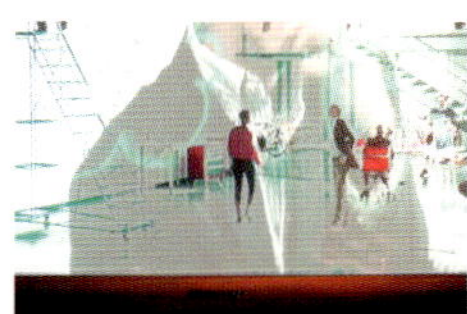
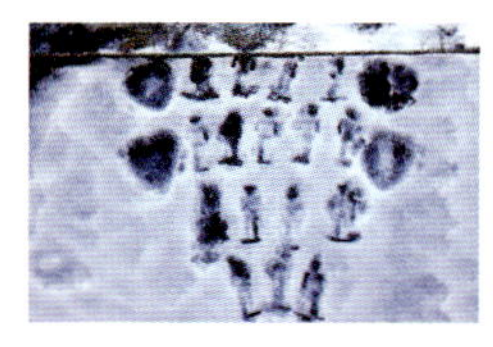

Transitioning TV image, New York, New York, January 2013; *Traces of lead soldiers removed from snow,* Cherry Hill Farm, Pennsylvania, January 2013

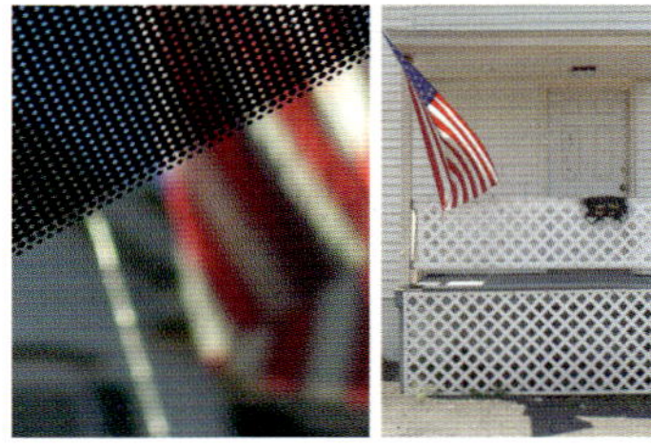

Post office flag from inside automobile, Springtown, Pennsylvania, December 2010; *Rear street apartment,* Quakertown, Pennsylvania, July 2010

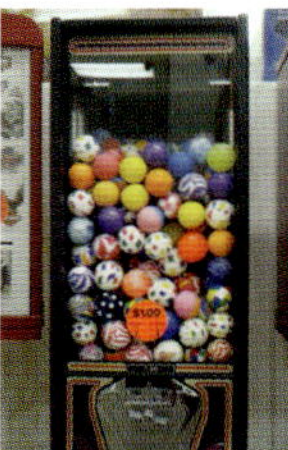
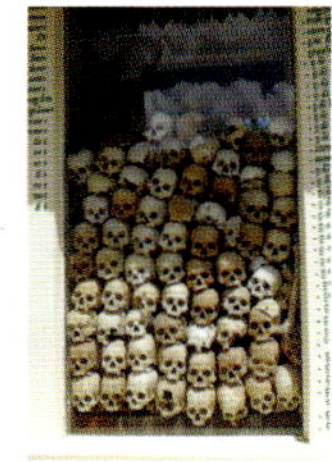

Gumball vending machine, Quakertown Farmers' Market, Pennsylvania, November 2011; *Memorial at Killing Fields,* Siem Reap, Cambodia, October 2011

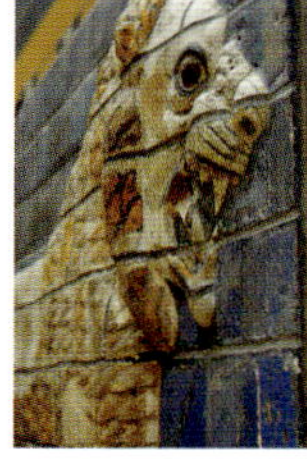
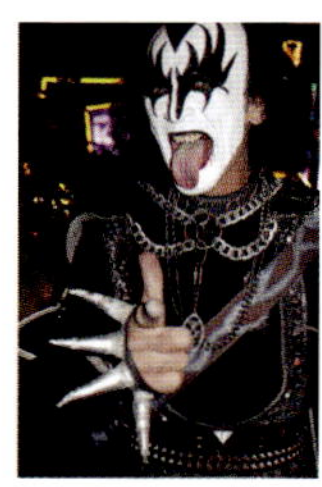

Ishtar Gate, Archeological Museum, Istanbul, Turkey, November 2012; *Kiss impersonator,* Las Vegas, Nevada, January 2012

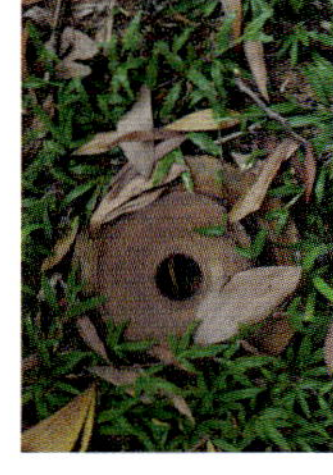
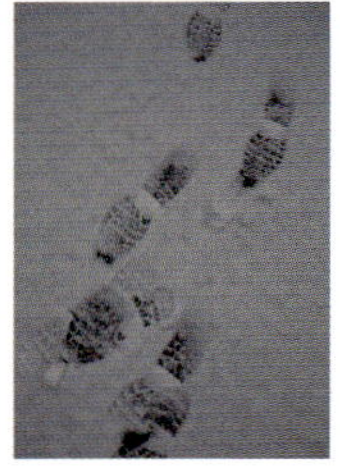

Disarmed land mine near Siem Reap, Cambodia, October 2011; *Snow footprints,* Cherry Hill Farm, Pennsylvania, February 2012

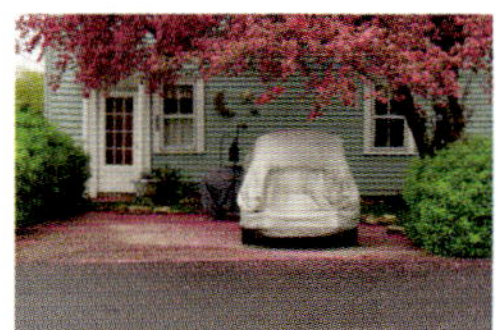
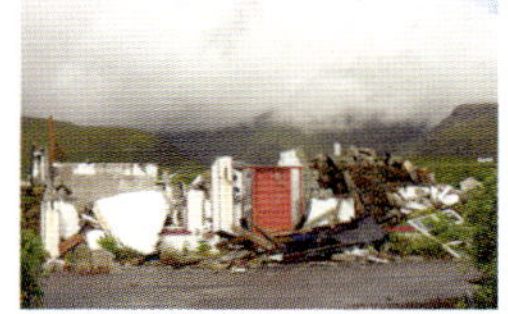

Springtime, Riegelsville, Pennsylvania, May 2013; *Destroyed House,* Dingle, Ireland, June 2013

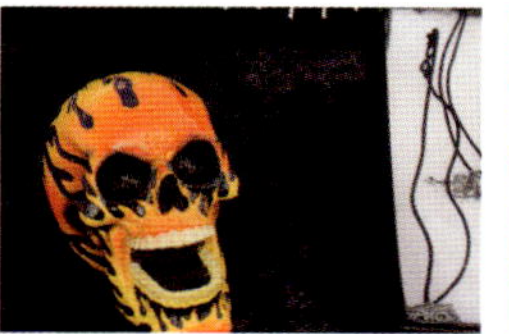
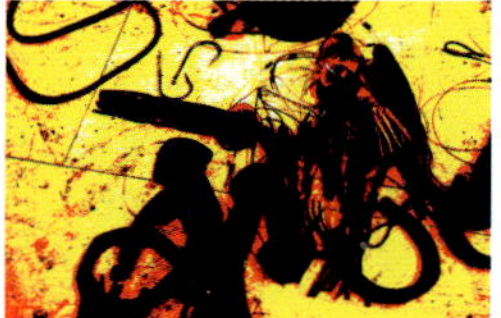

Amulet, Flea Market, Quakertown, Pennsylvania, April 2012; *Studio still life,* Cherry Hill Farm, Pennsylvania, March 2012

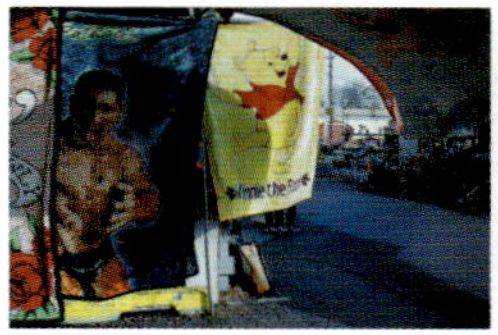

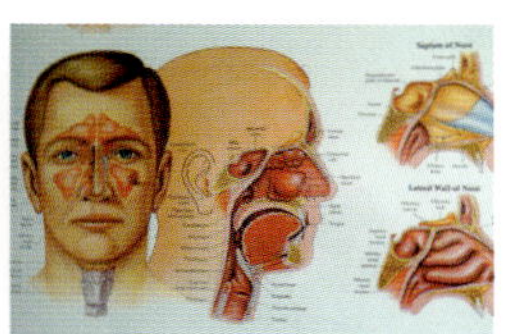

Blankets at Farmers' Market, Quakertown, Pennsylvania, January 2012; *Doctor's office chart*, New York, New York, January 2012

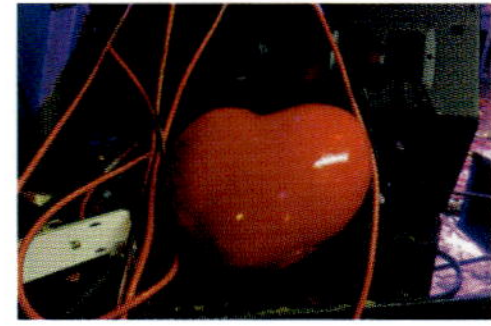

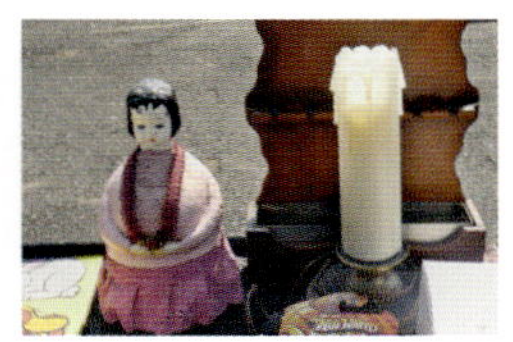

Bandstand heart, Soho club, New York, New York, December 2009; *Pin cushion and candle at flea market*, Quakertown, Pennsylvania, August 2011

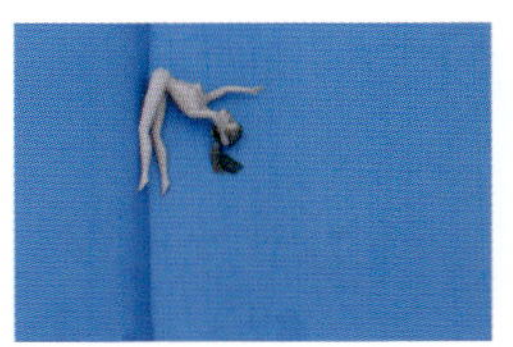

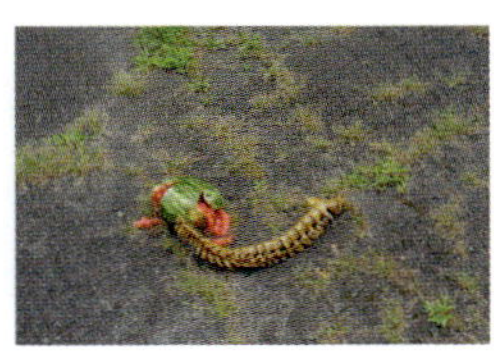

Barbie on pool float, Cherry Hill Farm, Pennsylvania, June 2011; *Human spine with smashed watermelon*, Cherry Hill Farm, Pennsylvania, August 2011

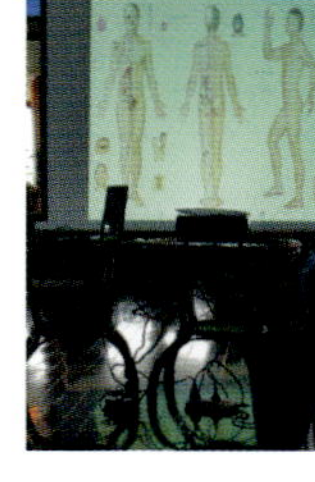

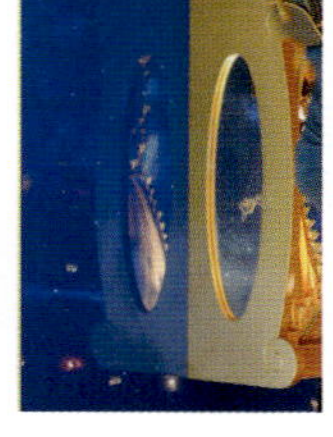

Slide lecture on ship, Yangtze River, China, October 2011; *Disney Store at Hong Kong Airport*, China, October 2011

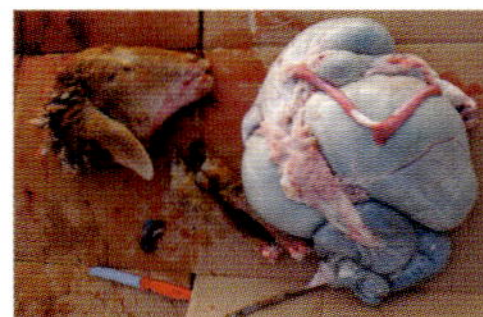

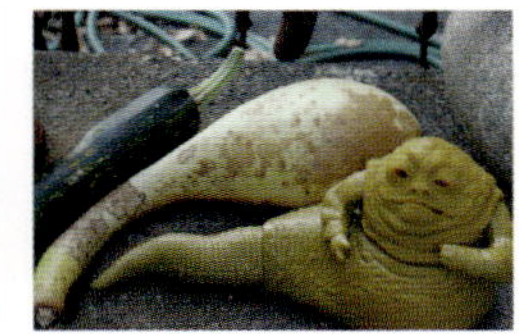

Halal preparation, Merzouga, Morocco, February 2011; *Gourds with Jabba the Hutt*, Cherry Hill Farm, Pennsylvania, September 2010

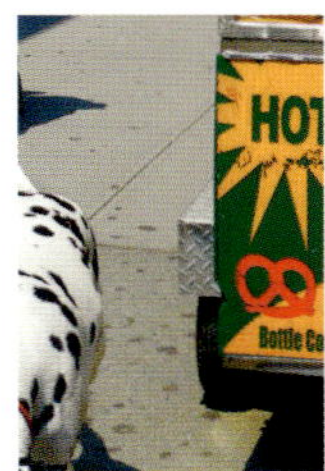

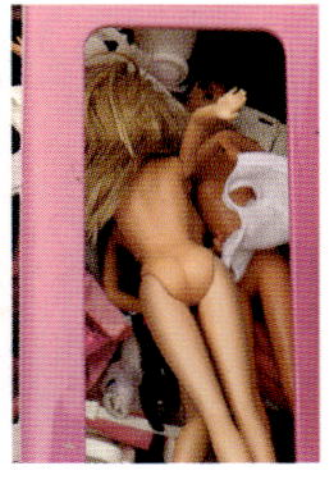

Sidewalk with Dalmatian, New York, New York, May 2011; *Barbie in telephone booth*, Cherry Hill Farm, Pennsylvania, June 2011

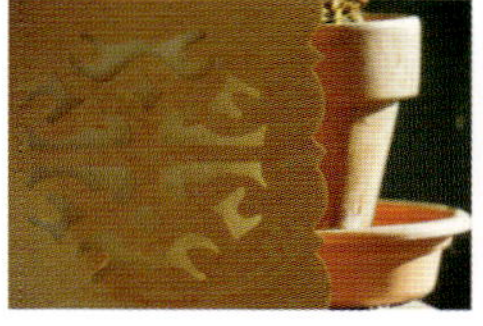

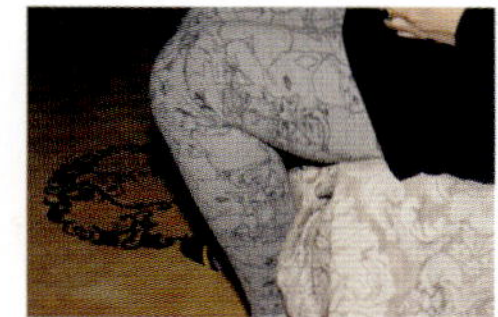

Flowerpots, Cherry Hill Farm, Pennsylvania, May 2013; *Leggings*, Cherry Hill Farm, Pennsylvania, November 2013

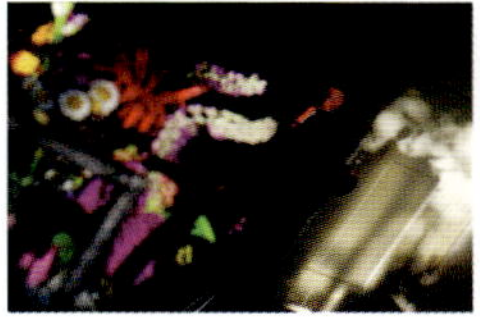

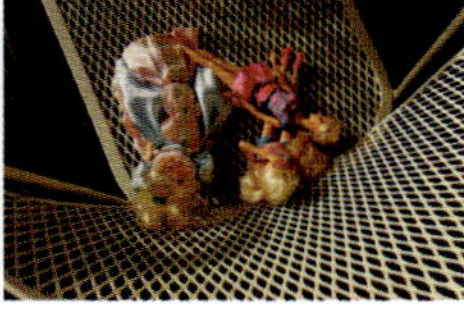

Summer flowers, Cherry Hill Farm, Pennsylvania, June 2012; *Barbies*, Cherry Hill Farm, Pennsylvania, September 2012

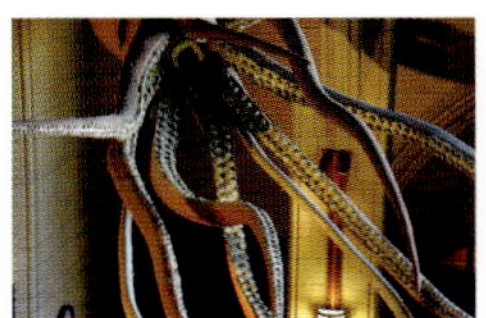

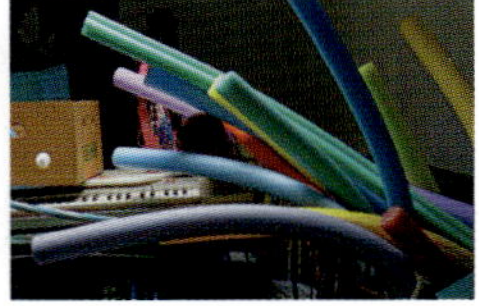

Giant squid, Peabody Museum, New Haven, Connecticut, May 2012; *Pool floats*, Cherry Hill Farm, Pennsylvania, June 2012

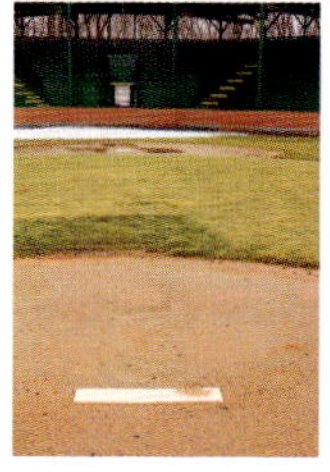 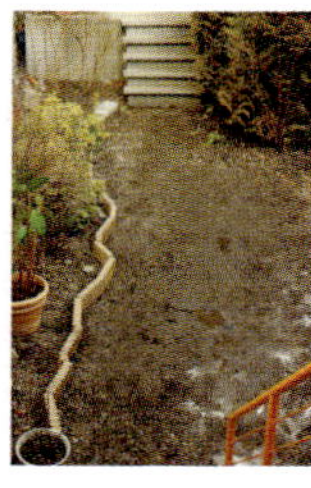

Pitcher's mound, Quakertown Memorial Park, Pennsylvania, February 2013; *Backyard, Red Hook,* Brooklyn, March 2013

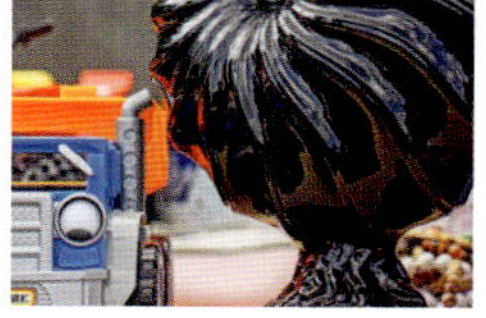 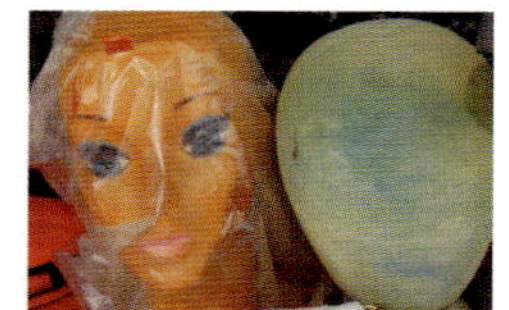

Flea market objects, both Quakertown, Pennsylvania, August 2012

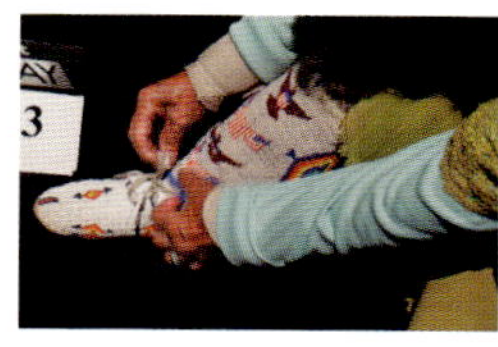 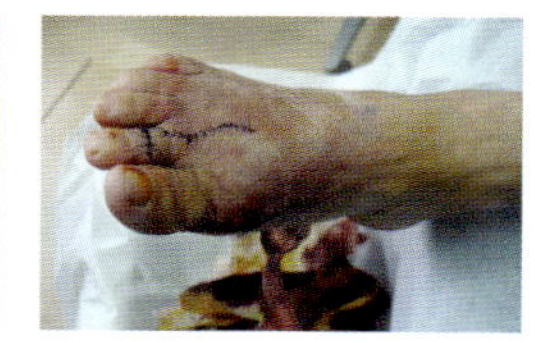

Native American beadwork, Lincoln Center, New York, New York, February 2013; *Post-surgery foot,* New York, New York, February 2013

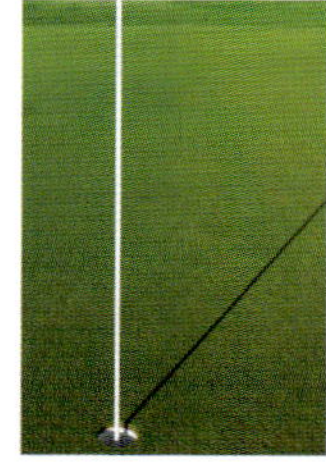 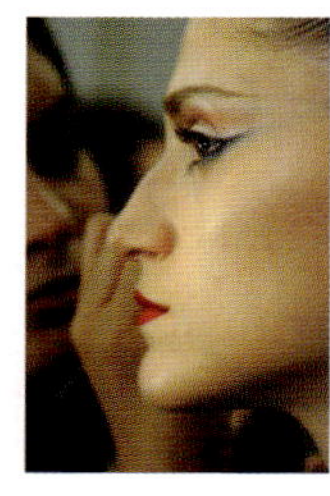

Putting green, Palm Springs, California, January 2012; *Daiane,* New York Fashion Week, New York, New York February 2012

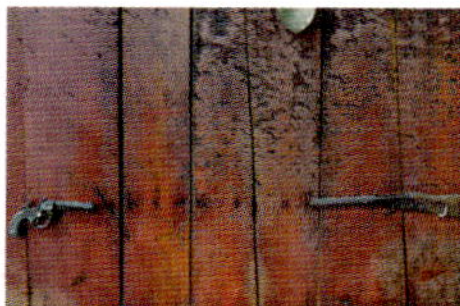 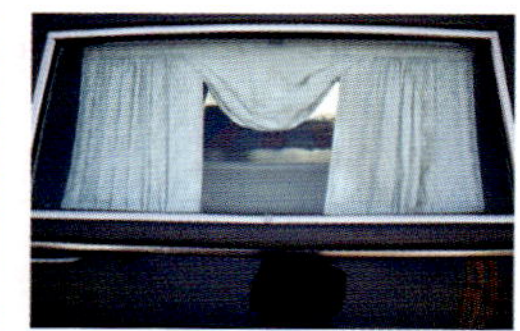

Toy guns on barn wall, Cherry Hill Farm, Pennsylvania, December 2011; *Hearse with flag-draped coffin inside,* Quakertown, Pennsylvania, December 2011

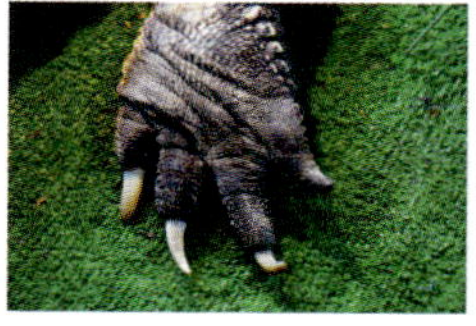

Alligator paw at Farmers' Market, Quakertown, Pennsylvania, June 2012; *Pool toy reflection,* Cherry Hill Farm, Pennsylvania, July 2012

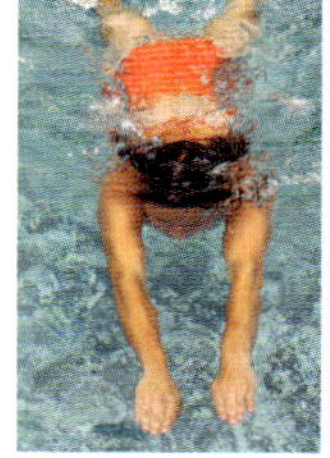 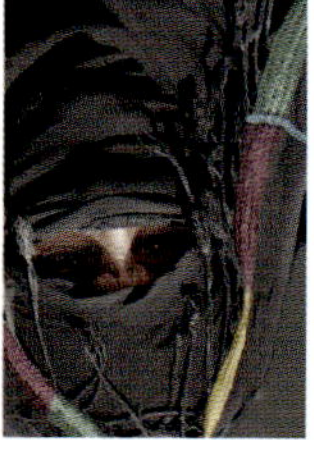

Swimmer, Cherry Hill Farm, Pennsylvania, August 2011; *Bedouin woman,* Merzouga, Morocco, February 2011

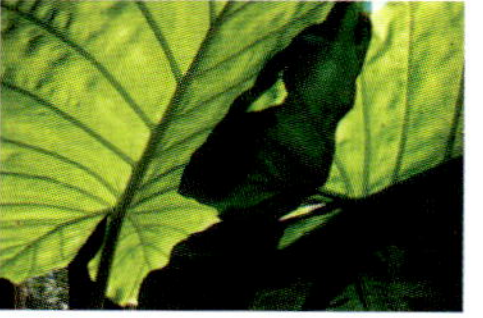 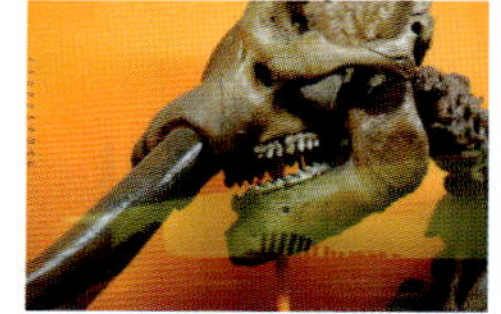

Shadow on Elephant ear plant, Cherry Hill Farm, Pennsylvania, January 2012; *Mastodon skull,* Peabody Museum, New Haven, Connecticut, May 2012

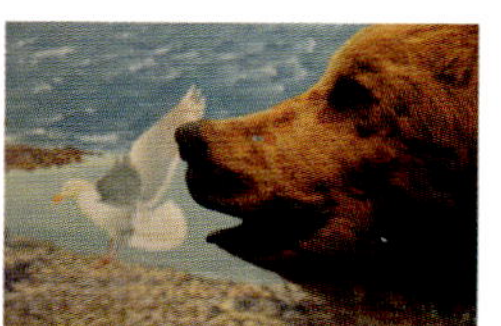 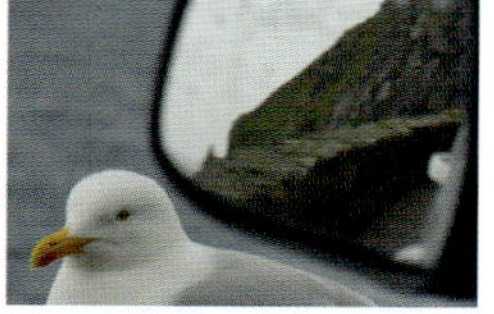

Diorama, Peabody Museum, New Haven, Connecticut, April 2012; *Mirror and gull,* Dingle, Ireland, June 2013

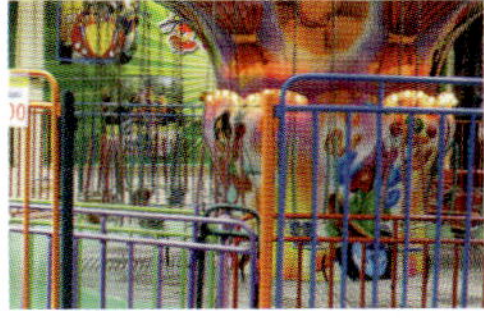
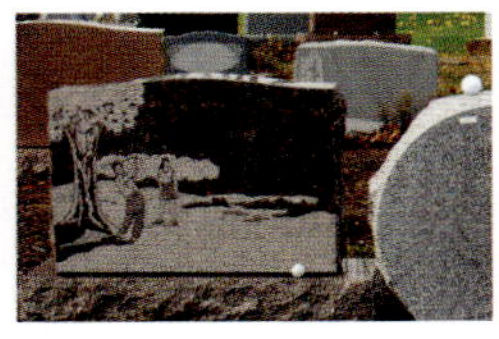

Children's ride, Amman, Jordan, January 2011; *Tombstone showroom yard,* Quakertown, Pennsylvania, November 2010

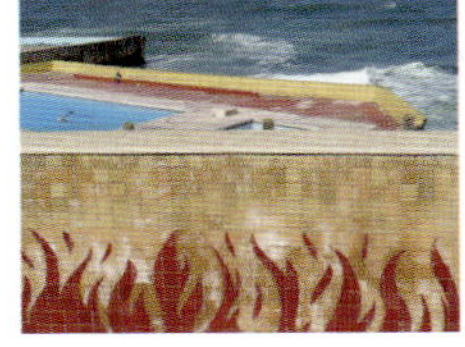
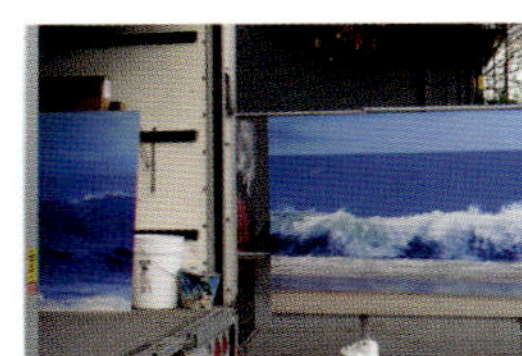

Wall, Casablanca, Morocco, February 2011; *Street vendor with seascape paintings,* New York, New York, December 2010

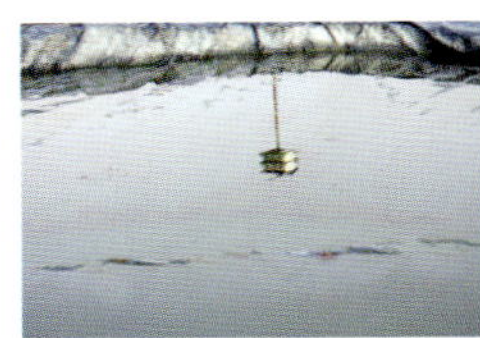
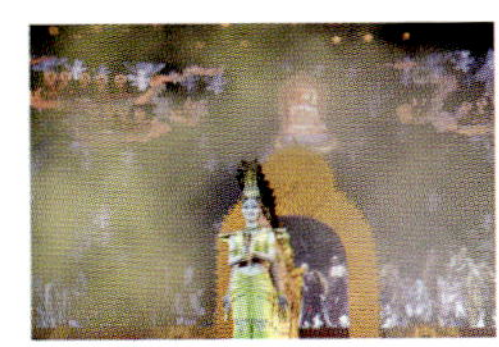

Bird house reflection, Cherry Hill Farm, Pennsylvania, March 2012; *Opera singer,* Beijing, China, October 2011

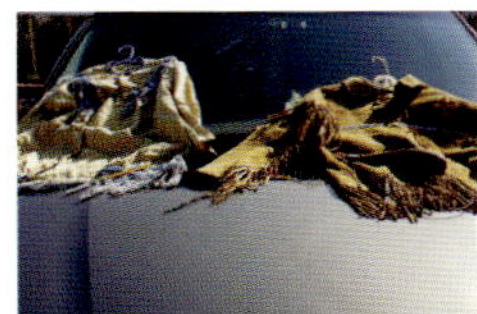
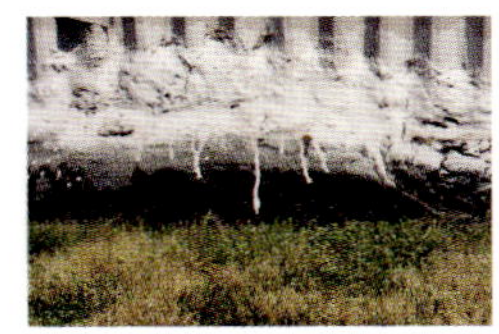

Western artifacts on a hood of car, flea market, Quakertown, Pennsylvania, February 2012; *Wall insulation,* Farmers' Market, Quakertown, Pennsylvania, March 2012

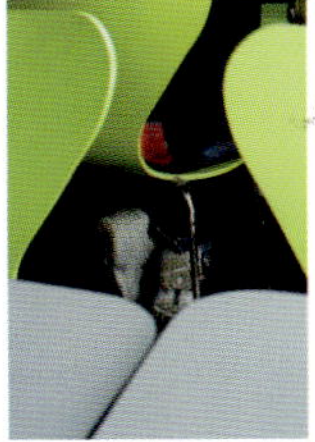

Chairs, Brooklyn Museum, New York, April 2013; *Flea market,* Quakertown, Pennsylvania, May 2013

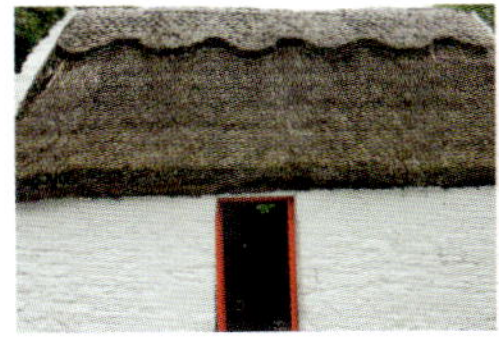
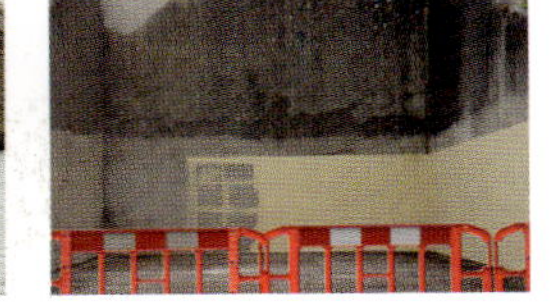

Two house structures, County Cork, Ireland, June 2013

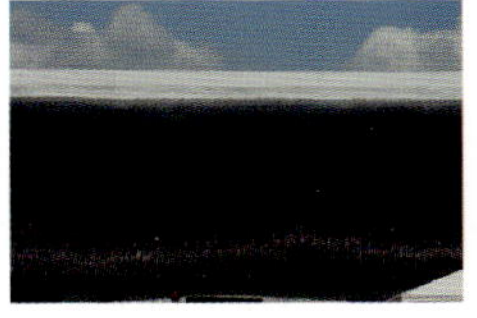
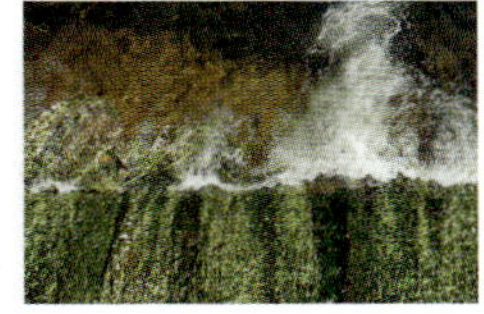

Barn at Russborough House, Russborough, Ireland June 2013; *Waterfall,* Ballynoe, Ireland, June 2013

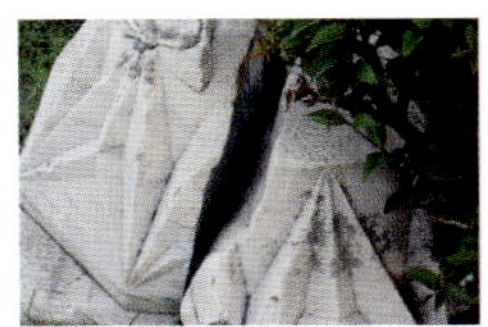
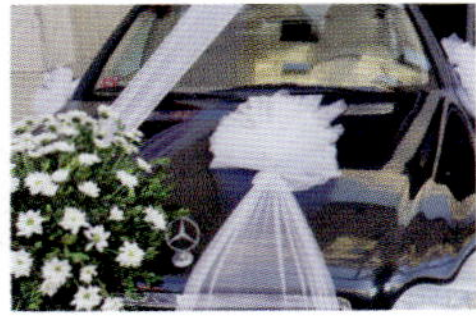

Base of column; wedding car, both Trabzon, Turkey, October 2012

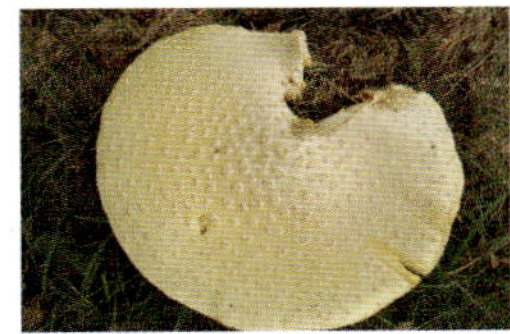
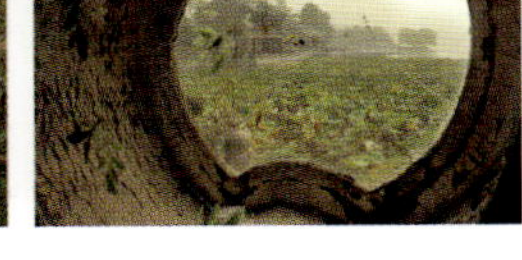

Mushroom, Cherry Hill Farm, Pennsylvania, September 2011; *Window at Summer Palace,* Beijing, October 2011

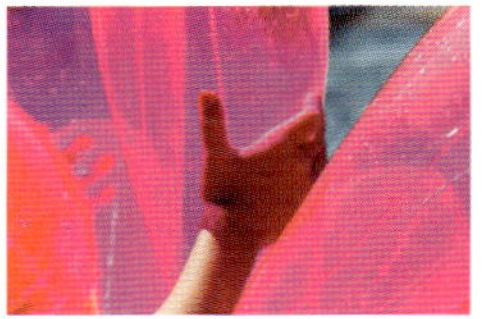
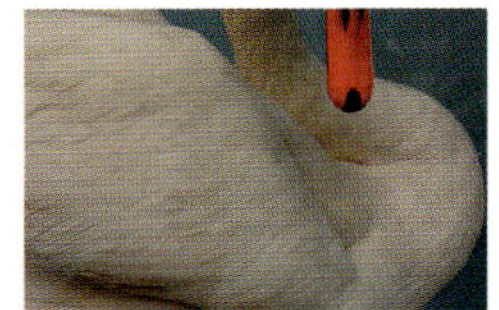

Pool toy, Cherry Hill Farm, Pennsylvania, July 2012; *Swan,* Peabody Museum, New Haven, Connecticut, May 2012

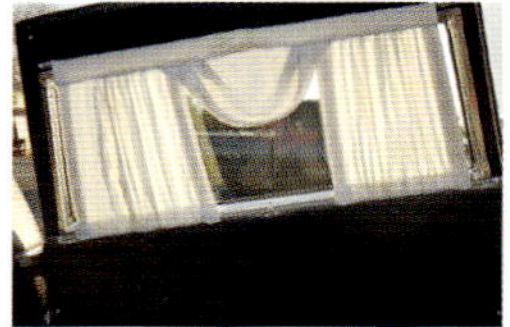
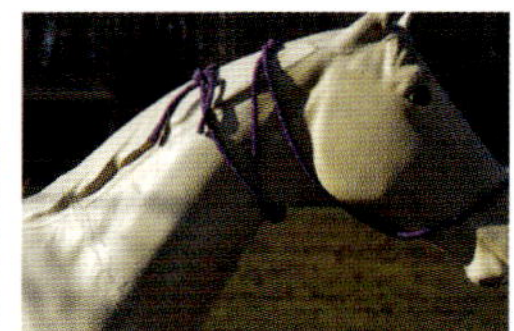

Open hearse door, Quakertown, Pennsylvania, December 2011; *Fiberglass horse,* Coopersburg, Pennsylvania, December 2011

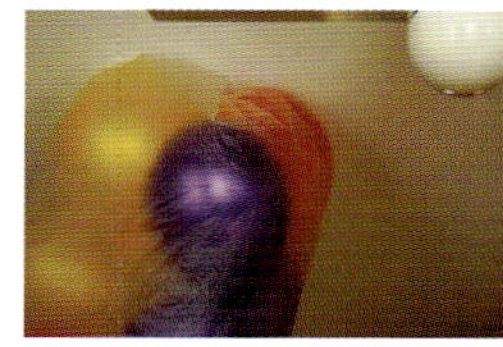
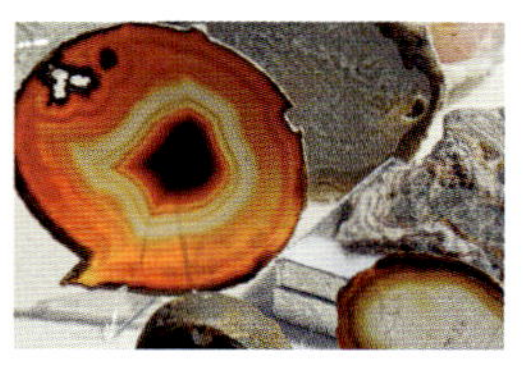

Balloons, Red Hook, Brooklyn, New York, March 2013; *Geode slices,* flea market, Quakertown, Pennsylvania, March 2013

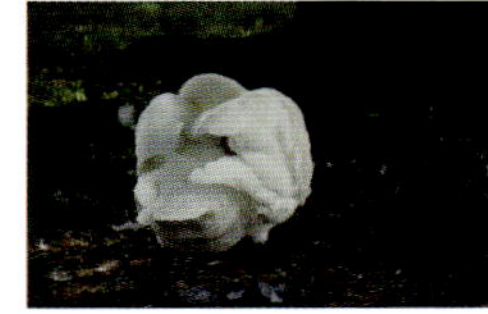
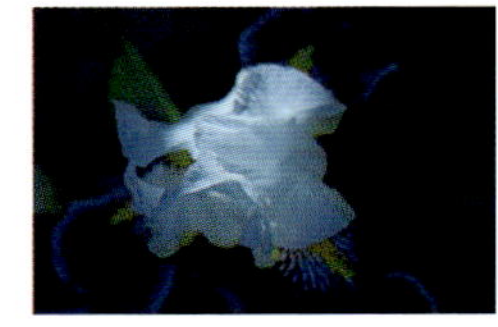

Swan, Trexler Nature Preserve, Trexlertown, Pennsylvania, September 2012; *Iris,* Cherry Hill Farm, May 2012

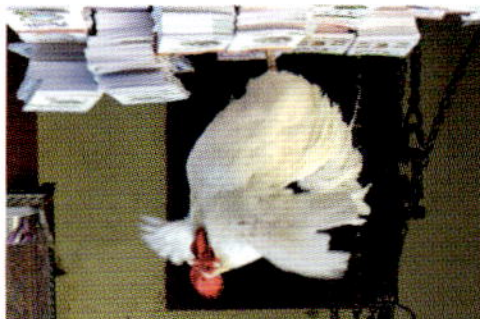
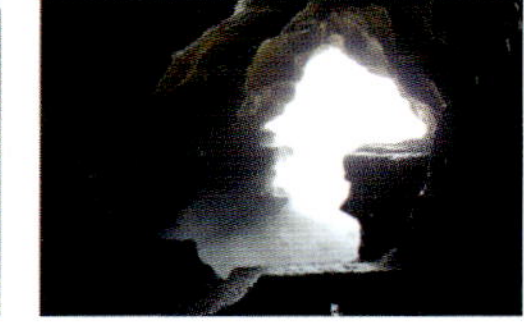

Rooster, Marrakesh, Morocco, February 2011; *Les Grottes d'Hercule,* Tangier, Morocco, February 2011

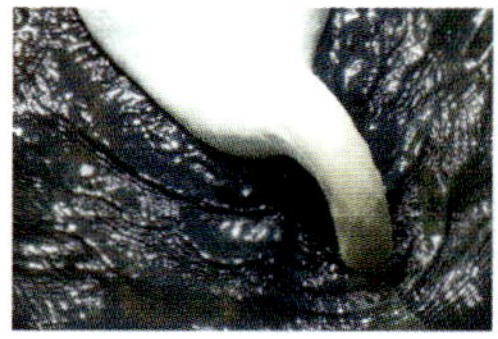
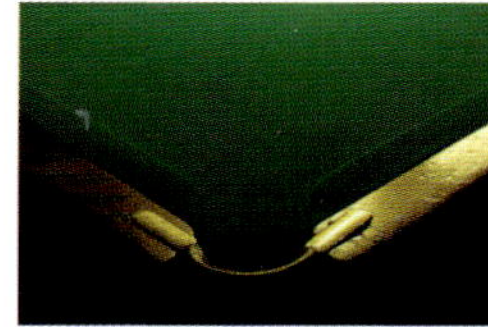

Swan's head, Caher, Ireland, June 2013; *Billiard table at Lismore Castle,* Ireland, June 2013

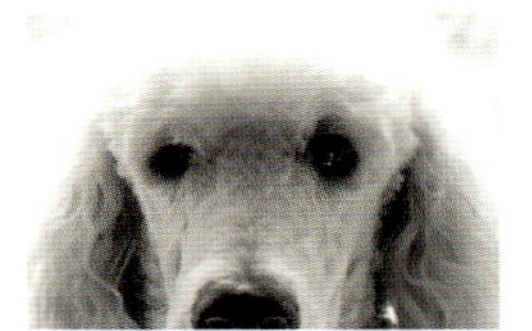
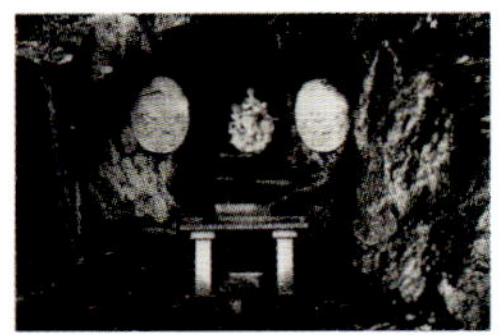

Bozart, New York, New York, January 2014; *Shrine, Stockbridge,* Massachusetts, October 2013

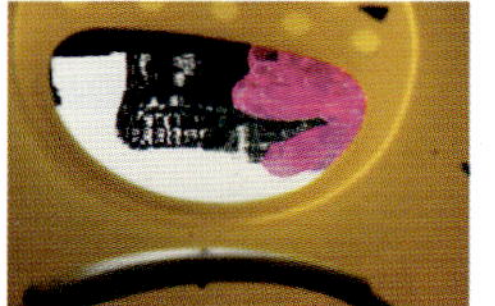
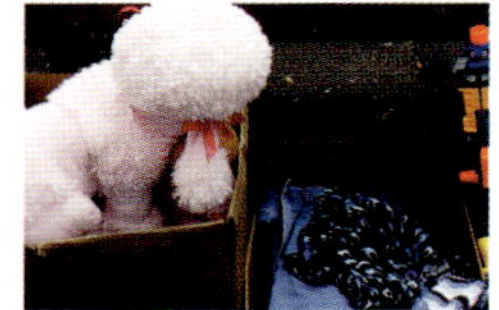

Reflection through pool toy, Cherry Hill Farm, Pennsylvania, July 2012; *Flea market poodle,* Quakertown, Pennsylvania, July 2012

STEPHEN POSEN

Born St. Louis, MO, 1939
Studio in New York City and
Bucks County, Pennsylvania

EDUCATION

Yale University, New Haven, CT,
M.F.A., 1964
Washington University, St. Louis, MO,
B.F.A., 1962

ONE-PERSON EXHIBITIONS

2012 Churner and Churner, New York
2006 The Drawing Center, New York
1990 Jason McCoy Gallery, New York
1986 Jason McCoy Gallery, New York
1978 Robert Miller Gallery, New York
1974 OK Harris Gallery, New York
1971 OK Harris Gallery, New York
1969 OK Harris Gallery, New York
2012 Churner and Churner, New York
2006 The Drawing Center, New York
1990 Jason McCoy Gallery, New York
1986 Jason McCoy Gallery, New York
1978 Robert Miller Gallery, New York
1974 OK Harris Gallery, New York
1971 OK Harris Gallery, New York
1969 OK Harris Gallery, New York

SELECTED GROUP EXHIBITIONS

2013 *Still Life: 1970s Photorealism,* Yale University Art Gallery, New Haven, CT

2009 *Picturing America Photorealism in the 1970s,* Deutsche Guggenheim, Berlin, Germany

2007 *Bloomingdales Collaboration, Zac Posen & Stephen Posen,* Bloomingdales, New York

2004 *American Photorealism,* Iwate Museum of Art. Traveled to: Iwaki City Art Museum, Kumamoto Prefectural Museum of Art, Hakodate Museum of Art, Hokkaido, Japan

2003 *Iperrealisti,* Chiostro Del Bramante, Rome, Italy

1997 *Intimate Universe [Revisited]: Seventy American Painters,* Robert Steele Gallery, New York

1989 *Two Centuries of Creativity,* 80 Washington Square East, New York

1986 *More Than Meets the Eye: The Art of Trompe L'Oeil,* Columbus Museum of Art, Columbus, OH. Traveled to: Norton Gallery and School of Art, West Palm Beach, FL

1985 *American Realism: Twentieth-Century Drawings and Watercolors,* San Francisco Museum of Modern Art. Traveled to: De Cordova and Dana Museum, Lincoln, MA; Archer M. Huntington Art Gallery, Austin, TX; Mary and Leigh Block Art Gallery, Evanston, IL; Williams College Museum of Art, Williamstown, MA, Akron Art Institute, OH, Madison Art Center, WI

1983 *American Super Realism from the Morton G. Neumann Family Collection,* Terra Museum of American Art, Evanston, IL

1981 *Contemporary American Realism since 1960,* Pennsylvania Academy of The Fine Arts. Traveled to: The Virginia Museum and Oakland Museum of Art

1981 *The Image in American Painting and Sculpture: 1950/80,* Akron Art Mueum, OH

1981 *Real, Really Real and Super Real: Directions in Contemporary American Realism,* San Antonio Museum of Art, TX. Traveled to: Indianapolis Museum of Art, Tucson Museum of Art, AZ, Museum of Art, Carnegie Institute, Pittsburgh, PA

1981 *Twenty Artists: Yale School of Art, 1950-70,* Yale University Art Gallery, New Haven, CT

1980 *Realism-Photorealism,* Philbrook Art Center, Tulsa, OK

1979 *Flowers IV,* Everson Museum of Art, Syracuse, NY

1979 *Reality of Illusion,* Denver Art Museum, CO. Traveled to: University Art Galleries, University of Southern California, Los Angeles, Honolulu Academy of Art, Hawaii, Oakland Museum, CA, University Art Museum, University of Texas, Austin, TX, Herbert F. Johnson Museum of Art, Ithaca, NY, Toledo Art Museum

1977 *Eight Contemporary American Realists,* Pennsylvania Academy of The Fine Arts, Philadelphia, PA

1977 *Materei Und Photographie Im Dialog,* Kunsthaus, Zurich, Switzerland

1977 *Illusion and Reality,* Australian National Gallery, Canberra, Australia. Traveled to: Western Australian Art Gallery, Perth, Queensland Art Gallery, Brisbane, Art Gallery of New South Wales, Sydney, Art Gallery of South Australia, Adelaide, National Gallery of Victoria, Melbourne, Tasmanian Museum and Art Gallery, Hobart, Australia

1975 *Trompe L'Oeil,* Taft Museum, Cincinnati, OH

1974 *New Realism Revisited,* New York State University/ Potsdam, Brainard Hall Art Gallery

1974 *Seventy-First American Exhibition,* The Art Institute of Chicago, Chicago, IL

1974 *Tokyo Biennale 1974*, Tokyo, Japan

1974 *New Realism,* The Art Institute of Chicago, Chicago, IL

1974 *Seven Realists,* Yale University Art Gallery, New Haven, CT

1973 *Hyperrealisme,* Galerie Isy Brachot, Brussels, Belgium

1973 *Hyperrealistes Americains,* Galerie Arditti, Paris, France

1973 *The Super-Realist Vision,* DeCordova Museum, Lincoln, MA

1973 *Amerikansk Realism,* Lunds Konsthall, Lund, Sweden

1973 *Art in Evolution,* Xerox Corporation, Rochester, NY

1973 *Realism Now,* New York Cultural Center, New York

1973 *Image Ready, Super-reality,* The Art Council of Great Britain, London

1973 *Realism Now,* Katonah Gallery, Katonah, NY

1972 32 *Realists,* Cleveland Institute of Art, Cleveland, OH
1972 *Documenta 5,* Kassel, Germany
1972 *Whitney Museum Painting Annual,* Whitney Museum, New York
1972 *Sharp Focus Realism,* Sidney Janis Gallery, New York
1972 *Contemporary reflections 1971-1972,* The Aldrich Museum of Contemporary Art, Ridgefield, CT
1971 *Highlights of the 1970-71 Art Season,* The Aldrich Museum, Ridgefield, CT
1971 *Radical Realism,* Contemporary Art Museum, Chicago, IL
1971 *New Realism,* State University College At Potsdam, NY
1969 *The Inflated Image,* Museum of Modern Art, New York

BOOKS AND CATALOGUES

ASHTON Dore, Stephen Posen Dancer/Mirror The Drawing Center's Drawing Papers 62, (cat) The Drawing Center, NY, 2006
ASHTON Dore, RUBINSTEIN Raphael, *Stephen Posen Drawings 2003-2005,* New York, Pragati, 2006
American Photorealism, (cat) Iwate Museum of Art, The Hokkaido Shimburn Press, Hokkaido, 2004
MERCURIO Gianni, *Iperrealisti,* (cat) Chiostro del Bramante, Viviani Arte, Rome, 2003
SEDOFSKY Lauren, *Stephen Posen. New Paintings,* (cat) Jason McCoy Gallery, New York, 1990
MARTIN Alvin, *American Realism: Twentieth-Century Drawings and Watercolors,* (cat) San Francisco Museum of Modern Art, San Francisco, 1985
SHESTACK Alan, SANDLER Irving, *Twenty Artists: Yale School of Art, 1950-70,* (cat) Yale University Art Gallery, Library of Congress Card Catalogue Number 80, New Haven, 1981
GOODYEAR Frank H. J., *Contemporary American Realism since 1960,* (cat) Pennsylvania Academy of the Fine Arts, Philadelphia, 1981
Real, Really Real and Super Real: Directions in Contemporary American Realism, (cat) San Antonio Museum of Art, TX, San Antonio, 1981
NAYLOR Colin and ORRIDGE P., *Genesis. Contemporary Artists.* St. Martin's Press, New York, 1977
GOODYEAR Frank H. J., *8 Contemporary American Realists,* (cat) Pennsylvania Academy of the Fine Arts, Philadelphia, 1977
STRINGER John, GOODYEAR Frank H. J, *Illusion and Reality,* (cat) Australian National Gallery, Gardner Printing & Publishing Pty. Ltd/Australian Gallery Director's Council, Sydney, 1977
BOYLE Richard J., GOODYEAR Frank H. J., *Eight Contemporary American Realists,* (cat) Pennsylvania Academy of the Fine Arts/Library of Congress Catalogue Number 77, Philadelphia, 1977
BATTCOCK Gregory, *Super Realism,* E.P. Dutton & Co., New York, 1975
CHASE Linda, *Tokyo Biennale 1974,* (cat) The Mainichi Newspaper/Japan International Art Promotion Association, Tokyo, 1974
LYNTON Norbert, *Image Ready, Super-reality,* (cat) The Art Council of Great Britain, London, NY, 1973
SAEGER Peter, *Neue Formen des Realismus,* Verlag M. DuMont Schauberg, Germany, 1973
Sharp Focus Realism, (cat) Sidney Janis Gallery, New York, 1972
BELLAMY Richard, *Art in Evolution,* (cat) Xerox Corporation, Rochester, NY, 1973
Photographers Sculptures Painters Printmakers 1972-73, Creative Artists Program Service, Gallery Association of New York State, NY, 1973
KULTERMANN Udo, WASMUTH Verlag Ernest, *Radical Realism,* Türingen, Germany, 1972
ALDRICH Larry, *Contemporary Reflections 1971-1972,* (cat) The Aldrich Museum of Contemporary Art, Ridgefield, CT, 1972
GOLDSMITH Benedict L., *New Realism,* (cat) State University College at Postdam, NY, 1971
WARD John L., *American Realism: 1945-1980,* UMI Research Press, Ann Arbor, 1989
ALLEN Martin, *American Realism.* Harry N. Abrams, New York, 1986
ARTHUR John, *Realism/Photorealism.* (cat) Philbrook Art Center, 1980

ARTICLES

ILIEV, Nico: *The Posens: A Family Affair, FLATT Book 6,* March 2014

GOOSSENS Tim, *Conversation with Stephen Posen, Document Magazine,* 2012

GOLDSTEIN Richard, *The Evolution of Stephen Posen, Bomb Magazine,* August 8, 2012

KIRSCHENBAUM Susan, *The Structuralists: Stephen Posen and Zac Posen in Whitewall, Contemporary Art and Lifestyle Magazine,* Fall 2008

HONIGMAN FINEL Ana, *All in the Family, Stylefile.com,* Tuesday, Sept. 11, 2007

LEFFINGWELL Edward, *Stephen Posen at the Drawing Center in Art in America,* Dec. 1, 2006

GORDON Vivian, *Mirror Dancers, Artnet.com,* May 2006

STOFFLET Mary, *Contemporary American Realism since 1960, Southwest Art,* May 1982

ALWYNNE Mackie, *Dialectic in Modernism: The Paintings of Stephen Posen, Art International,* Nov. 1979, pp. 56-61

ASHTON Dore, *Stephen Posen and Mixed Metaphor, Arts,* Oct., 1978, pp. 134-37

GOODYEAR Frank H. J. Frank, *Contemporary Realism: The Challenge of Definition, American Art Review,* Special Issue: Contemporary Realist, Nov. 1978

ALWYNNE Mackie, *Dialectic in Modernism: the Paintings of Stephen Posen, Art International,* Volume XXIII, editor James Fitzsimmons, Dec. 1979

CANADAY John, *Posen's Two Paintings a Year Are Well Worth Waiting For, The New York Times,* Sept. 21, 1975

PETER Frank, *The Soho Weekly News,* March 21, 1974

PERREAULT John, *New Wrinkles in Realism, The Village Voice,* March 14, 1974

ROSENBERG Harold, *The New Yorker,* February 5, 1972, p. 88

CHASE Linda, McBURNETT Ted, *Stephen Posen, Art in America,* Nov-Dec, 1972, pp. 85-87

CANADAY John, *The New York Times, Sunday Edition,* February 6, 1972, p. 23

PARSI, Jeanne, *Long Island Press,* January 30, 1972, p. 23

THORNTON Gene, *The New York Times,* January 25, 1972

KARP Ivan, *Rent is the Only Reality, Arts Magazine,* Dec. 1971, pp. 47-51, ill. *St. Louis Post Dispatch,* March 21, 1971

DOMINGO Willis, *Arts Magazine,* May 1971, p. 56

SCHWARTZ Barbara, *Art News,* April 1971, p. 66

SHIREY David, *Downtown Art Scene: Celebrities and Horses, The New York Times,* April 3, 1971, p. 24

PAULL Nina, *East Village Other,* March 23, 1971

PERRAULT John, *The Village Voice,* March 25, 1971

GRANTS AND AWARDS

1986-87 Guggenheim Fellow

1972 CAPS Grant

1964-66 Fulbright Grant to Florence, Italy

1964 Milliken Scholarship

SELECTED COLLECTIONS

The Chase Manhattan Bank, New York City

Georgia Museum of Art, Athens, GA

Guggenheim Museum, New York City

Heckscher Museum of Fine Arts, Huntington, NY

J.B. Speed Art Museum, Louisville, KY

Museum of Art at Brigham Young University, Provo, UT

Museum of Modern Art, New York City

The Nelson-Atkins Museum of Art, Kansas City, MO

The Pennsylvania Academy of the Fine Arts, Philadelphia, PA

State University of New York at Potsdam, NY

Virginia Museum of Fine Art, Richmond, VA

BIOGRAPHIES

STEPHEN POSEN received his BFA from Washington University and his MFA from Yale. Some of his solo and group exhibitions include Jason McCoy Gallery, Robert Miller Gallery, and O.K. Harris Gallery in New York; the San Francisco Museum of Modern Art; the Pennsylvania Academy of Fine Arts; the Akron Art Museum in Ohio, the Philbrook Art Center in Tuscon, Arizona; and the Chicago Art Institute. His work is in the collection of The Guggenheim Museum, NYC; the Pennsylvania Academy of Fine Art, Philadelphia; Chase Manhattan Bank; J.B. Speed Museum in Louisville, Kentucky; and the Virginia Museum of Fine Art, among others. He lives and works in New York City with his wife, Susan.

ALEXANDRA O. POSEN is a visual artist. She is a graduate of Brown University who studied physical theatre and mask work at the legendary l'Ecole Jacques Lecoq in Paris before returning to New York to form the performance group Atlas Mason and to work with a host of visual theater artists. She co-founded and was Creative Director of her brother's label leading it to become a significant global fashion brand. Since 2011, Posen has devoted herself to her studio practice where she creates mixed media artworks. She lives in Red Hook, Brooklyn with her artist husband, Nils Folke Anderson and their two children.

COLIN CHENEY is the internationally regarded poet whose first book, *Here Be Monsters,* was selected as a winner of the 2009 National Poetry Series Open Competition and published by Univ. of George Press. He is a recipient of the Ruth Lilly Fellowship from the Poetry Foundation and his poems have appeared widely in such journals as *American Poetry Review, Poetry, Gulf Coast, Ploughshares, Crazyhorse, Shenandoah,* and *Kenyon Review.* He is a graduate of Brown University with an MFA from New York University. He lives and works in Bangkok, Thailand.

SCOTT INDRISEK is the executive editor of Modern Painters and the former senior editor of Anthem magazine. His writing has appeared in *The Believer, Bookforum, BlackBook, Whitewall, ARTnews,* and many other publications. He lives in Bedford-Stuyvesant, Brooklyn with two erudite cats.

ZAC POSEN is the creative talent and head of House of Z LLC, the international fashion company. He was raised in Soho, New York, is a graduate of St. Ann's School in Brooklyn, and attended Central Saint Martin's at the University of the Arts, London. He is considered one of the premier fashion designers working today. He lives in New York City with his partner and their three dogs.

ACKNOWLEDGMENTS

For Susan, Alexandra and Zac:

Alexandra who shared her poetic insight as to the possibilities of the imagery.

Zac who understood the communicative power of the work.

Susan who gave her steadfast help in editing, together with her visual acuity and faith in my eye—and for sharing many of the places and times with me in the process.

And to those who engaged with me on my journey and those who shared their time with me in my studio: Tim Goossens, Toni Bryant, Larry Fink, Charles Traub, Rinko Kawauchi, Max Kozloff, Robert Frank, Bob Seidman, Judith Thurman, Nils Folke Anderson, Christopher Niquet, Christina Lessa.

And my gratitude to Marta Hallett and Belen Moreno whose welcoming eyes have made this book possible.

And to my loyal companion, Bozart, who is rarely inches from my heels and who occasionally ventures in front of my lens.